外研社

新概念英语

NEW CONCEPT ENGLISH

亚历山大（L. G. ALEXANDER）[英]　何其莘　著

3

Developing Skills
培养技能

智慧版

外语教学与研究出版社
FOREIGN LANGUAGE TEACHING AND RESEARCH PRESS
北京 BEIJING

京权图字：01-2020-6329

图书在版编目（CIP）数据

外研社新概念英语 ：智慧版．3，培养技能 ／（英）亚历山大（L. G. Alexander），何其莘著．-- 北京 ：外语教学与研究出版社，2022.6

ISBN 978-7-5213-3672-6

Ⅰ．①外… Ⅱ．①亚… ②何… Ⅲ．①英语－自学参考资料 Ⅳ．①H31

中国版本图书馆 CIP 数据核字（2022）第 104309 号

出版人 王 芳
责任编辑 咸珊珊
责任校对 赵 婧
封面设计 高 蕾
版式设计 孙莉明
出版发行 外语教学与研究出版社
社 址 北京市西三环北路 19 号（100089）
网 址 http://www.fltrp.com
印 刷 保定市中画美凯印刷有限公司
开 本 889×1194 1/16
印 张 19
版 次 2022 年 7 月第 1 版 2022 年 7 月第 1 次印刷
书 号 ISBN 978-7-5213-3672-6
定 价 68.90 元

购书咨询：（010）88819926 电子邮箱：club@fltrp.com
外研书店：https://waiyants.tmall.com
凡印刷、装订质量问题，请联系我社印制部
联系电话：（010）61207896 电子邮箱：zhijian@fltrp.com
凡侵权、盗版书籍线索，请联系我社法律事务部
举报电话：（010）88817519 电子邮箱：banquan@fltrp.com
物料号：336720001

记载人类文明
沟通世界文化
www.fltrp.com

外研社 **新概念英语**

NEW CONCEPT ENGLISH

DEVELOPING SKILLS *Students' Book* 培养技能 学生用书3

This simplified Chinese characters edition first published in 1997 jointly by Foreign Language Teaching and Research Press and Longman Asia Ltd.

双语版出版人：沈维贤
合作出版人：李朋义
合作编著者：亚历山大（L. G. Alexander），何其莘
策划编辑：赵嘉文，蔡女良
项目编辑：（朗文）王德厚，梅丹心；（外研社）孙蓓，任小玫
封面设计：梁若基

出版说明

《新概念英语》作为一套经典的英语学习图书，自出版以来一直深受广大学习者的喜爱。这套图书通过系统科学的编写体系、精妙生动的美文语篇，帮助学习者掌握英语听、说、读、写 4 项基本技能，培养语言实际运用能力，提升文化和审美素养，在学习中充分发挥自己的潜能。

《新概念英语》编写之初多用于课堂教学，但广大学习者多年的学习实践和成果证明，这套图书的教学理念和语言材料也同样适合不同类型、各种水平的学习者自学使用，可满足长、短期学习和备考等多种学习需求。

随着数字化学习时代的到来，为了给读者带来更好的学习体验，进一步提升学习效果，外研社推出了《新概念英语智慧版》，在保留《新概念英语》全部内容的基础上，为读者提供更加丰富的数字化资源和学习功能，包括在线音频、要点概述视频，以及单词学习与练习、朗读与跟读课文等适用各种学习情景的在线学习功能。

《新概念英语智慧版》具有以下特色：

- 延续经典，精益求精：保留原书全部内容，同时进一步完善注释、译文及体例等细节；
- 全新设计，美观实用：扩大版面，双色印刷，时尚悦目，带来更友好的阅读体验；
- 体系完整，编排科学：语言知识的衔接和复现设计严谨；每课配有词汇表、课文注释、参考译文、语言点讲解和练习，符合国内读者的学习习惯；
- 专业录音，培养语感：各课均配有在线音频，由英语母语专家朗读，反复听读可培养英语语感，练就地道发音；
- 数字资源，助读助学：通过要点概述在线视频，讲解重要知识点，配合纸质图书和其他数字资源，助力提升学习效果；
- 正版验证，提升体验：刮开封底二维码标签的涂层，验证并激活正版图书，即可获取丰富的在线学习资源。（验证激活步骤详见第 xvii 页）

2022 年 7 月

CONTENTS 目录

To the teacher and student

Language learning and the intermediate student

When a student has completed a pre-intermediate course, he enters a period of consolidation and expansion. What has been learnt so far must be practised constantly. At the same time, the student must learn to come to terms with wider English. He will still have intensive practice in the four skills, *understanding*, *speaking*, *reading* and *writing*, but many of the exercises he will be doing will be less mechanical.

At this level, there is less need for pattern control and contextualization. Now that the foundations have been laid, the student is in a position to cope with new sentence patterns as and when they occur. However, it is still necessary for the student to work from specially written multi-purpose texts if he is to be trained systematically in speech and writing.

Students working at this level often wish to sit for academic examinations like the Cambridge First Certificate. Now it is a curious paradox that formal examinations often hinder rather than help a student to learn a language. However, there should be no need to work at cross-purposes: it is quite possible for the student to go on learning a language and to prepare for an examination at the same time. It must be clearly understood that a formal examination with its bias towards the written language will only exert a pernicious influence on language learning when it is regarded as an end in itself. When the teacher makes it his aim to get his class through an examination and no more, he will undoubtedly fail to teach the language properly. An examination must always be regarded as something secondary, a by-product which the student will take in his stride. It must never be regarded as an end in itself. An intermediate course should not only enable a student to go on learning English systematically, but should, incidentally, enable him to pass an examination without special preparation.

About this course

Basic aims

1 To provide a comprehensive course for adult or secondary students who have completed a pre-intermediate course. The course contains sufficient material for one academic year's work. It is assumed that the student will receive about four hours' instruction each week: i.e. four one-hour lessons on four separate occasions, or two 'double periods' each consisting of two hours or ninety minutes. The student will receive most of his training in the classroom and will be required to do a certain amount of extra work in his own time.

2 To continue the student's training in the four skills: *understanding*, *speaking*, *reading* and *writing* — in that order. In this respect, the course sets out to do two things: to provide material which will be suitable for aural/oral practice and which can also be used to train the student systematically to write English.

3 To provide the student with a book which will enable him to *use* the language.

4 To provide the teacher with material which will enable him to conduct each lesson with a minimum of preparation.

5 To enable the teacher and the student to work entirely from a single volume without the need for additional 'practice books'.

6 To enable students to sit for the Cambridge First Certificate examination at the end of the course if they wish to do so. This aim must be regarded as coincidental to the main purpose of training students in the four language skills.

For whom the course is intended

This course should be found suitable for:

1 Adult or secondary students who have completed *Practice and Progress:* an integrated course for pre-intermediate students, or who have completed any other pre-intermediate course.

2 Schools and language institutes where 'wastage' caused by irregular attendance and late starters is a problem.

3 Intermediate students who wish to study on their own.

How much knowledge has been assumed

The material in *Practice and Progress*, the pre-intermediate course which precedes this one, has been designed to 'overlap' this course. Students who have completed it will have no difficulty whatever in continuing where they left off.

Students who have learnt English from other courses and who now wish to continue their studies with this course should have a fair working knowledge of the items listed below.

Assumed knowledge

Listening comprehension

1 The ability to understand short passages of English (narrative and descriptive) spoken at normal speed.

2 The ability to answer questions which require short or extended answers.

3 The ability to ask questions to elicit short or extended answers.

4 The ability to use orally a fair number of elementary sentence patterns.

5 The ability to reproduce orally the substance of a short passage of English after having heard it several times and read it.

Reading

1 The ability to read a short passage of English (up to 200 words in length) aloud. The student should have a fair grasp of the *rhythm* of the language (stress and intonation) even if he is unable to pronounce unfamiliar words correctly.

2 Students should have a passive vocabulary range of around 2,000 words and should be able to read works of fiction and non-fiction to this level.

Writing

1 *Word order*
The ability to write *simple*, *compound* and *complex* sentences.

2 *Comprehension*
The ability to answer in writing simple questions on a passage of English.

3 *Summary writing*
The ability to connect ideas from notes that have been provided so as to form a complete paragraph.

4 *Composition*
The ability to write a short composition of about 150 words based on ideas that have been provided.

5 *Letter writing*
Knowledge of the lay-out of the personal letter. The ability to write a short letter based on ideas that have been provided.

Command of language

1 *Grammar* (*Key structures*)
The course presupposes that the student has covered the elementary and pre-intermediate ground work. It is clearly recognized, however, that further instruction and practice are required.

2 *Usage* (*Special difficulties*)
The student should be familiar with a number of words that are often confused or misused and a limited number of idiomatic expressions.

A description of the course

General arrangement of material

This course is divided into three units, the first two of which are preceded by searching tests. Each unit consists of twenty passages which become longer and more complex as the course progresses. Detailed instructions to the student, together with worked examples, precede each unit.

The passages are multi-purpose texts. Each passage will be used to train the student in the following: listening comprehension; oral practice; reading aloud; tell the story; extended oral exercises; dictation; comprehension; summary writing; composition; grammar.

Instructions and worked examples

These precede each unit and should be read very carefully. The successful completion of this course depends entirely on the student's ability to carry out the instructions given.

Pre-unit tests

A searching test, based on material already studied, precedes Units 1 and 2. This will make it possible for students to find their own level and enable them to begin at any point in the book. At the same time, the student who works through the course systematically from beginning to end is not expected to make too sudden a jump between units. The tests should enable the teacher to assess how much the students have learnt. If they are found to be too long, they should be divided into manageable compartments.

The passages

An attempt has been made to provide the student with passages which are as interesting and as varied in subject-matter as possible. Each passage will be used as the basis for listening comprehension and written work. The approximate length of the passages in each unit is as follows:

Unit 1: 250 words.
Unit 2: 350 words.
Unit 3: 530 words.

Oral exercises

Oral exercises are not included in the book itself and must be supplied by the teacher. They may be along the lines suggested in the section on *How to use this course.*

Comprehension questions

The student will elicit specific information from each passage.

Summary writing

Work has been graded as follows:

Unit 1: The students will be trained to write notes by means of comprehension questions on the passages. The students will answer the comprehension questions in note form and then connect their notes to form a paragraph. Connecting words have not been provided.

Units 2 & 3: The students will now be in a position to elicit specific information from each passage and write a summary of his own.

Composition

Work has been graded as follows:

Unit 1: Alternating exercises

a Expanding sentences to form a paragraph of about 150 words.

b Writing compositions in three paragraphs on set plans in which the ideas have been provided. About 200 words.

Unit 2: Alternating exercises

a Expanding ideas to construct a plan. Writing a composition of about 250 words which is based on each plan.

b Writing compositions in three or four paragraphs based on set plans in which ideas have been provided. About 250 words.

Unit 3: Writing compositions of about 300 words on topics suggested by the passages. The student will be required to construct his own plan and to provide his own ideas.

Letter writing

Work has been graded as follows:

Unit 1: Writing letters based on ideas which have been provided.
Units 2 & 3: Writing letters on set topics.

Vocabulary exercises

Exercises in explaining words and phrases as they are used in the passages are given in all three units.

Key structures and Special difficulties

All the exercises on Key structures (Essential grammar) and Special difficulties (Usage) are derived from each passage. There are grammar exercises in Units 1 and 2 only. The exercises given are based largely on patterns which were fully explained in the pre-intermediate course *Practice and Progress.*

Cross-references

Cross-references have been included to enable the student to refer to material he has already learnt and to draw useful comparisons. Students who previously studied *Practice and Progress* are advised to refer to it when in difficulty. In the text, cross-references are in heavy type and are indicated in the following manner.

a **1 KS (= KEY STRUCTURES)** These letters are followed by a lesson number and sometimes a paragraph reference: e.g. **1 KS 47b**. The figure '**1**' indicates that the reference is to a section in the previous volume *Practice and Progress*.

b **KS (= KEY STRUCTURES)** The omission of the figure '**1**' indicates that the reference is to a section of the present volume.

c **1 SD (= SPECIAL DIFFICULTIES)** These letters are followed by a lesson number and sometimes a paragraph reference: e.g. **1 SD 52c**. The figure '**1**' indicates that the reference is to a section in the previous volume *Practice and Progress.*

d **SD (= SPECIAL DIFFICULTIES)** The omission of the figure '**1**' indicates that the reference is to a section of the present volume.

Multiple choice questions

Multiple choice is a *testing* device, not a *teaching* device. Its purpose here is to train students for the kind of objective testing which is usual in public examinations. Multiple choice exercises cover the following: reading comprehension, structure and vocabulary.

How to use this course

TEACHERS! PLEASE READ THIS INTRODUCTION CAREFULLY!

Allocation of time

Ideally, two classroom lessons of approximately 50 minutes each should be spent on each text. The first lesson should be devoted to Guided conversation; the second to Composition and language study. This means that there is enough material in this book for 120 lessons. However, you may choose to spend only *one* classroom lesson on each text — in which case, *every* lesson may be devoted to Guided conversation and a selection of exercises may be set as homework. Your first task is to decide how much time you have in your programme in relation to the material available in the course.

The suggestions given below outline the basic steps in each lesson. You may decide to follow them closely, adapt them to suit your style of teaching, or reject them altogether — BUT PLEASE READ THEM FIRST!

Lesson 1 : Guided conversation

Books required:

Developing Skills (for teachers and students)

The stages of the Lesson

1 Listening comprehension	about 15 minutes
2 Question and answer practice	about 10 minutes
3 Tell the story	about 10 minutes
4 Topics for discussion	about 15 minutes

Let's see what each step involves:

1 Listening comprehension (about 15 minutes)

There are eight recommended steps for presenting each text which will train students to understand spoken English. The steps are as follows:

a Introduce the story
b Understand the situation
c Listening objective
d Play the recording or read the text
e Answer the question
f Intensive reading
g Play the recording or read the text again
h Reading aloud

Every one of these steps must be very brief:

a Introduce the story

The teacher introduces the story with a few words, so the student clearly understands what's going on and is not obliged to guess. English should be used entirely as far as possible. For example (Text 1):
Today we'll listen to a story about a puma that has escaped.

b Understanding the situation

The students are asked to look at the cartoon to see if they can understand what is going on in the text. The teacher may ask a few questions in English to help the students understand the picture.
For example (Text 1):
Look at the picture and tell me what is happening here.
What is the man holding?

c Listening objective

The teacher gives the students 'a listening objective', by setting them a question they will try to find the answer to. This means, the students will listen to the text *actively* rather than *passively*.
For example (Text 1):
Listen to the story, then tell me: Where must the puma have come from?
The Coursebook always provides a question of this kind.

d Play the recording or read the text

The teacher plays the recording or reads the text just once while the students simply listen without interruption. They should try to 'hear' the answer to the question given in *c* above.

e Answer the question

Now the teacher asks the question (*c* above) again and the students try to answer it: *Now you've heard the story, where must the puma have come from?* Don't let students shout out the answer. Train them to raise their hands if they think they know the answer. Get one student to answer, then ask the others, *How many of you agree with him/her? Put up your hands if you agree with him/her. You don't agree* (to another student), *so what do you think the answer is? How many of you agree with him/her? Put up your hands.* This keeps the students guessing and involves *the whole class*. Students should be trained to listen right from the start without 'preparation' or 'translation'. They will soon get used to the sound of English and to understanding the meaning of what they hear.

f Intensive reading

Now the teacher plays the recording or reads the text again, pausing after every sentence to check the students understand. This is an extremely important part of the lesson as the students must fully understand the text at the end of the presentation. Rather than give direct explanations, try to get as much information as possible from the students (think of it as 'a corkscrew operation'!). Explanations should be given entirely in English, but don't carry direct-method teaching to absurd lengths. Use gesture and mime where possible. If some of your students still don't understand, ask the best students in the class for a 'confirmatory translation' of a particular word or phrase for the benefit of other students who haven't grasped the meaning. Remember, if you don't translate a particular difficulty, then someone in the class will. However, translation should always be regarded as a last resort.

g Play the recording or read the text again

Play the recording or read the text again right through without interruption. This time, the students will understand it without difficulty because of the careful explanation you provided in *f* above.

h Reading aloud

Ask a few students to read the text aloud, taking turns round the class. You will be able to tell from this how well particular students can pronounce correctly the English they have already heard.

This presentation should not take more than about fifteen minutes. DON'T SPEND TOO MUCH TIME ON ANY ONE ACTIVITY!

Students working at home on their own should listen to the recording of each text as often as is necessary for them to become thoroughly familiar with it.

2 Question and answer practice (about 10 minutes)

Once the text has been presented, proceed with question and answer practice. This is in two parts:

a The teacher asks a variety of questions and the students answer them
b The students ask a variety of questions

a The teacher asks a variety of questions and the students answer them

The questions you ask should be highly varied (including both yes/no questions and Wh-questions). They should be asked rapidly round the class and the students should be trained to answer naturally (i.e. don't insist on complete answers where they would not normally be given in the course of ordinary conversation). The essence of this exercise is *pace*, so it's better to get the students to answer individually rather than in chorus. Here, for example, are a few questions which relate to Text 1:

TEACHER: What are pumas like?
They're like cats, aren't they?
Where are they found? etc.

b The students ask a variety of questions

In order to prevent incorrect forms like *Where he went?*, students are trained to ask two questions at a time. The first of these is a yes/no question and the second a Wh-question. For example:

TEACHER: Ask me if pumas are like cats.
STUDENT: Are pumas like cats?
TEACHER: What … like?
STUDENT: What are pumas like? (Not *What pumas are like?* or *What pumas like?*)

This section consists of numbered notes which form a summary of the

3 Tell the story (about 10 minutes)

text. Write notes on the blackboard (or have them written up and covered before the lesson begins) and ask individual students round the class to tell you the story. This gives students semi-prepared practice in speaking without interruption. Point out only the main errors made *after* students finish speaking. Don't constantly interrupt them!

Here, for example, are some notes which relate to Text 1:

1 Hunt—village.
2 Woman—blackberries—large cat.
3 Ran away—experts confirmed—not attack.
4 Search difficult—morning/evening.
5 Trail—dead deer—rabbits.
6 Paw prints—fur.
7 Cat-like noises—business man.
8 *Was* a puma—where from?
9 Not zoo—private collector.

4 Topics for discussion (about 15 minutes)

The final part of the Guided conversation lessons should be devoted to free conversation. Students should be invited to 'have a go' at expressing their own ideas, no matter how many mistakes they make. The topics become progressively harder *within* each lesson and one or all of them may be attempted. Individual students should be invited to make one or two statements about the topics. As conversational skill develops, you may occasionally arrange to spend more time on free conversation (omitting, for example, such exercises as 'Tell the story'). Here, for example, are a few topics suggested by Text 1:

a Which animals do you like or dislike most and why?
b Tell us about a visit to the zoo.
c Is it right to put animals in cages? Why?/Why not?

Lesson 2: Composition and language study

As has already been indicated, this entire lesson may be omitted and a selection of written exercises may, instead, be set as homework. If this approach is adopted, then the Summary and Composition exercises *must always be set*. Needless to say, more satisfactory results will be obtained where a complete classroom lesson can be devoted to written exercises.

Books required:

Developing Skills (for teachers and students)

The exercises may be tackled in the order in which they are given. While the students are writing, you may go round the class helping individuals. Exercise not completed in class time may be set as homework. The written exercises become more demanding and time-consuming as the student progresses through the course. However, it is not necessary to complete every single exercise.

Dictations

Depending on the amount of time available, dictations should be given frequently. A few sentences taken from a passage the students have already studied may be dictated. The students may correct their own work by comparing their version with the passage. Dictation is an excellent exercise in syntax, spelling and listening comprehension.

Multiple choice exercises

Multiple choice exercises provide extra practice in reading comprehension, structure and vocabulary.

Homework

The written exercises become more demanding and time-consuming as the student progresses through the course. At a later stage, exercises which have not been completed in class may be set as homework.

Pre-unit tests

These should always be set before the students move on to a new unit.

Future work

If the student wishes to proceed further, he may go on to the following book after completing this one. They are designed to 'overlap' each other so that the student can continue without difficulty:

Fluency in English:
An integrated course for advanced students

致教师和学生

语言学习和中级水平的学生

学生学完中级以下水平的教程后，就进入巩固和扩展阶段。以前学到的语言技能要不断地练习，同时学生还要学会进一步地深入学习。理解、口语、阅读和写作 4 项技能还要进行强化训练，但是许多练习不再像以前那样机械。

到了这个阶段，按句型的难度和在语境中练习句型已不是那么必不可少。由于基础已经打下，学生一旦遇到新的句型也就能够对付。但是，如果要系统地训练学生在说和写方面的能力，还需要使用专门编写的多功能课文。

中级水平的学生常常希望参加专业性的考试，如剑桥初级证书考试。现在有一种怪现象，即正规考试往往妨碍而不是有助于学生学习一门语言。但是，学习和考试并非一定是相互矛盾的：学生完全有可能在学习语言的同时，作好应试的准备。必须清醒地认识到：正规考试侧重于书面用语，如果把应付正规考试作为最终目标，那么必然对英语学习产生有害的影响。如果教师把自己所教的班能通过某种考试作为教学的唯一目的，他必然教不好语言。要永远把考试放在第二位，把它当成是学生在学习中顺理成章必然会取得的一种副产品，而决不能把它当成最终目的。一本中级水平的教程不仅应能使学生系统地学好英语，而且应使他无需专门的准备就能通过某种考试。

关于本教程的说明

基本目的

1　为完成中级以下教程的成年人或中学生提供一本综合性的教程。这本教程中的内容足够 1 学年使用。假定学生每周上课约 4 个课时，即互不相连的 4 个课时，每课时为 1 小时，或两个“双课时”，每个双课时为 2 小时或 90 分钟。学生主要在课上接受训练，在课下仅做一点额外的作业。

2　继续训练学生的 4 项技能：**理解、口语、阅读、写作**——按此顺序进行训练。从这方面来讲，这本教程准备做两件事：为听 / 说练习提供适合的材料，同时，这些材料也可用于系统地训练学生的写作能力。

3　为学生提供一本令他能够**使用**语言的教程。

4　为教师提供一本只需很少的备课时间即可登台讲授的教程。

5　为教师和学生提供一本单卷本的教程，而无需其他附加的“练习手册”。

6　学完本册书后，能使有意参加“剑桥初级证书”考试的学生达到应试的水平。必须认识到这个目标与训练学生的 4 项语言技能的主要目标是一致的。

适用对象

本教程适用于：

1　已经学完中级以下水平综合教程《实践与进步》或任何中级以下教程的成年人或中学生。

2　那些由于学生上课出勤率不高、学英语起步较晚而造成“损失”的中学和语言学校。

3　愿意自学中级教程的学生。

应具备的知识范围

本教程的前一册是中级以下水平综合教程《实践与进步》，其内容编排与本册有所重叠。学完前一册的学生接着学本册，不会有什么困难。

学完其他教程而想接着学本册教程的学生应对下列语言知识具有扎实的基础。

应有的知识

听力理解

1　能听懂以正常速度讲述的英文片段（叙述与描写性的）。

2　能就所提问题给出简短或较长的回答。

3　能提出问题以要求对方给出简短或较长的回答。

4　能口头使用相当数量的基本句型。

5　对一篇短文能在听几遍和读过一遍后，口头复述出其大意。

阅读

1　能大声朗读长度不超过 200 个词的英语短文。学生即使对不熟悉的单词读音不准，也应能掌握好语言的节奏（重音和语调）。

2　应具有 2,000 单词的认知能力，并能读懂相应程度的小说类和非小说类作品。

写作

1　语序

能写出简单句、并列句和复合句。

2　理解

能笔头回答就一篇短文提出的简单问题。

3　摘要写作

能把提供的要点连起来组成一个完整的段落。

4　作文

能根据所给的要点写出 150 个词左右的短文。

5　书信写作

懂得私人信件的格式。能根据所给内容写出短信。

对语言的掌握程度

1　语法（关键句型）

学习本书的先决条件是学生已具有初级和中级以下水平的基础知识。但应清楚地认识到，进一步的讲解和训练仍是必要的。

2　惯用法（难点）

学生应熟悉相当数量的易混淆和易用错的词，以及少量的习惯用语。

教程内容

材料的总体安排

本书分 3 个单元，前两个单元各有一份摸底测验。每一单元有 20 篇课文，长度和难度逐渐加大。每一单元前都有学生须知和实例示范。

每篇课文均为多功能课文，可用来对学生进行下列训练：听力理解、口头练习、朗读、讲故事、口头发挥练习、听写、理解、摘要写作、作文和语法。

学生须知和实例示范

应认真阅读每一单元前的学生须知和实例示范。学生能否学好本教程，完全取决于学生能否按须知去做。

单元前测试

第 1、2 单元前各有一份根据已学材料编写的摸底测验，通过摸底测验可以让学生了解自己的水平，以便知道自己应从本书中哪一个地方开始学习。另一方面，由头到尾系统地学习本教程的学生不宜从一个单元突然跳到另一单元。测验也可使教师评估学生学得如何。如果认为测验内容太多，可以分为长短适宜的几部分，分几次进行。

课文

为学生提供的课文力求做到富有趣味性，题材多样化。每篇课文都可用来进行听力理解和笔头练习。各单元课文的长度大致如下：

第 1 单元：250 个词；
第 2 单元：350 个词；
第 3 单元：530 个词。

口头练习

本书没有编排口头练习，需要教师自己去补充。可按《本教程使用说明》中的有关原则自行编写。

指导理解的问题

学生从每篇课文中找出具体资料便可理解课文。

摘要写作

此项练习按难易程度分成以下几步：

第 1 单元：通过对课文提理解性的问题，训练学生写出要点。学生先用要点的形式，以笔头回答理解性问题，然后把这些要点组成一个段落。本书没有提供用于连接的词语。

第 2、3 单元：此时学生应能从每篇课文中找出具体资料，独立写出课文摘要。

作文

此项练习按难易程度分成以下几步：

第 1 单元：交替练习
a　把句子扩展组成 150 个词左右的段落。
b　按所给梗概，写出 200 个词左右的 3 个段落，组成一篇作文。

第 2 单元：交替练习
a　将所要表达的思想组成一个提纲。根据提纲写出一篇 250 个词左右的作文。
b　根据由提供的思路所组成的梗概，写出 250 个词左右、由 3 段或 4 段组成的作文。

第 3 单元：就各课提出的题目，写出约 300 个词的作文。学生要自行构思，自拟提纲。

书信写作

按难易程度可分以下几步：

第 1 单元：按所给的内容写出信文。
第 2、3 单元：按所给的题目写出信文。

词汇练习

3 个单元中都编有解释每篇课文中词语和短语的练习。

关键句型和难点

关键句型（基本语法）和难点（惯用法）的所有练习都是根据课文中出现的语言现象编写的。仅在第 1、2 单元中有语法练习。练习以句型为主，这些句型均已在中级以下水平教程《实践与进步》中作过详细的解释。

参见

本书加入了相互参见的提示，为的是便于学生参考学过的内容，并进行有益的对比。已学过《实践与进步》的学生，遇到困难时，请按参见提示去查阅。书中参见提示用黑体印刷，具体标记如下：

a　**1 KS**（= **KEY STRUCTURES**）后面紧跟的是某课的序号，有时还标出段落序号，例如：**1 KS 47b** 中的“1”指的是前一册书《实践与进步》。

b　**KS** 前没有数字“1”表示是本册中有关章节的关键句型。

c　**1 SD**（= **SPECIAL DIFFICULTIES**）后面跟着的是某课的序号，有时还标出段落序号。例如：**1 SD 52c** 中的“1”指的是前一册书《实践与进步》。

d　**SD** 前没有数字“1”，表示是本册书中有关章节的难点。

选择题

选择题是一种测试手段，不是教学手段。其目的是训练学生适应公共考试中常见的那种客观测试方法。选择题包括以下几方面的题目：理解、句型和词汇。

《新概念英语智慧版》支持扫码验证正版图书（仅限中国大陆地区），扫码下载外研社官方APP，激活正版音频，获取更多学习资源。

获取方式：

1　刮开封底标签涂层，扫描二维码，填写手机号和手机验证码，点击“认证激活”，验证正版图书 。

2　激活成功后，下载外研社官方 APP。

3　下载完成后，用激活时的手机号登录 APP，进入首页后点击“学习”—“我的图书”，或者“我的”—“我的图书”，即可看到已激活图书。

4　点击图书封面进入，即可开始学习。

5　如果验证正版图书失败，请拨打外研社官方客服电话 400-898-7008 反馈问题。

扫码关注外研社
新概念英语官方公众号

本教程使用说明

请各位教师仔细阅读本说明！

时间分配

理想的安排是，每篇课文用两个课时，每课时约 50 分钟。第 1 课时用于进行教师引导下的会话，第 2 课时用于作文和语言学习。这样，本书足够 120 个课时使用。但是，每篇课文也可只用 1 个课时——在这种情况下，上课时间可完全用于教师引导下的对话，并可选一部分练习作为课外作业。教师的首要任务是根据教学计划规定的时间确定如何运用教程。

下列建议简要地说明了每课书的讲课步骤。你可以遵照执行，也可以加以修订以适应你的教学方式；也可以拒之不用——**不过，请你先读一下本说明！**

第 1 课时：教师引导下的会话

所需书目

DevelopingSkills《培养技能》（师生均用此书）

讲课步骤

1	听力训练	约 15 分钟
2	问答练习	约 10 分钟
3	复述故事	约 10 分钟
4	专题讨论	约 15 分钟

现把这 4 个步骤分别说明如下：

1　听力训练（大约 15 分钟）

我们推荐介绍课文的 8 个步骤，以训练学生听懂英语口语的能力。这些步骤是：

a　介绍故事
b　了解情景
c　听力训练目标
d　播放录音或朗读课文
e　回答问题
f　精读
g　再次播放录音或朗读课文
h　大声朗读

每一个步骤都必须简洁：

a　介绍故事

教师用几句话介绍课文，这样学生就能清楚知道课文讲的是什么事情，而不需要去猜测。应尽可能使用英语。以第 1 课为例：

Today we'll listen to a story about a puma that has escaped.（今天我们要听一个故事，讲的是一只在逃的美洲狮。）

b　了解情景

要求学生看插图，以便检查学生是否了解课文中所发生的事情。教师可以用英语向学生提几个问题，以帮助学生理解插图。以第 1 课为例

Look at the picture and tell me what is happening here.（看图，然后告诉我这里发生了什么事情。）

What is the man holding?（那男人手中拿着什么？）

c　听力训练目标

通过给学生提个问题，让他们去寻找答案，教师便为学生确立一个“听力训练目标”。这就意味着学生会**积极地**而不是**消极地**去听课文录音。以第 1 课为例：

Listen to the story, then tell me: Where must the puma have come from?（听故事，然后告诉我，这只美洲狮肯定来自何处？）

教程中总是提供这样的一个问题。

d　播放录音或朗读课文

教师播放录音或朗读课文，学生静听一遍课文，中间不要停顿。他们应试图找到 c 项中所列问题的答案。

e　回答问题

现在教师再一次问 c 项的问题，让学生试着回答：“现在你听了这个故事，这只美洲狮肯定是哪里来的？”训练学生不集体回答。如果他们认为自己知道答案，请他们举手。问一个学生，然后再问其他的人：“你们中有多少人同意他 / 她的回答？”“如果你们同意，请举手。”“[对另一个学生] 如果你不同意，那么你认为答案是什么？”“你们中有多少人同意他 / 她的回答？”这样就能让学生不断地猜测，而且把**全班学生**都调动了起来。从一开始就要训练学生不做任何准备去听，也不通过翻译。他们很快会适应英语的语音，并理解他们听到的内容。

f　精读

现在教师重放录音或重读课文，每句话后停顿，以检查学生是否理解。这是课堂教学中非常重要的一个环节，因为在介绍课文结束时，学生应该彻底明白课文的意思。教师不要直接讲解，而应尽量从学生那里获取信息（可以把这种方法看作是“用螺丝起子拔瓶塞的行动”）。讲解应全部用英文，但不要把直接教学法绝对化。在可能的情况下，使用手势和模拟动作。如果班上仍有一些学生不理解，教师应该请班上学得最好的学生给出一个单词或词组的译文，以照顾尚未理解词义的学生。请记住，如果你不把一个难点译成中文，班上的其他人会这样做的。但是，翻译始终应被看成是最后的一着。

g　再次播放录音或朗读课文

不停顿地再次播放录音或朗读课文，因为有了 f 项中的精心解释，这次学生会很容易听懂。

h　大声朗读

在班上让学生轮流大声朗读课文。从朗读中你可以看出不同的学生是否能够准确地读出他们听到的英语。

介绍课文不应超过 15 分钟左右的时间。

不要在任何一项活动中花费太多的时间！

在家里自学的学生应尽量多听录音，使自己完全熟悉课文。

2　问答练习（大约 10 分钟）

在介绍课文之后，开始问答练习。这个练习分为两部分：

a　教师提出多种多样的问题，学生回答

b　学生提出多种多样的问题

a　教师提出多种多样的问题，学生回答

你提的问题必须形式多样（包括一般疑问句和用 Wh- 开头的疑问句）。提问的速度要快，全班每个人都应问到。应训练学生作出自然的回答（例如，不要坚持用完整的句子来回答问题，因为在日常对话中常常不用完整的句子）。这项练习的关键是**速度**，因此，最好让学生单个回答，而不要集体回答。这里是有关第 1 课的几个问题：

教师　What are pumas like?（美洲狮像什么？）

　　　They're like cats, aren't they?（它们像猫，是不是？）

　　　Where are they found?（它们产于什么地方？）

b　学生提出多种多样的问题

为了避免诸如 *Where he went?* 这种不正确的形式，要训练学生每次提两个问题。其中的第 1 个是一般疑问句，第 2 个是 Wh- 开头的疑问句。例如：

教师　Ask me if pumas are like cats.（问我美洲狮是否和猫相像。）

学生　Are pumas like cats?（美洲狮像猫吗？）

教师　What ... like?（……像什么？）

学生　What are pumas like?（美洲狮像什么？）（而不是 *What pumas are like?* 或 *What pumas like?*）

3　复述故事（大约 10 分钟）

这个步骤是给学生有编号的要点，这些要点是组成课文的摘要。先把要点写到黑板上（或在课前先写到黑板上，然后把它们遮挡起来），然后让全班学生逐个为你复述故事。这种练习可以使学生在半准备状态下不停顿地进行口语练习。在学生**说完**之后，可以指出他们复述过程中出现的主要语言错误。不要不停地打断他们。

下面是与第 1 课有关的要点。

1　Hunt—village.

2　Woman—blackberries—large cat.

3　Ran away—experts confirmed—not attack.

4　Search difficult—morning/evening.

5　Trail—dead deer—rabbits.

6　Paw prints—fur.

7　Cat-like noises—business man.

8　Was a puma—where from?

9　Not zoo—private collector.

4　专题讨论（大约 15 分钟）

在“教师引导下的会话”课上，最后一部分时间应用于自由活动。应邀请学生试着表达自己的思想，不论他们会在表达时出现多少语言错误。每一课的讨论题会渐渐变得越来越难，可以讨论其中一题，也可以讨论所有题目。每个学生都应有机会对这些题目讲上一两句话。随着学生对话能力的加强，你可以偶尔在自由会话这部分多用一些时间（可省略诸如“复述故事”这样的练习）。

下面是第 1 课课文可提供的讨论题：

a Which animals do you like or dislike most and why?（你最喜欢或最不喜欢哪一种动物？为什么？）

b Tell us about a visit to the zoo.（告诉我们你参观动物园的情况。）

c Is it right to put animals in cages? Why?/Why not?（把动物放进笼子里对吗？为什么对？为什么不对？）

第 2 课时：作文和语言学习

如上所述，第 2 课时可以完全不上，而将一部分笔头练习作为课外作业。如采取这种方法，在课外作业中**必须**布置摘要写作与作文练习。如果在课堂上用一整课时做笔头练习，效果当然更好，这是毋庸置疑的。

所需书目

Developing Skills《培养技能》（师生均用此书）

课堂上做笔头练习时，可以按练习编排顺序进行。在学生做练习时，教师可以在课堂上来回走动，进行个别辅导。课堂上未做完的练习，可留作课外作业。随着学习不断深入，笔头练习会越来越难，越来越费时间。但并不要求每题必做。

听写

如果时间允许，应经常做听写练习。可以从学生已学过的课文中抽出几个句子做听写练习。学生可参照原文，自行批改。听写是句法、拼写和听力方面极好的一项训练办法。

选择练习

选择题在阅读理解、句型和词汇方面提供额外的训练。

课外作业

随着学习内容不断加深，笔头作业会越来越难，越来越费时间。学到后面几课，凡在课堂上完不成的作业可留作课外作业。

单元前的测验

此项测验必须安排在学生开始新的单元学习之前进行。

继续学习

凡想继续学习的学生，学完本书后，可以接着学习以下教程。各册教程的内容互相“重叠”，因而学生继续学习不会觉得困难：

Fluency in English《流利英语》：高级水平综合教程

Pre-unit Test 1

IF YOU CAN DO THIS TEST GO ON TO UNIT 1

Key structures

A Word order.

Rewrite these sentences using the joining words in parentheses.

1 My hotel room overlooked a courtyard. There was a fountain. There were several trees. (*in which ... and*)

2 Uncle Charles looked everywhere for his glasses. He could not find them. (*Though*)

3 During Christmas, there was extra work at the post office. A great number of students were employed to help. (*so much ... that*)

4 I don't want to see that film. It had poor reviews. (*because*)

5 Wages have gone up. Prices will rise. The cost of living will be higher than ever. (*Now that ... and*)

6 The police searched everywhere. The missing boy could not be found. His dog could not be found. (*Although ... neither ... nor*)

7 James Sullivan will give a lecture at the local library next week. His book on the Antarctic was published recently. (*whose*)

8 Fares have increased. The railway company is still losing money. The employees have demanded higher wages. (*In spite of the fact that ... because*)

9 He gave me a fright. I knocked the teapot over. (*such ... that*)

10 The climbers reached the top of the mountain. They spent the night there. (*not only ... but ... as well*)

B Composition.

Write two paragraphs in about 150 words using the ideas given below.

1 Circus act — a man was walking on a tightrope — rode a one-wheel bicycle — carried two others on his shoulders — the crowd clapped his performance.

2 The man returned to give a repeat performance — tightrope again — he did a hand-stand on the one-wheel bicycle — lost his balance — the crowd gasped — the man grabbed the tightrope — he was still holding on to the bicycle — climbed on again and rode to the other side.

C Verbs.

a *What happened? What has happened? What has been happening?*

Give the correct form of the verbs in parentheses.

The mummy of an Egyptian woman who ________ (die) in 800 B.C. just ________ (have) an operation. As there ________ (be) strange marks on the X-ray plates taken of the mummy, doctors ________ (try) to find out whether the woman ________ (die) of a rare disease. The only way to do this ________ (be) to operate. The operation, which ________ (last) for over four hours, ________ (prove) to be very difficult. The doctors ________ (remove) a section of the mummy and ________ (send) it to a laboratory. They also ________ (find) something which the X-ray plates not ________ (show). The doctors not ________ (decide) yet how the woman ________ (die). They ________ (fear) that the mummy would fall to pieces when they ________ (cut) it open, but fortunately, this not ________ (happen). The mummy successfully ________ (survive) the operation.

b *What happened? What was happening? What used to happen?*

Give the correct form of the verbs in parentheses. Use *would* in place of *used to* where possible:

I ________ (travel) by air a great deal when I ________ (be) a boy. My parents ________ (live) in South America and I ________ (fly) there from Europe in the holidays. An air hostess ________ (take) charge of me and I never ________ (have) an unpleasant experience. I am used to travelling by air and only on one occasion have I ever felt frightened. After taking off, we ________ (fly) low over the city and slowly ________ (gain) height, when the plane suddenly ________ (turn) round and ________ (fly) back to the airport. While we ________ (wait) to land, an air hostess ________ (tell) us to keep calm, and to get off the plane quietly as soon as it had touched down.

c *What will happen?*

Give the correct form of the verbs in parentheses.

Busmen have decided to go on strike next week. The strike is due to begin on Tuesday. No one knows how long it ________ (last). The busmen have stated that the strike ________ (continue) until general agreement ________ (reach) about pay and working conditions. Most people believe that the strike ________ (last) for a week. Many owners of private cars ________ (offer) 'free rides' to people on their way to work. This ________ (relieve) pressure on the trains to some extent. Meanwhile, a number of university students have volunteered to drive buses while the strike ________ (last). All the young men are expert drivers, but before they ________ (drive) any of the buses, they ________ (have to) pass a special test.

d *What will happen? What will be happening? What will have been happening?*

Give the correct form of the verbs in parentheses.

I have just received a letter from my old school informing me that my former headmaster, Mr. Reginald Page, ________ (retire) next week. Pupils of the school, old and new, ________ (send) him a present to mark the occasion. All those who have contributed towards the gift ________ (sign) their names in a large album which ________ (send) to the headmaster's home. We all ________ (remember) Mr. Page for his patience and understanding and for the kindly encouragement he gave us when we went so unwillingly to school. A great many former pupils ________ (attend) a farewell dinner in his honour next Thursday. It is a curious coincidence that the day before his retirement, Mr. Page ________ (teach) for a total of forty years. After he ________ (retire) he ________ (devote) himself to gardening. For him, this ________ (be) an entirely new hobby.

e *What happened? What had happened? What had been happening?*

Give the correct form of the verbs in parentheses.

As the man tried to swing the speedboat round, the steering wheel came away in his hands. He ________ (wave) desperately to his companion who ________ (water ski) for the last fifteen minutes. Both men hardly ________ (have) time to realize what was happening when they ________ (throw) violently into the sea. The speedboat ________ (strike) a buoy, but it ________ (continue) to move very quickly across the water. Both men just ________ (begin) to swim towards the shore, when they ________ (notice) with dismay that the speedboat was moving in a circle. It now ________ (come) towards them at tremendous speed. In less than a minute, it ________ (roar) past them only a few feet away.

f Give the correct form of the verbs in parentheses.

1 Captain Scott ________ (find) that Amundsen ________ (reach) the South Pole before him.
2 We just ________ (move) to a new house but we ________ (be) dissatisfied with it.
3 When I ________ (meet) him two weeks ago, he ________ (tell) me that he just ________ (return) from the south of France.
4 Many new records ________ (set up) in the next Olympic Games.
5 He always ________ (go) for a walk every morning before his illness.
6 By next June, I ________ (study) English for three years.
7 While the two thieves ________ (argue) someone ________ (steal) their car.

g Give the correct form of the verbs in parentheses.

Though people have often laughed at stories told by seamen, it now ________ (know) that many 'monsters' which at times ________ (sight) are simply strange fish. Occassionally, unusual creatures ________ (wash) to the shore, but they rarely ________(catch) out at sea. Some time ago, however, a peculiar fish ________ (catch) near Madagascar. A small fishing boat ________ (carry) miles out to sea by the powerful fish as it pulled on the line. When it eventually ________ (bring) to shore, it ________ (find) to be over thirteen feet long. The fish, which since ________ (send) to a museum where it ________ (examine) by a scientist, ________ (call) an oarfish. Such creatures rarely ________ (see) alive by man as they live at a depth of six hundred feet.

h Write a report of this conversation as it might appear in a newspaper.

'At the time the murder was committed, I was travelling on the 8 o'clock train to London,' said the man.

'Do you always catch such an early train?' asked the inspector.

'Of course I do,' answered the man. 'I must be at work at 10 o'clock. My employer will confirm that I was there on time.'

'Would a later train get you to work on time?' asked the inspector.

'I suppose it would, but I never catch a later train.'

'At what time did you arrive at the station?'

'At ten to eight. I bought a paper and waited for the train.'

'And you didn't notice anything unusual?'

'Of course not.'

i If.

Give the correct form of the verbs in parentheses.

1 If they ________ (not bring) to the surface soon they may lose their lives.

2 If explosives are used, vibrations ________ (cause) the roof of the mine to collapse.

3 If there had not been a hard layer of rock beneath the soil, they ________ (complete) the job in a few hours.

j Give the correct form of the verbs in parentheses.

I tried to wake up my wife by ________ (ring) the doorbell, but she was fast asleep, so I got a ladder from the shed in the garden, put it against the wall, and began ________ (climb) towards the bedroom window. I was almost there when a sarcastic voice below said, 'I don't think the windows need ________ (clean) at this time of the night.' I looked down and nearly fell off the ladder when I saw a policeman. I immediately regretted ________ (answer) in the way I did, but I said, 'I enjoy ________ (clean) windows at night.'

'So do I,' answered the policeman in the same tone. 'Excuse my ________ (interrupt) you. I hate ________ (interrupt) a man when he's busy ________ (work), but would you mind ________ (come) with me to the station?'

'Well, I'd prefer ________ (stay) here,' I said. 'You see, I've forgotten my key.'

D Other verbs.

a Supply the correct form of *have to* or *should* in these sentences.

1 I'm sorry I couldn't get here on time. I ________ (go) to the bank.

2 I ________ (go) to the dentist yesterday but I forgot all about it.

3 We ________ (begin) work at 9 o'clock but we never do.

b Write these sentences again using *have* with the verbs in italics.

1 '*I shall deliver* the parcel,' said the shop assistant.

2 Are you going to *clean* this suit?

3 When will you *dye* this jacket?

c Supply the correct form of *can* or *able to* in the following sentences.

1 ________ you show me the way to the station please?

2 I gave him a few lessons and he ________ soon swim.

3 They ________ jump into the sea before the boat sank.

4 You ________ not leave this room until you get permission.

E A and The.

Put in *a(n)* or *the* where necessary.

After reading ________ article entitled ' ________ Cigarette Smoking and Your Health', I lit ________ cigarette to calm my nerves. I smoked with ________ concentration and ________ pleasure as I was sure that this would be my last cigarette. For ________ whole week I did not smoke at all and during this time my wife suffered terribly. I had all ________ usual symptoms of someone giving up ________ smoking: ________ bad temper and ________ enormous appetite. My friends kept on offering me ________ cigarettes and ________ cigars. They made no effort to hide their amusement whenever I produced ________ packet of ________ sweets from my pocket.

F Supply the missing words in the following.

Perhaps the ________ extraordinary building of the nineteenth century was the Crystal Palace which was built in Hyde Park for the Great Exhibition of 1851. The Crystal Palace was different ________ all other buildings ________ the world, for it was made of iron and glass. It was one of the ________ (big) buildings ________ all time and a ________ of people from ________ countries came to see it. A great ________ goods were sent to the exhibition from various parts of the world. There was also a great ________ of machinery on display.

G Supply the missing words in these sentences.

1 There will be a dance tonight ________ the Green Park Hotel.
2 The players ________ our team are all ________ red shirts.
3 He returned ________ England ________ August 10th.
4 I'll meet you ________ the corner ________ Wednesday.
5 I always feel tired ________ the end of the day.
6 As soon as he got ________ the taxi, he asked the driver to take him ________ the station.
7 We'll go for a walk ________ the afternoon.
8 He's incapable ________ controlling the class.
9 He is not interested ________ anything outside his work.
10 I don't want to be involved ________ this unpleasant affair.
11 He failed ________ his attempt to reach the top of the mountain.
12 The surgeon decided to operate ________ the patient.
13 I am not satisfied ________ your explanation.
14 I think someone is knocking ________ the door.
15 His debts amount ________ £500.

Special difficulties

A Words often confused.

Choose the correct words in the following sentences.

1 You can divide this apple (among) (between) the two of you.
2 He arrived late as (usually) (usual).
3 Mr. Simpson has been appointed (director) (headmaster) of the school.
4 What shall we do with this old (clothing) (clothes)?
5 I always wear out (clothes) (cloths) quickly.
6 His instructions were not very (clear) (clean).
7 You should wait until the road is (clear) (clean) before crossing.
8 Did you (wash) (wash up) your hands?
9 I don't feel in the (mood) (temper) for a walk.
10 Whatever you do, don't lose your (temper) (mood).
11 This coffee is (too) (enough) hot for me to drink.

12 The questions were (fairly) (enough) difficult, but I managed to answer them.
13 He is (enough old) (old enough) to know what is right.
14 You should use (petrol) (benzine) to get those stains off.

B Write sentences using each of the following.

1 Get up, get over, get away, get out.
2 Keep off, keep out, keep in, keep up.
3 Take in, take up, take off, take away.
4 Run into, run out of, run away, run after.
5 Make up, make for, make out, make up for.

C Write sentences using the following.

1 Turn yellow.
2 Go sour.
3 Grow dark.
4 Fall ill.
5 Come true.
6 Get angry.

D Complete the following sentences using *so ... I* or *neither ... I.*

1 She reads a lot and ________ .
2 You shouldn't work so hard and ________ .
3 You are mistaken and ________ .
4 You will regret it and ________ .
5 Tom telephoned him yesterday and ________ .
6 She hasn't been well and ________ .

Unit 1

Unit 1

INSTRUCTIONS TO THE STUDENT

Before you begin each exercise, read these instructions carefully. Read them *each time* you begin a new piece. They are very important.

How to work — Summary writing

Unit 1 contains twenty passages. You will be asked to write a summary of a part of each piece. In Unit 4 of *Practice and Progress* you were given the main points and asked to join them up. Connections were provided in the text. Now you will be expected to find the main points yourself and supply your own connections. The Comprehension questions which are given should be answered *in note form*. Your notes should be very brief.

1 Read the passage two or three times. Make sure you understand it.
2 Read the instructions which will tell you where your summary should begin and end, and exactly what you will have to do.
3 Read again the part of the passage you will have to summarize.
4 Answer each of the Comprehension questions in note form to get your points.
5 You will find parentheses at the side of the questions. These show you how the answers might be joined to form sentences, but you will have to use your own joining words. You may ignore the parentheses if you wish to join the points in your own way.
6 When joining your points, you may refer to the passage if necessary, but try to use *your own words* as far as possible. Your answer should be in one paragraph.
7 Read through your work and correct your mistakes.
8 At the end of your summary, write the number of words that you have used. Remember that words like 'the', 'a', etc. count as single words. Words which are joined by a hyphen also count as single words. You may write fewer than 80 words, but you must not go over the word limit.

Example

Work through this example carefully and then try to do the exercises in Unit 1 in the same way.

Silent enemies

Few countries will admit officially that they employ spies. However, from time to time, a spy is caught and the public sometimes gets a glimpse of what is going on behind the political scenes. Spies are rarely shot these days. They are frequently tried and imprisoned. If a spy is important enough, he is sometimes handed back to an enemy country in exchange for an equally important spy whom the enemy have caught. Few people have the opportunity to witness such exchanges, for they are carried out in secret.

On cold winter morning on December 17th last year, a small blue car stopped on a bridge in a provincial town in northern Germany. Three men dressed in heavy black coats got out and stood on the bridge. While they waited there, they kept on looking over the side. Fifteen minutes later, a motor boat sailed past and drew up by the river bank. Three men got out of the boat and looked up at the bridge. The men on the bridge silently walked down the stone steps leading to the river bank. No words were spoken when they met the men from the boat. After a while, the motorboat moved off and three men returned to the bridge. Now, only two of them were wearing black coats. The third was dressed in a light grey jacket. Anyone who had been watching the scene might not have realized that two master spies had been exchanged on that cold winter morning.

Summary writing

In not more than 85 words describe what happened on the morning of December 17th from the time a small blue car stopped on a bridge. Do not include anything that is not in the last paragraph.

Answer these questions in note form to get your points:

1 Did the car stop or not?
2 How many men got out?
3 How were they dressed?
4 Where did they stand?
5 Where did they keep looking?
6 Did a motorboat appear or not?
7 Where did it stop?
8 Where did the men go?
9 Why did they go to the river bank?
10 Did the boat move off or not?
11 Who accompanied the men in black coats?
12 How was he dressed?
13 Did they return to the bridge or not?
14 Had two master spies been exchanged or not?

A possible answer

Points

1 Car stopped.
2 Three men got out.
3 Black coats.
4 Stood — bridge.
5 Looked over side.
6 Motorboat appeared.
7 Stopped — river bank.
8 Men — down steps.
9 Met boat.
10 Boat moved off.
11 Man accompanied by others.
12 Grey jacket.
13 Returned — bridge.
14 Spies exchanged.

Summary writing

After the car stopped, three men *in* black coats got out *and* stood on the bridge. They kept looking over the side *until* a motorboat appeared. *When* it stopped by the river bank, the men on the bridge silently climbed down the stone steps *to* meet the men from the boat. *As soon as* the boat moved off, a man *in* a grey jacket accompanied by two men in black coats returned to the bridge. Two master spies had been exchanged. (81 words)

Vocabulary

In this exercise, you will be asked to explain words and phrases. You may use a phrase to explain a word if necessary. Try to find another word to replace the word or phrase in the passage.

Example

Study the example below to find out how this is done.

Give another word or phrase to replace the following words as they are used in the passage: employ (l.1); from time to time (l.1); gets a glimpse (l.2); rarely (l.2); frequently (l.3); handed (l.3); witness (l.5).

A possible answer

employ: provide work for.
from time to time: now and again.
gets a glimpse of: is able to see briefly.
rarely: seldom.
frequently: often.
handed: given.
witness: see.

Composition

Composition exercises are based on ideas suggested by each passage. You will be given two types of composition exercise:

1 You will be asked to expand a number of uncompleted sentences so that you write a paragraph of about 150 words. You are free to expand each sentence *in any way you please* providing that what you write fits in logically with the rest of the passage.

2 You will be given a full plan which contains notes for an essay in three paragraphs: an Introduction, Development, and Conclusion. You should write a composition of about 200 words based on these notes. You are quite free to add ideas of your own or ignore ideas that are to be found in the plan.

Examples

Work through these examples carefully and then try to do the composition exercises in Unit 1 in the same way.

1 Composition

Write an imaginary account of how one of the spies mentioned in the passage was caught. Expand the following into a paragraph of about 150 words.

Colonel Hepworth had been employed ________ In time, he rose to the position of ________ Soon after his appointment ________ No one suspected the Colonel until ________ Even then, it was impossible to ________ because ________ However, Hepworth was ________ The police noticed that he ________ and ________ One evening, they ________ and found him ________ After Hepworth was ________ it was learnt that ________ He had ________ . (54 words)

A possible answer

Colonel Hepworth had been employed *in the War Office for years*. In time, he rose to the position of *Chief Private Secretary to the Minister*. Soon after his appointment, *important people in the War Office began complaining that many State secrets had become known to the enemy*. No one suspected the Colonel until *a stranger telephoned the police and claimed that he had received large sums of money from Hepworth to obtain information about airbases*. Even then, it was impossible to *make any arrest* because *nothing could be proved against him*. However, Hepworth was *watched closely*. The police noticed that he *often stayed behind in the evenings* and *was often the last person to leave the War Office*. One evening, they *suddenly burst into his room* and found him *holding a pile of secret documents*. After Hepworth was *arrested*, it was learnt that *his real name was Christopher Bulin*. He had *become famous for his work as a spy during the war*.

(about 160 words)

Now here is the same question with a different set of facts and different presentation:

2 Composition

In about 200 words, write an imaginary account of how one of the spies mentioned in the passage was caught. Use the ideas given below. Do not write more than three paragraphs.

Title: The spy.

Introduction: Officer — War Office — trusted.

Development: Expensive car — large sums of money to spend — flat — parties — money 'inherited' — police checked story — false — flat watched — visited by members of Uranian Embassy.

Conclusion: Police entered flat — documents — transmitter — 'officer' confessed.

A possible answer

The spy

Andrew Whibley worked as an officer in the War Office. Though he did not have an important position, he was trusted by everybody.

One day, Whibley arrived at his office in a very expensive car. Although his salary was small, he appeared to have large sums of money to spend. He rented an expensive flat and gave parties for many of his friends. When he was asked how he had suddenly got so much money to spend, Whibley explained that he had inherited a large fortune from an aunt who had died a few months before. However, War Office officials were suspicious and they asked the police to check Whibley's story. The police soon discovered that Whibley had not been telling the truth. They kept a close watch on his flat and noticed that members of the Uranian Embassy often went there.

The police entered Whibley's flat when he was out and discovered copies of several secret documents and a radio transmitter which had been hidden inside a piano. After Whibley was arrested, he confessed that he had been receiving large sums of money from the Uranian Embassy to obtain official secrets.

(about 200 words)

Letter writing

Follow the instructions given under each passage.

Key structures and Special difficulties

When you finish your **Letter writing** exercise, go on to the language exercises that follow. In this unit, you will be given the opportunity to revise briefly each one of the **Key structures** dealt with in *Practice and Progress*. You may refer to *Practice and Progress* if you have forgotten anything. New **Special difficulties** are introduced after the **Key structures.** The work you do in grammar is based on material contained in the passages. Refer to the passages frequently. They will help you to understand the grammar and to do the exercises.

Multiple choice questions

This is a form of comprehension test in which you are asked to choose the correct answer from a number of suggested answers. This exercise tests your ability to understand the *meaning* of the passage you have read and also to recognize grammatical and lexical errors in English.

LESSON 1

A puma at large 逃遁的美洲狮

Listen then answer the question below.

听录音，然后回答以下问题。

Where must the puma have come from?

evidence began to accumulate

Pumas are large, cat-like animals which are found in America. When reports came into London Zoo that a wild puma had been spotted forty-five miles south of London, they were not taken seriously. However, as the evidence began to accumulate, experts from the Zoo felt obliged to investigate, for the descriptions given by people who claimed to have seen the puma were extraordinarily similar.

The hunt for the puma began in a small village where a woman picking blackberries saw 'a large cat' only five yards away from her. It immediately ran away when she saw it, and experts confirmed that a puma will not attack a human being unless it is cornered. The search proved difficult, for the puma was often observed at one place in the morning and at another place twenty miles away in the evening. Wherever it went, it left behind it a trail of dead deer and small animals like rabbits. Paw prints were seen in a number of places and puma fur was found clinging to bushes. Several people complained of 'cat-like noises' at night and a businessman on a fishing trip saw the puma up a tree. The experts were now fully convinced that the animal *was* a puma, but where had it come from? As no pumas had been reported missing from any zoo in the country, this one must have been in the possession of a private collector and somehow managed to escape. The hunt went on for several weeks, but the puma was not caught. It is disturbing to think that a dangerous wild animal is still at large in the quiet countryside.

New words and expressions 生词和短语

puma (title)	/'pju:mə/	n.	美洲狮
spot (l.2)	/spɒt/	v.	看出，发现
evidence (l.4)	/'evɪdəns/	n.	证据
accumulate (l.4)	/ə'kju:mjʊleɪt/	v.	积累，积聚
oblige (l.5)	/ə'blaɪdʒ/	v.	使……感到必须
hunt (l.7)	/hʌnt/	n.	追猎；寻找
blackberry (l.8)	/'blækbəri/	n.	黑莓
human being (l.9)	/ˌhju:mən-'bi:ɪŋ/		人类
corner (l.9)	/'kɔ:nə/	v.	使走投无路，使陷入困境
trail (l.11)	/treɪl/	n.	一串，一系列
print (l.12)	/prɪnt/	n.	印痕
cling (l.12)	/klɪŋ/ (clung /klʌŋ/, clung)	v.	粘
convince (l.14)	/kən'vɪns/	v.	使……信服
somehow (l.16)	/'sʌmhaʊ/	adv.	不知怎么搞的，不知什么原因
disturbing (l.17)	/dɪ'stɜ:bɪŋ/	adj.	令人不安的

Notes on the text 课文注释

1 at large 是介词短语，此处表示"逍遥自在"、"行动自由"的意思。

2 When reports came into London Zoo that a wild puma had been spotted forty-five miles south of London, 当伦敦动物园接到报告说，在伦敦以南 45 英里的地方发现一头野生美洲狮时。这个从句中以 that 引导的从句是 reports 的同位语，用于进一步说明报告的内容。

3 feel obliged to do sth. 是“感到不得不做某事”的意思。

4 it left behind it a trail of, 它身后留下一串……。

a trail of 作 left 的宾语，behind it 是状语，提到宾语之前是为了使句子结构更紧凑。

5 puma fur was found clinging to bushes 中，clinging 是现在分词，此处作主语 puma fur 的主语补足语。下文中 As no pumas had been reported missing ... 一句中，missing 也是现在分词作主语补足语。

6 in the possession of, 为……所有。

参考译文

美洲狮是一种体形似猫的大动物，产于美洲。当伦敦动物园接到报告说，在伦敦以南 45 英里处发现一头野生美洲狮时，这些报告并没有受到重视。可是，随着证据越来越多，动物园的专家们感到有必要进行一番调查，因为凡是声称见到过美洲狮的人们所描述的情况竟是出奇地相似。

搜寻美洲狮的工作是从一座小村庄开始的。那里的一位妇女在采摘黑莓时看见“一只大猫”离她仅 5 码远，她刚看见它，它就立刻逃走了。专家证实，美洲狮除非被逼得走投无路，否则是决不会伤人的。事实上搜寻工作很困难，因为常常是早晨在甲地发现那只美洲狮，晚上却在 20 英里外的乙地发现它的踪迹。无论它走到哪儿，一路上总会留下一串死鹿以及死兔子之类的小动物。在许多地方看见了爪印，灌木丛中也发现了粘在上面的美洲狮毛。有人抱怨说夜里听见了“像猫一样的叫声”；一位商人去钓鱼，看见那只美洲狮在树上。专家们如今已经完全肯定那只动物就是美洲狮，但它是从哪儿来的呢？由于全国的动物园没有一家报告丢了美洲狮，因此那只美洲狮一定是某位私人收藏家豢养的，不知怎么设法逃出来了。搜寻工作进行了好几个星期，但始终未能逮住那只美洲狮。想到在宁静的乡村里有一头危险的野兽继续逍遥流窜，真令人担心。

Summary writing 摘要写作

In not more than 80 words describe how experts came to the conclusion that the animal seen by many people really was a puma. Do not include anything that is not in the passage.

Answer these questions in note form to get your points:

1 What sort of reports were received by London Zoo?
2 Were the reports similar in nature or not?
3 Who saw it first?
4 Did it stay in one place, or did it move from place to place?
5 What did it leave behind it?
6 Were paw prints and puma fur found as well or not?
7 What was heard at night?
8 Was the animal seen up a tree or not?
9 Were experts now sure that the animal really was a puma or not?

Vocabulary 词汇

Give another word or phrase to replace the following words as they are used in the passage: spotted (l.2); accumulate (l.4); obliged to (l.5); claimed (l.6); extraordinarily similar (l.6); immediately (l.8); convinced (l.14).

Composition 作文

Describe the occasion when the woman picking blackberries saw the puma. Expand the following into a paragraph of about 150 words.

Mrs. Stone had spent the whole morning ... It was nearly lunchtime, so she decided ... She was just ... when she heard a noise in ... Then she saw an animal which ... She knew it was not a cat because ... The animal suddenly ... and she thought it was going to ... She dropped her basket and ... Hearing the sound, the animal ... after which, Mrs. Stone ... and ran all the way home. She told her neighbours that ... but they did not believe her. She also telephoned the police but they ... (85 words)

Letter writing 书信写作

On a full page, show the exact position of each of the following:

The address and date; the beginning of the letter; the Introduction; the Purpose; the Conclusion; the letter-ending; the signature; the postscript. Supply all necessary full stops and commas.

Key structures 关键句型

Simple, Compound and Complex Statements. 简单句、并列句和复合句 (**1 KS 73**)（参见第 2 册第 73 课关键句型）

Exercise 练习

Underline all the joining words in the passage. Note carefully how simple statements have been joined to make compound or complex statements.

Special difficulties 难点

过去曾有一种传统的规定，认为英文句子不允许以介词结尾。现在，这种所谓的禁忌早已破除。在现代英语中，除正体书面语体外，以介词结尾的句子很多，在口语中更为常见。

Where had it come from? (l.14)

Instead of saying:	*It is better to say:*
About whom are you talking?	Who(m) are you talking about?
That is the film about which I told you.	That is the film I told you about.

(Compare **1 SD 28**)（对比第 2 册第 28 课难点）

Exercises 练习

A Complete these sentences by adding a suitable word to the end of each one:

1 What are you looking ________ ?

2 Where is your mother going ________ ?

3 Whom has the letter been sent ________ ?

4 This is the house I was born ________ .

5 What does your decision depend ________ ?

B Write these sentences again changing the position of the words in italics. Where possible, omit the words *whom* or *which*.

1 He is the man *about* whom we have heard so much.

2 The shelf *on* which you put those books has collapsed.

3 *From* whom did you receive a letter?

4 This is the road *by* which we came.

5 Where is the pencil *with* which you were playing?

Multiple choice questions 选择题

Choose the correct answers to the following questions.

Comprehension 理解

1 Experts eventually decided to investigate ________ .

(*a*) because they did not believe that pumas existed in England

(*b*) because they wanted a puma for London Zoo

(*c*) when a woman saw a puma in a small village

(*d*) because people's descriptions of the puma had a lot in common

2 What particular piece of evidence persuaded the experts that a puma had been seen in the village?

(*a*) The puma had not attacked the woman.

(*b*) The woman had described the animal she had seen as 'a large cat'.

(*c*) A puma had come very close to a human being.

(*d*) The puma had behaved like a cat.

3 What was the problem the experts were unable to solve?

(*a*) How the puma had managed to cover such great distances within a day.

(*b*) How the puma had escaped from a zoo.

(*c*) Whom the puma had belonged to.

(*d*) How the puma had climbed a tree.

Structure 结构

4 The accumulating evidence made the experts ________ the animal was a puma. (ll.4-6)

(*a*) to think (*b*) thinking (*c*) think (*d*) thought

5 People said ________ the puma. (ll.5-6)

(*a*) to have seen (*b*) to see (*c*) they saw (*d*) they had seen

6 ________ , it immediately ran away. (ll.8-9)

(*a*) Observing her (*b*) On being observed

(*c*) Having been observed (*d*) On her being observed

7 Pumas never attack a human being except ________ cornered. (l.9)

(*a*) they are (*b*) being (*c*) that they are (*d*) when they are

8 The experts were now fully convinced that the animal ________ a puma. (ll.13-14)

(*a*) must be (*b*) should have been (*c*) can only be (*d*) could only have been

Vocabulary 词汇

9 The woman saw 'a large cat' ________ five yards away from her. (ll.7-8)

(*a*) at least (*b*) four or (*c*) no more than (*d*) within

10 A puma will not attack a human being unless it feels itself to be ________ . (l.9)

(*a*) in a corner (*b*) in a trap (*c*) at an angle (*d*) under cover

11 A businessman on a fishing trip is probably someone who ________ . (l.13)

(*a*) sells fish (*b*) fishes for pleasure

(*c*) nets fish (*d*) earns his living as a fisherman

12 A private collector is a man who collects ________ . (ll.15-16)

(*a*) for his own benefit (*b*) on his own

(*c*) in private (*d*) unknown to the public

LESSON

2 Thirteen equals one 十三等于一

Listen then answer the question below.

听录音，然后回答以下问题。

Was the vicar pleased that the clock was striking? Why?

our vicar woke up with a start

Our vicar is always raising money for one cause or another, but he has never managed to get enough money to have the church clock repaired. The big clock which used to strike the hours day and night was damaged many years ago and has been silent ever since.

One night, however, our vicar woke up with a start: the clock was striking the hours! Looking at his watch, he saw that it was one o'clock, but the bell struck thirteen times before it stopped. Armed with a torch, the vicar went up into the clock tower to see what was going on. In the torchlight, he caught sight of a figure whom he immediately recognized as Bill Wilkins, our local grocer.

'Whatever are you doing up here Bill?' asked the vicar in surprise.

'I'm trying to repair the bell,' answered Bill. 'I've been coming up here night after night for weeks now. You see, I was hoping to give you a surprise.'

'You certainly did give me a surprise!' said the vicar. 'You've probably woken up everyone in the village as well. Still, I'm glad the bell is working again.'

'That's the trouble, vicar,' answered Bill. 'It's working all right, but I'm afraid that at one o'clock it will strike thirteen times and there's nothing I can do about it.'

'We'll get used to that, Bill,' said the vicar. 'Thirteen is not as good as one, but it's better than nothing. Now let's go downstairs and have a cup of tea.'

New words and expressions 生词和短语

equal (title)	/ˈiːkwəl/	v.	等于	raise (l.1)	/reɪz/	v.	募集，筹（款）
vicar (l.1)	/ˈvɪkə/	n.	牧师	torchlight (l.8)	/ˈtɔːtʃlaɪt/	n.	手电筒光

Notes on the text 课文注释

1 woke up with a start: ...

with a start, 由于受到惊动，惊醒了。冒号后面是一个解释性的分句，是对 start 所作的具体说明。

2 recognize as, 认出是。

3 Whatever are you doing up here? 你究竟在这上面干什么？

whatever 用于疑问句中，用以加强 what 的语气，作“究竟什么”解，口语中很常用。

4 You certainly did give me a surprise! 你确实使我感到意外！

在英语中助动词 do 可以用来表示强调。此时助动词 do 放在谓语动词之前。

5 Thirteen is not as good as one, but it's better than nothing.

敲 13 下虽然不如敲 1 下好，但总比 1 下不敲强多了。

参考译文

我们教区的牧师总是为各种各样的事筹集资金，但始终未能筹足资金把教堂的钟修好。教堂的钟很大，以前不分昼夜打点报时，但在很多年前遭到毁坏，从此便无声无息了。

一天夜里，我们的牧师突然被惊醒了，大钟又在“打点”报时了！他一看表，才 1 点钟，可是那钟一连敲了 13 下才停。牧师拿着一支电筒走上钟楼想去看看究竟发生了什么事情。借着电筒光，他看见一个人，马上认出那是本地杂货店店主比尔·威尔金斯。

“你究竟在这上面干什么，比尔？”牧师惊讶地问。

“我想把这口钟修好，”比尔回答说，“好几个星期了，我天天夜里到钟楼上来。嗯，我是想让你大吃一惊。”

“你确实使我大吃了一惊！”牧师说，“也许同时你把村里所有的人都吵醒了。不过，钟又能报时了，我还是很高兴的。”

“问题就在这里，牧师，”比尔回答说，“不错，钟是能报时了，但是，恐怕每到 1 点钟，它总要敲 13 下，对此我已无能为力了。”

“大家慢慢就习惯了，比尔，”牧师说，“13 下是不如 1 下好，但总比 1 下也不敲强。来，咱们下楼去喝杯茶吧。”

Summary writing 摘要写作

In not more than 80 words describe what happened from the moment the vicar woke up. Do not include anything that is not in the passage.

Answer these questions in note form to get your points:

1 What woke the vicar up?
2 What was the time?
3 How many times did the clock strike?
4 Where did the vicar go?
5 What did he take with him?
6 Whom did he see in the clock tower?
7 What did Bill Wilkins say he was trying to do?
8 Had Bill Wilkins succeeded in repairing the clock or not?
9 Was the vicar pleased or angry?
10 What did he offer the grocer?

Vocabulary 词汇

Give another word or phrase to replace the following words as they are used in the passage: vicar (l.1); repaired (l.3); damaged (l.4); silent (l.4); with a start (l.5); caught sight of (ll.8-9).

Composition 作文

Write a composition of about 200 words using the ideas given below:

Title: A sticky business.

Introduction: A small village — the church clock suddenly stopped — no one could explain why.

Development: The vicar climbed into the clock tower — found that the clock had been invaded by bees — full of honey and wax.

Conclusion: A bee keeper was called — removed the queen bee — the other bees followed — the clock was cleaned — working again.

Letter writing 书信写作

Write six phrases which could be used to begin letters to friends.

Key structures 关键句型

What is happening? What always happens? 现在进行时、一般现在时表示习惯性的动作

(1 KS 74)（参见第 2 册第 74 课关键句型）

Note that with the word *always* we can sometimes say:

Our vicar is always raising money. (l.1)

He is always getting into trouble.

She is always writing letters.

Exercise 练习

Underline the verbs in the passage that tell us *what is happening* now. Note how they have been used.

Special difficulties 难点

Phrases with In. (Compare **1 SD 43, 80**)（对比第 2 册第 43, 80 课难点）

Study these examples:

'Whatever are you doing up here Bill?' asked the vicar *in surprise*. (l.10)

Please write *in ink*, not *in pencil*.

We have a great deal *in common*.

The swimmer seemed to be *in difficulty*, but he managed to reach the shore *in the end*.

I didn't feel well so I spent the day *in bed*.

We have received fifty applications *in all*.

The thieves were disturbed and left *in a hurry*.

I can't borrow any more money; I'm already *in debt*.

Mary's *in love* with a sailor.

There wasn't a person *in sight*.

He didn't realize that he was *in danger*.

The little boy was *in tears*.

Exercise 练习

Use a phrase with *in* in place of the words in italics.

1 I left home *very quickly* so as not to miss the train.
2 I suppose I shall finish this *eventually*.
3 In the early morning there was not a person *to be seen*.
4 Shall I write *with a pen* or *with a pencil*?
5 They haven't many interests *which they share*.
6 Why is that little girl *crying*?

Multiple choice questions 选择题

Choose the correct answers to the following questions.

Comprehension 理解

1 The church clock did not work because ________ .

(*a*) it was too expensive to repair

(*b*) it disturbed the vicar's sleep

(*c*) Bill Wilkins only worked at night

(*d*) the bell had been out of order for many years

2 The vicar was surprised to see Bill Wilkins in the clock tower because ________ .

(*a*) Bill Wilkins had been hoping to surprise him

(*b*) it was an unusual time and place to find him

(*c*) he had expected to find a figure

(*d*) the clock had struck thirteen times

3 The vicar offered Bill Wilkins a cup of tea because ________ .

(*a*) he thought that Bill Wilkins was thirsty

(*b*) thanks to him, the clock would now strike once an hour

(*c*) he was grateful for the trouble Bill Wilkins had taken

(*d*) he was pleased to have been woken up for nothing

Structure 结构

4 In the past the big clock ________ the hours. (ll.3-4)

(*a*) struck always (*b*) always struck (*c*) was always striking (*d*) has always been striking

5 It was not until the thirteenth stroke ________ the bell stopped. (l.7)

(*a*) before (*b*) when (*c*) so that (*d*) that

6 The vicar asked Bill ________ doing in the church tower. (l.10)

(*a*) what was he (*b*) what he was (*c*) what he is (*d*) whatever was he

7 'I ________ it all right, but I'm afraid ...' (ll.15-16)

(*a*) shall mend (*b*) am mending (*c*) have mended (*d*) mended

8 'We'll get used to ________ that, Bill.' (l.17)

(*a*) hearing (*b*) hear (*c*) the sound (*d*) having heard

Vocabulary 词汇

9 Money which is collected for a cause is known as ________ . (ll.1-2)

(*a*) cash (*b*) a fund (*c*) a scholarship (*d*) an investment

10 A grocer is a man who ________ . (l.9)

(*a*) runs a shop (*b*) eats a lot (*c*) sells bread (*d*) surprises people

11 'I've been coming here ________ for weeks now.' (l.11)

(*a*) every night (*b*) all night (*c*) the following night (*d*) several nights

12 ' ________ , I'm glad the bell is working again.' (l.14)

(*a*) Yet (*b*) Good (*c*) Just the same (*d*) Even now

LESSON

3 An unknown goddess 无名女神

Listen then answer the question below.

听录音，然后回答以下问题。

How did the archaeologists know that the statue was a goddess?

a very modern-looking woman

Some time ago, an interesting discovery was made by archaeologists on the Aegean island of Kea. An American team explored a temple which stands in an ancient city on the promontory of Ayia Irini. The city at one time must have been prosperous, for it enjoyed a high level of civilization. Houses — often three storeys high — were built of stone. They had large rooms with beautifully decorated walls. The city was even equipped with a drainage system, for a great many clay pipes were found beneath the narrow streets.

The temple which the archaeologists explored was used as a place of worship from the fifteenth century B.C. until Roman times. In the most sacred room of the temple, clay fragments of fifteen statues were found. Each of these represented a goddess and had, at one time, been painted. The body of one statue was found among remains dating from the fifteenth century B.C. Its missing head happened to be among remains of the fifth century B.C. This head must have been found in Classical times and carefully preserved. It was very old and precious even then. When the archaeologists reconstructed the fragments, they were amazed to find that the goddess turned out to be a very modern-looking woman. She stood three feet high and her hands rested on her hips. She was wearing a full-length skirt which swept the ground. Despite her great age, she was very graceful indeed, but, so far, the archaeologists have been unable to discover her identity.

New words and expressions 生词和短语

goddess (title)	/ˈgɒdɪs/	*n.*	女神
archaeologist (l.1)	/ˌɑːkiˈɒlədʒɪst/	*n.*	考古学家
Aegean (l.2)	/iːˈdʒiːən/	*adj.*	爱琴海的
explore (l.2)	/ɪkˈsplɔː/	*v.*	考察，勘探
promontory (l.3)	/ˈprɒməntəri/	*n.*	海角
prosperous (l.4)	/ˈprɒspərəs/	*adj.*	（经济上）繁荣的，昌盛的
civilization (l.5)	/ˌsɪvəlaɪˈzeɪʃən/	*n.*	文明
storey (l.5)	/ˈstɔːri/	*n.*	楼层
drainage (l.7)	/ˈdreɪnɪdʒ/	*n.*	排水
worship (l.9)	/ˈwɜːʃɪp/	*n.*	崇拜
sacred (l.10)	/ˈseɪkrɪd/	*adj.*	宗教的，神圣的
fragment (l.10)	/ˈfrægmənt/	*n.*	碎片
remains (l.12)	/rɪˈmeɪnz/	*n.*	（复数）遗物，遗迹，废墟
classical (l.13)	/ˈklæsɪkəl/	*adj.*	（希腊和罗马）古文化的
reconstruct (l.14)	/ˌriːkənˈstrʌkt/	*v.*	修复
rest (l.16)	/rest/	*v.*	倚放，放置
hip (l.16)	/hɪp/	*n.*	屁股，臀部
full-length (l.16)	/ˌfʊlˈleŋθ/	*adj.*	（裙衣）拖地长的
graceful (l.17)	/ˈgreɪsfəl/	*adj.*	优雅的
identity (l.17)	/aɪˈdentɪti/	*n.*	身份

Notes on the text 课文注释

1 the Aegean island of Kea, 爱琴海的基亚岛。爱琴海是东地中海的一部分，位于希腊半岛和小亚细亚之间。它包括希腊半岛以外的许多岛屿。基亚岛位于希腊半岛东南方的海域里。

2 Ayia Irini, 阿伊亚 · 依里尼，意为“圣依里尼”，Irini 是希腊文，意为“和平”。

3 The city at one time must have been prosperous, for it enjoyed a high level of civilization. 这座古城肯定一度很繁荣，因为它曾享有高度的文明。must have been 是对过去的推测。at one time, 一度。

4 Roman times, 罗马时代。指古罗马（约公元前 200 年—公元 400 年）时期，那时罗马人在欧洲建立了帝国。

5 date from, 追溯到。

6 Classical times, 指古希腊，古罗马时代。

7 the goddess turned out to be ..., 那位女神原来是……。

参考译文

不久之前，在爱琴海的基亚岛上，考古工作者有一项有趣的发现。一个美国考古队在阿伊亚 · 依里尼海角的一座古城里考察了一座庙宇。这座古城肯定一度很繁荣，因为它曾享有高度的文明。房子一般有 3 层楼高，用石块修建，里面房间很大，墙壁装饰华丽。城里甚至还敷设了排水系统，因为在狭窄的街道底下发现了许许多多陶土制作的排水管道。

考古工作者考察的这座庙宇从公元前 15 世纪直至罗马时代一直是祭祀祈祷的场所。在庙中最神圣的一间殿堂里发现了 15 尊陶制雕像的碎片。每一尊雕像代表一位女神，而且一度上过色。其中有一尊雕像，她的躯体是在公元前 15 世纪的历史文物中发现的，而她那身首异处的脑袋却碰巧是在公元前 5 世纪的文物中找到的。她的脑袋一定是在古希腊罗马时代就为人所发现，并受到了精心的保护。即使在当时，它也属历史悠久的珍奇之物。考古工作者把这些碎片重新拼装起来后，惊奇地发现那位女神原来是一位相貌十分摩登的女郎。她身高 3 英尺，双手叉腰，身穿一条拖地长裙，尽管上了年纪，但体态确实优美。不过，考古工作者至今未能确定这位女神的身份。

Summary writing 摘要写作

In not more than 80 words describe what archaeologists discovered in an ancient temple on the island of Kea. Do not include anything that is not in the last paragraph.

Answer these questions in note form to get your points:

1 Where did the archaeologists find clay fragments?]
2 What did they represent?
3 Had they once been painted or not?]
4 Where was the body of one statue found?
5 Where was its head found?]
6 Were the fragments reconstructed or not?
7 How tall did the goddess turn out to be?]
8 Where did her hands rest?
9 What was she wearing?]
10 Is her identity known or not?]

Vocabulary 词汇

Give another word or phrase to replace the following words as they are used in the passage: explored (l.2); ancient (l.3); prosperous (l.4); storeys (l.5); beneath (l.7); fragments (l.10); remains (l.12).

Composition 作文

Write an imaginary account of how the archaeologists explored the sacred room of the ancient temple.
Expand the following into a paragraph of about 150 words.

After walking round the ancient city, the archaeologists ... This temple ... On entering the sacred room, the archaeologists ... After this, workmen began digging and soon discovered ... They also found ... The archaeologists carefully ... They were astonished to find that ... The goddess was ... She ... Although the archaeologists ... they were unable to find out her name. (52 words)

Letter writing 书信写作

Write six phrases which could be used to end letters to friends.

Key structures 关键句型

What happened? 一般过去时 (1 KS 75)（参见第 2 册第 75 课关键句型）

Exercise 练习

Suppose that each of the following verbs were used to describe *what happened* yesterday. What would be their correct form?

Yesterday I ... leave, lay, lie, choose, raise, rise, beat, bite, catch, hear, sing, think, show, run, lose, begin, fall, feel.

Special difficulties 难点

Words often misused and confused

A *Happen.* Study these examples:

Its missing head *happened to be* among remains of the fifth century B.C. (By chance.) (ll.12-13)

I *happened to find* the ticket in my pocket. (By chance.)

It happened that I found the ticket in my pocket. (By chance.)

I couldn't find out what had *happened*. (What had taken place.)

B *Storey* and *Story*. Study this example:

Houses – often three storeys high – were built of stone. (ll.5-6)

C *Worship* and *Warship.* Study these examples:

The temple ... was used as a place of *worship.* (ll.9-10)

The *Arethusa* used to be a *warship.*

Exercises 练习

A Complete the following making a sentence out of each.

1 She happened ________ .

2 It happened ________ .

3 Tell me what ________ .

4 If you happen ________ .

B Use the words *storey*, *story*, *worship*, and *warship* in sentences of your own.

Multiple choice questions 选择题

Choose the correct answers to the following questions.

Comprehension 理解

1 The interesting discovery made by the archaeologists was ________ .
(*a*) that the city had once been prosperous
(*b*) that the temple had been used as a place of worship
(*c*) that they found the fifteen statues had been painted
(*d*) that they were not the first to have found the head of the goddess

2 The city 'enjoyed a high level of civilization'. This is confirmed by the fact that ________ .
(*a*) some of the houses were built only one storey high
(*b*) a great number of fragments were found in the temple
(*c*) the city had been built on clay
(*d*) advanced techniques had been employed in building and decorating

3 In seeking to establish the identity of the reconstructed statue, the archaeologists ________ .
(*a*) tried to determine which goddess it represented
(*b*) pieced together the fragments they found
(*c*) discovered that it was more modern than any of the other statues
(*d*) wondered whether it belonged to the fifth or the fifteenth century

Structure 结构

4 The city had once known ________ . (l.4)
(*a*) a prosperity (*b*) the prosperous (*c*) the prosperity (*d*) prosperity

5 The temple ________ used as a place of worship since Roman times. (ll.9-10)
(*a*) was (*b*) has not been (*c*) had been (*d*) was not

6 They found ________ that the goddess turned out to be ... (ll.14-15)
(*a*) surprisingly (*b*) with surprise (*c*) to their surprise (*d*) a surprise

7 ________ being very old, she was very graceful. (ll.16-17)
(*a*) Although (*b*) In spite of (*c*) Even (*d*) Even though

8 So far, the archaeologists ________ to discover her identity. (l.17)
(*a*) have been impossible (*b*) have not been able
(*c*) cannot have been (*d*) could not

Vocabulary 词汇

9 In the most ________ room of the temple ... (l.10)
(*a*) holy (*b*) religious (*c*) frightening (*d*) colourful

10 The head was carefully preserved. It was ________ . (l.13)
(*a*) well done (*b*) conserved (*c*) maintained (*d*) in good condition

11 The goddess ________ to be a very modern-looking woman. (l.15)
(*a*) appeared (*b*) proved (*c*) resolved (*d*) changed

12 But, ________ the archaeologists have been unable ... (l.17)
(*a*) beforehand (*b*) until now (*c*) for a long time (*d*) at this distance

LESSON 4

The double life of Alfred Bloggs

艾尔弗雷德·布洛格斯的双重生活

Listen then answer the question below.

听录音，然后回答以下问题。

Why did Alf want a white-collar job?

... he then changed

These days, people who do manual work often receive far more money than people who work in offices. People who work in offices are frequently referred to as 'white-collar workers' for the simple reason that they usually wear a collar and tie to go to work. Such is human nature, that a great many people are often willing to sacrifice higher pay for the privilege of becoming white-collar workers. This can give rise to curious situations, as it did in the case of Alfred Bloggs who worked as a dustman for the Ellesmere Corporation.

When he got married, Alf was too embarrassed to say anything to his wife about his job. He simply told her that he worked for the Corporation. Every morning, he left home dressed in a smart black suit. He then changed into overalls and spent the next eight hours as a dustman. Before returning home at night, he took a shower and changed back into his suit. Alf did this for over two years and his fellow dustmen kept his secret. Alf's wife has never discovered that she married a dustman and she never will, for Alf has just found another job. He will soon be working in an office. He will be earning only half as much as he used to, but he feels that his rise in status is well worth the loss of money. From now on, he will wear a suit all day and others will call him 'Mr. Bloggs', not 'Alf'.

New words and expressions 生词和短语

manual (l.1)	/'mænjuəl/	*adj.*	体力的	corporation (l.8)	/ˌkɔːpə'reɪʃən/	*n.*	公司
collar (l.4)	/'kɒlə/	*n.*	衣领	overalls (l.11)	/'əʊvərɔːlz/	*n.*	（复数）工作服
sacrifice (l.5)	/'sækrəfaɪs/	*v.*	牺牲，献出	shower (l.12)	/'ʃaʊə/	*n.*	淋浴
privilege (l.6)	/'prɪvɪlɪdʒ/	*n.*	好处	secret (l.12)	/'siːkrɪt/	*n.*	秘密
dustman (l.7)	/'dʌstmən/	*n.*	清洁工	status (l.15)	/'steɪtəs/	*n.*	地位

Notes on the text 课文注释

1 People who work in offices are frequently referred to as 'white-collar workers'，那些坐在办公室的人，往往被称为“白领工人”。white-collar workers 往往指脑力劳动者，而体力劳动者则被称为 blue-collar workers，蓝领工人。

2 for the simple reason that ... 这里 that 引导的从句是 the reason 的同位语。

3 Such is human nature, that ...

such 位于句首，起强调作用，后面要用倒装语序，that 引导的是 such 的同位语从句。

4 as it did in the case of Alfred Bloggs who worked as a dustman for the Ellesmere Corporation. 正如给埃

尔斯米尔公司当清洁工的艾尔弗雷德·布洛格斯的情况所造成的怪现象那样。as it did 中的 it 是指上一句中 that 从句所指的情况，而 did 是替代 give rise to curious situations。

5 half as much as he used to, 只相当于过去的一半。

参考译文

如今，从事体力劳动的人的收入一般要比坐办公室的人高出许多。坐办公室的人之所以常常被称作“白领工人”，就是因为他们通常是穿着硬领白衬衫、系着领带去上班。许多人常常情愿放弃较高的薪水以换取做白领工人的殊荣，此乃人之常情。而这常常会引起种种奇怪的现象，在埃尔斯米尔公司当清洁工的艾尔弗雷德·布洛格斯就是一个例子。

艾尔弗结婚时，感到非常难为情，而没有将自己的职业告诉妻子。他只说在埃尔斯米尔公司上班。每天早晨，他穿上一身漂亮的黑色西装离家上班，然后换上工作服，当 8 个小时清洁工。晚上回家前，他洗个淋浴，重新换上那身黑色西服。两年多以来，艾尔弗一直这样，他的同事也为他保守秘密。艾尔弗的妻子一直不知道她嫁给了一个清洁工，而且她永远也不会知道了，因为艾尔弗已找到新职，不久就要坐在办公室里工作了。他将来挣的钱只有他现在的一半。不过他觉得，地位升高了，损失点儿钱也值得。从此，艾尔弗可以一天到晚穿西服了。别人将称呼他为“布洛格斯先生”，而不再叫他“艾尔弗”了。

Summary writing 摘要写作

In not more than 80 words describe how Alfred Bloggs prevented his wife from finding out that he worked as a dustman. Do not include anything that is not in the last paragraph.

Answer these questions in note form to get your points:

1 What did Alfred Bloggs tell his wife when they got married?]
2 How did he dress each morning before he left home?
3 Did he change into overalls or not?
4 How did he spend the day?]
5 What did he do before going home at night?]
6 For how long did this last?
7 Did his fellow dustmen keep his secret or not?]
8 Will his wife ever learn the truth?
9 Where will her husband be working in future?]

Vocabulary 词汇

Give another word or phrase to replace the following words as they are used in the passage: receive (l.1); sacrifice (l.5); privilege (l.6); curious (l.7); embarrassed (l.9); discovered (l.13); status (l.15).

Composition 作文

Write a composition of about 200 words using the ideas given below. Do not write more than three paragraphs.

Title: Nearly caught.

Introduction: Alf and three other dustmen were collecting rubbish — arrived at Mrs. Frost's house.

Development: Alf's wife was visiting Mrs. Frost at the time — Alf was just getting out of the dustcart — saw his wife leaving Mrs. Frost's house — hid in dustcart — dustmen helped him — his wife talked to Mrs. Frost on the doorstep.

Conclusion: The dustcart drove away just as Mrs. Bloggs came towards it.

Letter writing 书信写作

Write a letter of about 80 words to an acquaintance whom you do not know very well asking him to lend you a book you know he possesses. Supply a suitable Introduction and Conclusion. Use the following ideas to write your *Purpose*: ask for loan of book — its title — why you want it — how long you will keep it — you will take good care of it.

Key structures 关键句型

What has happened? What has been happening? 现在完成时与现在完成进行时 (1 KS 76)

（参见第 2 册第 76 课关键句型）

Exercises 练习

A Find two verbs in the passage which tell us *what has happened* and note how they have been used.

B Write sentences using each of the following words or phrases: since last April; up till now; just; ever; yet.

Special difficulties 难点

A Alf was too embarrassed to say anything to his wife. (l.9) 间接宾语 (Compare **1 SD 3**)

（对比第 2 册第 3 课难点）

Study these examples:

He explained the difficulty *to me*.

I described the scene *to my wife*.

He said nothing *to me* about it.

Did you suggest this idea *to him*?

I confided the secret *to my sister*.

B Words often misused: Worth

Study these examples:

His rise in status is well worth the loss of money. (l.15)

That film is not worth seeing. (Compare **1 KS 68a**)（对比第 2 册第 68 课关键句型 a）

Exercises 练习

A Write sentences using the following combinations of words.

1 describe/film/aunt. 2 say/nothing/her. 3 explain/the position/me. 4 propose/idea/us.

B Choose the correct words in the following:

1 (Is) (Does) it worth five pounds?

2 Is this worth (buying) (to buy)?

3 Your car (does) (is) not worth £5,000.

4 I don't think it is worth (to go) (going) to all that trouble.

Multiple choice questions 选择题

Choose the correct answers to the following questions.

Comprehension 理解

1 What does the case of Alfred Bloggs illustrate?

(*a*) That people often care more about the status of a job than the salary.

(*b*) That 'white-collar workers' usually wear a suit to go to work.

(*c*) That manual workers prefer to keep their job a secret.

(*d*) That office workers usually earn less than manual workers.

2 What did Alfred Bloggs do for over two years?

(*a*) He told his wife he worked for the Corporation, when in fact he did not.

(*b*) He disguised himself as a dustman.

(*c*) He led a double life.

(*d*) He earned twice as much as he used to.

3 Why did Alfred Bloggs consider wearing a suit all day and being called 'Mr. Bloggs' so important?

(*a*) His new job is worth more than his previous one in every respect.

(*b*) He will no longer need a shower before returning home from work.

(*c*) He can now tell his wife about his previous job without embarrassment.

(*d*) He feels that other people will respect him more.

Structure 结构

4 They usually wear a collar and tie ________ ... (l.4)

(*a*) as they work (*b*) to work (*c*) going to work (*d*) in order to work

5 Alf was ________ anything to his wife. (l.9)

(*a*) so embarrassed he said (*b*) very embarrassed and said

(*c*) very embarrassed, so he said (*d*) so embarrassed he did not say

6 He told her that he worked for the Corporation ________ ... (ll.9-10)

(*a*) simply (*b*) in a simple way (*c*) and no more (*d*) only

7 Before he ________ home at night, he took a shower ... (ll.11-12)

(*a*) was returning (*b*) returned (*c*) had returned (*d*) will return

8 His earnings were only half the amount ________ ... (l.14)

(*a*) as they used to (*b*) they used to (*c*) they used to be (*d*) they were used to

Vocabulary 词汇

9 Manual workers often receive much higher ________ than people who work in offices. (ll.1-2)

(*a*) gains (*b*) fees (*c*) payments (*d*) wages

10 His ________ kept his secret. (l.12)

(*a*) brothers (*b*) workmates (*c*) companions (*d*) comrades

11 His rise in status more than ________ the loss of money. (l.15)

(*a*) pays back (*b*) rewards (*c*) compensates for (*d*) values

12 He wanted to be ________ 'Mr. Bloggs', not 'Alf'. (ll.15-16)

(*a*) addressed as (*b*) named (*c*) cried out (*d*) shouted

LESSON

5 The facts 确切数字

... to obtain these important facts

Listen then answer the question below.

听录音，然后回答以下问题。

What was the consequence of the editor's insistence on facts and statistics?

Editors of newspapers and magazines often go to extremes to provide their readers with unimportant facts and statistics. Last year a journalist had been instructed by a well-known magazine to write an article on the president's palace in a new African republic. When the article arrived, the editor read the first sentence and then refused to publish it. The article began: 'Hundreds of steps lead to the high wall which surrounds the president's palace.' The editor at once sent the journalist a fax instructing him to find out the exact number of steps and the height of the wall.

The journalist immediately set out to obtain these important facts, but he took a long time to send them. Meanwhile, the editor was getting impatient, for the magazine would soon go to press. He sent the journalist two more faxes, but received no reply. He sent yet another fax informing the journalist that if he did not reply soon he would be fired. When the journalist again failed to reply, the editor reluctantly published the article as it had originally been written. A week later, the editor at last received a fax from the journalist. Not only had the poor man been arrested, but he had been sent to prison as well. However, he had at last been allowed to send a fax in which he informed the editor that he had been arrested while counting the 1,084 steps leading to the fifteen-foot wall which surrounded the president's palace.

New words and expressions 生词和短语

editor (l.1)	/ˈedɪtə/	*n.*	编辑	publish (l.6)	/ˈpʌblɪʃ/	*v.*	出版
extreme (l.1)	/ɪkˈstriːm/	*n.*	极端	fax (l.7)	/fæks/	*n.*	传真
statistics (l.2)	/stəˈtɪstɪks/	*n.*	（复数）统计数字	impatient (l.10)	/ɪmˈpeɪʃənt/	*adj.*	不耐烦的
journalist (l.3)	/ˈdʒɜːnəlɪst/	*n.*	新闻记者	fire (l.12)	/ˈfaɪə/	*v.*	解雇
president (l.4)	/ˈprezɪdənt/	*n.*	总统	originally (l.13)	/əˈrɪdʒɪnəli/	*adv.*	起初，原先，从前
palace (l.4)	/ˈpælɪs/	*n.*	王宫；宏伟的住宅				

Notes on the text 课文注释

1 go to extremes, 走极端。

2 provide ... with ... 作"向……提供……"解。

3 to write an article on, 写一篇有关……的文章。

4 lead to ... 作"通往……"解。

5 go to press, 付印。

6 Not only had the poor man been arrested, but he had been sent to prison as well. 这是 not only ... but ... as well 引导的并列句子，如果将 not only 置于句首，后面主谓语应采取倒装结构。

参考译文

报刊杂志的编辑常常为了向读者提供一些无关紧要的事实和统计数字而走向极端。去年，一位记者受一家有名的杂志的委托写一篇关于非洲某个新成立共和国总统府的文章。稿子寄来后，编辑看了第一句话就拒绝予以发表。文章的开头是这样的："几百级台阶通向环绕总统府的高墙。"编辑立即给那位记者发去传真，要求他核实一下台阶的确切数字和围墙的高度。

记者立即出发去核实这些重要的事实，但过了好长时间不见他把数字寄来。在此期间，编辑等得不耐烦了，因为杂志马上要付印。他给记者先后发去两份传真，但对方毫无反应。于是他又发了一份传真，通知那位记者说，若再不迅速答复，将被解雇。但记者还是没有回复。编辑无奈，勉强按原样发了稿。一周之后，编辑终于接到了记者的传真。那个可怜的记者不仅被捕了，而且还被送进了监狱。不过，他终于获准发回了一份传真。在传真中他告诉编辑，就在他数通向 15 英尺高的总统府围墙的 1,084 级台阶时，被抓了起来。

Summary writing 摘要写作

In not more than 80 words describe what happened from the time the journalist set out to get the facts. Do not include anything that is not in the last paragraph.

Answer these questions in note form to get your points:

1 Did the journalist immediately set out to get the facts after receiving instructions from his editor or not?
2 Did he send them at once or not?
3 Was the editor getting impatient or not?
4 How many faxes did the editor send?
5 What did the editor threaten to do?
6 Was the last fax answered or not?
7 Was the article omitted from the magazine, or was it printed in its original form?
8 When did the journalist send a fax?
9 Why had he been imprisoned?

Vocabulary 词汇

Give another word or phrase to replace the following words as they are used in the passage: journalist (l.3); instructed (l.3); well-known (l.3); publish (l.6); surrounds (l.7); fired (l.12); reluctantly (l.12).

Composition 作文

Describe how the journalist was arrested and what happened afterwards. Expand the following into a paragraph of about 150 words.

The journalist counted the number of steps as he ... On arriving outside the main gate, he ... He then ... in order to measure the wall. While he was busy measuring the wall, a policeman ... Though the journalist ... , the policeman refused to believe him. He was arrested and sent to prison because the police thought that ... When the journalist ... he made things worse for himself. This proved to the police that ...

(69 words)

Letter writing 书信写作

Write a letter of about 80 words to a friend who has recently got married. You read about the wedding in your local paper. Supply a suitable Introduction and Conclusion. Use the following ideas to write the *Purpose*: Surprise and pleasure at seeing newspaper report — glad to hear that he and his wife will be staying in your neighbourhood — hope to see them soon.

Key structures 关键句型

A, The and Some. (1 KS 78)（参见第 2 册第 78 课关键句型）

Exercises 练习

A Underline the words *a(n)* and *the* in the passage and note how they have been used.

B Write sentences using the following words and phrases:

1 Hudson river 2 information 3 cinema 4 industry 5 flour and milk 6 newspaper

Special difficulties 难点

Not only had the poor man been arrested ... (ll.13-14)

在英文中，如果表示否定的副词或副词词组放在句首，就必须后接"助动词+主语+句子的其他部分"。这种倒装结构特别用来加强语气。

Study these pairs of sentences:

I have never seen so many people.

Never have I seen so many people.

I had hardly finished speaking when the door opened.

Hardly had I finished speaking when the door opened.

(Compare **1 SD 38a**)（对比第 2 册第 38 课难点 a）

Exercise 练习

Write these sentences again beginning each one with the words in italics.

1 He has *not only* made this mistake before but he will make it again.

2 I realized what was happening *only then*.

3 I will *never* trust him again.

4 You *seldom* find traffic wardens who are kind and helpful.

Multiple choice questions 选择题

Choose the correct answers to the following questions.

Comprehension 理解

1 The editor acted as he did because ________ .

(*a*) he wanted an excuse to fire the journalist

(*b*) he had not read the article beyond the first sentence

(*c*) he was dissatisfied with the factual content of the article

(*d*) he wanted to please the president of the new African republic

2 The journalist took a long time to send the details required because ________ .
(*a*) it took him a long time to count all the steps
(*b*) he had not been allowed to fax the information he had obtained
(*c*) he did not realize how soon the magazine would go to press
(*d*) he had been arrested before he had had time to obtain the facts

3 Why had the journalist been arrested?
(*a*) Because his activities must have appeared suspicious.
(*b*) For having gone to extremes to provide unimportant facts.
(*c*) For climbing the palace wall in order to measure its height.
(*d*) Because the article was published in its original form.

Structure 结构

4 ________ the first sentence, the editor refused to publish the article. (ll.5-6)
(*a*) Reading (*b*) Having read (*c*) He read (*d*) Being read

5 The magazine ________ to press. (l.10)
(*a*) was (*b*) had gone (*c*) was about to go (*d*) was due

6 He sent the journalist two faxes, but did not receive ________ . (ll.10-11)
(*a*) the replies (*b*) the reply (*c*) no reply (*d*) a reply

7 He informed the journalist he would be fired unless he ________ . (ll.11-12)
(*a*) was replied (*b*) replied (*c*) would reply (*d*) did not reply

8 He informed ________ while carrying out his instructions. (ll.15-16)
(*a*) his arrest to the editor (*b*) the editor his arrest
(*c*) the editor of his arrest (*d*) the editor that his arrest had been

Vocabulary 词汇

9 Editors of newspapers and magazines often go to extremes to provide their ________ with unimportant facts and statistics. (ll.1-2)
(*a*) audience (*b*) lectures (*c*) public (*d*) common

10 The magazine would soon go to press. It would soon be ________ . (l.10)
(*a*) pressing (*b*) printed (*c*) typed (*d*) impressed

11 The poor man had been arrested. He was very ________ . (l.14)
(*a*) poor (*b*) stupid (*c*) innocent (*d*) unfortunate

12 He had at last been ________ to send a fax. (ll.14-15)
(*a*) admitted (*b*) let (*c*) left (*d*) given permission

LESSON

6 Smash-and-grab 砸橱窗抢劫

Listen then answer the question below.

听录音，然后回答以下问题。

How did Mr. Taylor try to stop the thieves?

too busy to notice any pain

The expensive shops in a famous arcade near Piccadilly were just opening. At this time of the morning, the arcade was almost empty. Mr. Taylor, the owner of a jewellery shop was admiring a new window display. Two of his assistants had been working busily since eight o'clock and had only just finished. Diamond necklaces and rings had been beautifully arranged on a background of black velvet. After gazing at the display for several minutes, Mr. Taylor went back into his shop.

The silence was suddenly broken when a large car, with its headlights on and its horn blaring, roared down the arcade. It came to a stop outside the jeweller's. One man stayed at the wheel while two others with black stockings over their faces jumped out and smashed the window of the shop with iron bars. While this was going on, Mr. Taylor was upstairs. He and his staff began throwing furniture out of the window. Chairs and tables went flying into the arcade. One of the thieves was struck by a heavy statue, but he was too busy helping himself to diamonds to notice any pain. The raid was all over in three minutes, for the men scrambled back into the car and it moved off at a fantastic speed. Just as it was leaving, Mr. Taylor rushed out and ran after it throwing ashtrays and vases, but it was impossible to stop the thieves. They had got away with thousands of pounds worth of diamonds.

New words and expressions 生词和短语

smash-and-grab	(title)	/ˌsmæʃ-ən-ˈɡræb/	n.	砸橱窗抢劫
arcade	(l.1)	/ɑːˈkeɪd/	n.	有拱廊的街道（两旁常设商店）
Piccadilly	(l.1)	/ˌpɪkəˈdɪli/	n.	皮卡迪利大街
jewellery	(l.3)	/ˈdʒuːəlri/	n.	珠宝（总称）
necklace	(l.5)	/ˈnek-ləs/	n.	项链
ring	(l.6)	/rɪŋ/	n.	戒指
background	(l.6)	/ˈbækɡraʊnd/	n.	背景
velvet	(l.7)	/ˈvelvɪt/	n.	天鹅绒，丝绒
headlight	(l.9)	/ˈhedlaɪt/	n.	（汽车等）前灯
blare	(l.9)	/bleə/	v.	发嘟嘟声，吼叫
staff	(l.12)	/stɑːf/	n.	全体工作人员
raid	(l.14)	/reɪd/	n.	抢劫
scramble	(l.14)	/ˈskræmbəl/	v.	爬行
fantastic	(l.15)	/fænˈtæstɪk/	adj.	非常大的
ashtray	(l.16)	/ˈæʃtreɪ/	n.	烟灰缸

Notes on the text 课文注释

1 Piccadilly，皮卡迪利大街，伦敦市中心一条著名的街。这条街从海德公园通向一个著名的广场，叫作“皮卡迪利广场”。

2 with its headlights on and its horn blaring, ... 这是 with 引导的独立主格结构，在句中表示伴随状况。

3 but he was too busy helping himself to diamonds to notice any pain.

但他只顾忙着抢劫钻石，根本顾不上疼痛了。这里 help oneself to sth. 是“擅自取用，侵占某物”的意思。

参考译文

皮卡迪利大街附近的一条著名拱廊街道上，几家高档商店刚刚开始营业。在早晨的这个时候，拱廊街上几乎空无一人。珠宝店主泰勒先生正在欣赏新布置的橱窗。他手下两名店员从早上 8 点就开始忙碌，这时刚刚布置完毕。钻石项链、戒指漂亮地陈列在黑色丝绒上面。泰勒先生站在橱窗外凝神欣赏了几分钟就回到了店里。

宁静突然被打破，一辆大轿车亮着前灯，响着喇叭，呼啸着冲进了拱廊街，在珠宝店门口停了下来。一人留在驾驶座上，另外两个用黑色长筒丝袜蒙面的人跳下车来。他们用铁棒把商店橱窗玻璃砸碎。这一切发生时，泰勒先生正在楼上。他与店员动手向窗外投掷家具，椅子、桌子飞落到拱廊街上。一个窃贼被一尊很重的雕像击中，但由于他忙着抢钻石首饰，竟连疼痛都顾不上了。这场抢劫只持续了 3 分钟，因为窃贼争先恐后地爬上轿车，以惊人的速度开跑了。就在轿车离开的时候，泰勒先生从店里冲了出来，跟在车后追赶，一边还往车上扔烟灰缸、花瓶。但他已无法抓住那些窃贼了。他们已经带着价值数千镑的首饰逃之夭夭了。

Summary writing 摘要写作

Write an account of the smash-and-grab raid *in not more than 80 words*. Do not include anything that is not in the last paragraph.

Answer these questions in note form to get your points:

1 Did a large car enter an arcade near Piccadilly or not?
2 Where did it stop?
3 How many thieves got out of the car?
4 Did they smash the window or not?
5 Where was the owner of the shop?
6 What did he and his staff throw at the thieves?
7 Did they hit any of the thieves or not?
8 How long did the raid last?
9 Did the thieves drive away or not?
10 Did the owner run after the car or did he stay in the shop?
11 What did he throw at the car?
12 Did the thieves get away or were they caught?
13 What had they stolen?

Vocabulary 词汇

Give another word or phrase to replace the following words as they are used in the passage: expensive (l.1); almost (l.2); assistants (l.4); gazing (l.7); several (l.7); stayed (l.10); smashed (l.11).

Composition 作文

In not more than 200 words continue the above passage using the ideas given below. Do not write more than three paragraphs.

Title: They got away.

Introduction: The thieves' car joined the traffic — Mr. Taylor took a taxi — followed the thieves' car.
Development: A mad chase through the streets — the thieves' car hit another car — did not stop — the police chased both taxi and thieves — Mr. Taylor's taxi stopped at traffic lights — the thieves got away — taxi driver was stopped by the police — he had been speeding — Mr. Taylor explained the situation.
Conclusion: The thieves' car was found ten minutes later — side street — abandoned — the thieves escaped on foot.

Letter writing 书信写作

Suppose that you had witnessed an incident similar to the one described in the passage. Write a letter of about 80 words to a friend describing what you saw. Supply a suitable Introduction and Conclusion. Use the following ideas to write the *Purpose:* Tuesday morning — busy street — a man smashed the window of an antique shop — chased by passers-by — you joined in — the man was caught.

Key structures 关键句型

What happened? What was happening? 一般过去时与过去进行时 (1 KS 79)（参见第 2 册第 79 课关键句型）

Exercises 练习

A Underline the verbs in the passage which tell us *what happened* and *what was happening*. Note how they have been used.

B Write sentences using the following words and phrases: just as; used to; while.

Special difficulties 难点

Word building

Study these sentences:

It was possible to stop the thieves.

It was impossible to stop the thieves. (l.16)

Note how the opposite of 'possible' has been formed. We can add *dis-*, *in-*, *im-*, *un-*, *il-*, or *ir-* to certain words to make opposites.

Exercise 练习

Write these sentences again giving the correct opposites of the words in italics.

1 He was extremely *polite*.
2 I *agree* with you.
3 His handwriting is quite *legible*.
4 This report is *accurate*.
5 Have you *locked* the door?
6 Have you learnt these *regular* verbs?

Multiple choice questions 选择题

Choose the correct answers to the following questions.

Comprehension 理解

1 While Mr. Taylor was admiring the new window display, ________ .

(*a*) his two assistants were arranging jewellery in the window

(*b*) some thieves were on their way to raid his shop

(*c*) he was standing inside his shop

(*d*) his staff were finishing their work for the day

2 The car headlights were on and its horn blaring ________ .

(*a*) as the thieves wanted to warn people out of their way

(*b*) as a special signal to the assistants

(*c*) so the thieves could see where they were going

(*d*) to break the early morning silence

3 The thieves chose to raid Mr. Taylor's shop because ________ .

(*a*) it was early in the morning and not many shops were open

(*b*) they did not expect Mr. Taylor and his staff to try and stop them

(*c*) it usually had a great deal of valuable jewellery on display

(*d*) they had a very fast car to get away in

Structure 结构

4 The expensive shops in ________ were just opening. (ll.1-2)

(*a*) Piccadilly's famous arcade (*b*) a Piccadilly famous arcade

(*c*) a famous Piccadilly arcade (*d*) the famous arcade of Piccadilly

5 He ________ the display for several minutes before re-entering his shop. (ll.7-8)

(*a*) was gazing at (*b*) gazed at (*c*) had gazed at (*d*) had been gazing at

6 Using bars made ________ iron, the thieves smashed the shop window. (l.11)

(*a*) of (*b*) from (*c*) by (*d*) with

7 He and his staff began ________ furniture out of the window. (l.12)

(*a*) to throw (*b*) by throwing (*c*) and threw (*d*) the throwing of

8 Had he not been so busy taking the diamonds, he ________ the blow. (ll.13-14)

(*a*) would feel (*b*) had been feeling (*c*) had felt (*d*) would have felt

Vocabulary 词汇

9 To make the car 'roar down the arcade', the driver must have ________ . (ll.9-10)

(*a*) accelerated (*b*) sped (*c*) run (*d*) reversed

10 Two others, their faces ________ black stockings, jumped out. (ll.10-11)

(*a*) covered with (*b*) overdressed with (*c*) overlooked by (*d*) made up in

11 ________ , Mr. Taylor was upstairs. (ll.11-12)

(*a*) For the time being (*b*) Meanwhile (*c*) As it happened (*d*) For a while

12 Chairs and tables were ________ into the arcade. (ll.12-13)

(*a*) flown (*b*) emptied (*c*) hurled (*d*) projected

LESSON

7 Mutilated Ladies* 残钞鉴别组

Listen then answer the question below.

听录音，然后回答以下问题。

Why did Jane cook John's wallet?

a beautifully-cooked wallet

Has it ever happened to you? Have you ever put your trousers in the washing machine and then remembered there was a large bank note in your back pocket? When you rescued your trousers, did you find the note was whiter than white? People who live in Britain needn't despair when they make mistakes like this (and a lot of people do)! Fortunately for them, the Bank of England has a team called Mutilated Ladies which deals with claims from people who fed their money to a machine or to their dog. Dogs, it seems, love to chew up money!

A recent case concerns Jane Butlin whose fiancé, John, runs a successful furniture business. John had a very good day and put his wallet containing £3,000 into the microwave oven for safekeeping. Then he and Jane went horse-riding. When they got home, Jane cooked their dinner in the microwave oven and without realizing it, cooked her fiancé's wallet as well. Imagine their dismay when they found a beautifully-cooked wallet and notes turned to ash! John went to see his bank manager who sent the remains of the wallet and the money to the special department of the Bank of England in Newcastle: the Mutilated Ladies! They examined the remains and John got all his money back. 'So long as there's something to identify, we will give people their money back,' said a spokeswoman for the Bank. 'Last year, we paid £1.5m on 21,000 claims.'

*Damaged bank notes. The Queen's head appears on English bank notes, and 'lady' refers to this.

New words and expressions 生词和短语

mutilate (title)	/ˈmjuːtɪleɪt/	*v.*	使残缺不全	safekeeping (l.10)	/ˌseɪfˈkiːpɪŋ/	*n.*	妥善保管
chew (l.8)	/tʃuː/	*v.*	咀嚼	Newcastle (l.14)	/ˈnjuːˌkɑːsl/	*n.*	纽卡斯尔（英国港市）
fiancé (l.9)	/fiˈɒnseɪ/	*n.*	未婚夫				
microwave (l.10)	/ˈmaɪkrəweɪv/	*n.*	微波；微波炉	identify (l.15)	/aɪˈdentɪfaɪ/	*v.*	鉴定，识别
oven (l.10)	/ˈʌvən/	*n.*	烤箱，烤炉	spokeswoman (l.16)	/ˈspəʊksˌwʊmən/	*n.*	女发言人

Notes on the text 课文注释

1 Mutilated Ladies, 这是英国银行专门负责识别和鉴定残缺或被毁纸币的小组，其中的 lady 是指英国纸币上印的女王头像。

2 a large bank note, 面额很大的纸币。

3 whiter than white, 这是英国有关洗衣粉的电视广告中常用的一句话。这里的意思是纸币上的字迹、图案均被洗掉了，可以译为“比白纸还白”。

4 they found a beautifully-cooked wallet and notes turned to ash, 他们发现一只煮得很好看的钱包，钞票

已烧成了灰。过去分词短语 turned to ash 作宾语 notes 的补足语，这后半句话可以看成 they found ... that notes had been turned to ash。

参考译文

这种事情在你身上出现过吗？你有没有把裤子塞进洗衣机，然后又想起在裤子的后兜有一张大面值的纸币？当你把裤子抢救出来时，你有没有发现那张纸币已经变得比白纸还白？当英国人犯这种错误时（而且确实很多人犯这种错误），他们不必感到绝望。对英国人来说，值得庆幸的是英国银行有一个残钞鉴别组，负责处理那些把钱塞进机器或塞给狗的人提出的索赔要求。看起来，狗很喜欢咀嚼钱币。

最近的一个案例与简·巴特林有关，她的未婚夫约翰拥有一家生意兴隆的家具店。有一天约翰的生意很好，他把一只装有 3,000 英镑的钱包放进微波炉内保存。然后，他和简一起去骑马。回家后，简用微波炉煮了晚饭，无意之中把她未婚夫的钱包也一起煮了。可以想象他们发现一只煮得很好看的钱包、钞票已化成灰时的沮丧心情。约翰去找银行经理，经理把约翰的钱包和纸币的残留物送到英国银行在纽卡斯尔的一个专门部门——残钞鉴别组。他们鉴定了这些残留物。约翰拿回了他损失的全部数额。"只要有东西可供识别，我们会把钱还给人家的，"银行的一位女发言人说。"去年，我们对 21,000 起索赔要求支付了 150 万英镑。"

Summary writing 摘要写作

In not more than 80 words describe what happened to John and Jane. Do not include anything that is not in the last paragraph.

Answer these questions in note form to get your points:

1 What sort of business does John Butlin run?
2 What did he do at the end of a very good day?

3 What did he and his fiancée do then?
4 What did Jane do after they got home?
5 What were they dismayed to find?

6 Who did John go and see?
7 What did the bank manager do?
8 What happened after that?

Vocabulary 词汇

Give another word or phrase to replace the following words as they are used in the passage: happened (l.1); remembered (l.2); fortunately (l.6); concerns (l.9); dismay (l.12); the remains (l.13); department (l.14).

Composition 作文

Describe what happened when Jane got the dinner out of the microwave.

Expand the following into a paragraph of about 150 words.

Jane opened the oven door and saw that her meal was ... She took the food out of the oven and ... They both rushed to the oven and ... At first, they didn't know what ... John wanted to ... but Jane wouldn't ... 'It's best not to ...,' Jane said. 'You can see that all the money ...' Jane told John to ..., so the next day ...

(60 words)

Letter writing 书信写作

Write a letter of about 80 words to a friend thanking him for his hospitality. Supply a suitable Introduction and Conclusion. Use the following ideas to write the *Purpose*: the pleasure of seeing your friend again — his kindness during your stay — things about the visit you will remember for a long time — hope you can return this hospitality one day.

Key structures 关键句型

What happened? 一般过去时 (1 KS 75)（参见第 2 册第 75 课关键句型）

Exercises 练习

A Look at the second paragraph. Underline all the verbs that tell us *what happened.*

B Write sentences using the following past forms: rescued, went, cooked, sent, examined, paid.

Special difficulties 难点

John runs a successful furniture business. (l.9) 名词和相对应的形容词

Study these examples:

His business is a *success*. He runs a *successful* business.

He's a bit of a *fool*. He often makes *foolish* decisions.

She has a lot of *energy*. She's very *energetic*.

The clock strikes at intervals of an *hour*. It strikes at *hourly* intervals.

You didn't take any *care* with this. You were completely *careless*.

Exercise 练习

Supply the missing words.

1 You won't feel any pain. The operation is completely ________ .

2 I admired the beauty of the countryside. The countryside is so ________ .

3 I visit my mother every day. My mother expects ________ visits.

4 Don't behave like a child. Don't be so ________ !

5 She's a wonderful athlete. That explains why she's so ________ .

Multiple choice questions 选择题

Choose the correct answers to the following questions.

Comprehension 理解

1 They call the team in Newcastle 'Mutilated Ladies' because ________ .

(*a*) their job involves mutilating bank notes

(*b*) their job is to identify pictures of the Queen on mutilated bank notes

(*c*) ladies are always mutilating bank notes by accident in the wash

(*d*) only ladies have the patience for this difficult job

2 The Bank of England offers a special service to people who ________ .

(*a*) feed their money to the dog　　(*b*) try to wash large bank notes

(*c*) mutilate bank notes on purpose　　(*d*) have damaged but identifiable bank notes

3 You don't get your money back unless ________ .

(*a*) you go to Newcastle and see the Mutilated Ladies

(*b*) there is enough evidence to prove your claim

(*c*) your bank manager agrees to help you

(*d*) you have done this sort of thing before

Structure 结构

4 Have you ever forgotten ________ in the pocket of your trousers ...? (ll.1-3)

(*a*) a large bank note (*b*) large bank note (*c*) any large bank note (*d*) some large bank note

5 If you ________ in Britain, you needn't despair. (ll.4-5)

(*a*) do live (*b*) are living (*c*) live (*d*) were living

6 John is ________ , and runs a furniture business. (l.9)

(*a*) fiancé of Jane Butlin (*b*) Jane Butlin's fiancé

(*c*) Jane Butlin who's fiancé (*d*) Jane Butlin whose fiancé

7 The wallet ________ £3,000 from the day's business. (l.10)

(*a*) containing (*b*) was containing (*c*) contained (*d*) content

8 John put his wallet into the microwave oven ________ . (l.10)

(*a*) to keep it safe (*b*) for keeping safe (*c*) for the safety (*d*) to be safe keeping

Vocabulary 词汇

9 John runs a furniture business. He ________ the business. (l.9)

(*a*) is in charge of (*b*) is in the charge of (*c*) charges (*d*) bears the charges of

10 Jane discovered that the £3,000 had ________ ash. (ll.12-13)

(*a*) turned (*b*) grown (*c*) made (*d*) become

11 The remains were ________ to the Mutilated Ladies. (ll.13-14)

(*a*) conveyed (*b*) dispatched (*c*) carried (*d*) fetched

12 People can get their money back ________ there is something to identify. (ll.15-16)

(*a*) depending (*b*) provided (*c*) supposed (*d*) allowing

LESSON 8

A famous monastery 著名的修道院

Listen then answer the question below.

听录音，然后回答以下问题。

What are the St. Bernard dogs used for?

These friendly dogs ...

The Great St. Bernard Pass connects Switzerland to Italy. At 2,473 metres, it is the highest mountain pass in Europe. The famous monastery of St. Bernard, which was founded in the eleventh century, lies about a mile away. For hundreds of years, St. Bernard dogs have saved the lives of travellers crossing the dangerous Pass. These friendly dogs, which were first brought from Asia, were used as watchdogs even in Roman times. Now that a tunnel has been built through the mountains, the Pass is less dangerous, but each year, the dogs are still sent out into the snow whenever a traveller is in difficulty. Despite the new tunnel, there are still a few people who rashly attempt to cross the Pass on foot.

During the summer months, the monastery is very busy, for it is visited by thousands of people who cross the Pass in cars. As there are so many people about, the dogs have to be kept in a special enclosure. In winter, however, life at the monastery is quite different. The temperature drops to –30° and very few people attempt to cross the Pass. The monks prefer winter to summer for they have more privacy. The dogs have greater freedom, too, for they are allowed to wander outside their enclosure. The only regular visitors to the monastery in winter are parties of skiers who go there at Christmas and Easter. These young people, who love the peace of the mountains, always receive a warm welcome at St. Bernard's monastery.

New words and expressions 生词和短语

monastery (title)	/ˈmɒnəstri/	*n.*	寺院，修道院
St. Bernard (l.1)	/ˌseɪnt-bəˈnɑːd/		圣伯纳德
pass (l.2)	/pɑːs/	*n.*	关隘
watchdog (l.7)	/ˈwɒtʃdɒg/	*n.*	看门狗
rashly (l.9)	/ˈræʃli/	*adv.*	莽撞地，冒失地
enclosure (l.12)	/ɪnˈkləʊʒə/	*n.*	围场，圈地
monk (l.14)	/mʌŋk/	*n.*	和尚，僧侣
privacy (l.14)	/ˈprɪvəsi/	*n.*	清静，隐居
skier (l.16)	/ˈskiːə/	*n.*	滑雪者
Easter (l.16)	/ˈiːstə/	*n.*	复活节

Notes on the text 课文注释

1 Now that a tunnel has been built through the mountains, 由于一条穿山隧道已经开通。
now that 是连词，当"既然"、"由于"讲，引导一个原因状语从句，说明一种新情况。

2 As there are so many people about, ...
about 为副词，作"在附近"、"到处"讲。也可用 around 表示。

3 The monks prefer winter to summer, 修道士们喜欢冬天而不喜欢夏天。prefer ... to ... 有"喜欢……而不喜欢……"的意思，to 的前后要用名词或动名词来表示所对比的事物或活动。

参考译文

圣伯纳德大山口连接着瑞士与意大利，海拔 2,473 米，是欧洲最高的山口。11 世纪建造的著名的圣伯纳德修道院位于离山口 1 英里远的地方。几百年来，圣伯纳德修道院驯养的狗拯救了许多翻越这道险要山口的旅游者的生命。这些最先从亚洲引进的狗，待人友好，早在罗马时代就给人当看门狗了。如今由于在山里开挖了隧道，翻越山口已不那么危险了，但每年还要派狗到雪地里去帮助那些遇到困难的旅游者。尽管修通了隧道，但仍有一些人想冒险徒步跨越圣伯纳德山口。

夏天的几个月里，修道院十分忙碌，因为有成千上万的人驾车通过山口，顺道来修道院参观。由于来人太多，狗被关在专门的围栏里。然而到了冬天，修道院里的生活则是另一番景象。气温下降到零下 30 度，试图翻越山口的人寥寥无几。修道士们喜欢冬天，而不太喜欢夏天。因为在冬天，他们可以更多地过上无人打扰的生活。狗也比较自由，被放出围栏，四处溜达。冬天常来修道院参观的只有一批批滑雪者。他们在圣诞节或复活节到那儿去。这些热爱高山清静环境的年轻人每年都受到圣伯纳德修道院的热烈欢迎。

Summary writing 摘要写作

In not more than 80 words give an account of life at St. Bernard's monastery in summer and in winter. Do not include anything that is not in the last paragraph.

Answer these questions in note form to get your points:

1 When is St. Bernard's monastery visited by thousands of people?
2 How do these people cross the Pass?
3 Why are the dogs kept in a special enclosure?
4 How low does the temperature drop in winter?
5 Are there few visitors then, or are there a great many?
6 Do the monks prefer the winter season or not?
7 What are the dogs free to do in winter?
8 What sort of people regularly visit the monastery in winter?
9 Do they stay there the whole winter, or do they stay only at certain times?
10 Are they warmly welcomed or not?

Vocabulary 词汇

Give another word or phrase to replace the following words as they are used in the passage: famous (l.2); founded (l.3); lies (l.4); now that (l.7); rashly attempt (ll.9-10); quite (l.13); drops (l.13).

Composition 作文

In not more than 200 words write an imaginary account of the way a traveller was rescued on St. Bernard's Pass in winter. Use the ideas given below. Do not write more than three paragraphs.

Title: Rescue.

Introduction: A monk took two dogs out for exercise — the dogs were restless — a search party was organized.

Development: The dogs led the monks through the snow — high winds the previous night — now heavy fog — temperature 20° below — they got near — heard cries — a man was trapped under the snow — the dogs dragged him out — he was taken to the monastery on a sledge.

Conclusion: The man was unconscious — recovered later — told them what had happened the previous night.

Letter writing 书信写作

Write a letter of about 80 words to a friend recommending a hotel in the Alps to him. Supply a suitable Introduction and Conclusion. Use the following ideas to write the *Purpose*: why you recommend it — you stayed there last year — fine views — healthy mountain air — comfortable — moderate prices — you intend to go this year as well.

Key structures 关键句型

Verb forms: review. 动词时态复习 **(1 KS 83)**（参见第 2 册第 83 课关键句型）

Exercises 练习

A Underline the verbs in the passage which tell us *what always happens, what happened* and *what has happened.* Note how they have been used.

B Write sentences using the following words and phrases: ago; for six months; when; since 1988.

Special difficulties 难点

The dogs are still sent out into the snow whenever a traveller is in difficulty. (ll.8-9)

请记住，ever 有时可同 who, what, when, where 等一起构成代词或连词，用来加强句子（特别是疑问句）的语气。

Compare these pairs of sentences:

He did what I asked him to do.

He did whatever I asked him to do.

Who told you that?

Whoever told you that?

I'll tell you when you make a mistake.

I'll tell you whenever you make a mistake.

Where has he gone?

Wherever has he gone?

Exercise 练习

Supply the missing words in the following sentences.

1 Now that he's grown up, he does ______ever he pleases.

2 ______ever I telephone, the line's engaged.

3 ______ever told you that, didn't know what he was talking about.

Multiple choice questions 选择题

Choose the correct answers to the following questions.

Comprehension 理解

1 St. Bernard dogs are best known for ________ .

(*a*) being a great summer tourist attraction

(*b*) having saved people's lives before the new tunnel was built

(*c*) being able to search people out who have been trapped in the snow

(*d*) the freedom they have to wander about in the winter

2 What is the main advantage of the new tunnel?

(*a*) It prevents people from endangering their lives by climbing the Pass.

(*b*) It brings thousands of tourists to the monastery each summer.

(*c*) It provides a fast and safe communication across the Swiss-Italian border.

(*d*) It brings the St. Bernard monks into greater contact with the world.

3 In what way does life at the St. Bernard monastery differ in winter?

(*a*) The great number of visitors must come to the monastery on skis.

(*b*) The dogs are free to save the lives of people lost in the snow.

(*c*) The monks are more welcoming to their visitors.

(*d*) The monks can pursue their occupation relatively undisturbed.

Structure 结构

4 The highest mountain pass in Europe is ________ ... (ll.1-2)

(*a*) of 2,473 metres (*b*) at 2,473 metres high (*c*) high 2,473 metres (*d*) 2,473 metres high

5 – a few people who are ________ to cross the Pass on foot. (ll.9-10)

(*a*) rash enough (*b*) so rash (*c*) too rash (*d*) very rash

6 ________ so many people about, the dogs have to be kept in an enclosure. (l.12)

(*a*) With (*b*) Being (*c*) Because (*d*) Having

7 The monks let ________ outside their enclosure. (l.15)

(*a*) them to wander (*b*) to them wandering (*c*) them wander (*d*) them wandering

8 Parties of skiers ________ the monastery in winter. (ll.15-16)

(*a*) visit to (*b*) are visiting at (*c*) visit (*d*) are visiting

Vocabulary 词汇

9 The great St. Bernard Pass lies ________ Switzerland and Italy. (l.1)

(*a*) within (*b*) between (*c*) about (*d*) along

10 The dogs are sent out into the snow ________ a traveller is in difficulty. (ll.8-9)

(*a*) if ever (*b*) in case (*c*) all the time (*d*) while

11 Thousands of people ________ over the Pass. (ll.11-12)

(*a*) trip (*b*) voyage (*c*) conduct (*d*) drive

12 They are allowed to ________ outside their enclosure. (l.15)

(*a*) graze (*b*) drift (*c*) roam (*d*) wonder

LESSON

9 Flying cats 飞猫

Listen then answer the question below.
听录音，然后回答以下问题。

How do cats try to protect themselves when falling from great heights?

They have nine lives

Cats never fail to fascinate human beings. They can be friendly and affectionate towards humans, but they lead mysterious lives of their own as well. They never become submissive like dogs and horses. As a result, humans have learned to respect feline independence. Most cats remain suspicious of humans all their lives. One of the things that fascinates us most about cats is the popular belief that they have nine lives. Apparently, there is a good deal of truth in this idea. A cat's ability to survive falls is based on fact.

Recently the New York Animal Medical Centre made a study of 132 cats over a period of five months. All these cats had one experience in common: they had fallen off high buildings, yet only eight of them died from shock or injuries. Of course, New York is the ideal place for such an interesting study, because there is no shortage of tall buildings. There are plenty of high-rise windowsills to fall from! One cat, Sabrina, fell 32 storeys, yet only suffered from a broken tooth. 'Cats behave like well-trained paratroopers,' a doctor said. It seems that the further cats fall, the less they are likely to injure themselves. In a long drop, they reach speeds of 60 miles an hour and more. At high speeds, falling cats have time to relax. They stretch out their legs like flying squirrels. This increases their air-resistance and reduces the shock of impact when they hit the ground.

New words and expressions 生词和短语

fascinate (l.1)	/ˈfæsɪneɪt/	*v.*	迷住，吸引住
affectionate (l.2)	/əˈfekʃənɪt/	*adj.*	充满深情的，柔情的
mysterious (l.2)	/mɪˈstɪəriəs/	*adj.*	神秘的，难以理解的
submissive (l.3)	/səbˈmɪsɪv/	*adj.*	服从的，顺从的
feline (l.4)	/ˈfiːlaɪn/	*adj.*	猫的
independence (l.4)	/ˌɪndɪˈpendəns/	*n.*	独立，独立性
high-rise (l.12)	/ˈhaɪraɪz/	*adj.*	高层的
windowsill (l.12)	/ˈwɪndəʊˌsɪl/	*n.*	窗台
paratrooper (l.13)	/ˈpærəˌtruːpə/	*n.*	伞兵
squirrel (l.16)	/ˈskwɪrəl/	*n.*	松鼠
air-resistance (l.16)	/ˌeə-rɪˈzɪstəns/	*n.*	空气阻力
impact (l.16)	/ˈɪmpækt/	*n.*	冲击力

Notes on the text 课文注释

1 Cats never fail to fascinate human beings. 在这句话中有一个否定词 never 和一个含有否定意义的动词 fail，这两个否定词就组成了双重否定，而双重否定往往用来表示肯定。这句话可以译成："猫总能引起人们的极大兴趣。"

2 be based on, 在……基础之上。

3 have ... in common, 有……共同之处。

4 the further cats fall, the less they are likely to injure themselves, 猫跌落的距离越长，它们就越不会伤害自己。“the + 形容词或副词比较级 ... the + 形容词或副词比较级”的结构常用来表示比较关系，往往可以译成“越……越……”。be likely to 是“很可能会”的意思。

参考译文

猫总能引起人们的极大兴趣。它们可以对人友好，充满柔情。但是，它们又有自己神秘的生活方式。它们从不像狗和马一样变得那么顺从。结果是人们已经学会尊重猫的独立性。在它们的一生中，大多数猫都对人存有戒心。最使我们感兴趣的一件事情就是一种通俗的信念——猫有九条命。显然，这种说法里面包含着许多真实性。猫在跌落时能够大难不死是有事实作为依据的。

最近，纽约动物医疗中心对 132 只猫进行了为期 5 个月的综合研究。所有这些猫都有一个共同的经历：它们都曾从高层建筑上摔下来过，但只有其中的 8 只猫死于撞击或跌伤。当然，纽约是进行这种有趣的试验的一个理想的地方，因为那里根本不缺乏高楼大厦，有的是高层的窗台从上往下坠落。有一只叫萨伯瑞娜的猫从 32 层楼上掉下来，但只摔断了一颗牙。“猫就像训练有素的跳伞队员，”一位医生说。看起来，猫跌落的距离越长，它们就越不会伤害自己。在一个长长的跌落过程中，它们可以达到每小时 60 英里甚至更快的速度。在高速下落中，猫有时间放松自己。它们伸展开四肢，就像飞行中的松鼠一样。这样就加大了空气阻力，并减小了它们着地时冲击力带来的震荡。

Summary writing 摘要写作

In not more than 80 words describe the study of cats made by the New York Animal Medical Centre. Do not include anything that is not in the last paragraph.

Answer these questions in note form to get your points:

1 How many cats did the New York Animal Medical Centre make a study of?]

2 What had all these cats done?

3 How many of these cats had been killed?]

4 What happened to a cat called Sabrina?

5 What do cats do when falling at speeds of 60 miles an hour or more?

6 What effect does this have?]

Vocabulary 词汇

Give another word or phrase to replace the following words as they are used in the passage: affectionate (l.2); as a result (l.4); remain (l.5); there is no shortage of (ll.11-12); behave (l.13); injure (l.14); increases (l.16); reduces (l.16).

Composition 作文

Write an account of cats as pets. Expand the following into a paragraph of about 150 words.

Human beings like to keep dogs and ... Dogs are ... , but cats like to ... Cats are especially lovable when they are still kittens. As kittens they ... That's how they learn to ... A lot of people keep cats so they ... As kittens grow into cats, they like to ... They like regular meal times and enjoy ... However, they also ... During the daytime and at night they like to ... They often have fights with other cats. Sometimes during the night ... Cats are very clean animals. You often see them ... Human beings ... (87 words)

Letter writing 书信写作

You borrowed a book from a friend but your baby tore some of the pages. Write a letter of about 80 words offering to replace it. Supply a suitable Introduction and Conclusion. Use the following ideas to write the *Purpose*: very sorry for what has happened — had left book on low table — baby got hold of it — tore several pages — you have bought another book and are sending it.

Key structures 关键句型

What always happens? 一般现在时用于表示习惯性动作 (**1 KS 74**)（参见第 2 册第 74 课关键句型）

Exercises 练习

A Underline all the verbs in the text that describe general truths (simple present tense).

B Give the correct form of the verbs in parentheses. Do not refer to the passage until you finish the exercise.

Most cats ________ (remain) suspicious of humans all their lives. One of the things that ________ (fascinate) us most about cats is the popular belief that they ________ (have) nine lives. Apparently, there ________ (be) a good deal of truth in this idea. A cat's ability to survive falls ________ (base) on fact.

Special difficulties 难点

... New York is the ideal place for such an interesting study. (l.11) 形容词的位置

Read these sentences:

This study of cats is so interesting.

It's such an interesting study.

These studies of cats are so interesting.

They're such interesting studies.

They found it so difficult to study the behaviour of cats.

They had such difficulty studying the behaviour of cats.

Exercise 练习

Supply *so, such, such a,* or *such an.*

1 The film was ________ funny, we laughed all the way through it.

2 We all had ________ fun at the seaside. It's a pity you weren't there.

3 It's ________ unusual exhibition, I'm sure you'll enjoy it.

4 The twins are ________ alike, you can't tell the difference between them.

5 There was ________ loud noise, everyone jumped.

Multiple choice questions 选择题

Choose the correct answers to the following questions.

Comprehension 理解

1 We find cats endlessly fascinating because ________ .
(*a*) we feel there is a good deal we do not know about their lives
(*b*) we believe that cats have nine lives
(*c*) they are different from dogs and horses
(*d*) they can reach a speed of 60 miles an hour while falling

2 A recent study of 132 cats in New York proved ________ .
(*a*) that it is true that cats have nine lives
(*b*) that cats are related to flying squirrels
(*c*) that they are different from dogs and horses
(*d*) that cats falling from great heights are seldom killed

3 Cats can survive great falls mainly because ________ .
(*a*) the further they fall, the less likely they are to injure themselves
(*b*) a cat's ability to survive is based on fact
(*c*) a falling cat relaxes its legs and so increases its air-resistance
(*d*) they are unlikely to exceed a speed of about 60 miles an hour

Structure 结构

4 Cats have an unfailing fascination ________ most people. (l.1)
(*a*) with (*b*) to (*c*) for (*d*) at

5 Cats never become submissive ________ . (l.3)
(*a*) as dogs and horses (*b*) in the way that dogs and horses do
(*c*) as far as dogs and horses (*d*) as for dogs and horses

6 ________ popularly believed that cats have nine lives. (ll.6-7)
(*a*) There is (*b*) Is (*c*) This is (*d*) It is

7 New York is ideal for this study because ________ high-rise buildings. (ll.11-12)
(*a*) there is plenty of (*b*) of the number of (*c*) it has plenty (*d*) the number

8 Over a period of five months, there was ________ of 132 cats in New York. (l.9)
(*a*) a study (*b*) studied (*c*) some studies (*d*) studying

Vocabulary 词汇

9 Most cats are suspicious of human beings ________ their lives. (l.5)
(*a*) during (*b*) throughout (*c*) through (*d*) while

10 ________ there is a good deal of truth in this idea. (l.7)
(*a*) As a matter of fact (*b*) In the event (*c*) It would seem (*d*) Surprisingly enough

11 That cats can survive falls from great heights is ________ by the facts. (ll.7-8)
(*a*) explained (*b*) tested (*c*) supported (*d*) borne

12 One cat fell 32 storeys. ________ she only suffered a broken tooth. (ll.12-13)
(*a*) Even so (*b*) Although (*c*) Moreover (*d*) In spite of

LESSON 10

The loss of the *Titanic*

“泰坦尼克”号的沉没

Listen then answer the question below.

听录音，然后回答以下问题。

What would have happened if only two of the sixteen watertight compartments had been flooded?

the icy waters of the North Atlantic

The great ship, *Titanic*, sailed for New York from Southampton on April 10th, 1912. She was carrying 1,316 passengers and a crew of 891. Even by modern standards, the 46,000 ton *Titanic* was a colossal ship. At that time, however, she was not only the largest ship that had ever been built, but was regarded as unsinkable, for she had sixteen watertight compartments. Even if two of these were flooded, she would still be able to float. The tragic sinking of this great liner will always be remembered, for she went down on her first voyage with heavy loss of life.

Four days after setting out, while the *Titanic* was sailing across the icy waters of the North Atlantic, a huge iceberg was suddenly spotted by a lookout. After the alarm had been given, the great ship turned sharply to avoid a direct collision. The *Titanic* turned just in time, narrowly missing the immense wall of ice which rose over 100 feet out of the water beside her. Suddenly, there was a slight trembling sound from below, and the captain went down to see what had happened. The noise had been so faint that no one thought that the ship had been damaged. Below, the captain realized to his horror that the *Titanic* was sinking rapidly, for five of her sixteen watertight compartments had already been flooded! The order to abandon ship was given and hundreds of people plunged into the icy water. As there were not enough lifeboats for everybody, 1,500 lives were lost.

New words and expressions 生词和短语

Southampton (l.1)	/sauθ'æmptən/	*n.*	南安普敦（英国港市）
colossal (l.4)	/kə'lɒsəl/	*adj.*	庞大的
watertight (l.6)	/'wɔːtətaɪt/	*adj.*	不漏水的
compartment (l.6)	/kəm'pɑːtmənt/	*n.*	（轮船的）密封舱
flood (l.7)	/flʌd/	*v.*	充满水
float (l.7)	/fləut/	*v.*	漂浮
tragic (l.7)	/'trædʒɪk/	*adj.*	悲惨的
liner (l.7)	/'laɪnə/	*n.*	邮轮，客轮
voyage (l.8)	/'vɔɪ-ɪdʒ/	*n.*	航行
iceberg (l.10)	/'aɪsbɜːg/	*n.*	冰山
lookout (l.10)	/'luk-aut/	*n.*	瞭望员
collision (l.11)	/kə'lɪʒən/	*n.*	碰撞
narrowly (l.11)	/'nærəuli/	*adv.*	刚刚，勉强地
miss (l.11)	/mɪs/	*v.*	避开
slight (l.12)	/slaɪt/	*adj.*	轻微的
tremble (l.12)	/'trembəl/	*v.*	震颤
faint (l.13)	/feɪnt/	*adj.*	微弱的
horror (l.14)	/'hɒrə/	*n.*	恐惧
abandon (l.15)	/ə'bændən/	*v.*	抛弃
plunge (l.16)	/plʌndʒ/	*v.*	投入，跳入
lifeboat (l.16)	/'laɪfbəut/	*n.*	救生船

Notes on the text 课文注释

1 sail for, 驶往……。

2 even by modern standards, 即使依照现代标准来衡量。

by 作"依照"、"按照"讲。

3 regarded as unsinkable, 被认为是不会沉没的。regard ... as ... 当"把……当作……"讲。

4 she went down on her first voyage with heavy loss of life, 她首航就下沉，造成大批人员死亡。go down 是"下沉"的意思。

5 narrowly missing, 勉强避开。

6 Below, the captain realized to his horror, 在下面，船长惊恐地发现。below 是个副词。

参考译文

巨轮"泰坦尼克"号 1912 年 4 月 10 日从南安普敦起锚驶向纽约。船上载有 1,316 名乘客与 891 名船员。即使用现代标准来衡量，46,000 吨的"泰坦尼克"号也算得上一艘巨轮了。当时，这艘轮船不仅是造船史上建造的最大的一艘船，而且也被认为是不会沉没的。因为船由 16 个密封舱组成，即使有两个舱进水，仍可漂浮在水面上。然而，这艘巨轮首航就下沉，造成大批人员死亡。人们将永远记着这艘巨轮的沉没惨剧。

"泰坦尼克"号起航后的第 4 天，它正行驶在北大西洋冰冷的海面上。突然，瞭望员发现一座冰山。警报响过不久，巨轮急转弯，以避免与冰山正面相撞。"泰坦尼克"号这个弯拐得及时，紧贴着高出海面 100 英尺的巨大的冰墙擦过去。突然，从船舱下部传来一声轻微的颤音，船长走下船舱去查看究竟。由于这个声音非常轻，没人会想到船身已遭损坏。在下面，船长惊恐地发现"泰坦尼克"号正在急速下沉，16 个密封舱已有 5 个进水。于是，他发出了弃船的命令，几百人跳进了冰冷刺骨的海水里。由于没有足够的救生艇运载所有乘客，结果 1,500 人丧生。

Summary writing 摘要写作

Write an account of the sinking of the *Titanic in not more than 80 words*. Do not include anything that is not in the last paragraph.

Answer these questions in note form to get your points:

1 Where was the *Titanic* sailing?
2 What was seen by a lookout?

3 When did the ship turn sharply?
4 Did it sail alongside the iceberg, or did it collide with it?

5 What was heard from below?
6 What did the captain do?
7 What did he find?

8 When did everyone jump overboard?
9 Why were 1,500 people drowned?

Vocabulary 词汇

Give another word or phrase to replace the following words as they are used in the passage: colossal (l.4); regarded (l.5); compartments (l.6); flooded (l.7); float (l.7); avoid (l.11); narrowly (l.11).

Composition 作文

In not more than 200 words write an imaginary account of what happened on the *Titanic* immediately after the order to abandon ship was given. Use the ideas given below. Do not write more than three paragraphs.

Title: Abandon ship.

Introduction: Order to abandon ship unexpected — everybody unprepared.

Development: Immediate effect — panic and confusion — people rushing in all directions — crew came up from below — lifeboats lowered — people jumped overboard — struggle to get into lifeboats — lifeboats full.

Conclusion: *Titanic* sank rapidly — people in water — cries of despair — lifeboats moved away.

Letter writing 书信写作

Which of the following addresses is correct:

19 Kingsley Ave.
Sandford Park,
London, N.W.8,
England.
August 24th, 19 —

19 Kingsley Ave.,
Sandford Park,
London, N.W.8,
England.
24th Aug., 19 —

19 Kingsley Ave.,
Sandford Park,
London, N.W.8,
England
Aug. 24th, 19 —

Key structures 关键句型

What had happened? 过去完成时 (1 KS 86)（参见第 2 册第 86 课关键句型）

Exercises 练习

A Underline the verbs in the passage which tell us *what had happened*. Note how they have been used.

B Give the correct form of the verbs in parentheses. Do not refer to the passage until you finish the exercise.

1 At that time, she was the largest ship that ________ ever ________ (build).
2 After the alarm ________ (give), the great ship ________ (turn) sharply to avoid a direct collision.

Special difficulties 难点

Word building 构词法：在动词后面加上后缀 -er, -ist, -ness, -ion 或 -ity 往往可以组成名词

Study these sentences:

He works hard. He is a hard worker.
He plays the violin. He is a violinist.
He is very careless. I have never seen such carelessness.
Can you explain this? Can you give me an explanation?
He has a responsible position. He has a lot of responsibility.

Note how new words can be formed by adding *-er, -ist, -ness, -ion, -ity*.

Exercise 练习

Supply the missing words in the following sentences.

1 He studied physics at university. He is a p________ .
2 He works in a mine. He is a m________ .
3 Pasteur did a great service to ________ (human).
4 He is trying to make a good ________ (impress).
5 His paintings have been admired for their ________ (original).

Multiple choice questions 选择题

Choose the correct answers to the following questions.

Comprehension 理解

1 When the *Titanic* set out from Southampton ________ .

(*a*) she was carrying a very large cargo

(*b*) she was making a voyage which is only attempted by very large ships

(*c*) only two of her watertight compartments were flooded

(*d*) she was sailing on her maiden voyage

2 What happened once the iceberg had been spotted?

(*a*) The *Titanic* got lost in the icy waters of the North Atlantic.

(*b*) The alarm was given that there was a collision ahead.

(*c*) The *Titanic* quickly changed her course.

(*d*) The *Titanic* turned just as the iceberg rose steeply out of the water.

3 The *Titanic* sank because ________ .

(*a*) she had been badly damaged by an iceberg

(*b*) the captain was slow to realize the true nature of the damage

(*c*) no more than five of her watertight compartments had been flooded

(*d*) instead of trying to save her, people plunged into the water

Structure 结构

4 ________ were 1,316 passengers and a crew of 891. (ll.2-3)

(*a*) On her board (*b*) On board her (*c*) Boarding her (*d*) On boarding her

5 No one thought she ________ sink, for she had sixteen watertight compartments. (ll.5-6)

(*a*) would be possible to (*b*) would be able to (*c*) should (*d*) could possibly

6 She ________ four days when a huge iceberg was suddenly spotted. (ll.9-10)

(*a*) sailed (*b*) was sailing (*c*) has sailed (*d*) had been sailing

7 So faint ________ that no one thought ... (ll.13-14)

(*a*) the noise was (*b*) had been the noise (*c*) it was the noise (*d*) it had been the noise

8 As there were ________ lifeboats for everybody ... (ll.16-17)

(*a*) as little (*b*) so little (*c*) very few (*d*) too few

Vocabulary 词汇

9 The great ship ________ sharply to avoid a direct collision. (ll.10-11)

(*a*) veered (*b*) changed (*c*) went back (*d*) cornered

10 The *Titanic* turned ________ narrowly missing the immense wall ... (ll.11-12)

(*a*) in next to no time (*b*) on a sudden impulse

(*c*) with no time to spare (*d*) nearly on time

11 The captain went down to ________ . (l.13)

(*a*) explore (*b*) investigate (*c*) examine (*d*) inquire

12 There was not enough ________ in the lifeboats for everybody. (ll.16-17)

(*a*) room (*b*) place (*c*) volume (*d*) area

LESSON 11

Not guilty 无罪

Listen then answer the question below.

听录音，然后回答以下问题。

What was the Customs Officer looking for?

often made to feel guilty

Customs Officers are quite tolerant these days, but they can still stop you when you are going through the Green Channel and have nothing to declare. Even really honest people are often made to feel guilty. The hardened professional smuggler, on the other hand, is never troubled by such feelings, even if he has five hundred gold watches hidden in his suitcase. When I returned from abroad recently, a particularly officious young Customs Officer clearly regarded me as a smuggler.

'Have you anything to declare?' he asked, looking me in the eye.

'No,' I answered confidently.

'Would you mind unlocking this suitcase please?'

'Not at all,' I answered.

The Officer went through the case with great care. All the things I had packed so carefully were soon in a dreadful mess. I felt sure I would never be able to close the case again. Suddenly, I saw the Officer's face light up. He had spotted a tiny bottle at the bottom of my case and he pounced on it with delight.

'Perfume, eh?' he asked sarcastically. 'You should have declared that. Perfume is not exempt from import duty.'

'But it isn't perfume,' I said. 'It's hair gel.' Then I added with a smile, 'It's a strange mixture I make myself.'

As I expected, he did not believe me.

'Try it!' I said encouragingly.

The Officer unscrewed the cap and put the bottle to his nostrils. He was greeted by an unpleasant smell which convinced him that I was telling the truth. A few minutes later, I was able to hurry away with precious chalk marks on my baggage.

New words and expressions 生词和短语

guilty (title)	/ˈgɪlti/	adj.	犯罪的，违法的
tolerant (l.1)	/ˈtɒlərənt/	adj.	宽容的
declare (l.3)	/dɪˈkleə/	v.	申报
hardened (l.4)	/ˈhɑːdənd/	adj.	有经验的
professional (l.4)	/prəˈfeʃənəl/	adj.	职业的，专业的
smuggler (l.4)	/ˈsmʌgələ/	n.	走私者
officious (l.7)	/əˈfɪʃəs/	adj.	爱管闲事的
confidently (l.10)	/ˈkɒnfɪdəntli/	adv.	自信地
dreadful (l.14)	/ˈdredfəl/	adj.	可怕的，一团糟的
pounce (l.15)	/paʊns/	v.	猛抓，扑住
perfume (l.16)	/ˈpɜːfjuːm/	n.	香水
sarcastically (l.16)	/sɑːˈkæstɪkli/	adv.	讽刺地
exempt (l.16)	/ɪgˈzempt/	adj.	被免除的
duty (l.17)	/ˈdjuːti/	n.	税
gel (l.18)	/dʒel/	n.	凝胶
mixture (l.18)	/ˈmɪkstʃə/	n.	混合物
unscrew (l.22)	/ʌnˈskruː/	v.	拧开
nostril (l.22)	/ˈnɒstrɪl/	n.	鼻孔
chalk (l.24)	/tʃɔːk/	n.	粉笔
baggage (l.24)	/ˈbægɪdʒ/	n.	行李

Notes on the text 课文注释

1 the Green Channel, 绿色通道，指海关专供没有携带征税物品进关的旅客所走的通道。

2 hidden in his suitcase 是过去分词短语作定语，修饰 watches，它相当于一个定语从句：which are hidden in his suitcase。

3 looking me in the eye, 直盯着我的眼睛，这是现在分词短语作状语，表示方式，修饰 asked。

4 The officer went through, 这里 go through 作“检查”讲。

5 in a dreadful mess (或 in a mess), 乱七八糟，混乱透了。

6 I saw the Officer's face light up. 我看到那位官员的脸上露出了得意的神色。

7 You should have declared that. 你早该申报了。“should + 不定式的完成式”表示本该做而未做之事。

8 be exempt from 作“免除”、“豁免”解。

参考译文

现在的海关官员往往相当宽容。但是，当你通过绿色通道，没有任何东西需要申报时，他们仍可以拦住你。甚至是最诚实的人也常被弄得觉得有罪似的，而老练的职业走私犯即使在手提箱里藏着 500 只金表，却也处之泰然。最近一次，我出国归来，碰上一位特别好管闲事的年轻海关官员，他显然把我当成了走私犯。

“您有什么需要申报的吗？”他直盯着我的眼睛问。

“没有。”我自信地回答说。

“请打开这只手提箱好吗？”

“好的。”我回答说。

那位官员十分仔细地把箱子检查了一遍。所有细心包装好的东西一会儿工夫就乱成了一团。我相信那箱子再也关不上了。突然，我看到官员脸上露出了得意的神色。他在我的箱底发现了一只小瓶，高兴地一把抓了起来。

“香水，嗯？”他讥讽地说道，“你刚才应该申报，香水要上进口税的。”

“不，这不是香水，”我说，“是发胶。”接着我脸带微笑补充说：“这是一种我自己配制的奇特的混合物。”

果不出所料，他并不相信我。

“你就闻一闻吧！”我催促说。

海关官员拧开瓶盖，把瓶子放到鼻子底下。一股怪味袭来，使他相信了我说的是真话。几分钟后，我终于被放行，手提画着宝贵的粉笔记号的行李，匆匆离去。

Summary writing 摘要写作

In not more than 80 words describe the experiences of the writer while he was going through the Customs. Do not include anything that is not in the passage.

Answer these questions in note form to get your points:

1 Did the writer have anything to declare or not?
2 What did the Customs Officer make him do?

3 Did the Customs Officer search the case carefully or not?
4 What did he find?
5 What did he think was in the bottle?

6 What did the writer tell him the bottle contained?
7 Who had made it?

8 Did the Customs Officer believe him or not?
9 What did the writer encourage the Officer to do?

10 What convinced the Officer that the writer was telling the truth?
11 Did the Officer let the writer pass through the Customs or not?

Vocabulary 词汇

Give another word or phrase to replace the following words as they are used in the passage: troubled (l.5); clearly (l.7); packed (l.13); dreadful (l.14); cap (l.22); nostrils (l.22); convinced (l.23).

Composition 作文

Imagine that a man tries to smuggle something valuable through the Customs. Expand the following into a paragraph of about 150 words.

When the Customs Officer ... the man said that he had nothing to declare. The Officer asked the man to ... Although the case contained only ... and ... it was very heavy. This made the Officer suspicious, so he ... The case was soon empty and when the Officer ... he found that ... The Officer examined the case carefully and saw that ... He ... and removed the bottom part of the case which contained ... While the Officer was looking at ... the man tried to ... For a moment, the man disappeared among ... but he was soon ... and placed under arrest. (93 words)

Letter writing 书信写作

A friend has written to you asking you to lend him some money. Write a letter of about 80 words telling him you cannot afford to. Supply a suitable Introduction and Conclusion. Use the following ideas to write the *Purpose*: sorry you cannot help — have a great many expenses — you are in debt yourself — suggest someone who might help.

Key structures 关键句型

He said that ... He told me ... He asked ... 间接引语 **(1 KS 87)**（参见第 2 册第 87 课关键句型）

Exercise 练习

Answer these questions:

Lines 16-17 What did the Customs Officer tell the writer he should have done? Why did he tell the writer this?

Lines 18-19 What did the writer tell the Customs Officer?

Line 21 What did he tell the Customs Officer to do?

Special difficulties 难点

Capital letters 大写字母

Note how capital letters have been used in these sentences:

The train came into the station. It arrived at five o'clock.

George lives in Canada. He is Canadian. He is not an American.

I'll see you on Tuesday, January 14th.

Have you read *Great Expectations*?

Exercise 练习

Write this paragraph again using full stops and capital letters where necessary.

because tim jones cannot speak french or german he never enjoys travelling abroad last march, however, he went to denmark and stayed in copenhagen he said he spent most of his time at the tivoli which is one of the biggest funfairs in the world at the tivoli you can enjoy yourself very much even if you don't speak danish.

Multiple choice questions 选择题

Choose the correct answers to the following questions.

Comprehension 理解

1 What makes really honest people feel guilty when going through Customs?

(*a*) Having five hundred gold watches hidden in their suitcases.

(*b*) The particularly officious way Customs Officers always ask questions.

(*c*) The fact that they are treated as potential smugglers.

(*d*) Carrying things which are not exempt from import duty.

2 What made the Customs Officer's face light up?

(*a*) Knowing how difficult it would be for the writer to close his case.

(*b*) Seeing the bottle of hair gel which he could charge duty on.

(*c*) The idea of having found something which should have been declared.

(*d*) Discovering an unopened bottle of perfume at the bottom of the case.

3 The writer was in a hurry to get away because ________ .

(*a*) he had grown impatient at having taken so long to get through Customs

(*b*) he was anxious to get away from the unpleasant smell

(*c*) he was afraid he might still be stopped for smuggling

(*d*) he was trying to escape with precious chalk marks

Structure 结构

4 The Customs Officer asked him ________ he had anything to declare. (l.9)

(*a*) that (*b*) what (*c*) for (*d*) whether

5 'Have you anything to declare?' he asked, looking ________ . (l.9)

(*a*) direct to me (*b*) me directly (*c*) directly at me (*d*) in my direction

6 'Would you ________ please?' (l.11)

(*a*) unlock kindly this suitcase (*b*) kindly unlock this suitcase

(*c*) unlock this suitcase kindly (*d*) be kind to unlock this suitcase

7 He told him he ________ it. (l.16)

(*a*) ought to have declared (*b*) must have declared

(*c*) had to declare (*d*) needed to declare

8 ________ the cap, the Officer put the bottle to his nostrils. (l.22)

(*a*) Having unscrewed (*b*) Unscrewed (*c*) Being unscrewed (*d*) With unscrewed

Vocabulary 词汇

9 Customs Officers are quite tolerant these days. They are ________ . (l.1)

(*a*) tolerable (*b*) placid (*c*) easy-going (*d*) negligent

10 A hardened professional smuggler feels ________ his behaviour. (ll.4-5)

(*a*) unashamed of (*b*) unwronged by (*c*) unshocked by (*d*) guiltless of

11 As I expected, he was ________ . (l.20)

(*a*) incomprehensible (*b*) incredible (*c*) incredulous (*d*) sceptical

12 I was able to hurry away with precious chalk marks on my ________ . (ll.23-24)

(*a*) handbags (*b*) luggage (*c*) casement (*d*) equipment

LESSON

12 Life on a desert island 荒岛生活

Listen then answer the question below.

听录音，然后回答以下问题。

What was exceptional about the two men's stay on the desert island?

'ate like kings'

Most of us have formed an unrealistic picture of life on a desert island. We sometimes imagine a desert island to be a sort of paradise where the sun always shines. Life there is simple and good. Ripe fruit falls from the trees and you never have to work. The other side of the picture is quite the opposite. Life on a desert island is wretched. You either starve to death or live like Robinson Crusoe, waiting for a boat which never comes. Perhaps there is an element of truth in both these pictures, but few of us have had the opportunity to find out.

Two men who recently spent five days on a coral island wished they had stayed there longer. They were taking a badly damaged boat from the Virgin Islands to Miami to have it repaired. During the journey, their boat began to sink. They quickly loaded a small rubber dinghy with food, matches, and cans of beer and rowed for a few miles across the Caribbean until they arrived at a tiny coral island. There were hardly any trees on the island and there was no water, but this did not prove to be a problem. The men collected rainwater in the rubber dinghy. As they had brought a spear gun with them, they had plenty to eat. They caught lobster and fish every day, and, as one of them put it 'ate like kings'. When a passing tanker rescued them five days later, both men were genuinely sorry that they had to leave.

New words and expressions 生词和短语

desert island (title)	/ˌdezət-ˈaɪlənd/		荒岛
unrealistic (l.1)	/ˌʌnrɪəˈlɪstɪk/	*adj.*	不真实的
paradise (l.2)	/ˈpærədaɪs/	*n.*	天堂，乐土
wretched (l.6)	/ˈretʃɪd/	*adj.*	可怜的；艰苦的
starve (l.6)	/stɑːv/	*v.*	挨饿
element (l.7)	/ˈelɪmənt/	*n.*	成分
opportunity (l.8)	/ˌɒpəˈtjuːnɪti/	*n.*	机会
coral (l.9)	/ˈkɒrəl/	*n.*	珊瑚
Virgin Islands (l.10)	/ˈvɜːdʒɪn ˌaɪləndz/		维尔京群岛
Miami (l.10)	/maɪˈæmi/	*n.*	迈阿密（美国最南的城市）
dinghy (l.11)	/ˈdɪŋgi/	*n.*	救生筏，小船
Caribbean (l.12)	/ˌkærɪˈbiːən/	*n.*	加勒比海
spear gun (l.14)	/ˈspɪə-gʌn/		捕鱼枪
lobster (l.15)	/ˈlɒbstə/	*n.*	龙虾
tanker (l.15)	/ˈtæŋkə/	*n.*	油轮
genuinely (l.16)	/ˈdʒenjuɪnli/	*adv.*	由衷地
Robinson Crusoe (l.6)	/ˌrɒbɪnsən ˈkruːsəʊ/		鲁滨逊 · 克鲁索（小说《鲁滨逊漂流记》主人公）

Notes on the text 课文注释

1 imagine ... to be ..., 作"想象……是……"、"设想……是……"讲。不定式 to be 引导的短语作宾语补足语。

2 quite the opposite, 完全相反，截然不同。

3 starve to death, 饿死。

4 ... wished they had stayed there longer.

……还真希望在那里多待些日子。wish 引导的宾语从句常用虚拟语气。

5 as one of them put it, 正如其中一位所说的。

参考译文

我们许多人对于荒岛生活有一种不切实际的想法。我们有时想象荒岛是阳光终日普照的天堂。在那里，生活简单又美好。成熟的水果从树上掉下来，人们根本无需劳动。另一种想法恰恰相反，认为荒岛生活很可怕，要么饿死，要么像鲁滨逊那样，天天盼船来，却总不见船影。也许，这两种想象都有可信之处。但很少有人能有机会去弄个究竟。

最近有两个人在一座珊瑚岛上待了5天，他们真希望在那儿再多待一些日子。他们驾着一条严重损坏的小船从维尔京群岛去迈阿密修理。途中，船开始下沉，他们迅速把食物、火柴、罐装啤酒往一只救生筏上装。然后在加勒比海上划行了几英里，到了一座小珊瑚岛上。岛上几乎没有一棵树，也没有淡水，但这不算什么问题。他们用橡皮艇蓄积雨水。由于他们随身带了一支捕鱼枪，因此，吃饭不愁。他们天天捕捉龙虾和鱼，正如其中一位所说，吃得"像国王一样好"。5天后，一条油轮从那儿路过，搭救了他们。这二位不得不离开那个荒岛时，还真的感到遗憾呢！

Summary writing 摘要写作

In not more than 80 words explain how the two men came to spend five days on a desert island and say what they did there. Do not include anything that is not in the last paragraph.

Answer these questions in note form to get your points:

1 Was the men's boat damaged or not?
2 Where were they taking it?
3 What happened to it on the way?

4 What did the men load on to their rubber dinghy?
5 Where did they row?
6 Where did they arrive?

7 Where did the men collect water during their stay there?
8 How did they catch fish and lobster?

9 Did they eat 'like kings' for five days or not?
10 How were they rescued?

Vocabulary 词汇

Give another word or phrase to replace the following words as they are used in the passage: picture (l.1); wretched (l.6); starve to death (l.6); opportunity (l.8); repaired (l.10); loaded (l.11); dinghy (l.11).

Composition 作文

Imagine spending two weeks on an uninhabited desert island. In not more than 200 words describe what you did there. Use the ideas given below. Do not write more than three paragraphs.

Title: Shipwrecked.

Introduction: Shipwreck — everybody drowned — I clung to a plank — washed up on island.

Development: Slept for a long time — woke up — hungry and thirsty — explored island — uninhabited — found plenty of fruit — freshwater spring — tried to hunt wild animals — failed to catch anything — spent days swimming, lying in sun.

Conclusion: Boat on horizon — signalled and shouted — rescued.

Letter writing 书信写作

In not more than 60 words write a suitable *Purpose* and *Conclusion* to follow this introductory paragraph.

Dear Judy,

We arrived here late last night and are staying at a charming little hotel by the sea. The weather is perfect and I am sure we are going to enjoy our holiday.

Key structures 关键句型

If. 用 if 引导的从句 (1 KS 88)（参见第 2 册第 88 课关键句型）

Exercise 练习

Complete the following:

1 If you had told me earlier ________ .
2 If I were you ________ .
3 You will be disappointed if ________ .
4 You would change your mind if ________ .

Special difficulties 难点

Wish and If only.

在英语中，表示愿望可用动词 wish 或短语 if only。其中 wish 常指尚有可能发生的事情，而 if only 则强调所希望的状况并不存在。在 wish 和 if only 后面，要用过去时表示现在，用过去完成时表示过去。

Study these examples:

They wished they had stayed there longer. (l.9)
I wish you would do as you are told.
If only the weather would change.
I wish she could see me now.
I wish I had more time to spare.
If only you would try a little harder!
I wish I hadn't said anything about it.
If only we could have gone to the party!
I wish you hadn't spent so much money.

Exercise 练习

Complete the following:

1 It was silly of me not to buy that dress. I wish I ________ .
2 You are making a lot of noise. I wish you ________ .
3 It's a pity John's away. If only he ________ .
4 He plays the piano so well. I wish I ________ .
5 I never studied at all when I was at school. I wish I ________ .
6 I'm sorry I mentioned it to him. I wish I ________ .

Multiple choice questions 选择题

Choose the correct answers to the following questions.

Comprehension 理解

1 In what way are the pictures we form of life on a desert island unreal?

(*a*) They fail to present the wretchedness of such a situation.

(*b*) We forget that we would be too weak to work and only imagine the pleasure of idleness.

(*c*) They are either unduly optimistic or unduly pessimistic.

(*d*) They lack any truth at all as most of us have never visited one.

2 What was the equipment the men had brought that proved essential to their survival?

(*a*) Tools with which they had been going to repair their boat.

(*b*) Food, matches and tins of beer.

(*c*) Rainwater, lobster and fish.

(*d*) A spear gun and a rubber dinghy.

3 What made the men wish to stay on the desert island?

(*a*) Discovering how pleasant life can be fending for oneself.

(*b*) Having seen very few trees and no rainwater on the coral island.

(*c*) The fact that they were able to eat the same food as kings eat.

(*d*) Knowing they no longer needed to take their boat to Miami for repair.

Structure 结构

4 We sometimes think of a desert island ________ a sort of paradise. (l.2)

(*a*) to be (*b*) as being (*c*) is (*d*) be

5 But ________ have had the opportunity to find out. (ll.7-8)

(*a*) we few (*b*) hardly anybody (*c*) little people (*d*) not many

6 After ________ a few miles across the Caribbean, they arrived at a small coral island. (ll.11-12)

(*a*) they rowed (*b*) rowed (*c*) rowing (*d*) to row

7 ________ were scarce there and there was no water. (ll.12-13)

(*a*) The trees (*b*) Trees (*c*) Any trees (*d*) Trees on the island

8 Both men genuinely regretted ________ . (l.16)

(*a*) their leave (*b*) to have to leave (*c*) having to leave (*d*) they must have left

Vocabulary 词汇

9 A desert island is ________ place. (ll.1-2)

(*a*) an unpopular (*b*) an uninhabited (*c*) a deserted (*d*) a barren

10 The other side of the picture is ________ different. (ll.4-5)

(*a*) naturally (*b*) rather (*c*) really (*d*) entirely

11 But this was not ________ to be a problem. (l.13)

(*a*) demonstrated (*b*) thought (*c*) shown (*d*) found

12 And, as one of them ________ it, they 'ate like kings'. (l.15)

(*a*) expressed (*b*) placed (*c*) told (*d*) said

LESSON **13**

'It's only me' "是我，别怕"

Listen then answer the question below.
听录音，然后回答以下问题。

What did the man expect to find under the stairs?

She tried to explain the situation

After her husband had gone to work, Mrs. Richards sent her children to school and went upstairs to her bedroom. She was too excited to do any housework that morning, for in the evening she would be going to a fancy-dress party with her husband. She intended to dress up as a ghost and as she had made her costume the night before, she was impatient to try it on. Though the costume consisted only of a sheet, it was very effective. After putting it on, Mrs. Richards went downstairs. She wanted to find out whether it would be comfortable to wear.

Just as Mrs. Richards was entering the dining room, there was a knock on the front door. She knew that it must be the baker. She had told him to come straight in if ever she failed to open the door and to leave the bread on the kitchen table. Not wanting to frighten the poor man, Mrs. Richards quickly hid in the small storeroom under the stairs. She heard the front door open and heavy footsteps in the hall. Suddenly the door of the storeroom was opened and a man entered. Mrs. Richards realized that it must be the man from the Electricity Board who had come to read the meter. She tried to explain the situation, saying 'It's only me', but it was too late. The man let out a cry and jumped back several paces. When Mrs. Richards walked towards him, he fled, slamming the door behind him.

New words and expressions 生词和短语

costume (l.5)	/ˈkɒstjʊm/	*n.*	化装服
consist (l.6)	/kənˈsɪst/	*v.*	由……组成
sheet (l.7)	/ʃiːt/	*n.*	被单
effective (l.7)	/ɪˈfektɪv/	*adj.*	有明显效果的，有作用的
comfortable (l.8)	/ˈkʌmftəbəl/	*adj.*	舒适的
storeroom (l.12)	/ˈstɔːrʊm/	*n.*	储藏室
electricity (l.14)	/ɪˌlekˈtrɪsɪti/	*n.*	电
meter (l.14)	/ˈmiːtə/	*n.*	电表
pace (l.15)	/peɪs/	*n.*	一步
flee (l.16)	/fliː/ (fled /fled/, fled)	*v.*	逃走
slam (l.16)	/slæm/	*v.*	砰地关上

Notes on the text 课文注释

1 would be going, 是过去将来进行时，用来表示过去预计将要发生的动作。

2 fancy-dress party, 化装舞会。

3 dress up as, 化装成……。

4 try it on,
it 指 costume，try on 是"试穿"、"试戴"。

5 just as ..., 正当……的时候。

6 She had told him to come straight in if ever she failed to open the door and to leave the bread on the kitchen table. 她曾告诉过他，如果她没去开门，他可直接进来，把面包放在厨房的桌子上。if ever 在条件句中表示强调，可译作“任何时候”。to come straight in 指“直接进来”。

7 Not wanting to frighten the poor man, 不想去吓唬这个可怜的人。这是现在分词短语的否定形式，作目的状语。

参考译文

理查兹夫人等丈夫上班走后，把孩子送去上学，然后来到楼上自己的卧室。那天上午，她兴奋得什么家务活都不想做，因为晚上她要同丈夫一起去参加一个化装舞会。她打算装扮成鬼的模样。头天晚上她已把化装服做好，这时她急于想试试。尽管化装服仅由一个被单制成，却十分逼真。理查兹夫人穿上化装服后下了楼，想看看穿起来是否舒服。

理查兹夫人刚刚走进餐厅，前门就传来敲门声。她知道来人一定是面包师。她曾告诉过面包师，如果她不去开门，他可直接进门，把面包放在厨房的桌上。理查兹夫人不想吓唬这个可怜的人，便赶紧躲到了楼梯下的小储藏室里。她听见前门被打开，走廊里响起了重重的脚步声。突然储藏室门开了，一个男人走了进来。理查兹夫人这才想到一定是供电局来人查电表了。她说了声“是我，别怕！”然后想进行一番解释，但已来不及了。那人大叫了一声，惊退了几步。理查兹夫人朝他走去，只见他“砰”的一声关上门逃走了。

Summary writing 摘要写作

In not more than 80 words describe what happened from the moment Mrs. Richards entered the dining room. Do not include anything that is not in the passage.

Answer these questions in note form to get your points:

1 How was Mrs. Richards dressed?
2 Where was she going when someone knocked at the door?
3 Whom did she think it was?
4 Where did she hide?
5 Did she hear footsteps in the hall or not?
6 Who suddenly opened the storeroom door?
7 What did she say to him?
8 Did he get a bad fright or not?
9 Did she walk towards him or not?
10 Did he flee or did he stay there?
11 Did he slam the front door or not?

Vocabulary 词汇

Give another word or phrase to replace the following words as they are used in the passage: intended (l.4); impatient (l.6); try it on (l.6); whether (l.8); failed to (l.10); fled (l.16); slamming (l.16).

Composition 作文

Imagine that the man from the Electricity Board returned to Mrs. Richards' house with a policeman. Mrs. Richards was no longer dressed as a ghost. Expand the following into a paragraph of about 150 words.

Mrs. Richards immediately went upstairs and ... She felt sorry for the poor man from ... but at the same time, she was ... Suddenly, there was a knock at the front door and Mrs. Richards ... The electricity man had returned, accompanied ... so she ... The man told Mrs. Richards that ... and that ... Though Mrs. Richards explained that ... he refused to believe her. She told him to open the storeroom door but he ... so she ... While the electricity man and the policeman ... , Mrs. Richards fetched ... She showed it ... and ... (85 words)

Letter writing 书信写作

Put yourself in the position of the electricity man. Imagine you are writing a letter of about 80 words to your mother describing your experience. Supply a suitable Introduction and Conclusion. Use the following ideas to write the *Purpose*: you got a terrible shock — house haunted — ghost under stairs — it ran after you — you fled — the story is really true.

Key structures 关键句型

Must. (1 KS 89)（参见第二册第 89 课关键句型）

Exercises 练习

A Note how *must* has been used in lines 10 and 13.

B Write three pairs of sentences using the following:

1 *must go* and *must be*;

2 *mustn't* and *needn't*;

3 *had to* and *ought to have*.

Special difficulties 难点

It would be comfortable to wear. (l.8) 形容词 + 动词不定式

Instead of saying: I was *sorry when I learnt* that he had had an accident.

We can say: I was *sorry to learn* that he had had an accident.

Study these examples:

He was *delighted to learn* that his offer had been accepted.

I was *glad to hear* that he had arrived.

I was *pleased to hear* that you now feel better.

He was *anxious to leave* early.

Exercises 练习

A Write these sentences again changing the form of the words in italics.

1 I was glad *when I heard* that she had gone away for ever.

2 He said he was sorry *if he had* upset me.

3 You will be sad *when you hear* what I have to tell you.

B Write sentences using the following: pleased to; proud to; delighted to; shocked to.

Multiple choice questions 选择题

Choose the correct answers to the following questions.

Comprehension 理解

1 Mrs. Richards went upstairs because ________ .

(*a*) she did not need to do any housework

(*b*) she still had to finish the costume she was going to wear
(*c*) she wanted to change her clothes before doing the housework
(*d*) she wanted to change into her fancy-dress costume

2 Mrs. Richards did not go to the door because ________ .
(*a*) she was upstairs changing her clothes
(*b*) she did not want to make a bad impression on the baker
(*c*) she thought the baker might be taken in by her disguise
(*d*) the baker had already left the bread on the kitchen table

3 By saying 'It's only me', Mrs. Richards hoped ________ .
(*a*) the man would realize she was alone
(*b*) to persuade the man he was seeing a ghost
(*c*) the man would recognize her
(*d*) the man would not close the door of the storeroom

Structure 结构

4 After her husband had gone to work and the children ________ to school, she went upstairs ... (ll.1-2)
(*a*) had sent (*b*) were sent (*c*) had been sent (*d*) were sending

5 She wanted to find out how ________ to wear. (l.8)
(*a*) comfortable it was (*b*) comfortable it would be
(*c*) it was comfortable (*d*) it would be comfortable

6 ________ to frighten the poor man, Mrs. Richards quickly hid under the stairs. (ll.11-12)
(*a*) Not anxious about (*b*) Anxious not
(*c*) Being not anxious (*d*) Not being anxious for

7 Trying to explain the situation, she ________ 'It's only me'. (l.14)
(*a*) was saying (*b*) said (*c*) had said (*d*) has been saying

8 On seeing Mrs. Richards ________ towards him, he fled. (ll.15-16)
(*a*) to walk (*b*) having walked (*c*) walk (*d*) walked

Vocabulary 词汇

9 ________ Mrs. Richards was entering the dining room ... (l.9)
(*a*) At the very moment (*b*) So long as (*c*) Only when (*d*) During the time

10 – if she ever ________ the door and to leave the bread ... (ll.10-11)
(*a*) missed opening (*b*) forgot to open
(*c*) did not succeed in opening (*d*) happened not to open

11 It was the man from the Electricity Board who had come to take a meter- ________ . (ll.13-14)
(*a*) reading (*b*) measurement (*c*) regulation (*d*) study

12 The man ________ a cry. (l.15)
(*a*) escaped (*b*) gave (*c*) left (*d*) shouted

LESSON

14 A noble gangster 贵族歹徒

Listen then answer the question below.

听录音，然后回答以下问题。

How did Hawkwood make money in times of peace?

... made the remarkable discovery

There was a time when the owners of shops and businesses in Chicago had to pay large sums of money to gangsters in return for 'protection'. If the money was not paid promptly, the gangsters would quickly put a man out of business by destroying his shop. Obtaining 'protection money' is not a modern crime. As long ago as the fourteenth century, an Englishman, Sir John Hawkwood, made the remarkable discovery that people would rather pay large sums of money than have their life work destroyed by gangsters.

Six hundred years ago, Sir John Hawkwood arrived in Italy with a band of soldiers and settled near Florence. He soon made a name for himself and came to be known to the Italians as Giovanni Acuto. Whenever the Italian city-states were at war with each other, Hawkwood used to hire his soldiers to princes who were willing to pay the high price he demanded. In times of peace, when business was bad, Hawkwood and his men would march into a city-state and, after burning down a few farms, would offer to go away if protection money was paid to them. Hawkwood made large sums of money in this way. In spite of this, the Italians regarded him as a sort of hero. When he died at the age of eighty, the Florentines gave him a state funeral and had a picture painted which was dedicated to the memory of 'the most valiant soldier and most notable leader, Signor Giovanni Haukodue'.

New words and expressions 生词和短语

gangster	(title)	/ˈgæŋstə/	*n.*	歹徒，强盗
Chicago	(l.2)	/ʃɪˈkɑːgəʊ/	*n.*	芝加哥（美国城市）
protection	(l.3)	/prəˈtekʃən/	*n.*	保护
promptly	(l.3)	/ˈprɒmptli/	*adv.*	及时地
destroy	(l.4)	/dɪˈstrɔɪ/	*v.*	毁掉；消灭
remarkable	(l.7)	/rɪˈmɑːkəbəl/	*adj.*	不寻常的
band	(l.9)	/bænd/	*n.*	帮，团伙
Florence	(l.10)	/ˈflɒrəns/	*n.*	佛罗伦萨（意大利城市）
city-state	(l.11)	/ˌsɪtiˈsteɪt/	*n.*	（古代）城邦
hire	(l.11)	/haɪə/	*v.*	租出，雇给
prince	(l.11)	/prɪns/	*n.*	君主，诸侯
Florentine	(l.15)	/ˈflɒrəntaɪn/	*n.*	佛罗伦萨人
funeral	(l.16)	/ˈfjuːnərəl/	*n.*	葬礼
dedicate	(l.16)	/ˈdedɪkeɪt/	*v.*	奉献，题献给
memory	(l.16)	/ˈeməri/	*n.*	纪念
valiant	(l.16)	/ˈvæliənt/	*adj.*	英勇的

Notes on the text 课文注释

1 in return for ..., 作“作为……的报答”讲。

2 out of business, 倒闭，破产。

3 as long ago as, 作“追溯到”、“早在”讲。注意要与 as long as 区分开，后面这个短语作“只要”或“长达……之久”讲。

4 people would rather pay large sums of money than have their life work destroyed by gangsters, 人们情愿支付一大笔钱，也不愿自己毕生的心血毁于歹徒之手。
5 made a name for himself, 出名了。
6 be at war with ..., 与……处于战争状态。
7 in times of peace, 在和平时期。
8 a sort of hero, 某种英雄。sort of 作“可以说是一种”讲。

参考译文

曾经有一个时期，芝加哥的店主和商行的老板们不得不拿出大笔的钱给歹徒以换取“保护”。如果交款不及时，歹徒们就会很快捣毁他的商店，让他破产。勒索“保护金”并不是一种现代的罪恶行径。早在 14 世纪，英国人约翰·霍克伍德爵士就有过非凡的发现：人们情愿拿出大笔的钱，也不愿毕生的心血毁于歹徒之手。

600 年前，约翰·霍克伍德爵士带着一队士兵来到意大利，在佛罗伦萨附近驻扎下来，很快就出了名。意大利人叫他乔凡尼·阿库托。每次意大利各城邦之间打仗，霍克伍德便把他的士兵出租给愿给他出高价的君主。和平时期，当生意萧条时，霍克伍德便带领士兵进入某个城邦，纵火烧毁一两个农场，然后提出，如向他们缴纳保护金，他们便主动撤离。霍克伍德用这种方法挣了大笔的钱。尽管如此，意大利人还是把他视作某种英雄。他 80 岁那年死去时，佛罗伦萨人为他举行了国葬，并为他画像以纪念这位“骁勇无比的战士、杰出的领袖乔凡尼·阿库托先生”。

Summary writing 摘要写作

In not more than 80 words write an account of Sir John Hawkwood's career from the time he arrived in Italy. Do not include anything that is not in the last paragraph.

Answer these questions in note form to get your points:

1 Where did Sir John Hawkwood settle six hundred years ago?
2 Whom did he hire soldiers to in times of war?
3 Would he threaten to destroy a city-state in times of peace or not?
4 When would he spare a city-state?
5 Did the Italians regard him as a hero in spite of this or not?
6 How old was he when he died?
7 Who gave him a state funeral when he died?
8 Did they have a picture painted or not?
9 What was it dedicated to?

Vocabulary 词汇

Give another word or phrase to replace the following words as they are used in the passage: sums (l.2); promptly (l.3); obtaining (l.5); remarkable (l.7); settled (l.9); hire (l.11); demanded (l.12).

Composition 作文

In not more than 200 words write an imaginary account of one of Sir John Hawkwood's exploits. Use the ideas given below. Do not write more than three paragraphs.

Title: Hawkwood defeated.

Introduction: News that Hawkwood and his men were approaching — panic — villagers prepared to defend farms.

Development: Farmers fought — poorly armed — many killed — Hawkwood destroyed farms — sent message to prince of city-state — demanded money — refused — battle followed — Hawkwood invaded city — many buildings were destroyed — people killed.

Conclusion: Hawkwood was driven off — never attacked this city again — later became the prince's friend.

Letter writing 书信写作

You had agreed to give a talk at your local library, but now find that you are unable to do so. Write a letter of about 80 words explaining why. Supply a suitable Introduction and Conclusion. Use the following ideas to write the *Purpose*: sorry for the inconvenience — you are being sent abroad by your firm — will be away for three weeks — hope to give a talk on a later occasion.

Key structures 关键句型

Have. **(1 KS 90)**（参见第 2 册第 90 课关键句型）

Exercises 练习

A Note how *have* has been used in lines 8 and 16.

B Write sentences using *have* with the following:

1 a smoke;

2 got a headache;

3 repaired.

Special difficulties 难点

People would rather pay large sums of money than ... (ll.7-8)

Instead of saying:	*We can say*:
I prefer to wait here.	I would rather wait here.
	Or: I would sooner wait here.
I prefer not to wait here.	I would rather not wait here.
	Or: I would sooner not wait here.
It would be better if he waited here.	I'd rather *he waited* here.
It would be better if he didn't wait here.	I'd rather *he didn't wait* here.

Exercise 练习

Give the correct form of the verbs in parentheses.

1 I'd rather ________ (go) to the cinema.

2 I'd rather he ________ (leave) earlier.

3 I'd rather you ________ not ________ (speak) to him.

4 I'd rather not ________ (speak) about it.

5 I'd rather my father ________ (settle) the account.

6 She'd rather you ________ not ________ (tell) anyone about it.

Multiple choice questions 选择题

Choose the correct answers to the following questions.

Comprehension 理解

1 What 'protection' did Chicago gangsters give to those who paid them?
(*a*) They saved those people's businesses from destruction.
(*b*) They left those people's business premises unharmed.
(*c*) They protected those people against criminals like Sir John Hawkwood.
(*d*) They did not take those people's lives.

2 Sir John Hawkwood's Italian name, 'Giovanni Acuto', was one which ________ .
(*a*) he gave himself in order to become better known to the Italians
(*b*) he earned through his sharp practice of selling his 'protection'
(*c*) he needed in order to hire his soldiers to Italian princes
(*d*) was given him in recognition of his services to the Italian states

3 The Italians regarded Hawkwood as a sort of hero ________ .
(*a*) in that they could not help admiring his boldness and bravery
(*b*) as he helped the citizens in peacetime when business was bad for them
(*c*) despite the protection money he offered to those whose farms he burnt
(*d*) for he lived so long and was given a state funeral by the Florentines

Structure 结构

4 Obtaining 'protection money' is a crime which ________ practised for a long time. (l.5)
(*a*) has been (*b*) is (*c*) was (*d*) is being

5 People prefer paying large sums of money ________ their life work destroyed by gangsters. (ll.7-8)
(*a*) than have (*b*) to have (*c*) to having (*d*) than they have

6 Princes used to hire ________ Hawkwood. (ll.11-12)
(*a*) his soldiers from (*b*) soldiers from (*c*) soldiers of (*d*) some soldiers of

7 They would refuse to go away ________ protection money was paid to them. (ll.13-14)
(*a*) unless (*b*) provided that (*c*) except that (*d*) without

8 ________ at the age of eighty, the Florentines gave him ... (ll.15-16)
(*a*) On dying (*b*) Having died (*c*) On his death (*d*) Dead

Vocabulary 词汇

9 Six hundred years have ________ since Sir John Hawkwood arrived in ... (ll.9-10)
(*a*) past (*b*) passed (*c*) been (*d*) departed

10 – princes who were ________ to pay the high price he demanded. (ll.11-12)
(*a*) agreeable (*b*) accepting (*c*) desirable (*d*) prepared

11 Hawkwood made large sums of money ________ . (l.14)
(*a*) by the way (*b*) with such manners (*c*) on this road (*d*) like this

12 'the most ________ soldier and most notable leader ...' (ll.16-17)
(*a*) valuable (*b*) worthy (*c*) brave (*d*) hardy

LESSON

15 Fifty pence worth of trouble

五十便士的麻烦

Listen then answer the question below.

听录音，然后回答以下问题。

Did George get anything for his fifty pence? What?

The fire brigade was called

Children always appreciate small gifts of money. Mum or dad, of course, provides a regular supply of pocket money, but uncles and aunts are always a source of extra income. With some children, small sums go a long way. If fifty pence pieces are not exchanged for sweets, they rattle for months inside money boxes. Only very thrifty children manage to fill up a money box. For most of them, fifty pence is a small price to pay for a nice big bar of chocolate.

My nephew, George, has a money box but it is always empty. Very few of the fifty pence pieces and pound coins I have given him have found their way there. I gave him fifty pence yesterday and advised him to save it. Instead he bought himself fifty pence worth of trouble. On his way to the sweet shop, he dropped his fifty pence and it bounced along the pavement and then disappeared down a drain. George took off his jacket, rolled up his sleeves and pushed his right arm through the drain cover. He could not find his fifty pence piece anywhere, and what is more, he could not get his arm out. A crowd of people gathered round him and a lady rubbed his arm with soap and butter, but George was firmly stuck. The fire brigade was called and two fire fighters freed George using a special type of grease. George was not too upset by his experience because the lady who owns the sweet shop heard about his troubles and rewarded him with a large box of chocolates.

New words and expressions 生词和短语

appreciate (l.1)	/əˈpriːʃieɪt/	v.	欣赏，感激
pocket money (l.2)	/ˈpɒkɪt-ˌmʌni/		零用钱
rattle (l.5)	/ˈrætl/	v.	叮当作响
thrifty (l.6)	/ˈθrɪfti/	adj.	节俭的
nephew (l.8)	/ˈnefjuː/	n.	侄子，外甥
bounce (l.11)	/baʊns/	v.	弹起，跳起
pavement (l.11)	/ˈpeɪvmənt/	n.	人行道
stick (l.14)	/stɪk/ (stuck /stʌk/, stuck)	v.	卡住，夹住，不能再动
brigade (l.14)	/brɪˈgeɪd/	n.	旅，（消防）队
grease (l.15)	/griːs/	n.	润滑油

Notes on the text 课文注释

1 with some children, 介词 with 此处作“对于”讲。

2 go a long way, 可以维持很久。

3 If fifty pence pieces are not exchanged for sweets, 如果 50 便士的硬币没有用来换糖果的话。exchange ... for ... 作“以……换……”讲，注意英语中的便士有两种复数形式 pence 和 pennies，但用法不同。如：a fifty pence 是指 1 个 50 便士的硬币，而 fifty pennies 是指 50 个 1 便士的硬币。

4 have found their way there, 其中 there 是指储蓄罐。find one's way 在这里作“进入”讲，即“放到（储蓄罐）里”。

5 what is more, 更有甚者。是固定词组，此处用作插入语。

参考译文

孩子们总是喜欢得到一些零花钱。爸爸妈妈当然经常会给孩子零花钱，但是，叔舅婶姨也是孩子们额外收入的来源。对于有些孩子来说，少量的钱可以花很长一段时间。如果 50 便士不拿来换糖吃，则可以放在储蓄罐里叮当响上好几个月。但是能把储蓄罐装满的只有屈指可数的几个特别节俭的孩子。对大部分孩子来说，用 50 便士来买一大块好的巧克力，是算不了什么的。

我的外甥乔治有一个储蓄罐，但总是空空的。我给了他不少 50 便士的硬币，但没有几个存到储蓄罐里。昨天，我给了他 50 便士让他存起来，他却拿这钱给自己买了 50 便士的麻烦。在他去糖果店的路上，50 便士掉在地上，在人行道上跳了几下，掉进了阴沟里。乔治脱掉外套，卷起袖子，将右胳膊伸进了阴沟盖。但他摸了半天也没找到那 50 便士硬币，他的胳膊反倒退不出来了。这时在他周围围上了许多人，一位女士在乔治胳膊上抹了肥皂、黄油，但乔治的胳膊仍然卡得紧紧的。有人打电话叫来消防队，两位消防队员使用了一种特殊的润滑剂才使乔治得以解脱。不过，此事并没使乔治过于伤心，因为糖果店老板娘听说了他遇到的麻烦后，赏给了他一大盒巧克力。

Summary writing 摘要写作

In not more than 80 words describe George's experiences after his uncle gave him fifty pence. Do not include anything that is not in the last paragraph.

Answer these questions in note form to get your points:

1 Where was George going?
2 Where did he lose his fifty pence?
3 Did he take his jacket off or not?
4 Where did he put his arm?
5 Did he find his fifty pence, or did he fail to find it?
6 Could he get his arm out or not?
7 Did a crowd of people gather round him or not?
8 What did a lady try to do?
9 Did she succeed or did she fail?
10 How did the fire fighters finally free George?
11 What did the owner of the sweet shop present him with?

Vocabulary 词汇

Give another word or phrase to replace the following words as they are used in the passage: appreciate (l.1); gifts (l.1); extra income (l.3); rattle (l.5); price (l.7); gathered (l.13); was firmly stuck (l.14).

Composition 作文

Suppose you were among the crowd of people that gathered round George. Write an imaginary account of what happened. Expand the following into a paragraph of about 150 words.

I was walking along the street when I ... I could hear people shouting and ... On arriving at the scene, I ... A lady carrying a large bar of soap and a saucepan full of water ... She asked the boy if ... Then she rubbed his arm with butter, but ... Meanwhile, someone had telephoned ... The boy had begun to cry, but when ... At first, the fire fighters decided to ... but they changed their minds and ... The boy was soon free and though his arm hurt, he ... (83 words)

Letter writing 书信写作

Write a letter of about 80 words to your eight-year-old nephew asking him what he would like you to buy him for his birthday. Supply a suitable Introduction and Conclusion. Use the following information to write the *Purpose*: you want to get him something he will really like — a few suggestions — ask him to let you know what he wants — you will send it by post so that it arrives on his birthday.

Key structures 关键句型

Can. (1 KS 91)（参见第 2 册第 91 课关键句型）

Exercises 练习

A Note how the following have been used in the passage.
manage to (l.6) and *could not* (l.12).

B Write sentences using each of the following.

1 was able to;
2 could;
3 managed to.

Special difficulties 难点

Only very thrifty children manage to fill up a money box. (ll.5-6) up 的用法

Note the use of *up* in these sentences:

We *drove up* to the farmhouse.

The children *ran up* the garden path to greet their father.

I didn't like my composition so I *tore* it *up*.

He has *built up* a large collection of stamps.

Exercise 练习

Complete these sentences using the correct form of the following verbs: *do, save, wind, sail, wrap, button, go, eat.*

1 If I can ________ up enough money, I shall go abroad.
2 The steamboat ________ up the river.
3 It was very cold so I ________ up my coat before going out.
4 ________ up what is on your plate and I'll give you some more.
5 I ________ up to a policeman and asked him the way to the station.
6 He ________ the fish up in a piece of newspaper.
7 My watch has stopped because I forgot to ________ it up.
8 It takes children a long time to learn how to ________ up their shoelaces.

Multiple choice questions 选择题

Choose the correct answers to the following questions.

Comprehension 理解

1 What do most children do with the money they are given?

(*a*) They put it in their pockets.

(*b*) They wait until their money boxes are full before spending it.

(*c*) They go straight to a sweet shop and spend it.

(*d*) They spend a little of it on chocolate.

2 When the writer gave him fifty pence, George ________ .

(*a*) did not hear the writer's advice

(*b*) decided that saving it was more trouble than it was worth

(*c*) waited until the next day before deciding to spend it on sweets

(*d*) set out for the sweet shop, but lost it on his way

3 Once the fire fighters had come to George's rescue ________ .

(*a*) George had his arm greased and was able to get it out of the drain

(*b*) George took his fire fighters and got some chocolate at the sweet shop

(*c*) the lady who had failed to rescue George gave him a box of chocolates

(*d*) George was rewarded by the owner of the sweet shop for his trouble

Structure 结构

4 Fifty pence is not ________ to pay for a bar of chocolate. (ll.6-7)

(*a*) many (*b*) much (*c*) plenty (*d*) big

5 I gave him fifty pence yesterday and advised him he ________ it. (ll.9-10)

(*a*) saves (*b*) should save (*c*) would save (*d*) was saving

6 He ________ to the sweet shop when he dropped his fifty pence. (ll.10-11)

(*a*) had gone (*b*) was going to go (*c*) went (*d*) was going

7 He could not find his fifty pence anywhere ________ get his arm out. (ll.12-13)

(*a*) nor could he (*b*) nor he could (*c*) neither he could (*d*) either he could not

8 A lady put ________ . (ll.13-14)

(*a*) on his arm soap and butter (*b*) his arm on soap and butter

(*c*) soap and butter on his arm (*d*) on his arm with soap and butter

Vocabulary 词汇

9 With some children, small sums ________ . (ll.3-4)

(*a*) last a long time (*b*) are very durable (*c*) have far to go (*d*) gain in value

10 A crowd of people gathered ________ and a lady ... (ll.13-14)

(*a*) on a tour (*b*) in turn (*c*) in a circle (*d*) in a cycle

11 George was ________ stuck. (l.14)

(*a*) strictly (*b*) well and truly (*c*) hardly (*d*) by no means

12 George was not too ________ by his experience. (ll.15-16)

(*a*) moved (*b*) distressed (*c*) excited (*d*) embarrassed

LESSON

16 Mary had a little lamb

玛丽有一头小羔羊

Listen then answer the question below.

听录音，然后回答以下问题。

Was Dimitri right to apologize to his neighbour? Why not?

the little black lamb was almost white

Mary and her husband Dimitri lived in the tiny village of Perachora in southern Greece. One of Mary's prize possessions was a little white lamb which her husband had given her. She kept it tied to a tree in a field during the day and went to fetch it every evening. One evening, however, the lamb was missing. The rope had been cut, so it was obvious that the lamb had been stolen.

When Dimitri came in from the fields, his wife told him what had happened. Dimitri at once set out to find the thief. He knew it would not prove difficult in such a small village. After telling several of his friends about the theft, Dimitri found out that his neighbour, Aleko, had suddenly acquired a new lamb. Dimitri immediately went to Aleko's house and angrily accused him of stealing the lamb. He told him he had better return it or he would call the police. Aleko denied taking it and led Dimitri into his backyard. It was true that he had just bought a lamb, he explained, but *his* lamb was black. Ashamed of having acted so rashly, Dimitri apologized to Aleko for having accused him. While they were talking it began to rain and Dimitri stayed in Aleko's house until the rain stopped. When he went outside half an hour later, he was astonished to find that the little black lamb was almost white. Its wool, which had been dyed black, had been washed clean by the rain!

New words and expressions 生词和短语

prize (l.2)	/praɪz/	*adj.*	珍贵的，宝贵的	deny (l.11)	/dɪ'naɪ/	*v.*	否认
tie (l.3)	/taɪ/	*v.*	拴，系	ashamed (l.13)	/ə'ʃeɪmd/	*adj.*	感到羞耻的，惭愧的
theft (l.9)	/θeft/	*n.*	偷盗行为，偷盗案	apologize (l.13)	/ə'pɒlədʒaɪz/	*v.*	道歉
accuse (l.10)	/ə'kjuːz/	*v.*	指控	dye (l.16)	/daɪ/	*v.*	染

Notes on the text 课文注释

1. it would not prove difficult, 是不难做到的。

   prove 是连系动词，作"证明是"讲，本句子与 it would not be difficult 相同。

2 accuse sb. of (doing) sth. 作"指责，指控某人做某事"解。

3 he had better return it, 他最好把羔羊还给迪米特里。

   had better 用来表达一种建议，建议在将来某一具体场合采取的动作。这个短语比 should 和 ought to 的语气更强烈，常带有威胁、告诫或催促的意思。

4 denied taking it ...,

   deny 后面可接动名词作宾语，也可接宾语从句。

5 apologize to sb. for (doing) sth., 是"因（做）某事向某人道歉"的意思。

参考译文

玛丽与丈夫迪米特里住在希腊南部一个叫波拉考拉的小村庄里。玛丽最珍贵的财产之一就是丈夫送给她的一只白色小羔羊。白天，玛丽把羔羊拴在地里的一棵树上，每天晚上把它牵回家。可是，一天晚上，那只小羔羊失踪了。绳子被人割断，很明显小羔羊是被人偷走了。

迪米特里从地里回来，妻子把情况跟他一说，他马上出去找偷羔羊的人。他知道在这样一个小村庄里抓住小偷并不困难。把失窃的事告诉几个朋友后，迪米特里发现他的邻居阿列科家突然多了一只小羔羊。迪米特里立刻去了阿列科家，气呼呼地指责他偷了羔羊，告诉他最好把羊交还，否则就去叫警察。阿列科不承认，并把迪米特里领进院子。不错，他的确刚买了一只羔羊，阿列科解释说，但他的羔羊是黑色的。迪米特里为自己的鲁莽而感到不好意思，向阿列科道了歉，说是错怪了他。就在他俩说话的时候，天下起了雨，迪米特里便待在阿列科家里避雨，一直等到雨停为止。半小时后，当他从屋里出来时，他惊奇地发现小黑羔羊全身几乎都变成了白色。原来羊毛上染的黑色被雨水冲掉了！

Summary writing 摘要写作

In not more than 80 words describe what happened from the time when Dimitri learnt that his wife's white lamb had been stolen. Do not include anything that is not in the last paragraph.

Answer these questions in note form to get your points:

1 What did Mary tell Dimitri when he came home?]
2 What did Dimitri learn about his neighbour, Aleko?
3 Where did Dimitri go?
4 What did he accuse Aleko of?]
5 Did Aleko show Dimitri his new lamb or not?
6 What colour was it?
7 What did Dimitri do when he saw it was black?]
8 Why did Dimitri stay in Aleko's house for half an hour?
9 Why did he get a surprise when he went outside?]
10 Had the lamb been dyed or not?]

Vocabulary 词汇

Give another word or phrase to replace the following words as they are used in the passage: tiny (l.1); fetch (l.4); missing (l.5); acquired (l.10); denied (l.11); apologized (l.13); dyed (l.16).

Composition 作文

In not more than 200 words continue the above passage. Use the ideas given below. Do not write more than three paragraphs.

Title: Not so black.

Introduction: Dimitri took a close look at the lamb — surprised — it was white — recognized it as his own.

Development: Angry scene — accusation — Aleko still denied theft — violent argument — finally Aleko admitted it — Dimitri called the police — Aleko was arrested — Dimitri took the lamb home.

Conclusion: Excitement in the village — villagers were amused by the event — discussed it at great length for a long time.

Letter writing 书信写作

The following events have prompted you to write letters. Write suitable introductions of about 25 words each.

1 A prize you have won.
2 An examination you have passed.

Key structures 关键句型

He accused him of stealing the lamb. **(1 KS 92)**（参见第 2 册第 92 课关键句型）

Exercises 练习

A Note the form of the verbs in italics: accused him of *stealing* (ll.10-11); Aleko denied *taking* it (l.11); ashamed of *having* acted (l.13); apologized to Aleko for *having* accused (l.13); it began *to rain* (l.14).

B Write sentences using the following:

1 We continued ...
2 Let's go ...
3 This shirt needs ...
4 Excuse my ...

Special difficulties 难点

He had better return it. (l.11)

Instead of saying:	*We can say*:
It would be advisable for you to leave now.	You had better leave now.
It would not be advisable for you to telephone him.	You had better not telephone him.

Exercise 练习

Rewrite the following sentences using *had better* in place of *it would be advisable.*

1 It would be advisable for us to have lunch.
2 It would be advisable for her to renew her passport.
3 It would not be advisable for you to ask so many questions.
4 It would not be advisable for us to stay any longer.
5 It would be advisable for the children to get an early night.
6 It would be advisable for me to consult my solicitor.

Multiple choice questions 选择题

Choose the correct answers to the following questions.

Comprehension 理解

1 Every evening, Mary used to go and ________ .
(*a*) cut the lamb from the rope it had been tied on
(*b*) untie the lamb so it could wander in the field at night
(*c*) bring her lamb back home for the night
(*d*) make sure that her lamb was not missing

2 It would not be difficult to find the thief because ________ .

(*a*) the lamb had been one of Mary's prize possessions

(*b*) news travels fast in a small community

(*c*) Dimitri had a lot of friends in the village

(*d*) the rain would soon wash the black dye off the lamb

3 When Aleko first showed Dimitri the lamb in his backyard ________ .

(*a*) he was truthful about how he had acquired the lamb but not about its colour

(*b*) Dimitri admitted that the lamb could not be his wife's

(*c*) it was clear that the lamb had been dyed black

(*d*) it started to rain before Dimitri had time to identify the lamb as his

Structure 结构

4 Mary and her husband Dimitri lived in Peracora, ________ tiny village in southern Greece. (ll.1-2)

(*a*) in a (*b*) the (*c*) in the (*d*) a

5 – was a little white lamb which had been ________ from her husband. (ll.2-3)

(*a*) present (*b*) presented (*c*) presenting (*d*) a present

6 On her husband's return, ________ what had happened. (ll.7-8)

(*a*) his wife told him (*b*) she told Dimitri (*c*) Mary told him (*d*) Dimitri was told

7 – it would not prove difficult in a village of ________ size. (ll.8-9)

(*a*) a such small (*b*) so small (*c*) the smallest (*d*) so small a

8 He told him if he ________ it, he would call the police. (l.11)

(*a*) was not returning (*b*) did not return (*c*) has not returned (*d*) had not returned

Vocabulary 词汇

9 One of Mary's most ________ possessions ... (l.2)

(*a*) valued (*b*) worthwhile (*c*) worthy (*d*) expensive

10 After ________ the theft to several of his friends ... (l.9)

(*a*) telling (*b*) reporting (*c*) expressing (*d*) counting

11 During their ________ , it began to rain. (ll.13-14)

(*a*) chat (*b*) argument (*c*) conversation (*d*) speech

12 When he went ________ half an hour later ... (ll.14-15)

(*a*) out of doors (*b*) into the open (*c*) in the open air (*d*) inside out

LESSON 17

The longest suspension bridge in the world

世界上最长的吊桥

Sailed into New York harbour in 1524

Listen then answer the question below.

听录音，然后回答以下问题。

How is the bridge supported?

Verrazano, an Italian about whom little is known, sailed into New York Harbour in 1524 and named it Angoulême. He described it as 'a very agreeable situation located within two small hills in the midst of which flowed a great river.' Though Verrazano is by no means considered to be a great explorer, his name will probably remain immortal, for on November 21st, 1964, the longest suspension bridge in the world was named after him.

The Verrazano Bridge, which was designed by Othmar Ammann, joins Brooklyn to Staten Island. It has a span of 4,260 feet. The bridge is so long that the shape of the earth had to be taken into account by its designer. Two great towers support four huge cables. The towers are built on immense underwater platforms made of steel and concrete. The platforms extend to a depth of over 100 feet under the sea. These alone took sixteen months to build. Above the surface of the water, the towers rise to a height of nearly 700 feet. They support the cables from which the bridge has been suspended. Each of the four cables contains 26,108 lengths of wire. It has been estimated that if the bridge were packed with cars, it would still only be carrying a third of its total capacity. However, size and strength are not the only important things about this bridge. Despite its immensity, it is both simple and elegant, fulfilling its designer's dream to create 'an enormous object drawn as faintly as possible'.

New words and expressions 生词和短语

suspension (title)	/səˈspenʃən/	*n.*	悬，吊
agreeable (l.3)	/əˈgriːəbəl/	*adj.*	宜人的
situation (l.3)	/ˌsɪtʃuˈeɪʃən/	*n.*	地点，地方
locate (l.3)	/ləʊˈkeɪt/	*v.*	位于
immortal (l.6)	/ɪˈmɔːtl/	*adj.*	永生的，流芳百世的
Brooklyn (l.8)	/ˈbrʊklɪn/	*n.*	布鲁克林（纽约区名）
Staten (l.8)	/ˈstætən/	*n.*	斯塔顿（岛）
span (l.9)	/spæn/	*n.*	跨度
cable (l.10)	/ˈkeɪbəl/	*n.*	缆索
concrete (l.11)	/ˈkɒŋkriːt/	*n.*	混凝土
suspend (l.13)	/səˈspend/	*v.*	悬挂
length (l.14)	/leŋθ/	*n.*	根，段
estimate (l.14)	/ˈestɪmeɪt/	*v.*	估计
capacity (l.15)	/kəˈpæsɪti/	*n.*	承受量
immensity (l.16)	/ɪˈmensɪti/	*n.*	巨大
elegant (l.16)	/ˈelɪgənt/	*adj.*	优美别致的
faintly (l.17)	/ˈfeɪntli/	*adv.*	微细地

Notes on the text 课文注释

1 describe ... as ... 作“把……描绘成……”、“认为……”讲。

2 located within two small hills in the midst of which flowed a great river, 位于两座小山之间，一条大河滔滔流过。

located ... 是过去分词短语作定语，修饰 situation; in the midst of which 引导一个定语从句，which 指 two small hills。in the midst of, 在……之中。

3 by no means, 无论如何都不，决不。

4 ... the longest suspension bridge ..., 注：维拉萨诺大桥现已不是世界上最长的吊桥。

5 be named after sb., 以某人的名字命名。

6 be taken into account, 被考虑到。

7 It has been estimated ..., 据估计，……。

8 be packed with ... 作"挤满……"、"装满……"解。

参考译文

1524 年，一位鲜为人知的意大利人维拉萨诺驾船驶进纽约港，并将该港命名为安古拉姆。他对该港作了这样的描述："地理位置十分适宜，位于两座小山的中间，一条大河从中间流过"。虽然维拉萨诺绝对算不上一个伟大的探险家，但他的名字将流芳百世，因为 1964 年 11 月 21 日建成的一座世界上最长的吊桥是以他的名字命名的。

维拉萨诺大桥由奥斯马·阿曼设计，连接着布鲁克林与斯塔顿岛，桥长 4,260 英尺。由于桥身太长，设计者不得不考虑了地表的形状。两座巨塔支撑着 4 根粗大的钢缆。塔身建在巨大的水下钢筋混凝土平台上。平台深入海面以下 100 英尺。仅这两座塔就花了 16 个月才建成。塔身高出水面将近 700 英尺。高塔支撑着钢缆，而钢缆又悬吊着大桥。4 根钢缆中的每根由 26,108 股钢绳组成。据估计，即使桥上停满了汽车，也只不过是桥的总承载力的 1/3。然而，这座桥的重要特点不仅是它的规模与强度。尽管此桥很大，但它的结构简单，造型优美，实现了设计者企图创造一个"尽量用细线条勾画出一个庞然大物"的梦想。

Summary writing 摘要写作

Describe the Verrazano Bridge *in not more than 80 words.* Do not include anything that is not in the last paragraph.

Answer these questions in note form to get your points:

1 What is the name of the bridge which joins Brooklyn to Staten Island?
2 What is its span?
3 How many towers has it got?
4 What do these towers support?
5 What are the towers built on?
6 How far under the sea do the platforms go?
7 How far above the surface do the towers rise?
8 What is the bridge suspended from?
9 How many lengths of wire does each of these cables contain?
10 Is the bridge very strong or not?
11 Is it simple and elegant or not?

Vocabulary 词汇

Give another word or phrase to replace the following words as they are used in the passage: agreeable situation (l.3); in the midst (ll.3-4); considered (l.5); remain immortal (l.6); span (l.9); taken into account (l.9); support (l.10).

Composition 作文

Describe any bridge you know well. Expand the following into a paragraph of about 150 words.

The bridge I know best is called ... It joins ... to ... From far away it looks ... but when you get near ... It is made of ... and supported by ... which ... If you stand on the bridge early in the morning, you can see ... At this time everything is quiet. During the day, however, ... I enjoy standing on the bridge at night when ... In the darkness, you can see ... In the stillness ... are the only sounds that can be heard. (77 words)

Letter writing 书信写作

A friend who is coming to visit you has written to you asking for detailed information on how to get to your house. Write a reply in about 80 words. Supply a suitable Introduction and Conclusion. Use the following information to write the *Purpose*: which train to catch — where to get off — which bus to catch and where — any familiar landmark — where to get off — which road to take — where your house is.

Key structures 关键句型

The Verrazano Bridge was designed by Othmar Ammann. 被动语态 (1 KS 93)（参见第 2 册第 93 课关键句型）

Exercise 练习

Change the form of the verbs in these sentences. Omit the words in italics. Do not refer to the passage until you finish the exercise.

1 Verrazano is an Italian about whom *we* know little.
2 *They* do not consider Verrazano to be a great explorer.
3 *They* named the greatest bridge in the world after him.
4 *He* had to take into account the shape of the earth.
5 *They* have estimated that if the bridge were packed with cars ...

Special difficulties 难点

He is by no means considered to be a great explorer. (ll.4-5) 动词不定式 (Compare 1 SD 84)（对比第 2 册第 84 课难点）

Instead of saying: I find that he is quite unsuitable for the job.

We can say: I find him to be quite unsuitable for the job.

Exercise 练习

Write these sentences again changing the form of the phrases in italics:

1 I believed *that he owned* property abroad.
2 The Minister declared *that the treaty was* invalid.
3 I know *that he is* a person of high integrity.
4 I guess *that he is* about twenty-seven years old.
5 We estimated *that this picture is* worth at least £500.

Multiple choice questions 选择题

Choose the correct answers to the following questions.

Comprehension 理解

1 Verrazano's name will probably remain immortal because ________ .
(*a*) it was after he discovered New York Harbour that a bridge was built
(*b*) he named the river that the new bridge crosses
(*c*) he was an explorer of considerable means
(*d*) it has been given to the world's longest suspension bridge

2 The Verrazano Bridge was built with so wide a span because ________ .
(*a*) it had to cover a wide stretch of water
(*b*) of the unusual shape of the earth around Brooklyn and Staten Island
(*c*) the water that lies between Brooklyn and Staten Island is very deep
(*d*) the number of wires in each cable is so great

3 In designing the Verrazano Bridge, Othmar Ammann ________ .
(*a*) had to account for the curvature of the earth's surface
(*b*) spent over a year building the platforms that form the bridge's base
(*c*) had to consider the number of vehicles that might cross the bridge at any one time
(*d*) wished to reduce the size of the bridge as much as possible

Structure 结构

4 He described it ________ situated. (ll.2-3)
(*a*) as being very agreeably　(*b*) was very agreeable to be
(*c*) very agreeably having been　(*d*) very agreeably as being

5 The Verrazano Bridge, ________ the design of Othmar Ammann. (l.8)
(*a*) is　(*b*) was　(*c*) were　(*d*) has been

6 The length of the bridge is ________ the shape of the earth. (ll.9-10)
(*a*) so that　(*b*) such that　(*c*) that which　(*d*) thus

7 The towers are built on ________ which are sunk beneath the water. (ll.10-11)
(*a*) ferro-concrete immense platforms
(*b*) immense made of ferro-concrete platforms
(*c*) and made of ferro-concrete immense platforms
(*d*) immense ferro-concrete platforms

8 Even if the bridge were packed with cars, it could still ________ three times the load. (ll.14-15)
(*a*) be carrying　(*b*) be able to carry　(*c*) only carry　(*d*) carry

Vocabulary 词汇

9 'a very agreeable situation with two small hills lying ________ ' (ll.3-4)
(*a*) on either side　(*b*) on every side　(*c*) besides　(*d*) side by side

10 The Verrazano Bridge ________ Brooklyn with Staten Island. (l.8)
(*a*) attaches　(*b*) unifies　(*c*) links　(*d*) relates

11 A bridge which is hung from cables is known as a ________ bridge. (ll.12-13)
(*a*) suspended　(*b*) suspense　(*c*) suspension　(*d*) suspender

12 If the bridge were loaded with as many cars as it could ________ , it would still ... (ll.14-15)
(*a*) sustain　(*b*) endure　(*c*) receive　(*d*) take

LESSON

18 Electric currents in modern art

现代艺术中的电流

Listen then answer the question below.

听录音，然后回答以下问题。

How might some of the exhibits have been dangerous?

some people—including myself —were surprised

Modern sculpture rarely surprises us any more. The idea that modern art can only be seen in museums is mistaken. Even people who take no interest in art cannot have failed to notice examples of modern sculpture on display in public places. Strange forms stand in gardens, and outside buildings and shops. We have got quite used to them. Some so-called 'modern' pieces have been on display for nearly eighty years.

In spite of this, some people — including myself — were surprised by a recent exhibition of modern sculpture. The first thing I saw when I entered the art gallery was a notice which said: 'Do not touch the exhibits. Some of them are dangerous!' The objects on display were pieces of moving sculpture. Oddly shaped forms that are suspended from the ceiling and move in response to a gust of wind are quite familiar to everybody. These objects, however, were different. Lined up against the wall, there were long thin wires attached to metal spheres. The spheres had been magnetized and attracted or repelled each other all the time. In the centre of the hall, there were a number of tall structures which contained coloured lights. These lights flickered continuously like traffic lights which have gone mad. Sparks were emitted from small black boxes and red lamps flashed on and off angrily. It was rather like an exhibition of prehistoric electronic equipment. These peculiar forms not only seemed designed to shock people emotionally, but to give them electric shocks as well!

New words and expressions 生词和短语

current	(title)	/ˈkʌrənt/	*n.*	电流
sculpture	(l.1)	/ˈskʌlptʃə/	*n.*	雕塑
mistaken	(l.2)	/mɪˈsteɪkən/	*adj.*	错误的
gallery	(l.9)	/ˈgæləri/	*n.*	美术馆
exhibit	(l.9)	/ɪgˈzɪbɪt/	*n.*	展品，陈列品
oddly	(l.10)	/ˈɒdli/	*adv.*	古怪地
attach	(l.12)	/əˈtætʃ/	*v.*	连，系
sphere	(l.13)	/sfɪə/	*n.*	球体
magnetize	(l.13)	/ˈmægnɪtaɪz/	*v.*	使磁化
repel	(l.13)	/rɪˈpel/	*v.*	排斥
flicker	(l.15)	/ˈflɪkə/	*v.*	闪烁
emit	(l.15)	/ɪˈmɪt/	*v.*	放射
flash	(l.16)	/flæʃ/	*v.*	闪光
prehistoric	(l.16)	/ˌpriːhɪˈstɒrɪk/	*adj.*	史前的，老掉牙的
electronic	(l.16)	/ɪˌlekˈtrɒnɪk/	*adj.*	电子的
peculiar	(l.17)	/pɪˈkjuːliə/	*adj.*	奇异的
shock	(l.17)	/ʃɒk/	*v.*	令人震惊，刺激人
emotionally	(l.17)	/ɪˈməʊʃənəli/	*adv.*	感情上

Notes on the text 课文注释

1 The idea that ... is mistaken.

此处 that 引导的从句作 idea 的同位语。

2 take no interest in ..., 作“对……不感兴趣”解。

3 cannot have failed to notice, 不至于没注意到。
"cannot + have + 过去分词”表示对于过去的事所作的不肯定的推测。

4 move in response to a gust of wind, 随风飘荡。
in response (to) 作“回答”、“响应”、“作出反应”讲。此处是“(展品)随风而动”的意思。

5 be familiar to ... 是“为……所熟悉”的意思。

6 Lined up against the wall, 靠墙排列着。

7 like traffic lights which have gone mad, 就像失去控制的红绿灯一样。
go mad 作“发疯”、“发狂”讲。

8 on and off (亦作 off and on) 作“断断续续地”、“有时”讲。

9 These peculiar forms not only seemed designed ..., 其中 seemed 是系动词，seemed designed 作用与 were designed 是一样的。

参考译文

现代雕塑不再使我们感到惊讶了。那种认为现代艺术只能在博物馆里才能看到的观点是错误的。即使是对艺术不感兴趣的人也不会注意不到在公共场所展示的现代艺术品。公园里、大楼和商店外竖立着奇形怪状的雕塑，对这些，我们已经司空见惯了。有些所谓的“现代”艺术品在那里已经陈列了近 80 年了。

尽管如此，最近举办的一次现代雕塑展览还是使一些人（包括我在内）大吃了一惊。走进展厅首先看到的是一张告示，上面写着：“切勿触摸展品，某些展品有危险”。展品都是些活动的雕塑。人们所熟悉的是悬挂在天花板上、造型奇特、随风飘荡的雕塑品。这些展品却使人大开眼界。靠墙排列着许多细长的电线，而电线又连着金属球。金属球经过磁化，相互之间不停地吸引或排斥。展厅中央是装有彩色灯泡的许多高高的构件，灯泡一刻不停地闪烁，就像失去了控制的红绿灯。小黑盒子里迸出火花，红色灯泡发怒似地忽明忽暗。这儿倒像是在展览古老的电子设备。好像设计这些奇形怪状的展品不仅是为了给人感情上的强烈刺激，而且还想给人以电击似的！

Summary writing 摘要写作

In not more than 80 words describe what the writer saw from the moment he entered the art gallery. Do not include anything that is not in the last paragraph.

Answer these questions in note form to get your points:

1 What did the writer see when he entered the art gallery?]
2 Why did it forbid people to touch the exhibits?]
3 What did the exhibition consist of?]
4 What did the writer see against the wall?]
5 What did the spheres do?]
6 What did the tall structures in the centre of the hall contain?]
7 What did the coloured lights do?]
8 What was emitted from black boxes?]
9 Did red lamps go on and off or not?]

Vocabulary 词汇

Give another word or phrase to replace the following words as they are used in the passage: on display (l.4); oddly (l.10); suspended (l.11); response (l.11); familiar (l.11); attached (l.12); flickered continuously (l.15).

Composition 作文

In not more than 200 words describe an exhibition of modern paintings (real or imaginary). Use the ideas given below. Do not write more than three paragraphs.

Title: An interesting exhibition.

Introduction: Work of many artists exhibited — great public interest — you went to the art gallery.

Development: Description of some of the pictures on display — the picture you liked best — the strangest picture of them all.

Conclusion: People's comments overheard — your opinion of the paintings at the exhibition.

Letter writing 书信写作

Write a letter of about 80 words to a friend accepting an invitation to go with him to an exhibition. Supply a suitable Introduction and Conclusion. Use the following information to write the *Purpose*: thank him for invitation — looking forward to meeting him again soon — particularly interested in the exhibition — why — where you will meet your friend: time and place.

Key structures 关键句型

Preposition. 介词 (1 KS 94)（参见第 2 册第 94 课关键句型）

Exercise 练习

Supply the missing words in the following sentences. Do not refer to the passage until you finish the exercise.

1 Even people who take no interest ________ art cannot have failed to notice examples of modern sculpture ________ display in public places.

2 We have got quite used ________ them.

3 Oddly shaped forms that are suspended ________ the ceiling and move ________ response ________ a gust of wind are quite familiar ________ everybody.

4 There were long thin wires attached ________ metal spheres.

Special difficulties 难点

Spelling

Note the spelling of the words in italics:

I'll *pay* the bill. He never *pays* his bills.

He owns a *donkey*. I own two *donkeys*.

You'll wake up the *baby*. *Babies* often cry.

Will he *try* again? He never *tries* very hard.

Exercise 练习

Add *s* or *ies* to the following words. Make any other necessary changes.

lady, supply, valley, qualify, story, day, say, reply, marry, way, chimney, hurry, stay, enjoy, buy, body, bury, fry.

Multiple choice questions 选择题

Choose the correct answers to the following questions.

Comprehension 理解

1 Modern sculpture rarely surprises us any more because ________ .

(*a*) even if not in museums, we see it in and around other public places

(*b*) despite people's lack of interest in art, it is put on display

(*c*) people not only display it in their houses but in their gardens also

(*d*) museums have been exhibiting it for nearly eighty years

2 What surprised the writer when he visited a recent exhibition of modern sculpture?

(*a*) The fact that people were forbidden to touch the exhibits.

(*b*) The oddly shaped forms that were suspended from the ceiling.

(*c*) The way in which electrical energy was used to produce mobile effects.

(*d*) The prehistoric electronic equipment used to activate the exhibits.

3 The pieces of sculpture on display at the exhibition were ________ .

(*a*) noticed because they were dangerous

(*b*) either hung on wires or built into the middle of the hall

(*c*) flickering continuously with different coloured lights

(*d*) such that one could not pass them unnoticed though it seemed wiser to pass them untouched

Structure 结构

4 – 'modern' pieces ________ on display nearly eighty years ago. (ll.6-7)

(*a*) have been (*b*) are first (*c*) were first (*d*) had been

5 The first thing I saw ________ to the art gallery ... (l.9)

(*a*) on my arrival (*b*) on entering (*c*) at the entrance (*d*) having arrived

6 The notice prohibited people ________ the exhibits. (ll.9-10)

(*a*) to touch (*b*) from touching (*c*) touching (*d*) not to touch

7 The spheres had been magnetized ________ attracted or repelled each other ... (l.13)

(*a*) so that they (*b*) so they were (*c*) so as they had (*d*) in order that they

8 These peculiar forms ________ to shock people emotionally and to ... (ll.17-18)

(*a*) both seemed designed (*b*) seemed both designed

(*c*) seemed both designed and (*d*) seemed designed both

Vocabulary 词汇

9 – forms that are suspended from the ceiling and move ________ are ... (ll.10-11)

(*a*) at one blow (*b*) all of a sudden (*c*) with a light touch (*d*) at the slightest breath

10 Small black boxes ________ sparks ... (l.15)

(*a*) gave off (*b*) sent by (*c*) gave over (*d*) throw off

11 There were a number of tall structures ________ in different colours. (l.14)

(*a*) enlightened (*b*) illuminated (*c*) alighted (*d*) burning

12 These peculiar forms not only seemed ________ to shock people ... (ll.17-18)

(*a*) drawn (*b*) planned (*c*) intended (*d*) created

LESSON 19 A very dear cat 一只贵重的宝贝猫

Listen then answer the question below.

听录音，然后回答以下问题。

Why was Rastus ‘very dear’ in more ways than one?

Rastus was in safe hands

Kidnappers are rarely interested in animals, but they recently took considerable interest in Mrs. Eleanor Ramsay’s cat. Mrs. Eleanor Ramsay, a very wealthy old lady, has shared a flat with her cat, Rastus, for a great many years. Rastus leads an orderly life. He usually takes a short walk in the evenings and is always home by seven o’clock. One evening, however, he failed to arrive. Mrs. Ramsay got very worried. She looked everywhere for him but could not find him.

Three days after Rastus’ disappearance, Mrs. Ramsay received an anonymous letter. The writer stated that Rastus was in safe hands and would be returned immediately if Mrs. Ramsay paid a ransom of £1,000. Mrs. Ramsay was instructed to place the money in a cardboard box and to leave it outside her door. At first, she decided to go to the police, but fearing that she would never see Rastus again—the letter had made that quite clear—she changed her mind. She withdrew £1,000 from her bank and followed the kidnapper’s instructions. The next morning, the box had disappeared but Mrs. Ramsay was sure that the kidnapper would keep his word. Sure enough, Rastus arrived punctually at seven o’clock that evening. He looked very well, though he was rather thirsty, for he drank half a bottle of milk. The police were astounded when Mrs. Ramsay told them what she had done. She explained that Rastus was very dear to her. Considering the amount she paid, he was dear in more ways than one!

New words and expressions 生词和短语

dear	(title)	/dɪə/	*adj.*	亲爱的；珍贵的；昂贵的
kidnapper	(l.1)	/ˈkɪdnæpə/	*n.*	绑架者，拐骗者
considerable	(l.2)	/kənˈsɪdərəbəl/	*adj.*	相当大的
wealthy	(l.3)	/ˈwelθi/	*adj.*	富的，有钱的
orderly	(l.4)	/ˈɔːdəli/	*adj.*	有规律的
disappearance	(l.9)	/ˌdɪsəˈpɪərəns/	*n.*	失踪
anonymous	(l.9)	/əˈnɒnəməs/	*adj.*	匿名的
ransom	(l.10)	/ˈrænsəm/	*n.*	赎金
cardboard	(l.11)	/ˈkɑːdbɔːd/	*n.*	硬纸板
withdraw	(l.13)	/wɪðˈdrɔː/ (withdrew /wɪðˈdruː/, withdrawn /wɪðˈdrɔːn/)	*v.*	（从银行）取钱
punctually	(l.15)	/ˈpʌŋktʃuəli/	*adv.*	准时地
astound	(l.16)	/əˈstaʊnd/	*v.*	使吃惊

Notes on the text 课文注释

1 share ... with ..., 作“与……分享”、“合用……”解。

2 be in safe hands, 在可靠的人那里。

3 she changed her mind, 她改变了主意。

4 keep one's word, 遵守诺言。

5 sure enough, 无疑，果然。

6 Considering ... he was dear in more ways than one!

considering ... 是介词短语，作“考虑到……”、“就……而言”解，此处作原因状语。

dear 不仅作为“可爱”讲，还可作“昂贵”讲。此处有一语双关之意。

in more ways than one (way) 作“在更多方面”解。

参考译文

绑架者很少对动物感兴趣。最近，绑架者却盯上了埃莉诺·拉姆齐太太的猫。埃莉诺·拉姆齐太太是一个非常富有的老妇人，多年来，一直同她养的猫拉斯特斯一起住在一所公寓里。拉斯特斯生活很有规律，傍晚常常出去溜达一会儿，并且总是在7点钟以前回来。可是，有一天晚上，它出去后再也没回来。拉姆齐太太急坏了，四处寻找，但没找着。

拉斯特斯失踪3天后，拉姆齐太太收到一封匿名信。写信人声称拉斯特斯安然无恙，只要拉姆齐太太愿意支付1,000英镑赎金，便可以立即将猫送还。他让拉姆齐太太把钱放在一个纸盒里，然后将纸盒放在门口。一开始拉姆齐太太打算报警，但又害怕再也见不到拉斯特斯了——这点，信上说得十分明白——于是便改变了主意。她从银行取出1,000英镑，并照绑架者的要求做了。第二天早晨，放钱的盒子不见了，但拉姆齐太太确信绑架者是会履行诺言的。果然，当天晚上7点整，拉斯特斯准时回来了。它看上去一切正常，只是口渴得很，喝了半瓶牛奶。拉姆齐太太把她所做的事告诉了警察，警察听后大为吃惊。拉姆齐太太解释说她心疼她的猫拉斯特斯。想到她所花的那笔钱，她的心疼就具有双重意义了。

Summary writing 摘要写作

In not more than 80 words describe how Mrs. Ramsay's cat, Rastus, was returned to her. Do not include anything that is not in the last paragraph.

Answer these questions in note form to get your points:

1 When did Mrs. Ramsay receive an anonymous letter?]
2 How much money did the kidnapper demand for the return of the cat?
3 What would happen if she went to the police?]
4 Where did she have to put the money?
5 Where did she have to put the box?]
6 How much did she draw from the bank?
7 Did she act on the kidnapper's instructions or not?]
8 Had the money disappeared the following morning or not?
9 When did Rastus return to Mrs. Ramsay?]

Vocabulary 词汇

Give another word or phrase to replace the following words as they are used in the passage: rarely (l.1); considerable (l.2); wealthy (l.3); worried (l.7); stated (l.9); changed her mind (l.13); word (l.15).

Composition 作文

Describe how the kidnapper came to know that Mrs. Ramsay was so fond of her cat and how he stole it. Expand the following into a paragraph of about 150 words.

In a bar one night, Mr. X was talking to a workman who told him that ... The workman added that Mrs.

Ramsay ... Every day, Mr. X stood outside ... As the cat ... that it had regular habits. He also found out as much as he could about Mrs. Ramsay and learnt that ... One evening, as the cat was leaving the block of flats ... He took the cat to ... During the next three days, he walked past Mrs. Ramsay's flat on several occasions and noticed that ... Now that he was sure ... he wrote ... in which he ... (94 words)

Letter writing 书信写作

Write a letter of about 80 words to a former teacher telling him briefly what you have been doing since you left school. Supply a suitable Introduction and Conclusion. Use the following information to write your *Purpose*: further studies since leaving school — how you got your present job — whether you like it and why — what you hope to do in the future.

Key structures 关键句型

Review of verb forms. 复习动词 (1 KS 95)（参见第 2 册第 95 课关键句型）

Exercise 练习

Underline all the verbs in the passage and note how they have been used.

Special difficulties 难点

The comma. 逗号的用法

Note how commas are used in the following sentences:

1 After we had visited the market, we returned home.

2 Mr. Griffiths, the Prime Minister, said that his party would win the next election.

3 I bought pens, pencils and paper.

4 It was raining heavily and I was sure no one would be at the race course. There were, however, hundreds of people there.

5 The small boat, which took eleven weeks to cross the Atlantic, arrived at Plymouth yesterday.

Exercise 练习

Insert commas where necessary in the following paragraph.

Before going home I went to the grocer's. Bill Smith the man who always serves me was very busy. This however did not worry me. On the contrary it gave me the opportunity to look round for several things I wanted. By the time my turn came I had already filled a basket with packets of biscuits cans of fruit bars of soap and two large bags of flour.

Multiple choice questions 选择题

Choose the correct answers to the following questions.

Comprehension 理解

1 Some kidnappers took considerable interest in Mrs. Ramsay's cat because ________ .

(*a*) Mrs. Ramsay could and would pay a lot to get her only companion back

(*b*) Mrs. Ramsay clearly loved her cat to have kept him so long

(*c*) Rastus was an orderly cat and would be easy to look after if kidnapped

(*d*) Mrs. Ramsay missed her cat whenever he was not back home on time

2 On what conditions did the kidnapper promise the safe return of Rastus?

(*a*) His name was not to be revealed and he wanted a ransom of £1,000.

(*b*) Mrs. Ramsay was not to inform the police and had to pay £1,000.

(*c*) Mrs. Ramsay had to leave her flat until the box with the money had gone.

(*d*) Mrs. Ramsay was to withdraw £1,000 from her bank and follow his instructions.

3 How was Rastus dear to Mrs. Ramsay in more ways than one?

(*a*) She was very fond of him and it had cost her a lot to get him back.

(*b*) Besides the high ransom paid on his behalf, he drank a lot of milk.

(*c*) He was so dear that she had not dared tell the police of the kidnapping.

(*d*) He was very valuable and she valued him greatly.

Structure 结构

4 Mrs. Eleanor Ramsay is a very wealthy lady who ________ a flat with her cat Rastus, for a great many years. (ll.2-4)

(*a*) shares (*b*) has shared (*c*) shared (*d*) had shared

5 She searched for him but could not find him ________ . (ll.7-8)

(*a*) nowhere (*b*) somewhere (*c*) everywhere (*d*) anywhere

6 Her first reaction ________ the police. (ll.11-12)

(*a*) was to call (*b*) was calling (*c*) she would call (*d*) being to call

7 But ________ never seeing Rastus again, she changed her mind. (ll.12-13)

(*a*) afraid (*b*) afraid of (*c*) for fear (*d*) afraid for

8 Considering ________ money she paid, he was dear ... (ll.17-18)

(*a*) the great (*b*) how many (*c*) how much of (*d*) what a lot of

Vocabulary 词汇

9 Rastus leads a ________ life. (l.4)

(*a*) correct (*b*) measured (*c*) regular (*d*) disciplined

10 He usually goes ________ in the evenings ... (ll.4-5)

(*a*) on a trek (*b*) for a stroll (*c*) for a trot (*d*) on foot

11 ________ , Rastus arrived punctually ... (l.15)

(*a*) Certainly (*b*) Without a doubt (*c*) As expected (*d*) As a matter of fact

12 He appeared very ________ , though ... (ll.15-16)

(*a*) healthy (*b*) satisfied (*c*) good-looking (*d*) sane

LESSON

20 Pioneer pilots 飞行员的先驱

the first person to greet him ...

Listen then answer the question below.

听录音，然后回答以下问题。

What was the name of the first plane to fly across the English Channel?

In 1908 Lord Northcliffe offered a prize of £1,000 to the first man who would fly across the English Channel. Over a year passed before the first attempt was made. On July 19th, 1909, in the early morning, Hubert Latham took off from the French coast in his plane the 'Antoinette IV'. He had travelled only seven miles across the Channel when his engine failed and he was forced to land on the sea. The 'Antoinette' floated on the water until Latham was picked up by a ship.

Two days later, Louis Bleriot arrived near Calais with a plane called 'No. XI'. Bleriot had been making planes since 1905 and this was his latest model. A week before, he had completed a successful overland flight during which he covered twenty-six miles. Latham, however, did not give up easily. He, too, arrived near Calais on the same day with a new 'Antoinette'. It looked as if there would be an exciting race across the Channel. Both planes were going to take off on July 25th, but Latham failed to get up early enough. After making a short test flight at 4.15 a.m., Bleriot set off half an hour later. His great flight lasted thirty-seven minutes. When he landed near Dover, the first person to greet him was a local policeman. Latham made another attempt a week later and got within half a mile of Dover, but he was unlucky again. His engine failed and he landed on the sea for the second time.

New words and expressions 生词和短语

pioneer (title) /ˌpaɪəˈnɪə/ *n.* 先驱

lord (l.1) /lɔːd/ *n.* 对（英国）贵族的尊称；勋爵

Calais (l.8) /ˈkæleɪ/ *n.* 加来（法国港市）

overland (l.9) /ˌəʊvəˈlænd/ *adj.* 陆上的

Notes on the text 课文注释

1 the English Channel, 英吉利海峡。
大西洋延伸的部分，长约 350 英里（约 560 公里），将英法两国的领土分开。

2 Over a year passed before the first attempt was made.
一年多时间之后，才有人进行第一次尝试。

3 pick up 此处作“（从海里）救起”解。

4 did not give up easily, 不轻易作罢。
give up 当“放弃”讲。

5 It looked as if there would be an exciting race across the Channel. 看起来似乎有一场精彩的飞越英吉利

海峡的比赛。as if 引导的从句作起系动词作用的 look 的表语，其中谓语动词 would be 表示与未来的事实不相符的虚拟结构。

6 got within half a mile of Dover, 到了离多佛尔不到半英里的地方。

7 Dover, 多佛尔港，是英吉利海峡的一个港口，对面是法国港口加来。多佛尔与加来相距约 21 英里（约 34 公里），是英吉利海峡最窄的部分。

参考译文

1908 年，诺斯克利夫勋爵拿出 1,000 英镑，作为对第一个飞越英吉利海峡的人的奖励。然而一年多过去了才有人出来尝试。1909 年 7 月 19 日凌晨，休伯特·莱瑟姆驾驶“安特瓦奈特 4 号”飞机从法国海岸起飞，但他只在海峡上空飞行了 7 英里，引擎就发生了故障，他只好降落在海面上。“安特瓦奈特”号飞机在海上漂浮，后来有船经过，莱瑟姆方才获救。

两天之后，路易斯·布莱里奥驾驶一架名为“11 号”的飞机来到加来附近。布莱里奥从 1905 年起便开始研制飞机，“11 号”飞机是他制作的最新型号。一周以前，他曾成功地进行了一次 26 英里的陆上飞行。但是莱瑟姆不肯轻易罢休。同一天，他驾驶一架新的“安特瓦奈特”号飞机来到了加来附近。看来会有一场激烈的飞越英吉利海峡的竞争。两架飞机都打算在 7 月 25 日起飞，但莱瑟姆那天起床晚了。布莱里奥凌晨 4 点 15 分作了一次短距离试飞，半小时后便正式出发了。他这次伟大的飞行持续了 37 分钟。当他在多佛尔着陆后，第一个迎接他的是当地一名警察。莱瑟姆一周以后也作了一次尝试，飞到了离多佛尔不到半英里的地方。这次他又遭厄运，因引擎故障第二次降落在海面上。

Summary writing 摘要写作

In not more than 80 words describe the attempts made by Bleriot and Latham to fly across the Channel from the time when they both arrived at Calais. Do not include anything that is not in the last paragraph.

Answer these questions in note form to get your points:

1 On what date did Bleriot and Latham arrive at Calais?

2 Did it look as if there would be a race or not?
3 When would it take place?
4 Why did Latham not take part in the race?

5 Did Bleriot make a short test flight before setting out or not?
6 How long did it take him to fly across the Channel?

7 Who greeted him when he arrived at Dover?

8 How near to Dover did Latham fly the following week?
9 Why did he have to land on the sea for the second time?

Vocabulary 词汇

Give another word or phrase to replace the following words as they are used in the passage: forced to land (l.6); picked up (l.7); completed (l.9); covered (l.10); test (l.13); set off (l.13); failed (l.15).

Composition 作文

Imagine yourself in Bleriot's position. In not more than 200 words write a first-person account of the flight across the Channel. Use the ideas given below. Do not write more than three paragraphs.

Title: My flight across the Channel.

Introduction: Early morning — no sign of Latham — test flight — all well.

Development: Started off — could no longer see ship following below — suddenly alone — worried about direction — sea and sky — high winds — engine very hot — it began to rain — rain cooled engine — land ahead.

Conclusion: Flew in a circle — looked for a place to land — on field — two minutes later: policeman: bonjour!

Letter writing 书信写作

Suppose that you are at this moment on board an aeroplane. Write a letter of about 80 words describing your impressions. Supply a suitable Introduction and Conclusion. Use the following ideas to write the *Purpose*: your feelings when the plane took off — how you feel now — height and speed — the view from the window — when you will arrive at your destination.

Special difficulties 难点

Review SD1-17 复习第1至17课难点

Exercises 练习

A Complete the following sentences.

1 What are you looking ________ ? **(SD 1)**（参见第1课）

2 We have received fifty applications ________ all. **(SD 2)**（参见第2课）

3 I happened to ________ . **(SD 3)**（参见第3课）

4 It happened ________ . **(SD 3)**（参见第3课）

5 The play was a ________ on Broadway. **(SD 7)**（参见第7课）

6 The play was very ________ on Broadway. **(SD 7)**（参见第7课）

7 I wish you ________ . **(SD 12)**（参见第12课）

8 I'd rather he ________ . **(SD 14)**（参见第14课）

9 If I can save up enough money, ________ . **(SD 15)**（参见第15课）

10 You had better ________ . **(SD 16)**（参见第16课）

11 I find him to ________ . **(SD 17)**（参见第17课）

B Write sentences using the following words. **(SD 4)**（参见第4课）

explain/position/me; describe/film/aunt.

C Write these sentences again beginning each one with the words in italics. **(SD 5)**（参见第5课）

1 He has *not only* made this mistake before, but he will make it again.

2 I realized what was happening *only then*.

D Write the opposites of these words: **(SD 6)**（参见第6课）

polite; agree; legible; accurate; locked; regular.

Multiple choice questions 选择题

Choose the correct answers to the following questions.

Comprehension 理解

1 In Hubert Latham's first attempt to fly the English Channel ________ .

(*a*) Lord Northcliffe offered a prize of £1,000

(*b*) his engine failed with only seven miles to go before reaching Dover

(*c*) his plane developed engine trouble only seven miles after take-off

(*d*) both Latham and his plane were rescued by a passing ship

2 When Bleriot made his successful crossing ________ .

(*a*) he was flying a plane he had made in 1905

(*b*) he had already flown overland the distance across the English Channel

(*c*) he set out for Dover half an hour before Latham did

(*d*) he was arrested as soon as he landed in England

3 Latham failed at his second attempt because ________ .

(*a*) he did not get up early enough

(*b*) he had to make another forced landing

(*c*) he only got within half a mile of Dover

(*d*) his plane had not been repaired properly

Structure 结构

4 The first man ________ across the English Channel would receive Lord Northcliffe's prize. (ll.1-2)

(*a*) who was going to fly (*b*) flying (*c*) to fly (*d*) having flown

5 The first attempt ________ over a year later. (ll.2-3)

(*a*) was not made till (*b*) was made in (*c*) was made after (*d*) was made until

6 He, too, ________ near Calais with a new 'Antoinette'. (ll.10-11)

(*a*) just arrived (*b*) was just arriving (*c*) had just arrived (*d*) arrived just

7 It ________ to be an exciting race across the Channel. (ll.11-12)

(*a*) would promise (*b*) would have promised

(*c*) was promising (*d*) promised

8 Latham made another attempt a week later. ________ he got within half a mile of Dover. (ll.14-15)

(*a*) This time (*b*) That time (*c*) When (*d*) Then

Vocabulary 词汇

9 He had travelled ________ seven miles when ... (ll.5-6)

(*a*) farther than (*b*) no longer than (*c*) no further than (*d*) a space of

10 The 'Antoinette' ________ until Latham was picked up ... (l.7)

(*a*) held water (*b*) was watertight (*c*) stayed at sea (*d*) rode the waves

11 After making a short test flight, Bleriot set off at quarter ________ five. (ll.12-13)

(*a*) to (*b*) of (*c*) before (*d*) past

12 His ________ flight lasted thirty-seven minutes. (ll.13-14)

(*a*) immense (*b*) long (*c*) grand (*d*) remarkable

Pre-unit Test 2

IF YOU CAN DO THIS TEST GO ON TO UNIT 2

Composition

a Describe the impressions of a man who returns to his home town after an absence of forty years. Expand the following into a paragraph of about 150 words:
After an absence of forty years, the man returned to the town where ... Now, as the train drew into the station, he remembered how, as a boy, he ... The station itself had not changed, but when ... he got a shock. The old church which used to ... was now surrounded by ... He noticed with dismay that new blocks of flats had ... After, he went to his old neighbourhood. He was pleased to find that ... Everything was exactly ... Even the little shop where ... He smiled with pleasure when he saw that ... When ..., he rapidly made his way to the house where ... (100 words)

b In about 200 words describe how soldiers searched for a prisoner of war who, after escaping from his camp, had been hidden by a friendly villager. Do not write more than three paragraphs. Use the ideas given below.
Soldiers coming — the prisoner hid on the roof — saw the soldiers arrive — they questioned the villager — the villager pretended not to understand — the soldiers — searched the house and fields — they got a ladder — they climbed on to the roof — the prisoner climbed down a drain pipe — through an open window — hid in a large wardrobe — the soldiers left.

Key structures

Verb forms.

a Supply the correct form of the verbs in parentheses.
Before ________ (go) to bed, I set the alarm clock to ring at six in the morning because I wanted to get up early. It ________ (seem) to me that I no sooner ________ (go) to sleep than the alarm ________ (ring). It ________ (be) exactly 6 o'clock. After ________ (spend) another ten minutes in bed, I ________ (get) up and ________ (dress). It ________ (be) still dark when I ________ (get) outside. There ________ (be) no buses so I ________ (hurry) to the station on foot. I ________ (walk) for ten minutes when I ________ (decide) to stop and have a cup of tea at a café which just ________ (open). You can imagine my surprise when I ________ (discover) that the time ________ (be) only a quarter to six! The night before I ________ (set) the alarm to ring an hour too soon!

b Give the correct form of the verbs in parentheses.
During the past hundred years, many wonderful cave paintings ________ (discover). Early artists ________ (use) simple materials and ________ (draw) on rocks. One of the first discoveries ________ (make) in 1879 in Altamira*. A young girl ________ (walk) in a cave when she ________ (stop) to light a candle. As soon as she ________ (do) so, she ________ (see) strange animals on the walls. Since then, a great many more paintings ________ (find). In one picture, some deer ________ (hunt) by men. The men ________ (shoot) arrows at them and the deer ________ (run) away. Today, we ________ (try) to understand these pictures. Nobody ________ (think) that they are childish. From them we ________ (learn) a great deal about early man.

* Altamira 阿尔塔米拉是一个史前洞穴，因其中华丽的彩绘和雕刻而著名。它位于西班牙北部的桑坦德以西约 32 公里处。

c Give the correct form of the verbs in parentheses.

When the great new dam has been built it ________ (supply) power for a third of the country's requirements. The dam ________ (take) ten years to build and the course of the river ________ (change). At present, twenty thousand workers ________ (employ) and by the time the dam ________ (complete), it ________ (cost) millions of pounds. As many people have had to leave their homes, the government ________ (build) new villages for them. The great dam ________ (improve) living standards. In future, farmers ________ (produce) more than half the country's needs; new factories ________ (build) and the whole country ________ (have) an adequate supply of electricity.

d Give the correct form of the verbs in parentheses. Supply speech marks and arrange the conversation into paragraphs.

After the crash, two angry drivers got out of their cars. ... ________ you always ________ (sleep) when you ________ (drive)? ________ (ask) the first driver sarcastically. You ________ (be) on the wrong side of the road. ... ________ you ________ (mean) to tell me, ________ (shout) the second driver, that you ________ (not notice) that this road ________ (repair)? Of course I ________ (drive) on the wrong side of the road when you ________ (hit) me. The other side ________ (be) full of holes. ... ________ you ________ (not see) the traffic sign? Listen, ________ (say) the first driver, ... ________ you ever ________ (drive) a car before? I ________ (drive) a car for twenty years. There ________ (be) good driving schools for people like you. There they ________ (teach) you lots of things — how to drive a car for instance. Now you really ________ (tell) me something, ________ (answer) the second man angrily. I happen to be a driving instructor.

e Suppose you were writing a newspaper report of the above conversation. Complete the following.

After the crash, two angry drivers got out of their cars. The first driver asked sarcastically whether the other man always ________ when he ________ He ________ on the wrong side of the road. Shouting angrily, the second driver asked the first one whether ________ He ________ on the wrong side of the road when the first man ________ him because the other side ________ full of holes. He asked him if he ________ The first driver then asked whether ________ He said that he ________ There ________ he added, good driving schools for people like the other driver. There they ________ you lots of things — how to drive a car for instance. Grateful for this information, the second man angrily informed the first one that he ________ to be a driving instructor.

f *If.*

Complete the following sentences.

1 If ________ you might have been knocked down by a car.
2 If ________ she will let you know.
3 If you were in my position, what ________ ?

g *Other verbs.*

Write sentences to bring out the difference in meaning between the following pairs.

1 *mustn't* and *needn't*
2 *had to* and *should have*
3 *have to* and *should*

4 *must be* and *must eat*
5 *could* and *was able to*
6 *could* and *managed to*

h Complete the following sentences.

1 On ________ he smiled with pleasure.
2 I am not looking forward to ________ .
3 Instead of ________ you should see a doctor.
4 Don't you think this room needs ________ ?
5 You should avoid ________ .

i A and The.

Supply *a(n)* or *the* where necessary in the following paragraph.

________ editors of newspapers and ________ magazines often go to extremes to provide their readers with ________ unimportant facts and ________ statistics. Last year ________ journalist had been instructed by ________ well-known magazine to write ________ article on ________ president's palace in ________ new African republic. When ________ article arrived, ________ editor read ________ first sentence and then refused to publish it ________ article began ' ________ hundreds of ________ steps lead to ________ high wall which surrounds ________ president's palace.' ________ editor at once sent ________ journalist ________ telegram instructing him to find out ________ exact number of ________ steps and ________ height of ________ wall.

j Supply the missing words in the following sentences.

1 ________ 5 o'clock, a man ________ a small green car stopped ________ 24 Burton Road. He got ________ and walked ________ the front door of the house. He knocked ________ the door and waited. A few minutes later, the door opened and he went ________ the house.
2 I got tired ________ sitting ________ the stuffy bar, so I decided to go outside and stand ________ deck. Just as I was going ________ the bar, a tall man came up ________ me. It was Tony Adams, an old friend whom I had not seen ________ my student days. I was surprised to meet him ________ all these years.
3 A tall lady ________ black gloves ________ a long cigarette holder ________ one hand and a bag ________ the other went ________ a small, expensive shop ________ a London arcade. She stayed ________ the shop ________ hours and bought a large number of things. The assistant kept looking ________ his watch. It was a quarter to six and the shop should have shut ________ 5 o'clock, but he did not dare to ask her to leave.
4 Many people do not approve ________ blood sports.
5 He was found guilty ________ murder and condemned ________ death.
6 Has it ever occurred ________ you that those twins are quite different ________ each other in many ways?
7 I consulted my lawyer ________ the matter and I shall act ________ his advice.
8 It is impossible to prevent them ________ quarrelling ________ each other.
9 He is responding ________ treatment and will soon be cured ________ his illness.

10 I tried to reason ________ him, but he was very rude ________ me.
11 He might be good ________ his job but you can't rely ________ him.
12 I am thinking ________ looking ________ a new job.

Special difficulties

Complete the following making a sentence out of each.

1 If he happens ________ .
2 It happens that ________ .
3 Not only ________ .
4 Never ________ .
5 Seldom ________ .
6 Don't be such a ________ .
7 Don't be so ________ .
8 The child is always ________ .
9 The child is always full of ________ .
10 Whatever ________ .
11 You can come whenever ________ .
12 Whenever ________ .
13 I now wish ________ .
14 I wish ________ yesterday.
15 I wish ________ soon.
16 I was delighted ________ .
17 We are proud ________ .
18 I would sooner ________ .
19 He would rather not ________ .
20 I would rather she ________ .
21 You had better ________ .
22 I find it ________ .
23 No one considers him to ________ .

Unit 2

Unit 2

INSTRUCTIONS TO THE STUDENT

In Unit 2 you will be given very little help to construct sentences in the various extended exercises you will be doing. Comprehension has been introduced as a separate exercise and is not directly related to summary writing.

Before you begin each exercise, study these instructions carefully. Read them *each time* you begin a new piece. They are very important.

How to work — Summary writing

Unit 2 contains twenty passages. You will be required to write a summary of a part of each passage. Previously you were helped to find the important points. Here you must find them entirely by yourself. You will have to make a list of points and a rough draft before you write the final version of your summary.

1 Read the passage carefully two or three times. Make sure you understand it.

2 Read the instructions which will tell you where your summary will begin and end and exactly what you will have to do. On the passage mark the places where you have to begin and end.

3 Taking great care to carry out the instructions, write a list of points *in note form*. These notes must be *brief*. Do not include any unnecessary information.

4 When joining your points, you may refer to the passage if necessary, but try to use *your own words* as far as possible. Your answer should be in one paragraph.

5 First connect your points to write a *rough draft* of the summary. *Do not count* the number of words until you have finished the rough draft.

6 In the rough draft, it is likely that you will go well over the word limit. Correct your draft carefully, bringing the number of words down to the set limit. Remember that words like 'the', 'a' etc. count as single words. Words which are joined by a hyphen also count as single words. You may write fewer than 80 words, but you must never write more.

7 Write a *fair copy* of your summary stating at the end the exact number of words you have used.

8 Neatly cross out your points and rough draft.

Example

Work through this example carefully and then try to do the exercises in Unit 2 in the same way.

Christmas

As Christmas approaches, excitement mounts to a pitch. There are presents to be bought, cards to be sent, and rooms to be decorated. Parents are faced with the difficult task of concealing presents from inquisitive young children. If the gifts are large, this is sometimes a real problem. On Christmas Eve, young children find the excitement almost unbearable. They are torn between the desire to go to bed early so that Santa Claus will bring their presents quickly, and the desire to stay up late in case they miss any of the fun. The desire for presents usually proves stronger. But though children go to bed early, they often lie awake for a long time, hoping to catch a glimpse of Father Christmas.

Last Christmas, my wife and I successfully managed to conceal a few large presents in the storeroom. I was dreading the moment when my son, Jimmy, would ask me where that new bicycle had come from, but fortunately he did not see it.

On Christmas Eve, it took the children hours to get to sleep. It must have been nearly midnight when my wife and I crept into their room and began filling stockings and pillow cases as quietly as we could. After this was done, I wheeled in the bicycle I had bought for Jimmy and left it beside the Christmas tree. We knew we would not get much sleep that night, for the children were sure to wake up early. At about five o'clock next morning, we were woken by loud sounds coming from the children's room. The children were blowing toy trumpets, banging tin drums and shouting excitedly. Before I had time to stagger out of bed, young Jimmy came sailing into the room on his brand-new bicycle, and his younger sister, Elizabeth, followed close behind pushing her new pram. Even the baby arrived. He crawled into the room dragging a large balloon behind him. All of a sudden it burst. That woke us up completely. We jumped out of bed and began to play with the children. The day had really begun with a bang!

Summary writing

In not more than 80 words describe what happened from the moment the writer and his wife crept into the children's room to the time when they began to play with the children. Use your own words as far as possible. Do not include anything that is not in the last paragraph.

A possible answer

Points (What happened)

1 Christmas Eve — crept — children's room.
2 Filled stockings, pillow cases.
3 Writer brought in bicycle.
4 Left it beside Christmas tree.
5 Early next morning woken by children.
6 Jimmy rode — parents' room.
7 Sister followed — pram.
8 Baby crawled — balloon.
9 It burst.
10 Parents — out of bed.
11 Played with children.

Rough draft (Joining the Points)

After creeping into the children's room on Christmas Eve, the writer and his wife filled stockings and pillow cases with presents. Then the writer wheeled in a bicycle which he left beside the Christmas tree. At about five o'clock next morning they were woken by loud sounds coming from the children's room. Suddenly, Jimmy rode into his parents' bedroom on his new bicycle. His sister followed him pushing her new pram. Last of all came the baby holding a large balloon. When it burst, the writer and his wife jumped out of bed and began to play with the children. (100 words)

Fair copy (Corrected draft)

After creeping into the children's room on Christmas Eve, the writer and his wife not only filled stockings and pillow cases with presents, but left a bicycle beside the Christmas tree. The children woke them up very early next morning. Jimmy rode into his parents' bedroom on his new bicycle, followed by his sister and the baby. When the balloon the baby was holding suddenly burst, the writer and his wife got up and began to play with the children. (80 words)

Comprehension

These questions are designed to find out if you have understood the passage.

1 After you have read a question, find the answer in the passage.

2 Write a short answer *in one complete sentence* to each question. Normally, part of the question must be included in your answer.

3 Use your own words as far as possible.

4 Work neatly. Number each question carefully.

Example

Study this example carefully before attempting the comprehension exercises in Unit 2.

Comprehension

Give short answers to these questions in your own words as far as possible. Use one complete sentence for each answer.

1 Why are children torn between two desires on Christmas Eve?

2 Why do children often lie awake on Christmas Eve?

3 Where did the writer and his wife conceal the large presents they had bought?

Possible answers

a Children are torn between two desires on Christmas Eve because they want to go to bed early to get their presents from Santa Claus, but they also want to stay up late to see the fun.

b Children often lie awake on Christmas Eve because they hope to see Father Christmas.

c The writer and his wife hid the large presents they had bought in the storeroom.

Vocabulary

You will again be asked to explain words and phrases. Here it will not be necessary to replace a word or phrase with one of your own. You must simply explain each word or phrase as it has been used in the passage.

Example

Study the example below to find out how this is done.

Vocabulary

Explain the meanings of the following words and phrases as they are used in the passage: mounts (l.1); task (l.2); concealing presents (l.2); inquisitive (l.2); catch a glimpse of (l.7); dreading (l.9); fortunately (l.10).

A possible answer

mounts: rises.
task: job.
concealing presents: hiding gifts.
inquisitive: curious.
catch a glimpse of: see briefly.
dreading: afraid of.
fortunately: luckily.

Composition

As in the previous unit, Composition exercises are based on ideas suggested by each passage. You will be given two types of exercise:

1 You will be provided with notes which you will be asked to expand into a plan. Your plan must contain: a title; an introduction; a development; and a conclusion. When you have made out your plan, write a composition of three or four paragraphs in about 250 words.

2 You will be provided with a plan which contains: a title; an introduction; a development; and a conclusion. You will write a composition of three or four paragraphs in about 250 words based on each plan. You are quite free to add ideas of your own or to ignore ideas that are to be found in the plan.

Examples

Here are examples of the two types of composition exercise you will be given:

1 In not more than 250 words write an imaginary account of how the family described in the passage spent Christmas Day.

Expand the ideas given below into a plan and provide a suitable title. Your composition should be in four paragraphs.

Ideas: Early morning — played with children — breakfast — exchanged presents — church — home again — dinner prepared — guests arrived — excitement — more presents — dinner — Christmas party — fun and games — afternoon — sat by fire — everybody exhausted but happy.

2 In not more than 250 words write an imaginary account of how the family described in the passage spent Christmas Day.

Use the ideas given below. Do not write more than four paragraphs.

Title: Christmas Day.

Introduction: Early morning — played with children — breakfast — exchanged presents — church.

Development: Home again — dinner prepared — guests arrived — excitement — more presents — dinner — Christmas party — fun and games.

Conclusion: Afternoon — sat by fire — everybody exhausted but happy.

Letter writing

Follow the instructions given under each passage.

Key structures and Special difficulties

When you finish the **Letter writing** exercise go on to the language exercises that follow. In this unit you will be given the opportunity to revise many of the **Key structures** and **Special difficulties** you learnt in *Practice and Progress.* You should refer to *Practice and Progress* if you have forgotten anything. The work you do in grammar is based on material contained in the passages. Refer to the passages frequently. They will help you to understand the grammar and to do the exercises.

Multiple choice questions

This is a form of comprehension test in which you are asked to choose the correct answer from a number of suggested answers. This exercise tests your ability to understand the *meaning* of the passage you have read and also to recognize grammatical and lexical errors in English.

LESSON

21 Daniel Mendoza 丹尼尔·门多萨

Listen then answer the question below.

听录音，然后回答以下问题。

How many unsuccessful attempts did Mendoza make before becoming Champion of all England?

The two men quarrelled bitterly

Boxing matches were very popular in England two hundred years ago. In those days, boxers fought with bare fists for prize money. Because of this, they were known as 'prizefighters'. However, boxing was very crude, for there were no rules and a prizefighter could be seriously injured or even killed during a match.

One of the most colourful figures in boxing history was Daniel Mendoza, who was born in 1764. The use of gloves was not introduced until 1860, when the Marquis of Queensberry drew up the first set of rules. Though he was technically a prizefighter, Mendoza did much to change crude prizefighting into a sport, for he brought science to the game. In his day, Mendoza enjoyed tremendous popularity. He was adored by rich and poor alike.

Mendoza rose to fame swiftly after a boxing match when he was only fourteen years old. This attracted the attention of Richard Humphries who was then the most eminent boxer in England. He offered to train Mendoza and his young pupil was quick to learn. In fact, Mendoza soon became so successful that Humphries turned against him. The two men quarrelled bitterly and it was clear that the argument could only be settled by a fight. A match was held at Stilton, where both men fought for an hour. The public bet a great deal of money on Mendoza, but he was defeated. Mendoza met Humphries in the ring on a later occasion and he lost for a second time. It was not until his third match in 1790 that he finally beat Humphries and became Champion of England. Meanwhile, he founded a highly successful Academy and even Lord Byron became one of his pupils. He earned enormous sums of money and was paid as much as £100 for a single appearance. Despite this, he was so extravagant that he was always in debt. After he was defeated by a boxer called Gentleman Jackson, he was quickly forgotten. He was sent to prison for failing to pay his debts and died in poverty in 1836.

New words and expressions 生词和短语

boxing (l.1)	/ˈbɒksɪŋ/	*n.*	拳击
boxer (l.2)	/ˈbɒksə/	*n.*	拳击手
bare (l.2)	/beə/	*adj.*	赤裸的
prizefighter (l.3)	/ˈpraɪzfaɪtə/	*n.*	职业拳击手（尤指古时赤手拳击手）
crude (l.4)	/kruːd/	*adj.*	粗野的
marquis (l.7)	/ˈmɑːkwɪs/	*n.*	侯爵
technically (l.8)	/ˈteknɪkli/	*adv.*	严格根据法律意义地
science (l.9)	/ˈsaɪəns/	*n.*	科学
popularity (l.10)	/ˌpɒpjʊˈlærɪti/	*n.*	名望
adore (l.10)	/əˈdɔː/	*v.*	崇拜，爱戴
alike (l.10)	/əˈlaɪk/	*adv.*	一样地
fame (l.11)	/feɪm/	*n.*	名声
eminent (l.12)	/ˈemɪnənt/	*adj.*	著名的，杰出的
bitterly (l.14)	/ˈbɪtəli/	*adv.*	厉害地
bet (l.15)	/bet/ (bet, bet)	*v.*	打赌
academy (l.18)	/əˈkædəmi/	*n.*	专业学校
extravagant (l.20)	/ɪkˈstrævəgənt/	*adj.*	浪费的，奢侈的
poverty (l.22)	/ˈpɒvəti/	*n.*	贫困

Notes on the text 课文注释

1 they were known as 'prizefighters', 他们被称作"职业拳击手"。be known as ..., 被称作……。

2 until 1860, when the Marquis of Queensberry drew up the first set of rules 中，以 when 引导的从句是定语从句，修饰前面的年代 1860 年。draw up 是"制定"、"草拟"的意思。a set of, 一套。Marquis of Queensberry, 昆斯伯里侯爵，是指第 8 位昆斯伯里侯爵约翰 · 修托 · 道格拉斯（1844—1900），苏格兰贵族。他制定的"昆斯伯里规则"至今仍是拳击的比赛规则。

3 change ... into ..., 把……变成……；bring ... to ..., 把……引进……。

4 in his day, 在他的全盛时期。

day 此处指"幸运或顺利的时期"。

5 He was adored by rich and poor alike. 人们不论贫富都很崇拜他。

rich and poor 是固定词组，意为"富人和穷人"。有的形容词可用作名词，但前面要加 the。

6 rise to fame, 成名。

7 Humphries turned against him, 汉弗莱斯与他反目为敌。

8 at Stilton, where both men fought for an hour 中，以 where 引导的从句作 Stilton 的定语。

9 bet on ..., 在……上押（赌金）。

10 It was not until his third match in 1790 that he finally beat Humphries ... 这是一个 it 的强调句。被强调的部分 not until his third match in 1790 放在 It was 之后，句子的其他部分放在引导词 that 之后。

11 be in debt, 负债。

参考译文

两百年前，拳击比赛在英国非常盛行。当时，拳击手们不戴手套，为争夺奖金而搏斗。因此，他们被称作"职业拳击手"。不过，拳击是十分野蛮的，因为当时没有任何比赛规则，职业拳击手有可能在比赛中受重伤，甚至丧命。

拳击史上最引人注目的人物之一是丹尼尔 · 门多萨，他生于 1764 年。1860 年昆斯伯里侯爵第一次为拳击比赛制定了规则，拳击比赛这才用上了手套。虽然门多萨严格来讲不过是个职业拳击手，但在把这种粗野的拳击变成一种体育运动方面，他作出了重大贡献。是他把科学引进了这项运动。门多萨在他的全盛时期深受大家欢迎，无论是富人还是穷人都对他崇拜备至。

门多萨在 14 岁时参加了一场拳击赛后一举成名。这引起了当时英国拳坛名将理查德 · 汉弗莱斯的注意。他主动提出教授门多萨，而年少的门多萨一学就会。事实上，门多萨不久便名声大振，致使汉弗莱斯与他反目为敌。两个人争吵不休，显而易见，只有较量一番才能解决问题。于是两人在斯蒂尔顿设下赛场，打斗了一个小时。公众把大笔赌注下到了门多萨身上，但他却输了。后来，门多萨与汉弗莱斯再次在拳击场上较量，门多萨又输了一场。直到 1790 年他们第 3 次对垒，门多萨才终于击败了汉弗莱斯，成了全英拳击冠军。同时，他建立了一所拳击学校，办得很成功，连拜伦勋爵也成了他的学生。门多萨挣来大笔大笔的钱，一次出场费就可多达 100 英镑。尽管收入不少，但他挥霍无度，经常债台高筑。他在被一个叫杰克逊绅士的拳击手击败后很快被人遗忘。他因无力还债而被捕入狱，最后于 1836 年在贫困中死去。

Comprehension 理解

Give short answers to these questions in your own words as far as possible. Use one complete sentence for each answer.

1 Why were boxers known as 'prizefighters' two hundred years ago?

2 Why was boxing very crude in those days?

3 What was Mendoza's chief contribution to boxing?

Vocabulary 词汇

Explain the meanings of the following words and phrases as they are used in the passage: bare (l.2); injured (l.5); drew up (l.8); crude (l.9); enjoyed tremendous popularity (ll.9-10); adored (l.10); alike (l.10).

Summary writing 摘要写作

In not more than 80 words write a brief account of Mendoza's career from the time he quarrelled with Humphries. Use your own words as far as possible. Do not include anything that is not in the last paragraph.

Composition 作文

In not more than 250 words write an imaginary account of the first fight between Mendoza and Humphries. Expand the ideas given below into a plan and provide a suitable title. Your composition should be in four paragraphs.

Ideas: The quarrel — Mendoza and Humphries: bets from supporters — atmosphere just before the fight — the fight itself — Mendoza's defeat — effect on him and his supporters.

Letter writing 书信写作

On a full page, show the exact position of each of the following:

The address and date; the beginning of the letter; the Introduction; the Purpose; the Conclusion; the letter-ending; the signature; the postscript. Supply all necessary full stops and commas.

Key structures and Special difficulties 关键句型和难点

Exercises 练习

1 *Boxing matches were very popular in England two hundred years ago.* (ll.1-2) Write two sentences using the words *ago* and *before*. **(1 KS 38b)**（参见第 2 册第 38 课关键句型 b）

2 ... *a prizefighter could be seriously injured.* (ll.4-5) Write two sentences using *could* and *was able to*. **(1 KS 43c)**（参见第 2 册第 43 课关键句型 c）

3 *The use of gloves was not introduced until 1860.* (l.7) Write a sentence using the construction *not ... until*. **(1 KS 9d)**（参见第 2 册第 9 课关键句型 d）

4 *He was adored by rich and poor alike.* (l.10) Note the use of *by* in this sentence. Write two sentences using *by* in the same way. **(1 KS 34)**（参见第 2 册第 34 课关键句型）

5 *Mendoza rose to fame.* (l.11) Write two sentences illustrating the use of *rose* and *raised*. **(1 SD 51a)**（参见第 2 册第 51 课难点 a）

6 ... *his young pupil was quick to learn.* (l.13) Write two sentences using the following: *pleased to* and *sorry to*. **(1 SD 13)**（参见第 2 册第 13 课难点）

7 *it was clear.* (l.14) Write three sentences bringing out the different meanings of the word *clear*. Write a sentence using the word *clean*. **(1 SD 81c)**（参见第 2 册第 81 课难点 c）

8 *He was sent to prison for failing to pay his debts.* (l.21) Note the form of the verb *fail* here. Write sentences using a verb after each of the following: *afraid of; without; apologize for; congratulate on.* **(1 KS 20)**（参见第 2 册第 20 课关键句型）

Multiple choice questions 选择题

Choose the correct answers to the following questions.

Comprehension 理解

1 Richard Humphries offered to train Mendoza because ________ .

(*a*) he wanted to learn the techniques that Mendoza had introduced to boxing

(*b*) for one so young, Mendoza had displayed an unusual grasp of the game

(*c*) he had attended the boxing match which led to Mendoza's early fame

(*d*) he was anxious to establish himself as a superior boxer to Mendoza

2 At the match between Humphries and Mendoza at Stilton ________ .

(*a*) Mendoza lost a great deal of money to the public

(*b*) after an hour's fighting Humphries became Champion of England

(*c*) Mendoza lost twice to Humphries

(*d*) the argument between the two men was settled in favour of Humphries

3 Apart from the money he earned at matches, Mendoza ________ .

(*a*) earned a lot from the Academy which he founded after becoming Champion

(*b*) earned so much money that he became a rich man

(*c*) greatly supplemented his income by teaching the art of boxing

(*d*) was given enormous sums by Lord Byron

Structure 结构

4 In those days, ________ 'prizefighters' because they fought with bare fists for prize money. (ll.2-3)

(*a*) they called boxers (*b*) boxers called

(*c*) boxers being called (*d*) they were called boxers

5 A prizefighter could suffer a serious injury or ________ during a ... (ll.4-5)

(*a*) even be killed (*b*) be even killed (*c*) even killed (*d*) was even killed

6 Mendoza ________ boxing into a sport. (ll.8-9)

(*a*) was much changed by (*b*) did a great deal to change

(*c*) changed a great deal of (*d*) much changed

7 He was so extravagant that he ________ people money. (l.20)

(*a*) always owed to (*b*) always owed (*c*) owed always (*d*) was always owing to

Vocabulary 词汇

8 One of the most ________ in boxing history was ... (ll.6-7)

(*a*) vivid personalities (*b*) famous people (*c*) painted images (*d*) imaginative characters

9 – after a boxing match at the ________ young age of fourteen. (l.11)

(*a*) marvellously (*b*) singly (*c*) exceptionally (*d*) unequally

10 Mendoza's ________ to fame was noted by Richard Humphries. (ll.11-12)

(*a*) rise (*b*) rose (*c*) raise (*d*) claim

11 Humphries soon became ________ Mendoza's success. (ll.13-14)

(*a*) jealous of (*b*) disinterested in (*c*) revolted by (*d*) changed by

12 Mendoza finally ________ Humphries and became Champion of England. (ll.17-18)

(*a*) conquered (*b*) gained (*c*) won (*d*) beat

LESSON

22 By heart 熟记台词

Listen then answer the question below.

听录音，然后回答以下问题。

Which actor read the letter in the end, the aristocrat or the gaoler?

'The light is indeed dim, sire'

Some plays are so successful that they run for years on end. In many ways, this is unfortunate for the poor actors who are required to go on repeating the same lines night after night. One would expect them to know their parts by heart and never have cause to falter. Yet this is not always the case.

A famous actor in a highly successful play was once cast in the role of an aristocrat who had been imprisoned in the Bastille for twenty years. In the last act, a gaoler would always come on to the stage with a letter which he would hand to the prisoner. Even though the noble was expected to read the letter at each performance, he always insisted that it should be written out in full.

One night, the gaoler decided to play a joke on his colleague to find out if, after so many performances, he had managed to learn the contents of the letter by heart. The curtain went up on the final act of the play and revealed the aristocrat sitting alone behind bars in his dark cell. Just then, the gaoler appeared with the precious letter in his hands. He entered the cell and presented the letter to the aristocrat. But the copy he gave him had not been written out in full as usual. It was simply a blank sheet of paper. The gaoler looked on eagerly, anxious to see if his fellow actor had at last learnt his lines. The noble stared at the blank sheet of paper for a few seconds. Then, squinting his eyes, he said: 'The light is dim. Read the letter to me.' And he promptly handed the sheet of paper to the gaoler. Finding that he could not remember a word of the letter either, the gaoler replied: 'The light is indeed dim, sire. I must get my glasses.' With this, he hurried off the stage. Much to the aristocrat's amusement, the gaoler returned a few moments later with a pair of glasses and the usual copy of the letter which he proceeded to read to the prisoner.

New words and expressions 生词和短语

run	(l.1)	/rʌn/ (ran /ræn/, run)	*v.*	（戏剧、电影等）连演，连映
lines	(l.3)	/laɪnz/	*n.*	（复数）（剧本中的）台词
part	(l.4)	/pɑːt/	*n.*	剧中的角色，台词
falter	(l.4)	/ˈfɔːltə/	*v.*	支吾，结巴说
cast	(l.6)	/kɑːst/ (cast, cast)	*v.*	选派……扮演角色
role	(l.7)	/rəʊl/	*n.*	角色
aristocrat	(l.7)	/ˈærɪstəkræt/	*n.*	贵族
imprison	(l.7)	/ɪmˈprɪzən/	*v.*	关押
Bastille	(l.7)	/bæsˈtiːl/	*n.*	巴士底狱
gaoler	(l.7)	/ˈdʒeɪlə/	*n.*	监狱长，看守
colleague	(l.10)	/ˈkɒliːg/	*n.*	同事
curtain	(l.11)	/ˈkɜːtn/	*n.*	（舞台上的）幕布
reveal	(l.12)	/rɪˈviːl/	*v.*	使显露
cell	(l.13)	/sel/	*n.*	单人监房，监号
blank	(l.14)	/blæŋk/	*adj.*	空白的
squint	(l.16)	/skwɪnt/	*v.*	眯着（眼）看，瞄
dim	(l.16)	/dɪm/	*adj.*	昏暗的
sire	(l.18)	/saɪə/	*n.*	（古用法）陛下
proceed	(l.20)	/prəˈsiːd/	*v.*	继续进行

Notes on the text 课文注释

1 on end, 连续不断地。

2 in many ways, 在许多方面。

3 go on repeating, 继续重复。go on 加上现在分词是“继续干”的意思。

4 Yet this is not always the case. 然而情况并非总是如此。

5 in the role of ..., 充当……角色。

6 Bastille, 巴士底狱。
曾是法国巴黎的监狱。1370 年始建时是一个要塞，1789 年被巴黎市民攻克并捣毁。

7 insisted that it should be written out in full, insist 后面所接的宾语从句，常用虚拟语气“should + 动词原形”，而 should 又经常可以省略。

8 play a joke on ..., 拿……开玩笑。

9 sire 是古代仆人对国王的一种尊称，现在仅用于故事和剧本。

10 Much to the aristocrat's amusement, 使贵族感到非常可笑的是……。
much 为副词，此处修饰其后的介词短语 to the aristocrat's amusement。much to + sb.'s sth. 是一个常见的状语短语，有“给某人带来很大的……”的意思。

参考译文

有些剧目十分成功，以至连续上演好几年。这样一来，可怜的演员们可倒霉了。因为他们需要一夜连着一夜地重复同样的台词。人们以为，这些演员一定会把台词背得烂熟，绝不会临场结巴的，但情况却并不总是这样。

有一位名演员曾在一出极为成功的剧目中扮演一个贵族角色，这个贵族已在巴士底狱被关押了 20 年。在最后一幕中，狱卒手持一封信上场，然后将信交给狱中那位贵族。尽管那个贵族每场戏都得念一遍那封信，但他还是坚持要求将信的全文写在信纸上。

一天晚上，狱卒决定与他的同事开一个玩笑，看看他反复演出这么多场之后，是否已将信的内容记熟了。大幕拉开，最后一幕戏开演，贵族独自一人坐在铁窗后阴暗的牢房里。这时狱卒上场，手里拿着那封珍贵的信。狱卒走进牢房，将信交给贵族。但这回狱卒给贵族的信没有像往常那样写有全文，而是一张白纸。狱卒热切地观察着，急于想了解他的同事是否记熟了台词。贵族盯着白纸看了几秒钟，然后，眼珠一转，说道：“光线太暗，请给我读一下这封信。”说完，他一下子把信递给了狱卒。狱卒发现自己连一个字也记不住，于是便说：“陛下，这儿光线的确太暗了，我得去把眼镜拿来。”他一边说，一边匆匆下台。贵族感到非常好笑的是：一会儿工夫，狱卒重新登台，拿来一副眼镜以及平时使用的那封信，然后为那囚犯念了起来。

Comprehension 理解

Give short answers to these questions in your own words as far as possible. Use one complete sentence for each answer.

1 Why are actors in successful plays in many ways unfortunate?

2 In which act of the play was the aristocrat given a letter to read?

3 Why did the gaoler decide to play a joke on the aristocrat?

Vocabulary 词汇

Explain the meanings of the following words and phrases as they are used in the passage: run (l.1); on end (l.1); are required (l.2); repeating (l.3); falter (l.4); role (l.7); hand (l.8); in full (l.9).

Summary writing 摘要写作

In not more than 80 words describe what happened after the curtain went up on the final act of the play. Use your own words as far as possible. Do not include anything that is not in the last paragraph.

Composition 作文

Write a composition of about 250 words using the ideas given below. Do not write more than four paragraphs.

Title: Six short weeks.

Introduction: A new play called *The World Tomorrow* to be shown. Highly advertised — public interest — cast of famous actors.

Development: First night — play not well — received — supposed to be funny — nobody laughed — people walked out — bad reviews.

Conclusion: The play ran for six weeks — last performance — small audience — actors struggled through — the audience found the last line of the play very funny: 'Our six short weeks have hastened to their end.' Even the actors laughed.

Letter writing 书信写作

Write five sentences which could be used to begin a letter and five sentences which could be used to end one.

Key structures and Special difficulties 关键句型和难点

Exercises 练习

1 *Some plays are so successful that they run for years on end.* (l.1) Write three sentences illustrating the use of *so ... that; such ... that;* and *such a ... that.* **(1 SD 35)**（参见第 2 册第 35 课难点）

2 *In the last act, a gaoler would always come on to the stage.* (ll.7-8) Which verb could be used in place of *would* here? Write two sentences illustrating the use of *would* and *used to.* **(1 KS 55b)**（参见第 2 册第 55 课关键句型 b）

3 *The noble was expected to read the letter at each performance. He always insisted that it should be written out in full.* (ll.8-9) Join these two sentences, then compare your answer with the sentence in the passage. **(1 KS 49)**（参见第 2 册第 49 课关键句型）

4 *He always insisted that it should be written out in full.* (l.9) Write sentences using the following: *He suggested that ...; He insisted that ...; He demanded that ... .* **(1 KS 63)**（参见第 2 册第 63 课关键句型）

5 *He had managed to learn the contents of the letter by heart.* (l.11) Write two sentences showing how *managed to* can be used as the opposite of *could not.* **(1 KS 67c)**（参见第 2 册第 67 课关键句型练习 c）

6 *He entered the cell. He presented the letter to the aristocrat.* (l.13) Join these two sentences, then compare your answer with the sentence in the passage. **(1 KS 25)**（参见第 2 册第 25 课关键句型）

7 *The noble stared at the blank sheet of paper.* (ll.15-16) Write sentences using the phrasal verbs *throw at* and *point at.* **(1 KS 33e)**（参见第 2 册第 33 课关键句型 e）

8 *I must get my glasses.* (l.18) Which verb can we use in place of *must* here? **(1 KS 17a)**（参见第 2 册第 17 课关键句型 a）

Multiple choice questions 选择题

Choose the correct answers to the following questions.

Comprehension 理解

1 Which of the following proverbs suits the gist of the story best?

(*a*) He laughs best, who laughs last.

(*b*) Speech is silver, but silence is golden.

(*c*) Look before you leap.

(*d*) Don't count your chickens before they are hatched.

2 The play in which the two actors took part ________ .

(*a*) had had a highly successful run of twenty years

(*b*) was about the plight of a nobleman

(*c*) ended with the imprisonment of the aristocrat

(*d*) had been performed so often that audiences were bored by it

3 When the aristocrat was presented with a blank sheet of paper, ________ .

(*a*) he improvised the words which he had forgotten

(*b*) the gaoler was eagerly waiting to take the aristocrat's part

(*c*) he pretended that the light was not good enough for him to read by

(*d*) he asked the gaoler to fetch him some glasses

Structure 结构

4 A gaoler would come on stage with a letter ________ to the prisoner. (ll.7-8)

(*a*) to be delivering (*b*) and delivered (*c*) to deliver (*d*) delivered

5 He always insisted ________ in full. (l.9)

(*a*) on its being written out (*b*) on writing it out

(*c*) to have it written out (*d*) that it would have to be written out

6 – to find out if he ________ the contents of the letter by heart. (ll.10-11)

(*a*) had known (*b*) was knowing (*c*) knew (*d*) know

7 But he gave ________ which had not been written out in full. (ll.13-14)

(*a*) the copy to him (*b*) a copy him (*c*) him a copy (*d*) him the copy

8 ________ remember a word of the letter, so he replied ... (ll.17-18)

(*a*) But neither could the gaoler (*b*) Nor the gaoler could

(*c*) Also the gaoler could not (*d*) Either the gaoler could not

Vocabulary 词汇

9 The gaoler decided to ________ his colleague. (l.10)

(*a*) have a joke with (*b*) play the fool with (*c*) make fun of (*d*) play a trick on

10 He wanted to see if his fellow actor had ________ learnt his lines. (ll.10-11)

(*a*) lastly (*b*) in the end (*c*) conclusively (*d*) finally

11 Then, ________ about him, he said, ... (l.16)

(*a*) searching (*b*) peering (*c*) blinking (*d*) staring

12 Agreeing that the light was dim, the gaoler ________ he would get his glasses. (l.18)

(*a*) spoke (*b*) informed (*c*) said (*d*) rejoined

LESSON

23 One man's meat is another man's poison

各有所爱

Listen then answer the question below.

听录音，然后回答以下问题。

What was it about snails that made the writer collect them for his friend on that day in particular?

... would consider octopus a great delicacy

People become quite illogical when they try to decide what can be eaten and what cannot be eaten. If you lived in the Mediterranean, for instance, you would consider octopus a great delicacy. You would not be able to understand why some people find it repulsive. On the other hand, your stomach would turn at the idea of frying potatoes in animal fat — the normally accepted practice in many northern countries. The sad truth is that most of us have been brought up to eat certain foods and we stick to them all our lives.

No creature has received more praise and abuse than the common garden snail. Cooked in wine, snails are a great luxury in various parts of the world. There are countless people who, ever since their early years, have learned to associate snails with food. My friend, Robert, lives in a country where snails are despised. As his flat is in a large town, he has no garden of his own. For years he has been asking me to collect snails from my garden and take them to him. The idea never appealed to me very much, but one day, after a heavy shower, I happened to be walking in my garden when I noticed a huge number of snails taking a stroll on some of my prize plants. Acting on a sudden impulse, I collected several dozen, put them in a paper bag, and took them to Robert. Robert was delighted to see me and equally pleased with my little gift. I left the bag in the hall and Robert and I went into the living room where we talked for a couple of hours. I had forgotten all about the snails when Robert suddenly said that I must stay to dinner. Snails would, of course, be the main dish. I did not fancy the idea and I reluctantly followed Robert out of the room. To our dismay, we saw that there were snails everywhere: they had escaped from the paper bag and had taken complete possession of the hall! I have never been able to look at a snail since then.

New words and expressions 生词和短语

poison (title)	/ˈpɔɪzən/	*n.*	毒药
illogical (l.1)	/ɪˈlɒdʒɪkəl/	*adj.*	不合逻辑的，无章法的
octopus (l.3)	/ˈɒktəpəs/	*n.*	章鱼
delicacy (l.3)	/ˈdelɪkəsi/	*n.*	美味，佳肴
repulsive (l.4)	/rɪˈpʌlsɪv/	*adj.*	令人反感的，令人生厌的
stomach (l.5)	/ˈstʌmək/	*n.*	胃
turn (l.5)	/tɜːn/	*v.*	感到恶心，反胃
fry (l.5)	/fraɪ/	*v.*	油炸
fat (l.6)	/fæt/	*n.*	（动物、植物）油
abuse (l.9)	/əˈbjuːs/	*n.*	辱骂，责骂
snail (l.9)	/sneɪl/	*n.*	蜗牛
luxury (l.10)	/ˈlʌkʃəri/	*n.*	奢侈品，珍品
associate (l.11)	/əˈsəʊʃieɪt/	*v.*	联想到
despise (l.11)	/dɪˈspaɪz/	*v.*	鄙视
appeal (l.13)	/əˈpiːl/	*v.*	引起兴致
shower (l.14)	/ˈʃaʊə/	*n.*	阵雨
stroll (l.14)	/strəʊl/	*n.*	溜达，散步
impulse (l.15)	/ˈɪmpʌls/	*n.*	冲动
dozen (l.15)	/ˈdʌzən/	*n.*	12 个，一打
fancy (l.19)	/ˈfænsi/	*v.*	喜爱，喜欢

Notes on the text 课文注释

1 One man's meat is another man's poison. 这是英语的一句谚语，意思是“对一方有利的未必对另一方也有利”。有时可译作“各有所爱”，同时也有汉语俗语“萝卜青菜各有所爱”的意思。

2 would turn at the idea of ..., turn 此处作“恶心”、“作呕”解。at the idea of ... 是“想到……”的意思。

3 to be brought up, 养育，抚养。stick to 有“坚持”的意思。

4 Cooked in wine, snails ..., 用酒烹制的蜗牛……，这是过去分词短语作状语，表示条件。

5 I happened to be walking in the garden. 我碰巧在花园里散步。happen 后面加不定式表示“碰巧做……”。

6 take (亦作 have) possession of, 是“占有”、“拥有”的意思。

参考译文

在决定什么能吃而什么不能吃的时候，人们往往变得不合情理。比如，如果你住在地中海地区，你会把章鱼视作美味佳肴，同时不能理解为什么有人一见章鱼就恶心。另一方面，你一想到用动物油炸土豆就会反胃，但这在北方许多国家却是一种普通的烹饪方法。不无遗憾的是，我们中的大部分人，生来就只吃某几种食品，而且一辈子都这样。

没有一种生物所受到的赞美和厌恶会超过花园里常见的蜗牛了。蜗牛加酒烧煮后，便成了世界上许多地方的一道珍奇的名菜。有不计其数的人们从小就知道蜗牛可做菜。但我的朋友罗伯特却住在一个厌恶蜗牛的国家中。他住在大城市里的一所公寓里，没有自己的花园。多年来，他一直让我把我园子里的蜗牛收集起来给他捎去。一开始，他的这一想法没有引起我多大兴趣。后来有一天，一场大雨后，我在花园里漫无目的地散步，突然注意到许许多多蜗牛在我的一些心爱的花木上慢悠悠地蠕动着。我一时冲动，逮了几十只，装进一只纸袋里，带着去找罗伯特。罗伯特见到我很高兴，对我的薄礼也感到满意。我把纸袋放在门厅里，与罗伯特一起进了起居室，在那里聊了好几个钟头。我把蜗牛的事已忘得一干二净，罗伯特突然提出一定要我留下来吃晚饭，这才提醒了我。蜗牛当然是道主菜。我并不喜欢这个主意，所以我勉强跟着罗伯特走出了起居室。使我们惊愕的是门厅里到处爬满了蜗牛：它们从纸袋里逃了出来，爬得满厅都是！从那以后，我再也不能看一眼蜗牛了。

Comprehension 理解

Give short answers to these questions in your own words as far as possible. Use one complete sentence for each answer.

1 In what part of the world is octopus considered a great delicacy?

2 Why do we stick to certain foods all our lives?

3 Why did the writer's friend find it difficult to obtain snails?

Vocabulary 词汇

Explain the meanings of the following words and phrases as they are used in the passage: illogical (l.1); instance (l.3); repulsive (l.4); stick (l.7); various (l.10); associate (l.11); appealed to (l.13).

Summary writing 摘要写作

In not more than 80 words describe what happened from the moment the writer collected snails from his garden. Use your own words as far as possible. Do not include anything that is not in the last paragraph.

Composition 作文

In not more than 250 words write a continuation of the passage. Expand the ideas given below into a plan and provide a suitable title. Your composition should be in three or four paragraphs.

Ideas: Snails — walls, ceiling — coat pockets — effort to collect them — ladders, etc. — marks everywhere — Robert amused — cooked the snails — a meal for one.

Letter writing 书信写作

In not more than 100 words write a letter of three paragraphs inviting a friend to spend a weekend with your family at your home in the country.

Key structures and Special difficulties 关键句型和难点

Exercises 练习

1 *People become quite illogical when ... .* (l.1) Write two sentences illustrating the use of the words *quite* and *quiet*. **(1 SD 53b)**（参见第 2 册第 53 课难点 b）

2 *If you lived in the Mediterranean, you would consider octopus a great delicacy.* (ll.2-3) Write this sentence again beginning 'If you had lived ...' **(1 KS 64b)**（参见第 2 册第 64 课关键句型 b）

3 *the normally accepted practice.* (l.6) Write two sentences using the words *practice* and *practise*. **(1 SD 69a)**（参见第 2 册第 69 课难点 a）

4 *The sad truth is that most of us ... .* (l.7) Write two sentences using *most* and *the most*. **(1 KS 54d)**（参见第 2 册第 54 课关键句型 d）

5 *There are countless people who, ever since their earliest years ... .* (ll.10-11) Write three sentences using the words *since*, *for* and *ago*. **(1 KS 29)**（参见第 2 册第 29 课关键句型）

6 *As his flat is in a large town ... .* (l.12) What does *as* mean in this sentence? Write three sentences illustrating the other meaning of *as*. **(1 SD 17a)**（参见第 2 册第 17 课难点 a）

7 *For years he has been asking me to collect snails.* (l.12) Write two sentences using *has been asking* and *has asked*. **(1 KS 52)**（参见第 2 册第 52 课关键句型）

8 *I happened to be walking in my garden.* (l.14) Write sentences using the following: *he happens, it happened that, happened*. **(SD 3a)**（参见第 3 课难点 a）

Multiple choice questions 选择题

Choose the correct answers to the following questions.

Comprehension 理解

1 In a country where snails are eaten, you would expect ________ .

(*a*) to find a great many snails in people's gardens

(*b*) to find that people cooked them in wine

(*c*) snails to be so popular that they are a luxury only the rich can afford

(*d*) people to be amazed by anyone who refused to eat them

2 The idea of collecting snails never appealed to the writer very much until ________ .
(*a*) the sight of the snails made him think of Robert
(*b*) a heavy shower of rain led him to look for them in his garden
(*c*) a sudden impulse made him decide to visit the country where Robert lived
(*d*) he felt obliged to remove them from his prize plants

3 When the writer arrived at Robert's flat ________ .
(*a*) Robert welcomed him warmly because of the snails he had brought
(*b*) Robert immediately invited him to dinner in order to eat the snails
(*c*) he forgot about giving Robert the snails until two hours later
(*d*) he gave Robert the snails, little thinking Robert would propose a dinner with snails as the main dish

Structure 结构

4 People are quite illogical when ________ deciding what ... (ll.1-2)
(*a*) it comes to (*b*) they come to (*c*) they come (*d*) coming to

5 Most of us have been brought up to eat certain kinds ________ . (l.7)
(*a*) food (*b*) of food (*c*) of the foods (*d*) foods

6 No creature ________ abused more often than ... (l.9)
(*a*) is being praised and (*b*) is praised nor
(*c*) has been praised or (*d*) has been praised and

7 Having left the bag in the hall, ________ into the living room. (ll.16-17)
(*a*) I accompanied Robert (*b*) Robert took me
(*c*) we went (*d*) I and Robert went

8 We saw the snails ________ from the paper bag ... (ll.19-20)
(*a*) escaping (*b*) escape (*c*) had escaped (*d*) to escape

Vocabulary 词汇

9 On the other hand, you would ________ at the idea ... (ll.5-6)
(*a*) be sick (*b*) sick (*c*) sicken (*d*) feel sick

10 Snails would, of course, be the main ________ . (ll.18-19)
(*a*) meal (*b*) food (*c*) plate (*d*) course

11 – I went into the living room where we talked for ________ . (l.17)
(*a*) round the clock (*b*) two hours or so (*c*) a second hour (*d*) some hours

12 There are ________ people, who ... (ll.10-11)
(*a*) numerable (*b*) numerous (*c*) numerical (*d*) numbered

LESSON

24 A skeleton in the cupboard

“家丑”

… some terrible secret

Listen then answer the question below.

听录音，然后回答以下问题。

Who was Sebastian?

We often read in novels how a seemingly respectable person or family has some terrible secret which has been concealed from strangers for years. The English language possesses a vivid saying to describe this sort of situation. The terrible secret is called ‘a skeleton in the cupboard’. At some dramatic moment in the story, the terrible secret becomes known and a reputation is ruined. The reader’s hair stands on end when he reads in the final pages of the novel that the heroine, a dear old lady who had always been so kind to everybody, had, in her youth, poisoned every one of her five husbands.

It is all very well for such things to occur in fiction. To varying degrees, we all have secrets which we do not want even our closest friends to learn, but few of us have skeletons in the cupboard. The only person I know who has a skeleton in the cupboard is George Carlton, and he is very proud of the fact. George studied medicine in his youth. Instead of becoming a doctor, however, he became a successful writer of detective stories. I once spent an uncomfortable weekend which I shall never forget at his house. George showed me to the guestroom which, he said, was rarely used. He told me to unpack my things and then come down to dinner. After I had stacked my shirts and underclothes in two empty drawers, I decided to hang one of the two suits I had brought with me in the cupboard. I opened the cupboard door and then stood in front of it petrified. A skeleton was dangling before my eyes. The sudden movement of the door made it sway slightly and it gave me the impression that it was about to leap out at me. Dropping my suit, I dashed downstairs to tell George. This was worse than ‘a terrible secret’; this was a *real* skeleton! But George was unsympathetic. ‘Oh, that,’ he said with a smile as if he were talking about an old friend. ‘That’s Sebastian. You forget that I was a medical student once upon a time.’

New words and expressions 生词和短语

skeleton (title)	/ˈskelɪtən/	*n.*	骷髅
seemingly (l.1)	/ˈsiːmɪŋli/	*adv.*	表面上地
respectable (l.1)	/rɪˈspektəbəl/	*adj.*	体面的，雅观的
conceal (l.2)	/kənˈsiːl/	*v.*	隐藏，隐瞒
vivid (l.3)	/ˈvɪvɪd/	*adj.*	生动的
dramatic (l.5)	/drəˈmætɪk/	*adj.*	令人激动的，扣人心弦的
ruin (l.6)	/ˈruːɪn/	*v.*	毁坏
heroine (l.8)	/ˈherəʊɪn/	*n.*	女主人公
fiction (l.10)	/ˈfɪkʃən/	*n.*	小说
varying (l.10)	/ˈveəriɪŋ/	*adj.*	不同的
medicine (l.13)	/ˈmedsən/	*n.*	医学
guestroom (l.15)	/ˈgest-rʊm/	*n.*	（家庭中的）来客住房
unpack (l.15)	/ʌnˈpæk/	*v.*	（从箱中）取出
stack (l.16)	/stæk/	*v.*	（整齐地）堆放，排放
underclothes (l.16)	/ˈʌndəkləʊðz/	*n.*	（复数）内衣

drawer (l.16)	/drɔː/	*n.*	抽屉
petrified (l.18)	/ˈpetrɪfaɪd/	*adj.*	惊呆的
dangle (l.18)	/ˈdæŋɡəl/	*v.*	悬挂
sway (l.18)	/sweɪ/	*v.*	摇摆
unsympathetic (l.21)	/ˌʌnsɪmpəˈθetɪk/	*adj.*	不表同情的，无动于衷的
medical (l.22)	/ˈmedɪkəl/	*adj.*	医学的

Notes on the text 课文注释

1 A skeleton in the cupboard, 直译为“柜中骷髅”，此系一成语，作“家丑”解。

2 conceal sth. from sb. 作“对某人隐瞒某事”解。

3 The reader's hair stands on end, 读者感到毛骨悚然。

4 to varying degrees, 在不同程度上。

5 stood in front of it petrified, 站在柜前吓呆了。

stand 此处表示处于某种状态，起系动词的作用，后面常接形容词、介词短语或过去分词，表示主语处于某种状态中的特征，可视作表语。

6 the impression that it was about to leap out ...,

that 引导的从句作 impression 的同位语。be about to do sth., 表示按照计划即将做的动作。

参考译文

在小说中，我们经常读到一个表面上受人尊重的人物或家族，却有着某种多年不为人所知的骇人听闻的秘密。英语中有一个生动的说法来形容这种情况。惊人的秘密被称作“柜中骷髅”。在小说的某个戏剧性时刻，可怕的秘密泄漏出来，接着便是某人的声誉扫地。当读者读到小说最后几页了解到书中女主人公，那位一向待大家很好的可爱的老妇人年轻时一连毒死了她的5个丈夫时，不禁会毛骨悚然。

这种事发生在小说中是无可非议的。尽管我们人人都有各种大小秘密，连最亲密的朋友都不愿让他们知道，但我们当中极少有人有柜中骷髅。我所认识的唯一的在柜中藏骷髅的人便是乔治·卡尔顿，他甚至引以为自豪。乔治年轻时学过医，然而，他后来没当上医生，却成了一位成功的侦探小说作家。有一次，我在他家里度周末，过得很不愉快。这事我永远不会忘记。乔治把我领进客房，说这间房间很少使用。他让我打开行装后下楼吃饭。我将衬衫、内衣放进两个空抽屉里，然后我想把随身带来的两套西服中的一套挂到大衣柜里去。我打开柜门，站在柜门前一下子惊呆了。一具骷髅悬挂在眼前，由于柜门突然打开，它也随之轻微摇晃起来，让我觉得它好像马上要跳出柜门朝我扑过来似的。我扔下西服冲下楼去告诉乔治。这是比“骇人听闻的秘密”更加惊人的东西，这是一具真正的骷髅啊！但乔治却无动于衷。“噢，是它呀！”他笑着说道，俨然在谈论一位老朋友。“那是塞巴斯蒂安。你忘了我以前是学医的了。”

Comprehension 理解

Give short answers to these questions in your own words as far as possible. Use one complete sentence for each answer.

1 Explain the saying 'a skeleton in the cupboard'.

2 What was the terrible secret of the dear old lady who had always been so kind to everybody?

3 What does George Carlton do for a living?

Vocabulary 词汇

Explain the meanings of the following words and phrases as they are used in the passage: seemingly (l.1); concealed (l.2); vivid saying (l.3); reputation (l.6); ruined (l.6); fiction (l.10); to varying degrees (l.10).

Summary writing 摘要写作

In not more than 80 words describe the writer's experiences from the moment he was shown to the guestroom. Use your own words as far as possible. Do not include anything that is not in the last paragraph.

Composition 作文

In not more than 250 words write a continuation of the above passage in the first person. Use the ideas given below. Do not write more than four paragraphs.

Title: A Weekend with Sebastian.

Introduction: George Carlton refused to remove skeleton — nowhere to put it.

Development: How I spent the night — very uncomfortable — took Sebastian out of the cupboard — walked around the house with him looking for somewhere to put him — maid just going to bed — saw Sebastian walking around — screamed — Carlton appeared — the scene.

Conclusion: Two years later I read about myself and Sebastian in one of Carlton's detective stories.

Letter writing 书信写作

In not more than 100 words write a letter of three paragraphs to your family doctor (who is also a personal friend) telling him that you have not been feeling well lately and asking him if you could make an appointment.

Key structures and Special difficulties 关键句型和难点

Exercises 练习

1 *We often read in novels* ... . (l.1) Note the position of *often* here. Write similar sentences using the words *frequently, rarely, always* and *never.* **(1 KS 2b)**（参见第 2 册第 2 课关键句型练习 b）

2 *we do not want even our closest friends to learn.* (ll.10-11) Note this pattern. Write two sentences in the same way using the verbs *teach* and *allow*. **(1 SD 11a)**（参见第 2 册第 11 课难点 a）

3 *few of us have skeletons in the cupboard.* (l.11) Write sentences illustrating the difference between: *few* and *a few; little* and *a little*. **(1 KS 32b)**（参见第 2 册第 32 课关键句型 b）

4 *he is very proud of the fact.* (l.12) Which words normally follow these words: *aware, ready, patient, afraid, fortunate, curious, dependent, different, skilful, familiar* and *close*. **(1 KS 70)**（参见第 2 册第 70 课关键句型）

5 *The sudden movement of the door made it sway.* (l.18) Note this use of *make*. Write two sentences using *make* and *let*. **(1 SD 57)**（参见第 2 册第 57 课难点）

6 *'Oh, that,' he said* ... . (l.21) Note this use of speech marks. **(1 SD 26)**（参见第 2 册第 26 课难点）

Write this piece of conversation again using speech marks.

You must see Arsenic and Old Lace again Tom said. It's a wonderful film. No thank you I answered. I don't think I could stand it. I saw it years ago said Tom. I shall never forget those dear old ladies. And I shall never forget that dreadful moment when Boris Karloff suddenly appeared at the window I said. I nearly jumped out of my seat.

Multiple choice questions 选择题

Choose the correct answers to the following questions.

Comprehension 理解

1 In what respect does fact differ from fiction concerning the secrets that people keep to themselves?

(*a*) They are rarely so terrible as to ruin our reputations if revealed.

(*b*) People's closest friends do not even suspect them of having them.

(*c*) People who have 'skeletons in the cupboard' are rarely found out.

(*d*) People who have skeletons in their cupboards are very proud of the fact.

2 Before opening the cupboard door, the writer had ________ .

(*a*) unpacked and gone down for dinner

(*b*) changed into some new clothes

(*c*) put his shirts and his underwear in a couple of drawers

(*d*) hung one of the two suits he had brought with him

3 What was the most frightening thing about the writer's experience?

(*a*) The sight of a skeleton hanging in the cupboard.

(*b*) The sudden movement of the door when he opened the cupboard.

(*c*) To discover that it was the skeleton of an old friend of George's.

(*d*) To have found a *real* skeleton rather than finding out a terrible secret.

Structure 结构

4 We often read in novels of a seemingly respectable person or family ________ some terrible secret ... (ll.1-2)

(*a*) having (*b*) has (*c*) whom has (*d*) that they have

5 The only person I have ever known ________ a skeleton in the cupboard ... (ll.11-12)

(*a*) he had (*b*) of having (*c*) that he has (*d*) to have

6 – George Carlton, and it is ________ he is very proud of. (l.12)

(*a*) the fact (*b*) something (*c*) that which (*d*) what

7 No sooner had I opened the cupboard door ________ I stood ... (ll.17-18)

(*a*) and (*b*) then (*c*) than (*d*) that

8 '________ that I was a medical student once upon a time?' (l.22)

(*a*) Why don't you remember (*b*) Have you forgotten

(*c*) Do you forget (*d*) Have you not remembered

Vocabulary 词汇

9 The English language ________ a vivid saying to ... (ll.3-4)

(*a*) owes (*b*) contains (*c*) holds (*d*) has

10 – the guestroom, which, he said, was ________ used. (l.15)

(*a*) little (*b*) a little (*c*) uncommonly (*d*) preciously

11 He told me to unpack my ________ and then ... (ll.15-16)

(*a*) items (*b*) objects (*c*) trunks (*d*) belongings

12 – gave me the impression that it ________ leaping out at me. (l.19)

(*a*) was on the point of (*b*) was concerned with (*c*) was thinking of (*d*) was almost

LESSON

25 The Cutty Sark “卡蒂萨克”号帆船

Listen then answer the question below.

听录音，然后回答以下问题。

What piece of bad luck prevented the *Cutty Sark* from winning the race?

A temporary rudder was made

One of the most famous sailing ships of the nineteenth century, the *Cutty Sark*, can still be seen at Greenwich. She stands on dry land and is visited by thousands of people each year. She serves as an impressive reminder of the great ships of the past. Before they were replaced by steamships, sailing vessels like the *Cutty Sark* were used to carry tea from China and wool from Australia. The *Cutty Sark* was one of the fastest sailing ships that has ever been built. The only other ship to match her was the *Thermopylae.* Both these ships set out from Shanghai on June 18th, 1872 on an exciting race to England. This race, which went on for exactly four months, was the last of its kind. It marked the end of the great tradition of ships with sails and the beginning of a new era.

The first of the two ships to reach Java after the race had begun was the *Thermopylae*, but on the Indian Ocean, the *Cutty Sark* took the lead. It seemed certain that she would be the first ship home, but during the race she had a lot of bad luck. In August, she was struck by a very heavy storm during which her rudder was torn away. The *Cutty Sark* rolled from side to side and it became impossible to steer her. A temporary rudder was made on board from spare planks and it was fitted with great difficulty. This greatly reduced the speed of the ship, for there was a danger that if she travelled too quickly, this rudder would be torn away as well. Because of this, the *Cutty Sark* lost her lead. After crossing the Equator, the captain called in at a port to have a new rudder fitted, but by now the *Thermopylae* was over five hundred miles ahead. Though the new rudder was fitted at tremendous speed, it was impossible for the *Cutty Sark* to win. She arrived in England a week after the *Thermopylae*. Even this was remarkable, considering that she had had so many delays. There is no doubt that if she had not lost her rudder she would have won the race easily.

New words and expressions 生词和短语

impressive (l.4)	/ɪmˈpresɪv/	*adj.*	给人深刻印象的
steamship (l.5)	/ˈstiːmˌʃɪp/	*n.*	蒸汽轮船
vessel (l.5)	/ˈvesəl/	*n.*	轮船，大木船
era (l.10)	/ˈɪərə/	*n.*	时期，时代
Java (l.11)	/ˈdʒɑːvə/	*n.*	爪哇（印度尼西亚岛屿）
rudder (l.13)	/ˈrʌdə/	*n.*	舵
roll (l.14)	/rəʊl/	*v.*	颠簸，摇摆
steer (l.14)	/stɪə/	*v.*	掌握方向
temporary (l.14)	/ˈtempərəri/	*adj.*	临时的
plank (l.15)	/plæŋk/	*n.*	大块木板
fit (l.15)	/fɪt/	*v.*	安装
Equator (l.17)	/ɪˈkweɪtə/	*n.*	赤道
delay (l.21)	/dɪˈleɪ/	*n.*	耽误

Notes on the text 课文注释

1 *Cutty Sark*, "卡蒂萨克"号，19 世纪一艘著名的帆船。现在这艘船在伦敦格林尼治作为展品被保护了起来。在轮船时代以前，它是那时候最快的帆船。

2 both these ships, 这两艘船。
也可写成 both of these ships 或 both ships。

3 The first of the two ships to reach Java ..., 两艘船中首先到达爪哇的……。不定式短语 to reach Java 此处作定语，修饰 first，中间被另一个修饰 first 的介词短语 of the two ships 所分开。

4 take the lead, 领先。
lose one's lead, 失去领先地位。

5 There is no doubt that if she had not lost her rudder she would have won the race easily. 毫无疑问，如果中途没有失去舵，"卡蒂萨克"号肯定能在比赛中轻易夺冠。这是一个虚拟语气的句子，是对过去的一种假设。

参考译文

人们在格林尼治仍可看到 19 世纪最有名的帆船之一"卡蒂萨克"号。它停在陆地上，每年接待成千上万的参观者。它给人们留下深刻的印象，使人们回忆起历史上的巨型帆船。在蒸汽船取代帆船之前，"卡蒂萨克"号之类的帆船被用来从中国运回茶叶，从澳大利亚运回羊毛。"卡蒂萨克"号是帆船制造史上建造的最快的一艘帆船。唯一可以与之一比高低的是"塞姆皮雷"号帆船。两船于 1872 年 6 月 18 日同时从上海启航驶往英国，途中展开了一场激烈的比赛。这场比赛持续了整整 4 个月，是这类比赛中的最后一次，它标志着帆船伟大传统的结束与一个新纪元的开始。

比赛开始后，"塞姆皮雷"号率先抵达爪哇岛。但在印度洋上，"卡蒂萨克"号驶到了前面。看来，它首先返抵英国是确信无疑的了，但它却在比赛中连遭厄运。8 月份，"卡蒂萨克"号遭到了一场特大风暴的袭击，失去了一只舵。船身左右摇晃，无法操纵。船员用备用的木板在船上赶制了一只应急用的舵，并克服重重困难将舵安装就位。这样一来，大大降低了船的航速。因为船不能开得太快，否则就有危险，应急舵也会被刮走。因为这个缘故，"卡蒂萨克"号落到了后面。跨越赤道后，船长将船停靠在一个港口，在那儿换了一只舵。但此时，"塞姆皮雷"号早已在 500 多英里之遥了。尽管换装新舵时分秒必争，但"卡蒂萨克"号已经不可能取胜了，它抵达英国时比"塞姆皮雷"号晚了 1 个星期。但考虑到路上的多次耽搁，这个成绩也已很不容易了。毫无疑问，如果中途没有失去舵，"卡蒂萨克"号肯定能在比赛中轻易夺冠。

Comprehension 理解

Give short answers to these questions in your own words as far as possible. Use one complete sentence for each answer.

1 Where can the *Cutty Sark* be seen?
2 What sort of cargo did ships like the *Cutty Sark* carry?
3 How long did the race between the *Cutty Sark* and the *Thermopylae* last?

Vocabulary 词汇

Explain the meanings of the following words and phrases as they are used in the passage: reminder (l.4); match (l.7); era (l.10); struck (l.13); steer (l.14); temporary (l.14); on board (l.15).

Summary writing 摘要写作

In not more than 80 words write an account of the race between the *Cutty Sark* and the *Thermopylae* after they set out from Shanghai. Use your own words as far as possible. Do not include anything that is not in the last paragraph.

Composition 作文

In not more than 250 words write a composition entitled 'Ships of the past'. Expand the ideas given below into a plan.

Ideas: Ancient ships — oars — galley slaves — Viking ships — Eric the Red — early sailing ships — Columbus — galleons — the Spanish Armada — warships — Nelson — the coming of steam — the *Great Eastern*.

Letter writing 书信写作

Imagine you are at present travelling on a ship. Write a letter in three paragraphs of about 100 words to your parents describing your journey so far.

Key structures and Special difficulties 关键句型和难点

Exercises 练习

1 *vessels like the* Cutty Sark *were used to carry tea.* (ll.5-6) Write three sentences using the following: *I use, I am used to, I used to.* **(1 SD 55a)**（参见第 2 册第 55 课难点 a）

2 *The* Cutty Sark *was one of the fastest sailing ships.* (ll.6-7) Write sentences using the words *fast* and *faster than.* **(1 KS 8)**（参见第 2 册第 8 课关键句型）

3 *these ships set out from Shanghai.* (l.8) Write two sentences using the phrasal verbs *set off* and *set up.* **(1 SD 12b)**（参见第 2 册第 12 课难点 b）

4 *This race ... was the last of its kind.* (l.9) Write two sentences using *its* and *it's.* **(1 SD 20b)**（参见第 2 册第 20 课难点 b）

5 *she had a lot of bad luck.* (l.13) Write sentences using *a lot of, a great many* and *a great deal of.* **(1 KS 56b)**（参见第 2 册第 56 课关键句型 b）

6 *A temporary rudder was made on board.* (ll.14-15) Which of the following words are preceded by *on* **(1 SD 80)**（参见第 2 册第 80 课难点）and which by *in*: *fire, ink, common, tears, foot, purpose, love, a hurry.* **(SD 2)**（参见第 2 课难点）

7 *if she travelled too quickly.* (l.16) Write two sentences showing the difference between *very* and *too.* **(1 SD 29c)**（参见第 2 册第 29 课难点 c）

8 *the captain called in at a port to have a new rudder fitted.* (ll.17-18) Note this use of *have*. Write these sentences again using *have* with the verbs in italics. **(1 KS 66)**（参见第 2 册第 66 课关键句型）
He is *building* a house.
She *had cleaned* his suit.

9 *it was impossible for the* Cutty Sark *to win.* (l.19) Write two sentences using the verbs *win* and *beat.* **(1 SD 51c)**（参见第 2 册第 51 课难点 c）

Multiple choice questions 选择题

Choose the correct answers to the following questions.

Comprehension 理解

1 The fame of the *Cutty Sark* rests mainly upon ________ .
(*a*) the number of tourists who come to visit her annually
(*b*) her likeness to other great sailing ships of the past

(*c*) her being one of the last and one of the fastest of a line of great sailing ships

(*d*) her victory in the race against the *Thermopylae*

2 The race which took place between the *Cutty Sark* and the *Thermopylae* was ________ .

(*a*) a landmark in the history of shipping

(*b*) held to celebrate the invention of the steamship

(*c*) held especially for sailing ships on the route from Shanghai to London

(*d*) unusually slow because the *Cutty Sark* lost her rudder en route

3 During the race, the most remarkable feat of the *Cutty Sark* was ________ .

(*a*) although last to reach Java, to take the lead on the Indian Ocean

(*b*) the fact that she managed to sail into port without a rudder

(*c*) the speed at which she was sailing while having a new rudder fitted

(*d*) the speed at which she made up the gap between her and the *Thermopylae*

Structure 结构

4 The *Cutty Sark* ________ at Greenwich. (ll.1-2)

(*a*) is still possible to see (*b*) is able still to be seen

(*c*) may still be seen (*d*) is still possibly seen

5 Before ________ , vessels like the *Cutty Sark* were used ... (ll.4-6)

(*a*) steamships replaced sail (*b*) the steamship replaced the sailing ship

(*c*) steamships replaced sailing (*d*) the steam replaced the sail

6 It seemed certain that she ________ the first ship home. (l.12)

(*a*) would go to be (*b*) would be going to be

(*c*) went (*d*) was going to be

7 The *Thermopylae* arrived in England only a week before ________ . (ll.19-20)

(*a*) she did (*b*) she was (*c*) herself (*d*) she had arrived

8 ________ her rudder, there is no doubt she would have won ... (l.21)

(*a*) That if she had not lost (*b*) Not having lost

(*c*) Were she not to lose (*d*) Had she not lost

Vocabulary 词汇

9 – on dry land and ________ thousands of visitors each year. (ll.2-3)

(*a*) appeals to (*b*) attracts (*c*) catches (*d*) pulls

10 On June 18th, 1872 both these ships ________ an exciting race from Shanghai to England. (l.8)

(*a*) set out on (*b*) departed for (*c*) entered (*d*) went for

11 On the Indian Ocean, the *Cutty Sark* went ________ the lead. (ll.11-12)

(*a*) into (*b*) on (*c*) for (*d*) after

12 Even this was remarkable, ________ the numerous delays. (ll.20-21)

(*a*) in respect of (*b*) according to (*c*) in view of (*d*) accounting

LESSON

26 Wanted: a large biscuit tin

征购大饼干筒

Listen then answer the question below.

听录音，然后回答以下问题。

Who won the prize for the biggest biscuit?

a biscuit on a wheelbarrow

No one can avoid being influenced by advertisements. Much as we may pride ourselves on our good taste, we are no longer free to choose the things we want, for advertising exerts a subtle influence on us. In their efforts to persuade us to buy this or that product, advertisers have made a close study of human nature and have classified all our little weaknesses.

Advertisers discovered years ago that all of us love to get something for nothing. An advertisement which begins with the magic word FREE can rarely go wrong. These days, advertisers not only offer free samples, but free cars, free houses, and free trips round the world as well. They devise hundreds of competitions which will enable us to win huge sums of money. Radio and television have made it possible for advertisers to capture the attention of millions of people in this way.

During a radio programme, a company of biscuit manufacturers once asked listeners to bake biscuits and send them to their factory. They offered to pay $10 a pound for the biggest biscuit baked by a listener. The response to this competition was tremendous. Before long, biscuits of all shapes and sizes began arriving at the factory. One lady brought in a biscuit on a wheelbarrow. It weighed nearly 500 pounds. A little later, a man came along with a biscuit which occupied the whole boot of his car. All the biscuits that were sent were carefully weighed. The largest was 713 pounds. It seemed certain that this would win the prize. But just before the competition closed, a lorry arrived at the factory with a truly colossal biscuit which weighed 2,400 pounds. It had been baked by a college student who had used over 1,000 pounds of flour, 800 pounds of sugar, 200 pounds of fat, and 400 pounds of various other ingredients. It was so heavy that a crane had to be used to remove it from the lorry. The manufacturers had to pay more money than they had anticipated, for they bought the biscuit from the student for $24,000.

New words and expressions 生词和短语

influence (l.1)	/ˈɪnfluəns/	*v.*	影响
pride (l.2)	/praɪd/	*v.*	骄傲
taste (l.2)	/teɪst/	*n.*	鉴赏力
exert (l.3)	/ɪɡˈzɜːt/	*v.*	施加
subtle (l.3)	/ˈsʌtl/	*adj.*	微妙的，难以捉摸的
advertiser (l.5)	/ˈædvətaɪzə/	*n.*	做广告的人
classify (l.6)	/ˈklæsɪfaɪ/	*v.*	分类
magic (l.8)	/ˈmædʒɪk/	*adj.*	有奇妙作用的
sample (l.9)	/ˈsɑːmpəl/	*n.*	样品
devise (l.10)	/dɪˈvaɪz/	*v.*	设计，想出
capture (l.11)	/ˈkæptʃə/	*v.*	吸引，赢得
manufacturer (l.12)	/ˌmænjuˈfæktʃərə/	*n.*	生产厂家，制造商
wheelbarrow (l.15)	/ˈwiːlˌbærəʊ/	*n.*	独轮手推车
boot (l.16)	/buːt/	*n.*	（汽车尾部的）行李箱
ingredient (l.20)	/ɪnˈɡriːdiənt/	*n.*	配料
crane (l.20)	/kreɪn/	*n.*	起重机
anticipate (l.21)	/ænˈtɪsɪpeɪt/	*v.*	预期，预料

Notes on the text 课文注释

1 No one can avoid being influenced by advertisements.
没有人能避免受广告的影响。
avoid 一词需接动名词作宾语，being influenced 是动名词一般式的被动形式。

2 Much as we may pride ourselves ..., 尽管我们可以自夸……，虽然我们可以为……而感到自豪。
这是一个让步状语从句，连词 much as 可以译成“虽然……”。

3 get something for nothing, 免费得到。

4 go wrong, 出差错，出毛病。

5 the response to this competition, 对这一竞赛的反响。

参考译文

没有人能避免受广告的影响。尽管我们可以自夸自己的鉴赏力如何敏锐，但我们已经无法独立自主地选购自己所需的东西了。这是因为广告在我们身上施加着一种潜移默化的影响。做广告的人在力图劝说我们买下这种产品或那种产品之前，已经仔细地研究了人的本性，并把人的弱点进行了分类。

做广告的人们多年前就发现我们大家都喜欢免费得到东西。凡是用“免费”这个神奇的词开头的广告很少会失败的。目前，做广告的人不仅提供免费样品，而且还提供免费汽车，免费住房，免费周游世界。他们设计数以百计的竞赛，竞赛中有人可赢得巨额奖金。电台、电视使做广告的人可以用这种手段吸引成百万人的注意力。

有一次，在电台播放的节目里，一个生产饼干的公司请听众自己烘制饼干送到他们的工厂去。他们愿意以每磅 10 美元的价钱买下由听众烘制的最大的饼干。这次竞赛在听众中引起了极其热烈的反响。不久，形状各异、大小不一的饼干陆续送到了工厂。一位女士用手推车运来一个饼干，重达 500 磅左右。相隔不一会儿，一个男子也带来一个大饼干，那饼干把汽车的行李箱挤得满满的。凡送来的饼干都仔细地称量。最重的一个达 713 磅，看来这个饼干获奖无疑了。但就在竞赛截止时间将到之际，一辆卡车驶进了工厂，运来了一个特大无比、重达 2,400 磅的饼干。它是由一个大学生烘制的，用去 1,000 多磅面粉、800 磅食糖、200 磅动物脂肪及 400 磅其他各种原料。饼干太重了，用了一台起重机才把它从卡车上卸下。饼干公司不得不付出比他们预计多得多的钱，因为为买下那学生烘制的饼干他们支付了 24,000 美元。

Comprehension 理解

Give short answers to these questions in your own words as far as possible. Use one complete sentence for each answer.

1 Why are we no longer free to choose the things we want?

2 Why have advertisers made a close study of human weaknesses?

3 How can advertisers capture the attention of millions of people?

Vocabulary 词汇

Explain the meanings of the following words and phrases as they are used in the passage: no longer (l.2); in their efforts to persuade us (l.4); classified (l.6); free (l.9); enable (l.10); capture (l.11).

Summary writing 摘要写作

In not more than 80 words write an account of the competition organized by a company of biscuit manufacturers. Use your own words as far as possible. Do not include anything that is not in the last paragraph.

Composition 作文

In not more than 250 words describe a radio show organized by a firm of soap manufacturers. Use the ideas given below and provide a suitable title. Do not write more than two paragraphs.

Introduction: A member of the audience will be asked a maximum of ten questions. Each time he answers a question correctly, he may accept a money prize or ask for a more difficult question. The minimum prize is £2 for a correct answer to the first question. This goes on doubling itself, reaching a maximum of £2,048 for ten correct answers.

Development and Conclusion: Man being questioned in front of audience — questions of all types (e.g. spelling difficult words, general knowledge, etc.). Excitement mounts up as man answers question after question until he reaches the last one.

Letter writing 书信写作

Write a letter of about 100 words in three paragraphs informing a friend of yours that you will be moving into his neighbourhood. Ask him to help you to find accommodation.

Key structures and Special difficulties 关键句型和难点

Exercises 练习

1 *No one can avoid being influenced by advertisements.* (l.1) Complete the following: **(1 KS 68)**（参见第 2 册第 68 课关键句型）

He enjoys ________ .

Imagine ________ .

It's no use ________ .

It's not worth ________ .

Would you mind ________ ?

2 *can rarely go wrong.* (l.8) Write sentences using the following: *go bad; turn yellow; grow quiet.* **(1 SD 75)**（参见第 2 册第 75 课难点）

3 *in this way.* (l.11) Write sentences to bring out the correct meaning of each of the following: *in the way, on the way,* and *by the way*. **(1 SD 5a)**（参见第 2 册第 5 课难点 a）

4 *... and send them to their factory.* (ll.12-13) Note this pattern. Write similar sentences using the verbs *lend* and *give*. **(1 SD 3)**（参见第 2 册第 3 课难点）

5 *One lady brought in a biscuit.* (l.15) Write two sentences showing the difference between *one* and *a*. **(1 SD 32)**（参见第 2 册第 32 课难点）

6 *It was heavy. A crane had to be used to remove it from the lorry.* (ll.20-21) Join these two sentences then compare your answer with the sentence in the passage. **(1 SD 35)**（参见第 2 册第 35 课难点）

Multiple choice questions 选择题

Choose the correct answers to the following questions.

Comprehension 理解

1 What among other things enables advertisers to sell a product more easily?

(*a*) Knowing that we will buy anything provided it tastes good.

(*b*) Giving every customer something free with each product he buys.

(*c*) Having so many free things all over the world to tempt people with.

(*d*) Having radio and television at their disposal to promote their products.

2 The people who entered the competition did so because ________ .

(*a*) they wanted to get something for nothing

(*b*) they hoped by winning easily to cover the cost of the baking ingredients

(*c*) they hoped to receive the prize money of $24,000

(*d*) the manufacturers had offered free biscuits to anyone who entered

3 What had the manufacturers failed to anticipate?

(*a*) The number of people who would take an interest in the competition.

(*b*) The number of ingredients required to bake a large biscuit with.

(*c*) That it was possible to bake a biscuit as large as the student's.

(*d*) That there was time to bake a huge biscuit before the competition closed.

Structure 结构

4 ________ of our good taste, we are no longer ... (ll.1-2)

(*a*) So proud may we be (*b*) Although we may pride ourselves a great deal

(*c*) Proud as we may be (*d*) Pride ourselves as we may

5 – discovered years ago that all of us ________ something for nothing. (ll.7-8)

(*a*) are loving to get (*b*) love getting (*c*) love to be getting (*d*) love when we get

6 An advertisement can rarely go wrong ________ with the magic word FREE. (l.8)

(*a*) which begins (*b*) to begin (*c*) if it will begin (*d*) what begins

7 It was nearly 500 pounds ________ . (l.15)

(*a*) weighed (*b*) weighing (*c*) in weight (*d*) of weight

8 It was so heavy that a crane ________ from the lorry. (ll.20-21)

(*a*) did they need remove it (*b*) they needed to remove it

(*c*) was needed to have removed it (*d*) was needed to have it removed

Vocabulary 词汇

9 In their efforts to persuade us to buy ________ ... (l.4)

(*a*) one or other product (*b*) that or this product

(*c*) some product or other (*d*) a product or two

10 The ________ to this competition was tremendous. (ll.13-14)

(*a*) answer (*b*) reply (*c*) attraction (*d*) reaction

11 – with a biscuit which ________ the boot of his car. (l.16)

(*a*) took complete possession of (*b*) took up all the space in

(*c*) completely covered (*d*) on the whole filled

12 The manufacturers had to pay more money than they ________ ... (ll.21-22)

(*a*) expected (*b*) hoped (*c*) intended (*d*) wished

LESSON

27 Nothing to sell and nothing to buy 不卖也不买

Listen then answer the question below.

听录音，然后回答以下问题。

What is the most important thing for a tramp?

... freedom from care

It has been said that everyone lives by selling something. In the light of this statement, teachers live by selling knowledge, philosophers by selling wisdom and priests by selling spiritual comfort. Though it may be possible to measure the value of material goods in terms of money, it is extremely difficult to estimate the true value of the services which people perform for us. There are times when we would willingly give everything we possess to save our lives, yet we might grudge paying a surgeon a high fee for offering us precisely this service. The conditions of society are such that skills have to be paid for in the same way that goods are paid for at a shop. Everyone has something to sell.

Tramps seem to be the only exception to this general rule. Beggars almost sell themselves as human beings to arouse the pity of passers-by. But real tramps are not beggars. They have nothing to sell and require nothing from others. In seeking independence, they do not sacrifice their human dignity. A tramp may ask you for money, but he will never ask you to feel sorry for him. He has deliberately chosen to lead the life he leads and is fully aware of the consequences. He may never be sure where the next meal is coming from, but he is free from the thousands of anxieties which afflict other people. His few material possessions make it possible for him to move from place to place with ease. By having to sleep in the open, he gets far closer to the world of nature than most of us ever do. He may hunt, beg, or steal occasionally to keep himself alive; he may even, in times of real need, do a little work; but he will never sacrifice his freedom. We often speak of tramps with contempt and put them in the same class as beggars, but how many of us can honestly say that we have not felt a little envious of their simple way of life and their freedom from care?

New words and expressions 生词和短语

philosopher (l.3)	/fɪˈlɒsəfə/	*n.*	哲学家
wisdom (l.3)	/ˈwɪzdəm/	*n.*	智慧
priest (l.3)	/priːst/	*n.*	牧师
spiritual (l.3)	/ˈspɪrɪtʃuəl/	*adj.*	精神上的
grudge (l.8)	/ɡrʌdʒ/	*v.*	不愿给，舍不得给
surgeon (l.8)	/ˈsɜːdʒən/	*n.*	外科大夫
passer-by (l.12)	/ˌpɑːsəˈbaɪ/	*n.*	过路人 （复数 passers-by）
dignity (l.13)	/ˈdɪɡnɪti/	*n.*	尊严
deliberately (l.14)	/dɪˈlɪbərɪtli/	*adv.*	故意地
consequence (l.15)	/ˈkɒnsɪkwəns/	*n.*	后果，结果
afflict (l.16)	/əˈflɪkt/	*v.*	使苦恼，折磨
ease (l.17)	/iːz/	*n.*	容易
nature (l.18)	/ˈneɪtʃə/	*n.*	大自然
contempt (l.20)	/kənˈtempt/	*n.*	蔑视
envious (l.21)	/ˈenviəs/	*adj.*	嫉妒的

Notes on the text 课文注释

1 in the light of, 依据，按照。

2 in terms of, 从……方面（说来），按照。

3 grudge paying 中，grudge 作“吝惜”、“不愿”解，后面要接名词或动名词。
这句话中的 this service 指上文 to save our lives。

4 The conditions of society are such that ...
such 此处为代词，作“这样”解。that 所引导的从句，可视为同位语从句。

5 be free from ..., 作“不受……影响”解，后面常接 pain（痛苦），trouble（苦恼），danger（危险）一类的词语。

6 By having to sleep in the open, 由于不得不在露天过夜，这一介词短语作原因状语。

7 in times of real need, 确实需要的时候。

8 put them in the same class as beggars, 把他们归为乞丐一类。the same ... as ..., 像……一样。

参考译文

据说每个人都靠出售某种东西来维持生活。根据这种说法，教师靠卖知识为生，哲学家靠卖智慧为生，牧师靠卖精神安慰为生。虽然物质产品的价值可以用金钱来衡量，但要估算别人为我们所提供的服务的价值却是极其困难的。有时，我们为了挽救生命，愿意付出我们所拥有的一切。但就在外科大夫给我们提供了这种服务后，我们却可能为所支付的昂贵费用而抱怨。社会上的情况就是如此，技术是必须付钱去买的，就像在商店里要花钱买商品一样。人人都有东西可以出售。

在这条普遍性的规律面前，好像只有流浪汉是个例外。乞丐出售的几乎是他本人，以引起过路人的怜悯。但真正的流浪汉并不是乞丐。他们既不出售任何东西，也不需要从别人那儿得到任何东西。在追求独立自由的同时，他们并不牺牲为人的尊严。流浪汉可能会向你讨钱，但他从来不要你可怜他。他是故意地选择过那种生活的，并完全清楚以这种方式生活的后果。他可能从不知道下顿饭有无着落，但他不像有些人那样被成千上万桩愁事所折磨。他几乎没有什么财产，这使他能够轻松自如地在各地奔波。由于被迫在露天睡觉，他比我们中许多人都离大自然近得多。为了生存，他可能会去打猎、乞讨，偶尔偷上一两回；确实需要的时候，他甚至可能干一点儿活，但他决不会牺牲自由。说起流浪汉，我们常常带有轻蔑并把他们与乞丐归为一类。但是，我们中有多少人能够坦率地说我们对流浪汉的简朴生活与无忧无虑的境况不感到有些羡慕呢？

Comprehension 理解

Give short answers to these questions in your own words as far as possible. Use one complete sentence for each answer.

1 Which of the two is it easier to estimate in terms of money: the value of material goods or the value of services?

2 How do beggars arouse the pity of passers-by?

3 How do tramps differ from beggars?

Vocabulary 词汇

Explain the meanings of the following words and phrases as they are used in the passage: value (l.4); estimate (l.5); perform (l.6); possess (l.7); grudge (l.8); precisely (l.8); skills (l.9).

Summary writing 摘要写作

In not more than 80 words give an account of a tramp's way of life. Use your own words as far as possible. Do not include anything that is not in the last paragraph.

Composition 作文

In not more than 250 words write an answer to the above passage criticizing a tramp's way of life. Expand the ideas given below into a plan and provide a suitable title. Your composition should be in four paragraphs.

Ideas: Tramps — free, but freedom paid for by others — selfish way of life — unwillingness to assume responsibility for others (home, children, work, etc.) — lazy parasites on society — if we all had the mentality of tramps, society would not exist.

Letter writing 书信写作

Write a letter of about 100 words in three paragraphs to a relation who lives abroad. Ask him whether it would be possible for you to get a job abroad for a few months to help to pay for a holiday you intend to have.

Key structures and Special difficulties 关键句型和难点

Exercises 练习

1 *It has been said that* ... . (l.1) Write two sentences using the following: *He is said* ... , *It is said that* ... . **(1 KS 58b)**（参见第 2 册第 58 课关键句型 b）

2 *teachers live by selling knowledge.* (l.2) Write sentences using the following words: *information, news, work* and *luggage.* **(1 KS 54a)**（参见第 2 册第 54 课关键句型 a）

3 *There are times* ... . (ll.6-7) Write sentences using the following: *it will be; there was; there has been.* **(1 SD 23)**（参见第 2 册第 23 课难点）

4 *we would willingly give everything we possess to save our lives.* (ll.7-8) Note the use of *to* here. Write sentences using the following: *so as not to; in order that my mother; so that.* **(1 SD 59)**（参见第 2 册第 59 课难点）

5 *skills have to be paid for.* (l.9) Write two sentences using the following: *to be found; to be sold.* **(1 KS 34)**（参见第 2 册第 34 课关键句型）

6 *He may never be sure where the next meal is coming from.* (l.15) Write these sentences again changing the position of the words in italics. Where possible omit the words *whom* and *which*. **(SD 1)**（参见第 1 课难点）

By whom was this book written?

This is not the sort of book *in* which I am interested.

7 *He has to sleep in the open. He gets far closer to the world of nature than most of us ever do.* (ll.17-18) Join these two sentences then compare your answer with the sentence in the passage. **(1 KS 20)**（参见第 2 册第 20 课关键句型）

Multiple choice questions 选择题

Choose the correct answers to the following questions.

Comprehension 理解

1 It is very difficult to estimate the true value of the services people perform for us because ________ .

(*a*) people's needs vary so much according to their circumstances

(*b*) we refuse to admit that surgeons perform a very necessary service (*c*) we seldom should give everything we possess for such services

(*d*) such services are paid for in the same way as material goods

2 In choosing to lead the life he leads, the tramp has decided ________ .

(*a*) he will never need to ask people for anything

(*b*) to sleep in the open in order to be closer to the world of nature

(*c*) he would rather lead the life of a criminal than do any work

(*d*) his freedom more than compensates for the inconveniences of such a life

3 In moments of truth we feel envious of a tramp's way of life because ________ .

(*a*) we feel that our way of life is undignified compared to a tramp's

(*b*) his life is not burdened with the anxieties we are often troubled by

(*c*) of the freedom he has from the struggle to keep alive

(*d*) we realize that it is better than having to beg for a livelihood

Structure 结构

4 Yet we might grudge ________ a surgeon for offering ... (l.8)

(*a*) a high fee we had paid (*b*) the high fee we would pay

(*c*) the high fee paying (*d*) to pay a high fee

5 They ________ require anything from others. (ll.12-13)

(*a*) do not have to sell anything or (*b*) have nothing to sell nor do they

(*c*) have to sell nothing nor they (*d*) have not sold anything and do not

6 With so few material possessions, he ________ to move from ... (ll.16-17)

(*a*) may be able (*b*) is able (*c*) can (*d*) is possible

7 We often speak contemptuously ________ tramps and ... (ll.19-20)

(*a*) for (*b*) on (*c*) to (*d*) of

8 But ________ of us can honestly say ... (l.20)

(*a*) who (*b*) which ones (*c*) how many (*d*) what one

Vocabulary 词汇

9 A surgeon is a man who ________ . (l.8)

(*a*) saves people's lives (*b*) gives people financial advice

(*c*) performs operations (*d*) insures people's lives against sickness or death

10 – make it possible for him to move ________ with ease. (ll.16-17)

(*a*) here and there (*b*) one way or another

(*c*) from square to square (*d*) in every sense

11 He may hunt, beg or steal occasionally to ________ ... (l.18)

(*a*) make a living (*b*) survive (*c*) be living (*d*) be alive

12 We often ________ tramps and put them down as beggars. (ll.19-20)

(*a*) convict (*b*) blame (*c*) look down on (*d*) condemn

LESSON 28

Five pounds too dear 五镑也太贵

colourful rugs from Persia

Listen then answer the question below.

听录音，然后回答以下问题。

Why was even five pounds 'too dear'?

Small boats loaded with wares sped to the great liner as she was entering the harbour. Before she had anchored, the men from the boats had climbed on board and the decks were soon covered with colourful rugs from Persia, silks from India, copper coffee pots, and beautiful handmade silverware. It was difficult not to be tempted. Many of the tourists on board had begun bargaining with the tradesmen, but I decided not to buy anything until I had disembarked.

I had no sooner got off the ship than I was assailed by a man who wanted to sell me a diamond ring. I had no intention of buying one, but I could not conceal the fact that I was impressed by the size of the diamonds. Some of them were as big as marbles. The man went to great lengths to prove that the diamonds were real. As we were walking past a shop, he held a diamond firmly against the window and made a deep impression in the glass. It took me over half an hour to get rid of him.

The next man to approach me was selling expensive pens and watches. I examined one of the pens closely. It certainly looked genuine. At the base of the gold cap, the words 'made in the U.S.A.' had been neatly inscribed. The man said that the pen was worth £50, but as a special favour, he would let me have it for £30. I shook my head and held up five fingers indicating that I was willing to pay £5. Gesticulating wildly, the man acted as if he found my offer outrageous, but he eventually reduced the price to £10. Shrugging my shoulders, I began to walk away when, a moment later, he ran after me and thrust the pen into my hands. Though he kept throwing up his arms in despair, he readily accepted the £5 I gave him. I felt especially pleased with my wonderful bargain — until I got back to the ship. No matter how hard I tried, it was impossible to fill this beautiful pen with ink and to this day it has never written a single word!

New words and expressions 生词和短语

wares (l.1)	/weəz/	n.	（复数）货物，商品
anchor (l.2)	/ˈæŋkə/	v.	停航下锚
deck (l.3)	/dek/	n.	甲板
silverware (l.5)	/ˈsɪlvəweə/	n.	银器
tempt (l.6)	/tempt/	v.	吸引；引诱
bargain (l.6)	/ˈbɑːɡɪn/	v.	讨价还价
disembark (l.8)	/ˌdɪsɪmˈbɑːk/	v.	下船上岸
assail (l.9)	/əˈseɪl/	v.	纠缠
marble (l.11)	/ˈmɑːbəl/	n.	小玻璃球
inscribe (l.16)	/ɪnˈskraɪb/	v.	刻写，雕
favour (l.16)	/ˈfeɪvə/	n.	好处，优惠
gesticulate (l.17)	/dʒeˈstɪkjʊleɪt/	v.	（讲话时）打手势
outrageous (l.18)	/aʊtˈreɪdʒəs/	adj.	出人预料的；令人不悦的
thrust (l.19)	/θrʌst/	v.	硬塞给

Notes on the text 课文注释

1 I had no sooner got off the ship than I was assailed ..., 我刚刚一下船就被……纠缠住了。no sooner ... than ... 作“刚……就……”讲。

2 go to great lengths to do sth., 竭力做某事。

3 get rid of, 摆脱。

4 as a special favour, 作为一种特殊的优惠。

5 throw up his arms in despair, 绝望地举起双手。

参考译文

当一艘大型客轮进港的时候，许多小船载着各种杂货快速向它驶来。大船还未下锚，小船上的人就纷纷爬上客轮。一会儿工夫，甲板上就摆满了色彩斑斓的波斯地毯、印度丝绸、铜咖啡壶以及手工制作的漂亮的银器。要想不对这些东西动心是很困难的。船上的许多游客开始同商贩讨价还价起来，但我打定主意上岸之前什么也不买。

我刚下船，就被一个人缠住了，他向我兜售一枚钻石戒指。我根本不想买，但我不能掩饰这样一个事实：其钻石之大给我留下了深刻的印象。有的钻石像玻璃球那么大。那人竭力想证明那钻石是真货。我们路过一家商店时，他将一颗钻石使劲地往橱窗上一按，在玻璃上留下一道深痕。我花了半个多小时才摆脱了他的纠缠。

向我兜售的第二个人是卖名贵钢笔和手表的。我仔细察看了一支钢笔，那看上去确实不假，金笔帽下方整齐地刻有“美国制造”字样。那人说那支笔值 50 英镑，作为特别优惠，他愿意让我出 30 英镑成交。我摇摇头，伸出 5 根手指表示我只愿出 5 英镑。那人激动地打着手势，仿佛我的出价使他不能容忍。但他终于把价钱降到了 10 英镑。我耸耸肩膀掉头走开了。一会儿，他突然从后面追了上来，把笔塞到我手里。虽然他绝望地举起双手，但他毫不迟疑地收下了我付给他的 5 英镑。在回到船上之前，我一直为我的绝妙的讨价还价而洋洋得意。然而不管我如何摆弄，那支漂亮的钢笔就是吸不进墨水。直到今天，那支笔连一个字也没写过！

Comprehension 理解

Give short answers to these questions in your own words as far as possible. Use one complete sentence for each answer.

1 What happened as the great liner was entering the harbour?

2 Why was the writer impressed by the size of the diamonds?

3 What did the diamond seller do to prove that his diamonds were real?

Vocabulary 词汇

Explain the meanings of the following words and phrases as they are used in the passage: loaded with wares (l.1); liner (l.1); rugs (l.4); bargaining (l.6); went to great lengths (l.11); impression (l.12); to get rid of him (l.13).

Summary writing 摘要写作

In not more than 80 words describe the writer's experiences after he had got rid of the diamond seller. Use your own words as far as possible. Do not include anything that is not in the last paragraph.

Composition 作文

In not more than 250 words write an imaginary account, mainly in dialogue form, of the scene that took place between the writer and the man who sold him the pen. Use the ideas given below.

Title: The bargain.

Introduction: Man approached with pens and watches — held them up — writer showed interest.

Development and Conclusion: Writer asked to see a pen — man handed him one — argument about the price — gradually reduced to £10 — writer walked away — man followed — made it clear that he was being robbed but accepted £5. Writer pleased, but man disappeared quickly.

Letter writing 书信写作

You have heard that a friend of yours wishes to sell his CD player. Write him a letter of about 100 words in three paragraphs. Express interest in the machine and ask him to tell you about its condition and how much he wants.

Key structures and Special difficulties 关键句型和难点

Exercises 练习

1 *I had no sooner got off the ship than I* ... .(l.9) Join these pairs of sentences with *no sooner* ... *than*. **(1 SD 38a)**（参见第 2 册第 38 课难点 a）

I opened the door. The telephone began to ring.

He finished his speech. Everyone began to clap.

2 *Some of them were as big as marbles.* (l.11) Write two sentences illustrating the use of *as* ... *as* and *not as* ... *as*. **(1 KS 32a)**（参见第 2 册第 32 课关键句型 a）

3 *As we were walking past a shop* ... . (l.12) Complete the following sentences. **(1 KS 7)**（参见第 2 册第 7 课关键句型）

While I was working in the garden ...

I was just going into the shop when ...

4 *It took me over half an hour to get rid of him.* (l.13) Write two sentences using *it takes* and *it has taken*. **(1 SD 50c)**（参见第 2 册第 50 课难点 c）

5 *'made in the U.S.A.'*. (l.15) Write sentences using each of the following: *made in, made by, made of* and *made from*. **(1 SD 10a)**（参见第 2 册第 10 课难点 a）

6 *to this day it has never written a single word.* (l.22) Write two sentences using the phrases *up till now* and *so far*. **(1 KS 28)**（参见第 2 册第 28 课关键句型）

Multiple choice questions 选择题

Choose the correct answers to the following questions.

Comprehension 理解

1 At what point did the tradesmen start trying to sell their merchandise?

(*a*) Once it had been brought to them by the small boats.

(*b*) While they were laying it out on the decks.

(*c*) As soon as the liner had anchored in the harbour.

(*d*) Once the tourists had arrived on board.

2 What happened once the writer got on shore?
(*a*) A man who had followed him off the ship tried to sell him a diamond.
(*b*) He was made to look at some diamonds against his will.
(*c*) A man started pestering him to buy a diamond.
(*d*) On his way to a shop, he met a man who was selling diamonds.

3 What made the writer finally buy the pen?
(*a*) He had been unable to make the man understand he did not want it.
(*b*) The man eventually agreed to his original offer.
(*c*) He decided it was the only way to get rid of the man.
(*d*) He was afraid the man might otherwise become violent.

Structure 结构

4 But I decided to disembark ________ anything. (ll.7-8)
(*a*) before I would buy (*b*) until I was buying (*c*) until I had bought (*d*) before buying

5 I was assailed by a man who wanted ________ a diamond ring. (l.9)
(*a*) that I bought (*b*) for me to buy (*c*) me to buy (*d*) my buying

6 – of buying one, but the man ________ that I was impressed ... (l.10)
(*a*) must have noticed (*b*) had to notice (*c*) must notice (*d*) could notice

7 The man said that although the pen was worth £50, as a special favour, ________ for £30. (ll.16-17)
(*a*) he would let it to me (*b*) he could have let me have it
(*c*) it would have been mine (*d*) he might give me

Vocabulary 词汇

8 It was difficult to ________ temptation. (ll.5-6)
(*a*) avoid (*b*) fight (*c*) resist (*d*) stand

9 ________ I was approached by a man who was selling ... (l.14)
(*a*) The later (*b*) On the next time (*c*) Afterwards (*d*) After

10 – and held up five fingers indicating I ________ to pay five pounds. (l.17)
(*a*) wished (*b*) was ready to (*c*) intended (*d*) expected

11 The man acted as if he found my offer ________ ... (l.18)
(*a*) irritating (*b*) preposterous (*c*) hilarious (*d*) unspeakable

12 ________ hard I tried, it was impossible to fill the pen. (ll.21-22)
(*a*) However (*b*) Whatever (*c*) Whichever (*d*) So ever

LESSON

29 Funny or not? 是否可笑？

a Russian might fail to see anything amusing

Listen then answer the question below.

听录音，然后回答以下问题。

What is the basis of 'sick' humour?

Whether we find a joke funny or not largely depends on where we have been brought up. The sense of humour is mysteriously bound up with national characteristics. A Frenchman, for instance, might find it hard to laugh at a Russian joke. In the same way, a Russian might fail to see anything amusing in a joke which would make an Englishman laugh to tears.

Most funny stories are based on comic situations. In spite of national differences, certain funny situations have a universal appeal. No matter where you live, you would find it difficult not to laugh at, say, Charlie Chaplin's early films. However, a new type of humour, which stems largely from the U.S., has recently come into fashion. It is called 'sick humour'. Comedians base their jokes on tragic situations like violent death or serious accidents. Many people find this sort of joke distasteful. The following example of 'sick humour' will enable you to judge for yourself.

A man who had broken his right leg was taken to hospital a few weeks before Christmas. From the moment he arrived there, he kept on pestering his doctor to tell him when he would be able to go home. He dreaded having to spend Christmas in hospital. Though the doctor did his best, the patient's recovery was slow. On Christmas Day, the man still had his right leg in plaster. He spent a miserable day in bed thinking of all the fun he was missing. The following day, however, the doctor consoled him by telling him that his chances of being able to leave hospital in time for New Year celebrations were good. The man took heart and, sure enough, on New Year's Eve he was able to hobble along to a party. To compensate for his unpleasant experiences in hospital, the man drank a little more than was good for him. In the process, he enjoyed himself thoroughly and kept telling everybody how much he hated hospitals. He was still mumbling something about hospitals at the end of the party when he slipped on a piece of ice and broke his left leg.

New words and expressions 生词和短语

largely (l.1)	/ˈlɑːdʒli/	*adv.*	在很大程度上
comic (l.7)	/ˈkɒmɪk/	*adj.*	喜剧的，可笑的
universal (l.8)	/ˌjuːnɪˈvɜːsəl/	*adj.*	普遍的
comedian (l.10)	/kəˈmiːdiən/	*n.*	滑稽演员，喜剧演员
distasteful (l.11)	/dɪsˈteɪstfəl/	*adj.*	讨厌的
pester (l.14)	/ˈpestə/	*v.*	一再要求，纠缠
dread (l.15)	/dred/	*v.*	惧怕
recovery (l.15)	/rɪˈkʌvəri/	*n.*	康复
plaster (l.16)	/ˈplɑːstə/	*n.*	熟石膏
console (l.17)	/kənˈsəʊl/	*v.*	安慰，慰问
hobble (l.19)	/ˈhɒbəl/	*v.*	瘸着腿走
compensate (l.19)	/ˈkɒmpənseɪt/	*v.*	补偿
mumble (l.21)	/ˈmʌmbəl/	*v.*	喃喃而语

Notes on the text 课文注释

1 whether we find a joke funny or not, 这是一个名词性的从句，在句子中作主语。

2 be bound up with, 与……联系在一起。

3 you would find it difficult not to laugh at, say, Charlie Chaplin's early films. 比如说，你看了查理·卓别林的早期电影很难不发笑。句中的 say 是插入语，可译作"比如说"。查理·卓别林是电影史上最有名的演员之一。他在诸如《淘金记》(1925)这类电影中扮演的流浪汉"小人物"在各种不利的条件下仍获得了成功。

4 stem from, 起源于。

5 come into fashion, 开始流行，时兴起来。

6 judge for yourself, 你自己来判断。

7 take heart, 振作精神。

8 the man drank a little more than was good for him. 这个人稍微多喝了一点酒。
此句 than 后面省略了主语 what，be good for sb. 是"对某人有益"的意思。

参考译文

我们觉得一则笑话是否好笑，很大程度上取决于我们是在哪儿长大的。幽默感与民族有着神秘莫测的联系。譬如，法国人听完一则俄罗斯笑话可能很难发笑。同样的道理，一则可以令英国人笑出泪来的笑话，俄罗斯人听了可能觉得没有什么可笑之处。

大部分令人发笑的故事都是根据喜剧情节编写的。尽管民族不同，有些滑稽情节却能产生普遍的效果。比如说，不管你生活在哪里，你看了查理·卓别林的早期电影很难不发笑。然而，近来一种新式幽默流行了起来，这种幽默主要来自美国。它被叫作"病态幽默"。喜剧演员根据悲剧情节诸如暴死、重大事故等来编造笑话。许多人认为这种笑话是低级庸俗的。下面是个"病态幽默"的实例，你可以据此自己作出判断。

圣诞节前几周，某人摔断了右腿被送进医院。从他进医院那一刻起，他就缠住医生，让医生告诉他什么时候能回家。他十分害怕在医院过圣诞。尽管医生竭力医治，但病人恢复缓慢。圣诞节那天，他的右腿还上着石膏，他在床上郁郁不乐地躺了一天，想着他错过的种种欢乐。然而，第二天，医生安慰他说，出院欢度新年的可能性还是很大的，那人听后振作了精神。果然，除夕时他可以一瘸一拐地去参加晚会了。为了补偿住院这一段不愉快的经历，那人喝得稍许多了一点。在晚会上他尽情娱乐，一再告诉大家他是多么讨厌医院。晚会结束时，他嘴里还在嘟哝着医院的事，突然踩到一块冰上滑倒了，摔断了左腿。

Comprehension 理解

Give short answers to these questions in your own words as far as possible. Use one complete sentence for each answer.

1 Why might a Frenchman find it hard to laugh at a Russian joke?

2 Why do people all over the world find Charlie Chaplin's early films amusing?

3 Where did 'sick humour' originate?

Vocabulary 词汇

Explain the meanings of the following words and phrases as they are used in the passage: brought up (l.2); mysteriously bound up with (ll.2-3); make (l.5); universal appeal (l.8); stems (l.10); come into fashion (l.10); distasteful (l.11).

Summary writing 摘要写作

Relate the story told in the passage *in not more than 80 words*. Use your own words as far as possible. Do not include anything that is not in the last paragraph.

Composition 作文

In not more than 250 words tell a funny story you know well. Make out a full plan and provide a suitable title. Your composition should be in three or four paragraphs.

Letter writing 书信写作

You cannot find your overcoat and think you may have left it at the house of a friend whom you visited recently. Write him a letter of about 100 words in three paragraphs asking him if you did in fact leave your overcoat at his house.

Key structures and Special difficulties 关键句型和难点

Exercises 练习

1 *depends on*. (l.1) Which words normally follow these verbs: *operate, differ, smell, encourage, lean, approve, delight, suffer, assure, escape, interested, concentrate, include*. **(1 KS 22)**（参见第 2 册第 22 课关键句型）

2 *A Frenchman ... might find it hard to laugh at a Russian joke*. (ll.3-4) Note this pattern. Write similar sentences using the following: *He found it ... ; She considered it ... ; He thought it ...* . **(1 SD 84)**（参见第 2 册第 84 课难点）

3 *to laugh at a Russian joke*. (l.4) Write two sentences illustrating the difference between *laugh* and *laugh at*. **(1 SD 82a)**（参见第 2 册第 82 课难点 a）

4 *fail to see anything amusing*. (l.5) Explain the meaning of *amusing* here. Write sentences using the following words: *amuse, enjoy, entertain*. **(1 SD 69b)**（参见第 2 册第 69 课难点 b）

5 *A man had broken his right leg. He was taken to hospital a few weeks before Christmas*. (l.13) Join these two sentences then compare your answer with the sentence in the passage. **(1 SD 28)**（参见第 2 册第 28 课难点）

6 *he kept on pestering his doctor*. (l.14) Write sentences using the following: *keep off, keep up with, keep out*. **(1 SD 78)**（参见第 2 册第 78 课难点）

7 *on New Year's Eve he was able to hobble along to a party*. (l.19) Write two sentences using *could* and *was able to*. **(1 KS 43c)**（参见第 2 册第 43 课关键句型 c）

Multiple choice questions 选择题

Choose the correct answers to the following questions.

Comprehension 理解

1 Whether you find 'sick humour' funny or not will depend on ________ .

(*a*) your having been brought up in America

(*b*) the joke being related to a fundamentally comic situation

(*c*) your ability to see the funny side of an unpleasant event

(*d*) your ability to laugh until you cry

2 The man spent Christmas Day feeling miserable because ________ .
(*a*) the doctor had failed to attend to him
(*b*) he was not able to be with his friends
(*c*) being unable to walk, he did not enjoy the celebrations at the hospital
(*d*) he thought he might also miss the New Year's Eve celebrations

3 The point of the joke taken to illustrate 'sick humour' is that ________ .
(*a*) no sooner was the man out of hospital than he had to go back in again
(*b*) the man should not have said how much he hated hospitals
(*c*) the man would be unable to walk for the rest of his life
(*d*) the man had not got a leg to stand on

Structure 结构

4 ________ , for instance, might find it hard to ... (ll.3-4)
(*a*) The French (*b*) A French (*c*) A man in France (*d*) If you were French

5 ________ amusing stories are based on comic situations. (l.7)
(*a*) Most (*b*) Most of (*c*) The majority (*d*) Mostly

6 A man ________ broken was taken to hospital ... (l.13)
(*a*) whose right leg had been (*b*) who had the right leg
(*c*) with one right leg (*d*) to whom the right leg had been

7 He had no sooner arrived there ________ pestering his doctor ... (ll.13-14)
(*a*) and then he began (*b*) than he began (*c*) he began (*d*) to begin

8 The man compensated for his unpleasant experiences in hospital ________ a little more than ... (ll.19-20)
(*a*) drinking (*b*) to drink (*c*) by drinking (*d*) and drunk

Vocabulary 词汇

9 Though the doctor ________ ... (l.15)
(*a*) worked very well (*b*) could not have been better
(*c*) was extremely skilled (*d*) did all he could

10 The doctor ________ him by ... (l.17)
(*a*) felt (*b*) advised (*c*) pleased (*d*) comforted

11 – and kept telling everyone ________ he hated hospitals. (l.21)
(*a*) at great lengths that (*b*) to their cost (*c*) to what extent (*d*) why

12 He was still mumbling something ________ at the end ... (ll.21-22)
(*a*) in the same way (*b*) to the same effect (*c*) of common sense (*d*) of some sort

LESSON

30 The death of a ghost “幽灵”之死

Listen then answer the question below.

听录音，然后回答以下问题。

Why did the two brothers keep the secret?

the ghost of Endley

For years, villagers believed that Endley Farm was haunted. The farm was owned by two brothers, Joe and Bob Cox. They employed a few farmhands, but no one was willing to work there long. Every time a worker gave up his job, he told the same story. Farm labourers said that they always woke up to find that work had been done overnight. Hay had been cut and cowsheds had been cleaned. A farm worker, who stayed up all night, claimed to have seen a figure cutting corn in the moonlight. In time, it became an accepted fact that the Cox brothers employed a conscientious ghost that did most of their work for them.

No one suspected that there might be someone else on the farm who had never been seen. This was indeed the case. A short time ago, villagers were astonished to learn that the ghost of Endley had died. Everyone went to the funeral, for the ‘ghost’ was none other than Eric Cox, a third brother who was supposed to have died as a young man. After the funeral, Joe and Bob revealed a secret which they had kept for over fifty years.

Eric had been the eldest son of the family, very much older than his two brothers. He had been obliged to join the army during the Second World War. As he hated army life, he decided to desert his regiment. When he learnt that he would be sent abroad, he returned to the farm and his father hid him until the end of the war. Fearing the authorities, Eric remained in hiding after the war as well. His father told everybody that Eric had been killed in action. The only other people who knew the secret were Joe and Bob. They did not even tell their wives. When their father died, they thought it their duty to keep Eric in hiding. All these years, Eric had lived as a recluse. He used to sleep during the day and work at night, quite unaware of the fact that he had become the ghost of Endley. When he died, however, his brothers found it impossible to keep the secret any longer.

New words and expressions 生词和短语

labourer (l.4)	/ˈleɪbərə/	*n.*	劳动者
overnight (l.6)	/ˌəuvəˈnaɪt/	*adv.*	一夜之间
hay (l.6)	/heɪ/	*n.*	干草
corn (l.8)	/kɔːn/	*n.*	谷物
moonlight (l.8)	/ˈmuːnlaɪt/	*n.*	月光
conscientious (l.9)	/ˌkɒnʃiˈenʃəs/	*adj.*	认真的
suspect (l.10)	/səˈspekt/	*v.*	怀疑
desert (l.16)	/dɪˈzɜːt/	*v.*	（军队中）开小差
regiment (l.16)	/ˈredʒɪmənt/	*n.*	（军队）团
action (l.19)	/ˈækʃən/	*n.*	战斗
recluse (l.21)	/rɪˈkluːs/	*n.*	隐士

Notes on the text 课文注释

1 every time（= whenever）作“每当……”解，引导时间状语从句。

2 stay up, 熬夜，不睡觉。

3 In time, it became an accepted fact that ..., 最后，……已成为公认的一个事实。
in time 作“终于”、“最后”讲。that 引导的从句为主语从句。

4 none other than ..., 不是别人正是……。

参考译文

多年来，村民们一直认为恩得利农场在“闹鬼”。恩得利农场属于乔·考科斯和鲍勃·考科斯兄弟俩所有。他们雇了几个农工，但谁也不愿意在那儿长期工作下去。每次雇工辞职后都叙述着同样的故事。雇工们说，常常一早起来发现有人在夜里把活干了，干草已切好，牛棚也打扫干净了。有一个彻夜未眠的雇工还声称他看见一个人影在月光下收割庄稼。随着时间的流逝，考科斯兄弟雇了一个尽心尽责的“鬼”，他们家的活大部分都让“鬼”给干了，这件事成了公认的事实。

谁也没想到农场里竟会有一个从未露面的人。但事实上确有此人。不久之前，村民们惊悉恩得利农场的“鬼”死了。大家都去参加了葬礼，因为那“鬼”不是别人，正是农场主的兄弟埃里克·考科斯。人们以为埃里克年轻时就死了。葬礼之后，乔和鲍勃透露了他们保守了长达 50 多年的秘密。

埃里克是这家的长子，年龄比他两个弟弟大很多，第二次世界大战期间被迫参军。他讨厌军旅生活，决定逃离所在部队。当他了解到自己将被派遣出国时，他逃回农场，父亲把他藏了起来，直到战争结束。由于害怕当局，埃里克战后继续深藏不露。他的父亲告诉大家，埃里克在战争中被打死了。除他父亲之外，只有乔与鲍勃知道这个秘密。但他俩连自己的妻子都没告诉。父亲死后，他们兄弟俩认为有责任继续把埃里克藏起来。这些年来，埃里克过着隐士生活，白天睡觉，夜里出来干活，一点不知道自己已成了恩得利农场的活“鬼”。他死后，他的弟弟们才觉得无法再保守这个秘密了。

Comprehension 理解

Give short answers to these questions in your own words as far as possible. Use one complete sentence for each answer.

1 Why did farm hands frequently give up their jobs at Endley farm?

2 Who was the ghost of Endley?

3 Why was everybody surprised to learn that Eric Cox had just died?

Vocabulary 词汇

Explain the meanings of the following words and phrases as they are used in the passage: was willing (l.3); labourers (l.4); claimed (l.7); an accepted fact (l.8); conscientious (l.9); astonished (l.11); revealed (l.13).

Summary writing 摘要写作

In not more than 80 words write an account of the life of Eric Cox from the time he joined the army. Use your own words as far as possible. Do not include anything that is not in the last paragraph.

Composition 作文

In not more than 250 words write an imaginary account of the night a farm worker saw a figure cutting corn. Write in the first person. Use the ideas given below. Do not write more than four paragraphs.

Title: The ghost of Endley.

Introduction: I noticed that work had been done overnight. I decided to stay up all night — sat in barn.

Development: I fell asleep — suddenly woke up — went to cowshed — it had already been cleaned — went out to fields — saw a figure working — rushed back to farmhouse — woke up others — we went out — no one there.

Conclusion: Sure it was a ghost — decided not to work at Endley Farm any longer — told story to villagers.

Letter writing 书信写作

You have already written several letters to a friend but he has failed to answer them. Write a letter of about 100 words in three paragraphs complaining that he has not written to you and asking him to give news of himself.

Key structures and Special difficulties 关键句型和难点

Exercises 练习

1 *Every time a worker gave up his job* ... . (ll.3-4) Explain the meaning of the phrasal verb *gave up* here. Write sentences using the following: *give in, give away* and *give oneself up*. **(1 SD 18a)**（参见第 2 册第 18 课难点 a）

2 *he told the same story*. (l.4) Write sentences using *say* or *tell* with the following words: *a lie, goodbye, the difference, so, the time*. **(1 SD 67)**（参见第 2 册第 67 课难点）

3 *that did most of their work*. (l.9) Write sentences using *do* or *make* with the following: *a speech, his best, a favour, a mistake*. **(1 SD 40)**（参见第 2 册第 40 课难点）

4 *After the funeral, Joe and Bob revealed a secret. They had kept it for over fifty years*. (ll.13-14) Join these two sentences then compare your answer with the sentence in the passage. **(1 SD 28)**（参见第 2 册第 28 课难点）

5 *He used to sleep during the day*. (l.21) Write two sentences using: *He used to work* ... ; *He was working* ... . **(1 KS 31)**（参见第 2 册第 31 课关键句型）

Multiple choice questions 选择题

Choose the correct answers to the following questions.

Comprehension 理解

1 While farmhands stayed at Endley Farm ________ .

(*a*) they woke up during the night to find their work had been done for them

(*b*) they often saw a figure working in the fields at night

(*c*) they did not have any work to do

(*d*) it never occurred to them that there was someone in hiding on the farm

2 Eric remained in hiding after the war because ________ .

(*a*) he feared the penalty he might receive for his desertion

(*b*) his father had told everyone he had died

(*c*) he was afraid of being sent abroad by the authorities

(*d*) he was fond of the life of a recluse

3 When did the identity of the 'ghost' become known?

(*a*) When the villagers attended the funeral.

(*b*) Fifty years after the outbreak of the Second World War.

(*c*) When the father of the three Cox brothers died.

(*d*) When Joe and Bob felt they would have to have their brother buried.

Structure 结构

4 Farm labourers said that on waking up ________ work had been done. (ll.4-5)

(*a*) to find (*b*) they would find (*c*) and finding (*d*) they had found

5 – employed a conscientious ghost, ________ most of their work for them. (ll.8-9)

(*a*) doing (*b*) to have done (*c*) which did (*d*) so as to do

6 As he hated ________ , he decided to desert ... (l.16)

(*a*) the life of army (*b*) life in the army (*c*) life of the army (*d*) the army for life

7 – Eric had been killed ________ fighting with his regiment. (ll.18-19)

(*a*) while (*b*) during (*c*) as if (*d*) because

8 Joe and Bob were the only other people who knew the secret ________ their wives. (ll.19-20)

(*a*) and did not even tell (*b*) which they did not even tell

(*c*) who did not tell (*d*) yet did not tell it to

Vocabulary 词汇

9 ________ , it became an accepted fact ... (l.8)

(*a*) At the time (*b*) On time (*c*) With time (*d*) At times

10 He was ________ during the Second World War. (ll.15-16)

(*a*) recruited (*b*) conscripted (*c*) armed (*d*) regimented

11 All these years, Eric had lived ________ . (ll.20-21)

(*a*) out of this world (*b*) a secret life

(*c*) without a companion (*d*) the life of a hermit

12 He used to work at night, ________ that he had become the ghost of Endley. (ll.21-22)

(*a*) never realizing (*b*) quite misunderstanding

(*c*) quite ignoring (*d*) never accounting for

LESSON

31 A lovable eccentric 可爱的怪人

add colour to the dull routine

Listen then answer the question below.

听录音，然后回答以下问题。

Why did the shop assistant refuse to serve Dickie?

True eccentrics never deliberately set out to draw attention to themselves. They disregard social conventions without being conscious that they are doing anything extraordinary. This invariably wins them the love and respect of others, for they add colour to the dull routine of everyday life.

Up to the time of his death, Richard Colson was one of the most notable figures in our town. He was a shrewd and wealthy businessman, but most people in the town hardly knew anything about this side of his life. He was known to us all as Dickie and his eccentricity had become legendary long before he died.

Dickie disliked snobs intensely. Though he owned a large car, he hardly ever used it, preferring always to go on foot. Even when it was raining heavily, he refused to carry an umbrella. One day, he walked into an expensive shop after having been caught in a particularly heavy shower. He wanted to buy a £300 watch for his wife, but he was in such a bedraggled condition that an assistant refused to serve him. Dickie left the shop without a word and returned carrying a large cloth bag. As it was extremely heavy, he dumped it on the counter. The assistant asked him to leave, but Dickie paid no attention to him and requested to see the manager. Recognizing who the customer was, the manager was most apologetic and reprimanded the assistant severely. When Dickie was given the watch, he presented the assistant with the cloth bag. It contained £300 in pennies. He insisted on the assistant's counting the money before he left — 30,000 pennies in all! On another occasion, he invited a number of important critics to see his private collection of modern paintings. This exhibition received a great deal of attention in the press, for though the pictures were supposed to be the work of famous artists, they had in fact been painted by Dickie. It took him four years to stage this elaborate joke simply to prove that critics do not always know what they are talking about.

New words and expressions 生词和短语

lovable (title)	/ˈlʌvəbəl/	*adj.*	可爱的
eccentric (title)	/ɪkˈsentrɪk/	*n.*	（行为）古怪的人
disregard (l.2)	/ˌdɪsrɪˈgɑːd/	*v.*	不顾，漠视
convention (l.2)	/kənˈvenʃən/	*n.*	习俗，风俗
conscious (l.3)	/ˈkɒnʃəs/	*adj.*	感觉到的，意识到的
invariably (l.3)	/ɪnˈveəriəbli/	*adv.*	总是，经常地
routine (l.5)	/ruːˈtiːn/	*n.*	常规；惯例
shrewd (l.7)	/ʃruːd/	*adj.*	精明的
eccentricity (l.9)	/ˌeksenˈtrɪsɪti/	*n.*	怪癖
legendary (l.9)	/ˈledʒəndəri/	*adj.*	传奇般的
snob (l.10)	/snɒb/	*n.*	势利小人，谄上欺下的人
intensely (l.10)	/ɪnˈtensli/	*adv.*	强烈地
bedraggled (l.13)	/bɪˈdrægəld/	*adj.*	拖泥带水的
dump (l.14)	/dʌmp/	*v.*	把……砰的一声抛下
apologetic (l.16)	/əˌpɒləˈdʒetɪk/	*adj.*	道歉的
reprimand (l.16)	/ˈreprɪmɑːnd/	*v.*	训斥
stage (l.22)	/steɪdʒ/	*v.*	策划
elaborate (l.22)	/ɪˈlæbərɪt/	*adj.*	精心构思的

Notes on the text 课文注释

1 set out to do sth., 打算，企图做某事。

2 draw attention to ..., 作“引起对……的注意”讲。

3 without being conscious that ..., 没有意识到……。

这是介词短语作状语，be conscious that ... 作“意识到 ……”解。

4 This invariably wins them the love and respect of others. 这常常赢来人们对他们的爱戴和尊敬。

win sb. sth., 作“使某人获得某事（物）”讲。

5 add ... to, 把……添加到……。

6 this side of his life, 他生活中这方面的情况。

这里指的是 He was a shrewd and wealthy businessman.

7 be caught in, 作“突然遇上，碰上”讲。

8 Recognizing who the customer was, the manager was most apologetic ...

由于经理认出这个顾客是谁了，便竭力赔礼道歉……。这句话用现在分词短语作原因状语，most 在这里起加强语气的作用，相当于 very。

9 insisted on the assistant's counting, 坚持让店员点清。

insist on 后接动名词，the assistant's 是动名词的逻辑主语。

参考译文

真正古怪的人从不有意引人注意。他们不顾社会习俗，意识不到自己的所作所为有什么特殊之处。他们总能赢得别人的喜爱与尊敬，因为他们给平淡单一的日常生活增添了色彩。

理查德·科尔森生前是我们镇上最有名望的人之一。他是个精明能干、有钱的商人，但镇上大部分人对他生活中的这一个方面几乎一无所知。大家都管他叫迪基。早在他去世前，他的古怪行为就成了传奇故事。

迪基痛恨势利小人。尽管他有一辆豪华小轿车，但却很少使用，常常喜欢以步代车。即使大雨倾盆，他也总是拒绝带伞。一天，他遇上一场瓢泼大雨，淋得透湿。他走进一家高级商店，要为妻子买一块价值300英镑的手表。但店员见他浑身泥水的样子，竟不肯接待他。迪基二话没说就走了。一会儿，他带着一个大布口袋回到店里。布袋很沉，他重重地把布袋扔在柜台上。店员让迪基走开，他置之不理，并要求见经理。经理认出了这位顾客，表示了深深的歉意，并严厉地训斥了店员。店员为迪基拿出了那块手表，迪基把布口袋递给他，口袋里面装着300镑的便士。他坚持要店员点清那些硬币后他才离去。这些硬币加在一起共有30,000枚！还有一次，他邀请一些著名评论家来参观他私人收藏的现代画。这次展览引起了报界的广泛注意，因为这些画名义上是名家的作品，事实上是迪基自己画的。他花了4年时间策划这出精心设计的闹剧，只是想证明评论家们有时并不了解他们所谈论的事情。

Comprehension 理解

Give short answers to these questions in your own words as far as possible. Use one complete sentence for each answer.

1 Why do eccentrics add colour to the dull routine of everyday life?

2 Why was Richard Colson one of the most notable figures of our town?

3 What did Colson set out to prove when he held an exhibition of modern paintings?

Vocabulary 词汇

Explain the meanings of the following words and phrases as they are used in the passage: deliberately (l.1); disregard (l.2); conventions (l.2); conscious (l.3); notable figures (l.7); shrewd (l.7); elaborate (l.22).

Summary writing 摘要写作

In not more than 80 words explain how Dickie bought a watch for his wife. Use your own words as far as possible. Do not include anything that is not in the last paragraph.

Composition 作文

In not more than 250 words write an actual or imaginary description of an eccentric person. Expand the ideas given below into a plan and provide a suitable title. Your composition should be in three or four paragraphs.

Ideas: Appearance — dress — behaviour — home — way he or she lives — strange actions (e.g. puts up strange notices to passers-by in his garden; stands for parliament — gives speeches saying what he would do if he were Prime Minister — gets a few votes, etc.) — The way other people behave towards him.

Letter writing 书信写作

An old friend of yours has just died. Write a letter of about 100 words in three paragraphs to his wife expressing your sympathy and asking if you can help her in any way.

Key structures and Special difficulties 关键句型和难点

Exercises 练习

1 *without being conscious*. (ll.2-3) Write sentences using verbs after each of the following: *instead of; apart from; interested in*. **(1 KS 20)**（参见第 2 册第 20 课关键句型）

2 *He owned a large car. He hardly ever used it. He preferred always to go on foot.* (ll.10-11) Join these three sentences then compare your answer with the sentence in the passage. **(1 KS 49)**（参见第 2 册第 49 课关键句型）

3 *he walked into an expensive shop*. (ll.11-12) Write two pairs of sentences illustrating the difference between: *into* and *out of; into* and *in*. **(1 KS 33b)**（参见第 2 册第 33 课关键句型 b）

4 *Dickie paid no attention*. (l.15) Write sentences using the following: *pay attention, care* and *take care*. **(1 SD 16b)**（参见第 2 册第 16 课难点 b）

5 *Recognizing who the customer was ...* . (l.16) Write sentences completing the following: *I don't know who ... ; Ask him why ... ; She asked if ...* . **(1 KS 39)**（参见第 2 册第 39 课关键句型）

6 *He insisted on the assistant's counting the money*. (l.18) Complete the following: *Would you mind my ... ; Imagine her ...* . **(1 KS 68b)**（参见第 2 册第 68 课关键句型 b）

7 *30,000 pennies in all*. (l.18) Write sentences using the following phrases: *in the end; in debt; in sight; in tears*. **(SD 2)**（参见第 2 课难点）

Multiple choice questions 选择题

Choose the correct answers to the following questions.

Comprehension 理解

1 Most people in the town would have regarded Dickie's behaviour as eccentric on the day he visited the shop because ________ .

(*a*) when he set out into the rain he did not take an umbrella

(*b*) he went to such lengths to show his dislike of snobbery (*c*) he spent so much money on a watch

(*d*) he had not counted the pennies before giving them to the assistant

2 When Dickie went into an expensive shop ________ .

(*a*) he wanted to shelter from the rain

(*b*) he did not look like a man who could afford a watch

(*c*) he had forgotten to bring his cloth bag with him

(*d*) he had been sent by his wife to buy a watch

3 The press paid a great deal of attention to Dickie's exhibition because ________ .

(*a*) it had taken him so long to prepare the paintings

(*b*) the critics admired Dickie's ability to copy the work of famous artists

(*c*) no one had known that Dickie was a painter

(*d*) it became known that Dickie had succeeded in deceiving the critics

Structure 结构

4 They disregard social conventions and are quite unaware ________ they are doing anything extraordinary. (ll.2-3)

(*a*) that what (*b*) of the fact that (*c*) if (*d*) when

5 As it ________ , he dumped it on the counter. (ll.14-15)

(*a*) was weighing (*b*) weighed a lot (*c*) weighed much (*d*) had weighed much

6 ________ £300 worth of pennies in the bag. (ll.17-18)

(*a*) There were (*b*) It was (*c*) They were (*d*) It had

7 He insisted ________ the money before he left. (l.18)

(*a*) that the assistant should count (*b*) the assistant to count

(*c*) to count (*d*) to be counted

8 He asked a number of important critics to come ________ his private ... (ll.19-20)

(*a*) and see (*b*) seeing (*c*) see (*d*) so they saw

Vocabulary 词汇

9 – and returned carrying a large ________ . (l.14)

(*a*) cloth case (*b*) clothes-basket (*c*) sack of clothing (*d*) bag made of cloth

10 But Dickie paid no attention to his ________ ... (l.15)

(*a*) question (*b*) inquiry (*c*) query (*d*) demand

11 The pictures were supposed to have been ________ by famous artists. (ll.20-21)

(*a*) worked (*b*) made (*c*) done (*d*) designed

12 Critics do not always ________ . (l.22)

(*a*) mean well (*b*) speak with understanding

(*c*) tell the truth (*d*) talk sense

LESSON

32 A lost ship 一艘沉船

Listen then answer the question below.

听录音，然后回答以下问题。

Did the crew of the *Elkor* find what they were looking for? Why?

tremendous excitement on board

The salvage operation had been a complete failure. The small ship, *Elkor*, which had been searching the Barents Sea for weeks, was on its way home. A radio message from the mainland had been received by the ship's captain instructing him to give up the search. The captain knew that another attempt would be made later, for the sunken ship he was trying to find had been carrying a precious cargo of gold bullion.

Despite the message, the captain of the *Elkor* decided to try once more. The sea bed was scoured with powerful nets and there was tremendous excitement on board when a chest was raised from the bottom. Though the crew were at first under the impression that the lost ship had been found, the contents of the chest proved them wrong. What they had in fact found was a ship which had been sunk many years before.

The chest contained the personal belongings of a seaman, Alan Fielding. There were books, clothing and photographs, together with letters which the seaman had once received from his wife. The captain of the *Elkor* ordered his men to salvage as much as possible from the wreck. Nothing of value was found, but the numerous items which were brought to the surface proved to be of great interest. From a heavy gun that was raised, the captain realized that the ship must have been a cruiser. In another chest, which contained the belongings of a ship's officer, there was an unfinished letter which had been written on March 14th, 1943. The captain learnt from the letter that the name of the lost ship was the *Karen*. The most valuable find of all was the ship's log book, parts of which it was still possible to read. From this the captain was able to piece together all the information that had come to light. The *Karen* had been sailing in a convoy to Russia when she was torpedoed by an enemy submarine. This was later confirmed by a naval official at the Ministry of Defence after the *Elkor* had returned home. All the items that were found were sent to the War Museum.

New words and expressions 生词和短语

salvage (l.1)	/ˈsælvɪdʒ/	*n.*	救助，营救；打捞
Barents (l.2)	/ˈbærənts/	*n.*	巴伦支（海）
sunken (l.6)	/ˈsʌŋkən/	*adj.*	沉没的
cargo (l.7)	/ˈkɑːɡəʊ/	*n.*	货物
bullion (l.7)	/ˈbʊljən/	*n.*	金条；银条
scour (l.8)	/skaʊə/	*v.*	彻底搜索
chest (l.9)	/tʃest/	*n.*	大箱子
contents (l.10)	/ˈkɒntents/	*n.*	（复数）所装的东西
belongings (l.12)	/bɪˈlɒŋɪŋz/	*n.*	（复数）所有物
item (l.15)	/ˈaɪtəm/	*n.*	物件
cruiser (l.16)	/ˈkruːzə/	*n.*	巡洋舰
find (l.18)	/faɪnd/	*n.*	找到的物品
log book (l.19)	/ˈlɒɡ-bʊk/	*n.*	航海日志
piece (l.19)	/piːs/	*v.*	拼成整体
convoy (l.20)	/ˈkɒnvɔɪ/	*n.*	护航
torpedo (l.21)	/tɔːˈpiːdəʊ/	*v.*	用鱼雷攻击
submarine (l.21)	/ˈsʌbməriːn/	*n.*	潜水艇
naval (l.21)	/ˈneɪvəl/	*adj.*	海军的
ministry (l.21)	/ˈmɪnɪstri/	*n.*	（政府的）部

Notes on the text 课文注释

1 on its way home, 返航途中。

2 for the sunken ship he was trying to find ...,

for 作“因为”讲，引导并列句；he was trying to find 是定语从句修饰主语 ship。

3 under the impression that, 以为，认为。

4 be of great interest, 很有趣。

5 parts of which it was possible to read,

which 指先行词 log book，所引导的是定语从句，it 是形式主语，不定式 to read 是真实主语，parts of which 作 read 的宾语。

6 piece together ...（或 piece ... together）作“综合”、“拼凑”讲。come to light, 被搞清，被知道。

7 War Museum, 军事博物馆。指伦敦的帝国军事博物馆，其中展出第一次世界大战和第二次世界大战的军事物品。

参考译文

打捞工作彻底失败了。小船“埃尔科”号在巴伦支海搜寻了几个星期之后，正在返航途中。返航前，该船船长收到了大陆上发来的电报，指示他们放弃这次搜寻。船长知道日后还会再作尝试，因为他试图寻找的沉船上载有一批珍贵的金条。

尽管船长接到了电报，他还是决定再试一试。他们用结实的网把海床搜索了一遍。当一只箱子从海底被打捞上来时，甲板上的人们激动不已。船员们开始认为沉船找着了，但海底沉箱内的物品证明他们弄错了。事实上，他们发现的是另一艘沉没多年的船。

木箱内装有水手艾伦·菲尔丁的私人财物，其中有书籍、衣服、照片以及水手收到的妻子的来信。“埃尔科”号船长命令船员尽量从沉船中打捞物品，但没发现什么值钱的东西，不过打捞出来的众多的物品还是引起了大家极大的兴趣。从捞起的一门大炮来看，船长认为那艘船一定是艘巡洋舰。另一只海底沉箱中装的是船上一位军官的财物，其中有一封写于 1943 年 3 月 14 日的信，但没有写完。从这封信中船长了解到沉船的船名是“卡伦”号。打捞到的东西中最有价值的是船上的航海日志，其中有一部分仍然清晰可读。据此，船长可以将所有的那些已经搞清的材料拼凑起来。“卡伦”号当年在为其他船只护航驶往俄国途中突然遭到敌方潜水艇鱼雷的袭击。这一说法在“埃尔科”号返航后得到国防部一位海军官员的证实。那次打捞到的所有物品均被送往军事博物馆。

Comprehension 理解

Give short answers to these questions in your own words as far as possible. Use one complete sentence for each answer.

1 Why did the captain of *Elkor* know that another attempt would be made later to find the sunken ship?

2 What did the crew think when a chest was raised from the bottom?

3 Who was Alan Fielding?

Vocabulary 词汇

Explain the meanings of the following words and phrases as they are used in the passage: instructing (l.4); give up the search (l.4); precious (l.6); tremendous (l.9); were at first under the impression (l.10); wrong (l.11).

Summary writing 摘要写作

In not more than 80 words describe how the items brought to the surface enabled the captain of *Elkor* to identify the lost ship. Use your own words as far as possible. Do not include anything that is not in the last paragraph.

Composition 作文

In not more than 250 words write the page of *Karen*'s log book which was dated March 14th, 1943. Use the ideas given below. Do not write more than four paragraphs.

Title: The last day.

Introduction: Journey has gone well so far — convoy successfully fought off an air attack — early morning — no ships lost.

Development and Conclusion: 10 a.m. First attack by U-boat — ship ahead, the *Dauntless* sunk — men in sea — *Karen* picked up survivors — 720 men — 50 lives lost — crowded on board — attack on U-boat — put it out of action with depth charges. 3.15 p.m. (last entry) — second U-boat attack ...

Letter writing 书信写作

In about 100 words write the unfinished letter referred to in the passage which was written on March 14th, 1943 by a ship's officer.

Key structures and Special difficulties 关键句型和难点

Exercises 练习

1 *which had been searching the Barents Sea*. (l.2) Write sentences using the following: *had been doing* and *had been working*. **(1 KS 62b)**（参见第 2 册第 62 课关键句型 b）

2 *received*. (l.4) Write two sentences illustrating the difference between *receive* and *take*. **(1 SD 4)**（参见第 2 册第 4 课难点）

3 *The sea bed was scoured with powerful nets. There was tremendous excitement on board. A chest was raised from the bottom. The crew were at first under the impression that the lost ship had been found. The contents of the chest proved them wrong.* (ll.8-11) Express these ideas again in not more than two sentences. Compare your answer with the sentences in the passage. **(1 KS 25, KS 49)**（参见第 2 册 25, 49 课关键句型）

4 *the contents of the chest*. (ll.10-11) How would the word *contents* be stressed in this sentence? **(1 SD 93)**（参见第 2 册第 93 课难点）

5 *clothing*. (l.12) Write three sentences using the following words: *cloth, clothes,* and *clothing*. **(1 SD 81a)**（参见第 2 册第 81 课难点 a）

6 *brought*. (l.15) Write three sentences using the following words: *bring, take,* and *fetch*. **(1 SD 29b)**（参见第 2 册第 29 课难点 b）

7 *realized*. (l.16) Write two sentences illustrating the difference between *realize* and *understand*. **(1 SD 20c)**（参见第 2 册第 20 课难点 c）

Multiple choice questions 选择题

Choose the correct answers to the following questions.

Comprehension 理解

1 Why had the salvage operation been a complete failure?
(*a*) They had failed to locate the ship they had been sent to look for.
(*b*) They had not succeeded in finding the Barents Sea.
(*c*) They had found the wrong ship.
(*d*) The captain had not understood his instructions.

2 In ordering as much as possible to be salvaged from the wreck, the captain ________ .
(*a*) expected to find some of the gold bullion
(*b*) hoped, among other things, to establish the identity of the ship
(*c*) thought he would find out that the ship had been a cruiser
(*d*) was looking for more information concerning the dead seaman

3 The log book was the most important find because it ________ .
(*a*) helped to explain how the warship had come to be sunk in the Barents Sea
(*b*) contained a written account of how the *Karen* had been torpedoed
(*c*) provided vital information as to the ship's whereabouts
(*d*) gave the Ministry of Defence information it had known nothing about

Structure 结构

4 The captain knew that ________ the only attempt. (l.5)
(*a*) it was not (*b*) his had not been (*c*) his would not be (*d*) it had not been

5 It was a ship which had been sunk many years before ________ in fact found. (l.11)
(*a*) what they had (*b*) that they had (*c*) had been (*d*) which was

6 They did not find ________ . (l.14)
(*a*) nothing of value (*b*) a valuable thing (*c*) any value (*d*) anything valuable

7 – parts of which ________ . (l.19)
(*a*) it could still be read (*b*) it could still read (*c*) could still be read (*d*) could still read

8 After the *Elkor* had returned home, a naval official ________ . (ll.21-22)
(*a*) had this later confirmed at the Ministry of Defence
(*b*) confirmed this at the Ministry of Defence
(*c*) at the Ministry of Defence confirmed this
(*d*) later at the Ministry of Defence confirmed this

Vocabulary 词汇

9 The ship's captain had received instructions to give up the search ________ a radio message from the mainland. (ll.3-4)
(*a*) on (*b*) by (*c*) with (*d*) in

10 There were books, clothing and photographs, ________ letters ... (ll.12-13)
(*a*) including (*b*) along with (*c*) added to (*d*) beside

11 – an unfinished letter which was ________ March 14th, 1943. (l.17)
(*a*) inscribed (*b*) marked (*c*) dated (*d*) posted on

12 – all the information that had ________ . (l.20)
(*a*) emerged (*b*) alighted (*c*) arisen (*d*) surfaced

LESSON

33 A day to remember 难忘的一天

Listen then answer the question below.

听录音，然后回答以下问题。

What incident began the series of traffic accidents?

just one of those days!

We have all experienced days when everything goes wrong. A day may begin well enough, but suddenly everything seems to get out of control. What invariably happens is that a great number of things choose to go wrong at precisely the same moment. It is as if a single unimportant event set up a chain of reactions. Let us suppose that you are preparing a meal and keeping an eye on the baby at the same time. The telephone rings and this marks the prelude to an unforeseen series of catastrophes. While you are on the phone, the baby pulls the tablecloth off the table, smashing half your best crockery and cutting himself in the process. You hang up hurriedly and attend to baby, crockery, etc. Meanwhile, the meal gets burnt. As if this were not enough to reduce you to tears, your husband arrives, unexpectedly bringing three guests to dinner.

Things can go wrong on a big scale, as a number of people recently discovered in Parramatta, a suburb of Sydney. During the rush hour one evening two cars collided and both drivers began to argue. The woman immediately behind the two cars happened to be a learner. She suddenly got into a panic and stopped her car. This made the driver following her brake hard. His wife was sitting beside him holding a large cake. As she was thrown forward, the cake went right through the windscreen and landed on the road. Seeing a cake flying through the air, a lorry driver who was drawing up alongside the car, pulled up all of a sudden. The lorry was loaded with empty beer bottles and hundreds of them slid off the back of the vehicle and on to the road. This led to yet another angry argument. Meanwhile, the traffic piled up behind. It took the police nearly an hour to get the traffic on the move again. In the meantime, the lorry driver had to sweep up hundreds of broken bottles. Only two stray dogs benefited from all this confusion, for they greedily devoured what was left of the cake. It was just one of those days!

New words and expressions 生词和短语

prelude (l.7)	/ˈpreljuːd/	n.	序幕，前奏	windscreen (l.16)	/ˈwɪndskriːn/	n.	（汽车的）挡风玻璃
unforeseen (l.8)	/ˌʌnfɔːˈsiːn/	adj.	意料之外的	alongside (l.17)	/əˌlɒŋˈsaɪd/	prep.	在……的旁边，与……并排
series (l.8)	/ˈsɪəriːz/	n.	系列				
catastrophe (l.8)	/kəˈtæstrəfi/	n.	大祸，灾难	slide (l.18)	/slaɪd/ (slid /slɪd/, slid)	v.	滑
crockery (l.9)	/ˈkrɒkəri/	n.	陶器，瓦器				
suburb (l.12)	/ˈsʌbɜːb/	n.	郊区	stray (l.21)	/streɪ/	adj.	迷失的，离群的
collide (l.13)	/kəˈlaɪd/	v.	猛撞	confusion (l.21)	/kənˈfjuːʒən/	n.	混乱
learner (l.14)	/ˈlɜːnə/	n.	初学者	greedily (l.21)	/ˈɡriːdɪli/	adv.	贪婪地
panic (l.14)	/ˈpænɪk/	n.	惊慌，恐慌	devour (l.22)	/dɪˈvaʊə/	v.	狼吞虎咽地吃

Notes on the text 课文注释

1 get out of control, 失去控制。

2 It is as if a single unimportant event set up a chain of reactions. 就好像一件无关紧要的小事引起了一连串的连锁反应。as if 引导的从句中用的是虚拟语气；set up, 引起，产生；a chain of, 一连串。

3 keep an eye on, 照看，照管。

4 you are on the phone, 你在接电话。

5 reduce you to tears, 使你流泪。

6 on a big scale, 大规模地。

7 rush hour,（上下班的）高峰时间。

8 draw up, 停住，停下来。

9 pull up, 停车。

10 get the traffic on the move, 使车辆动起来。

参考译文

我们大家都有过事事不顺心的日子。一天开始时，可能还不错，但突然间似乎一切都失去了控制。情况经常是这样的，许许多多的事情都偏偏赶在同一时刻出问题，好像是一件无关紧要的小事引起了一连串的连锁反应。假设你在做饭，同时又在照看孩子。这时电话铃响了，它预示着一连串意想不到的灾难的来临。就在你接电话时，孩子把桌布从桌子上扯了下来，将家中最好的陶瓷餐具半数摔碎，同时也弄伤了他自己。你急急忙忙挂上电话，赶去照看孩子和餐具。这时，饭又烧煳了。好像这一切还不足以使你急得掉泪似的，你的丈夫接着回来了，事先没打招呼就带来 3 个客人吃饭。

就像许多人最近在悉尼郊区帕拉马塔所发现的那样，有时乱子会闹得很大。一天傍晚交通最拥挤时，一辆汽车撞上前面一辆汽车，两个司机争吵起来。紧跟其后的一辆车上的司机碰巧是个初学者，她一惊之下突然把车停了下来。她这一停使得跟在后头的司机也来了个急刹车。司机的妻子正坐在他身边，手里托着块大蛋糕。她往前一冲，蛋糕从挡风玻璃飞了出去掉在马路上。此时，一辆卡车正要在这辆车旁停车，司机看见一块蛋糕从天而降，紧急刹车。卡车上装着空啤酒瓶，成百只瓶子顺势从卡车后面滑出车外落在马路上。这又引起了一场唇枪舌剑的争吵。与此同时，后面的车辆排成了长龙，警察花了将近一个小时才使车辆又开起来。在这段时间里，卡车司机不得不清扫那几百只破瓶子。只有两只野狗从这一片混乱中得到了好处，它们贪婪地吃掉了剩下的蛋糕。这就是事事不顺心的那么一天！

Comprehension 理解

Give short answers to these questions in your own words as far as possible. Use one complete sentence for each answer.

1 What can mark the beginning of an unforeseen series of catastrophes while you are preparing a meal?

2 Why are your husband's guests not welcome?

3 What began all the trouble in Parramatta recently?

Vocabulary 词汇

Explain the meanings of the following words and phrases as they are used in the passage: happens (l.3); precisely (l.4); preparing (l.6); catastrophes (l.8); smashing (l.9); in the process (l.9); reduce you to tears (l.10).

Summary writing 摘要写作

In not more than 80 words describe what happened from the time when the learner driver stopped her car. Use your own words as far as possible. Do not include anything that is not in the last paragraph.

Composition 作文

In not more than 250 words describe a similar 'chain of reactions'. Expand the ideas given below into a plan and provide a suitable title. Your composition should be in three or four paragraphs.

Ideas: Man loaded with parcels — looking for his car — saw one exactly like it — mistook it for his own — found his key with difficulty — tried to open the door — key wouldn't turn — forced the lock — broke the key — dropped the parcels — infuriated — deliberately broke the window of the car — the owner saw him — rushed towards him — called a policeman — the man arrested — tried to explain — was not believed.

Letter writing 书信写作

You have been trying to sell your car and an unknown person has written to you making an offer. Write a reply in about 100 words in three paragraphs accepting the offer and making arrangements for the sale.

Key structures and Special difficulties 关键句型和难点

Exercises 练习

1 *We have all experienced days ... .* (l.1) Write two sentences using the following: *he experienced; a lot of experience.* **(1 SD 31a)** （参见第 2 册第 31 课难点 a）

2 *A day may begin well enough.* (ll.1-2) Write sentences using the following: *good enough; enough money; fairly.* **(1 SD 86)** （参见第 2 册第 86 课难点）

3 *You are on the phone. The baby pulls the tablecloth off the table. He smashes half your best crockery. He cuts himself in the process.* (ll.8-9) Join these sentences together to make one sentence. Compare your answer with the sentence in the passage. **(1 KS 49)** （参见第 2 册第 49 课关键句型）

4 *people recently discovered.* (l.12) Write two sentences illustrating the difference between *discover* and *invent.* **(1 SD 61a)** （参见第 2 册第 61 课难点 a）

5 *His wife was sitting beside him.* (l.15) Write two sentences illustrating the difference between *beside* and *besides.* **(1 SD 18b)** （参见第 2 册第 18 课难点 b）

6 *a lorry driver who was drawing up alongside the car.* (l.17) Explain the meaning of *drawing up* in this sentence. Write sentences using *draw back* and *draw off.* **(1 SD 64)** （参见第 2 册第 64 课难点）

7 *the lorry driver had to sweep up hundreds of broken bottles.* (ll.20-21) Write two sentences illustrating the difference between *had to take* and *should have taken.* **(1 KS 65)** （参见第 2 册第 65 课关键句型）

Multiple choice questions 选择题

Choose the correct answers to the following questions.

Comprehension 理解

1 What would have most upset the woman the day everything went wrong for her?

(*a*) She had not expected her husband to arrive so early.

(*b*) The meal she had cooked for the three guests had got burnt.

(*c*) Her husband had not told her he was bringing anyone to dinner.
(*d*) She had not got enough crockery left to serve the meal with.

2 What might have prevented a chain of reactions following the initial collision?
(*a*) If the two drivers who had collided had not begun to argue.
(*b*) Had there been a more experienced driver behind the two cars.
(*c*) If, instead of panicking, the woman had made no attempt to stop.
(*d*) Had the wife of the man who braked not thrown a cake through the window.

3 There was a second angry argument because ________ .
(*a*) the lorry driver blamed the owner of the cake for his accident
(*b*) the traffic was extremely slow to get on the move again
(*c*) the lorry driver did not think he should be made to sweep up the glass
(*d*) two dogs had devoured what was left of the cake

Structure 结构

4 It is as if a single event that is ________ a chain of reactions. (ll.4-5)
(*a*) no importance set up (*b*) of no importance set up
(*c*) not any important sets up (*d*) not any importance sets up

5 – you are preparing a meal ________ keeping an eye on the baby. (ll.6-7)
(*a*) at the same time (*b*) as you are (*c*) as well (*d*) while

6 As if this ________ you to tears ... (l.10)
(*a*) has not already reduced (*b*) were not already reducing
(*c*) did not already reduce (*d*) would not already reduce

7 Immediately behind the two cars ________ happened to be a learner. (ll.13-14)
(*a*) was a woman who (*b*) a woman
(*c*) the woman (*d*) there was the woman who

8 The police spent nearly an hour ________ the traffic on the move again. (ll.19-20)
(*a*) to get (*b*) until getting (*c*) getting (*d*) having got

Vocabulary 词汇

9 You are preparing a meal and ________ the baby at the same time. (ll.6-7)
(*a*) looking at (*b*) seeing (*c*) watching (*d*) seeing to

10 She stopped her car ________ a sudden panic. (l.14)
(*a*) into (*b*) in (*c*) from (*d*) with

11 Hundreds of them ________ the back of the vehicle ... (ll.18-19)
(*a*) slipped off (*b*) slid down (*c*) slid over (*d*) slipped under

12 They greedily devoured the ________ of the cake. (ll.21-22)
(*a*) left (*b*) leave (*c*) leftover (*d*) remains

LESSON

34 A happy discovery 幸运的发现

Listen then answer the question below.

听录音，然后回答以下问题。

What was the 'happy discovery'?

No one discovers a rarity by chance

Antique shops exert a peculiar fascination on a great many people. The more expensive kind of antique shop where rare objects are beautifully displayed in glass cases to keep them free from dust is usually a forbidding place. But no one has to muster up courage to enter a less pretentious antique shop. There is always hope that in its labyrinth of musty, dark, disordered rooms a real rarity will be found amongst the piles of assorted junk that litter the floors.

No one discovers a rarity by chance. A truly dedicated bargain hunter must have patience, and above all, the ability to recognize the worth of something when he sees it. To do this, he must be at least as knowledgeable as the dealer. Like a scientist bent on making a discovery, he must cherish the hope that one day he will be amply rewarded.

My old friend, Frank Halliday, is just such a person. He has often described to me how he picked up a masterpiece for a mere £50. One Saturday morning, Frank visited an antique shop in my neighbourhood. As he had never been there before, he found a great deal to interest him. The morning passed rapidly and Frank was about to leave when he noticed a large packing case lying on the floor. The dealer told him that it had just come in, but that he could not be bothered to open it. Frank begged him to do so and the dealer reluctantly prised it open. The contents were disappointing. Apart from an interesting-looking carved dagger, the box was full of crockery, much of it broken. Frank gently lifted the crockery out of the box and suddenly noticed a miniature painting at the bottom of the packing case. As its composition and line reminded him of an Italian painting he knew well, he decided to buy it. Glancing at it briefly, the dealer told him that it was worth £50. Frank could hardly conceal his excitement, for he knew that he had made a real discovery. The tiny painting proved to be an unknown masterpiece by Correggio and was worth hundreds of thousands of pounds.

New words and expressions 生词和短语

antique (l.1)	/ˌænˈtiːk/	n.	古董，古玩
fascination (l.1)	/ˌfæsɪˈneɪʃən/	n.	魅力，迷惑力
forbidding (l.4)	/fəˈbɪdɪŋ/	adj.	望而生畏的，望而却步的
muster (l.4)	/ˈmʌstə/	v.	鼓起
pretentious (l.5)	/prɪˈtenʃəs/	adj.	自命不凡的，矫饰的
labyrinth (l.6)	/ˈlæbərɪnθ/	n.	迷宫
musty (l.6)	/ˈmʌsti/	adj.	陈腐的，发霉的
rarity (l.6)	/ˈreərɪti/	n.	稀世珍品
assorted (l.7)	/əˈsɔːtɪd/	adj.	各式各样的
junk (l.7)	/dʒʌŋk/	n.	破烂货，废品
litter (l.7)	/ˈlɪtə/	v.	杂乱地布满
dedicated (l.8)	/ˈdedɪkeɪtɪd/	adj.	专心致志的
bargain hunter (l.8)	/ˌbɑːgɪn-ˈhʌntə/		到处找便宜货买的人

dealer (l.10)	/ˈdiːlə/	*n.*	商人
cherish (l.10)	/ˈtʃerɪʃ/	*v.*	抱有，怀有
amply (l.11)	/ˈæmpəli/	*adv.*	足够地
masterpiece (l.13)	/ˈmɑːstəpiːs/	*n.*	杰作
mere (l.13)	/mɪə/	*adj.*	仅仅的
prise (l.17)	/praɪz/	*v.*	撬开
carve (l.17)	/kɑːv/	*v.*	镌刻
dagger (l.17)	/ˈdægə/	*n.*	短剑，匕首
miniature (l.19)	/ˈmɪnətʃə/	*adj.*	小巧的，小型的
composition (l.19)	/ˌkɒmpəˈzɪʃən/	*n.*	构图

Notes on the text 课文注释

1 muster up courage, 鼓起勇气。

2 above all, 最重要的。

3 be bent on, 决心要。

4 pick up, 在此处有“偶然发现”、“无意中获得”的意思。

5 apart from ..., 除……以外。

6 Correggio, 柯勒乔（1494 — 1534）。意大利著名画家，真名安托尼奥·阿来里。他对色彩对比、光和影的处理方法对 16 到 17 世纪意大利绘画产生了巨大影响。他最著名的作品陈列在意大利巴玛大教堂。

参考译文

古玩店对许多人来说有一种特殊的魅力。高档一点的古玩店为了防尘，把珍品漂亮地陈列在玻璃柜子里，那里往往令人望而却步。而对不太装腔作势的古玩店，无论是谁都不用壮着胆子才敢往里进。人们还常常有希望在发霉、阴暗、杂乱无章、迷宫般的店堂里，从杂乱地摆放在地面上的、一堆堆各式各样的破烂货里找到一件稀世珍品。

无论是谁都不会一下子就发现一件珍品。一个到处找便宜货买的人必须具有耐心，而且最重要的是看到珍品时要有鉴别珍品的能力。要做到这一点，他至少要像古董商一样懂行。他必须像一个专心致志进行探索的科学家那样抱有这样的希望，即终有一天，他的努力会取得丰硕的成果。

我的老朋友弗兰克·哈利戴正是这样一个人。他多次向我详细讲他如何只花 50 英镑便买到一位名家的杰作。一个星期六的上午，弗兰克去了我家附近的一家古玩店。由于他从未去过那儿，结果他发现了许多有趣的东西。上午很快过去了，弗兰克正准备离去，突然看见地板上放着一只体积很大的货箱。古董商告诉他那只货箱刚到不久，但他没有心思把它打开。经弗兰克恳求，古董商才勉强把货箱撬开了。箱内东西令人失望。除了一柄式样别致、雕有花纹的匕首外，货箱内装满了陶器，而且大部分都已破碎。弗兰克轻轻地把陶器拿出箱子，突然发现在箱底有一幅微型画，画面构图与线条使他想起了一幅他所熟悉的意大利画，于是他决定将画买下来。古董商漫不经心看了一眼那幅画，告诉弗兰克那画值 50 英镑。弗兰克几乎无法掩饰自己兴奋的心情，因为他明白自己发现了一件珍品。那幅不大的画原来是柯勒乔的一幅未被发现的杰作，价值几十万英镑。

Comprehension 理解

Give short answers to these questions in your own words as far as possible. Use one complete sentence for each answer.

1 What does a truly dedicated bargain hunter hope to find in the less pretentious kind of antique shop?

2 What qualities must a truly dedicated bargain hunter possess?

3 How much did Frank Halliday pay for his masterpiece?

Vocabulary 词汇

Explain the meanings of the following words and phrases as they are used in the passage: rare objects (l.2); displayed (l.3); piles (l.7); assorted junk (l.7); truly (l.8); bent on (l.10); amply (l.11).

Summary writing 摘要写作

In not more than 80 words describe how Frank Halliday came to discover an unknown masterpiece. Use your own words as far as possible. Do not include anything that is not in the last paragraph.

Composition 作文

In not more than 250 words write a description, real or imaginary, of an antique shop. Use the ideas given below. Do not write more than four paragraphs.

Title: An antique shop.

Introduction: Appearance outside — window display — the sort of people it attracts.

Development: Inside — the dealer — his appearance and character — the shop itself — how objects are displayed — a typical scene during the day — description of customers.

Conclusion: The pleasure of searching for unusual things.

Letter writing 书信写作

You intend to spend your holidays in a country which has a very warm (or very cold) climate. Write a letter of about 100 words in three paragraphs to a friend asking him to advise you about items of clothing you should take with you.

Key structures and Special difficulties 关键句型和难点

Exercises 练习

1 *when he sees it.* (l.9) Write sentences using the following: *the moment he arrives; until he comes;* and *before you leave.* **(1 KS 60c)** (参见第 2 册第 60 课关键句型 c)

2 Explain the difference in the use of *must be* in these two sentences:

To do this, he *must be* at least as knowledgeable as the dealer. (ll.9-10)

You *must be* very tired after driving so many miles. **(1 KS 17)** (参见第 2 册第 17 课关键句型)

3 Supply *a(n)* or *the* where necessary in the following. Do not refer to the passage until you finish the exercise.

One Saturday morning, ________ Frank visited ________ antique shop in my neighbourhood. As he had never been there before, he found ________ great deal to interest him. ________ morning passed rapidly and ________ Frank was about to leave when he noticed ________ large packing case lying on ________ floor. ________ dealer told him that it had just come in, but that he could not be bothered to open it. ________ Frank begged him to do so and ________ dealer reluctantly prised it open. ________ contents were disappointing. Apart from ________ interesting-looking carved dagger, ________ box was full of ________ crockery, much of it broken. (ll.13-18) **(1 KS 6, 30, 54)**

(参见第 2 册第 6, 30, 54 课关键句型)

4 *he noticed.* (l.15) Write two sentences illustrating the difference between *notice* and *remark*. **(1 SD 41)**

(参见第 2 册第 41 课难点)

Multiple choice questions 选择题

Choose the correct answers to the following questions.

Comprehension 理解

1 When Frank Halliday visited an antique shop in the writer's neighbourhood ________ .

(*a*) it was by no means the first time he had picked up a masterpiece for £50

(*b*) he displayed the kind of perseverance needed to find a rarity

(*c*) he spent a short time searching in the morning before deciding to leave

(*d*) he found most of what he looked at rather boring

2 How did Frank come to discover the miniature by Correggio?

(*a*) He was shown it by the dealer who did not realize its worth.

(*b*) He persuaded the dealer to open the box in which it happened to be.

(*c*) By concealing his excitement on being told the price wanted for it.

(*d*) By lifting a box of crockery which had been concealing the painting.

3 Frank decided to buy the miniature because ________ .

(*a*) it was an Italian painting he knew well

(*b*) it only cost £50

(*c*) he knew he had made a real discovery

(*d*) it was similar to a painting he knew well

Structure 结构

4 Rare objects are beautifully displayed in glass cases ________ them free from dust. (ll.2-4)

(*a*) which are keeping (*b*) which keep (*c*) who keep (*d*) and kept

5 But it is not necessary ________ up courage to enter an ordinary shop. (ll.4-5)

(*a*) for nobody to muster (*b*) to have mustered

(*c*) that one musters (*d*) for anyone to muster

6 A bargain hunter must have patience, and above all, ________ recognize the worth of ... (ll.8-9)

(*a*) can (*b*) is able to (*c*) be able to (*d*) be capable of

7 ________ there, he found a great deal to interest him. (ll.13-14)

(*a*) This being his first visit (*b*) Never having been before

(*c*) This being his first time to visit (*d*) Having never been before

8 The dealer told him it ________ him £50. (ll.20-21)

(*a*) cost (*b*) had cost (*c*) will cost (*d*) would cost

Vocabulary 词汇

9 Frank visited an antique shop ________ . (l.13)

(*a*) next door (*b*) in my county (*c*) near my home (*d*) owned by my neighbour

10 Frank was ________ leaving when ... (ll.14-15)

(*a*) almost (*b*) just (*c*) only (*d*) hardly

11 A case which needs prising open has probably been ________ ... (ll.15-17)

(*a*) nailed down (*b*) roped (*c*) locked (*d*) unlocked

12 The dealer gave it a brief ________ and told him ... (ll.20-21)

(*a*) peer (*b*) eye (*c*) glance (*d*) regard

LESSON

35 Justice was done 伸张正义

the cry was repeated several times

Listen then answer the question below.

听录音，然后回答以下问题。

The word 'justice' is given two different meanings in the text. What is the distinction between them?

The word 'justice' is usually associated with courts of law. We might say that justice has been done when a man's innocence or guilt has been proved beyond doubt. Justice is part of the complex machinery of the law. Those who seek it undertake an arduous journey and can never be sure that they will find it. Judges, however wise or eminent, are human and can make mistakes.

There are rare instances when justice almost ceases to be an abstract concept. Reward or punishment are meted out quite independent of human interference. At such times, justice acts like a living force. When we use a phrase like 'it serves him right', we are, in part, admitting that a certain set of circumstances has enabled justice to act of its own accord.

When a thief was caught on the premises of a large jewellery store one morning, the shop assistants must have found it impossible to resist the temptation to say 'it serves him right'. The shop was an old converted house with many large, disused fireplaces and tall, narrow chimneys. Towards midday, a girl heard a muffled cry coming from behind one of the walls. As the cry was repeated several times, she ran to tell the manager who promptly rang up the fire brigade. The cry had certainly come from one of the chimneys, but as there were so many of them, the fire fighters could not be certain which one it was. They located the right chimney by tapping at the walls and listening for the man's cries. After chipping through a wall which was eighteen inches thick, they found that a man had been trapped in the chimney. As it was extremely narrow, the man was unable to move, but the fire fighters were eventually able to free him by cutting a huge hole in the wall. The sorry-looking, blackened figure that emerged, admitted at once that he had tried to break into the shop during the night but had got stuck in the chimney. He had been there for nearly ten hours. Justice had been done even before the man was handed over to the police.

New words and expressions 生词和短语

justice (title)	/ˈdʒʌstɪs/	*n.*	正义，公正；司法
court (l.1)	/kɔːt/	*n.*	法院
law (l.1)	/lɔː/	*n.*	法律
innocence (l.2)	/ˈɪnəsəns/	*n.*	无辜
undertake (l.4)	/ˌʌndəˈteɪk/	*v.*	承担；着手做
arduous (l.4)	/ˈɑːdjuəs/	*adj.*	艰苦的，艰难的
abstract (l.7)	/ˈæbstrækt/	*adj.*	抽象的
concept (l.7)	/ˈkɒnsept/	*n.*	概念，观念
mete out (l.8)	/miːt-aʊt/		给予，处置
interference (l.8)	/ˌɪntəˈfɪərəns/	*n.*	干涉
accord (l.10)	/əˈkɔːd/	*n.*	一致
premises (l.11)	/ˈpremɪsɪz/	*n.*	（复数）房屋
convert (l.12)	/kənˈvɜːt/	*v.*	转变，改变
disused (l.13)	/ˌdɪsˈjuːzd/	*adj.*	不再用的，废弃的
fireplace (l.13)	/ˈfaɪəpleɪs/	*n.*	壁炉
muffled (l.13)	/ˈmʌfəld/	*adj.*	沉闷的，模糊不清的
chip (l.17)	/tʃɪp/	*v.*	砍，削，凿
blacken (l.20)	/ˈblækən/	*v.*	使变黑
emerge (l.20)	/ɪˈmɜːdʒ/	*v.*	（从某处）出现

Notes on the text 课文注释

1 beyond doubt, 确凿无疑。

2 however wise or eminent, 不管他们是多么精明、多么杰出。

however 为连接副词，作“不管……如何”解，所引导的让步状语从句中经常可以省略某些词，此处省略了 they are。

3 quite independent of human interference, 完全不受人的干预。be independent of, 不受。

4 it serves him right, 他罪有应得。

5 in part, 部分地，在某种程度上。

6 of its own accord, 自愿地，自动地。

7 impossible to resist the temptation to say ..., 情不自禁地说……。

参考译文

“正义”这个词常常是同法庭联系在一起的。当某人被证据确凿地证明无罪或有罪的时候，我们也许会说正义得到了伸张。正义是复杂的法律体系的组成部分。那些寻求正义的人走的是一条崎岖的道路，从来没有把握他们最终将找到正义。法官无论如何聪明与有名，毕竟也是人，也会出差错的。

在个别情况下，正义不再是一种抽象概念。奖惩的实施是不受人的意志支配的。在这种时候，正义像一种有生命的力量行使其职能。当我们说“他罪有应得”这句话的时候，我们部分地承认了某种特定的环境使得正义自动地起了作用。

一天上午，当一个小偷在一家大型珠宝店里被人抓住的时候，店员一定会忍不住说：“他罪有应得。”那是一座老式的、经过改造的房子，店里有许多废置不用的大壁炉和又高又窄的烟囱。快到中午的时候，一个女售货员听见从一堵墙里传出一种闷声闷气的叫声。由于这种喊叫声重复了几次，她跑去报告了经理，经理当即给消防队挂了电话。喊叫声肯定是从烟囱里传出来的，然而，因为烟囱太多，消防队员无法确定到底是哪一个。他们通过叩击烟囱倾听那人的喊叫声而确定了传出声音的那个烟囱。他们凿透了 18 英寸厚的墙壁，发现有个人卡在了烟囱里。由于烟囱太窄，那人无法动弹。消防队员在墙上挖了个大洞，才终于把他解救出来。那个看起来满脸沮丧、浑身漆黑的家伙从烟囱里一出来，就承认头天夜里他企图到店里行窃，但让烟囱卡住了。他已经在烟囱里被困了将近 10 个小时。甚至在那人还没被送交给警察之前，正义就已得到了伸张。

Comprehension 理解

Give short answers to these questions in your own words as far as possible. Use one complete sentence for each answer.

1 What is the word *justice* usually associated with?

2 Why can those who seek justice never be sure that they will find it?

3 When does justice seem to act like a living force?

Vocabulary 词汇

Explain the meanings of the following words and phrases as they are used in the passage: seek (l.4); arduous (l.4); eminent (l.6); instances (l.7); ceases (l.7); independent of (l.8); of its own accord (l.10).

Summary writing 摘要写作

In not more than 80 words describe how the thief came to be discovered up the chimney and how he was freed. Use your own words as far as possible. Do not include anything that is not in the last paragraph.

Composition 作文

In not more than 250 words write an imaginary account of the thief's experiences up to the time he was freed by fire fighters. Expand the ideas given below into a plan and provide a suitable title. Your composition should be in three or four paragraphs.

Ideas: Planning the theft — kept close watch on shop — noticed chimneys — one night climbed on to roof — chimney seemed wide — went down — stuck — climbed up again — went down another chimney — again got stuck — could neither climb up nor down — shouted for help — everything dark and silent — frightened — shouted next morning — freed by firefighters.

Letter writing 书信写作

You recently quarrelled with a friend. Write him a letter of about 100 words in three paragraphs apologizing for the incident and suggesting that you should both meet soon.

Key structures and Special difficulties 关键句型和难点

Exercises 练习

1 *We might say that justice has been done ...* . (ll.1-2)
Complete the following sentences. **(1 KS 15)**（参见第 2 册第 15 课关键句型）
He says that ________ .
He wants to know if ________ .
He believes that ________ .

2 *when a man's innocence or guilt has been proved beyond doubt.* (ll.2-3) Write sentences using the following: *The moment he has arrived ...; Now that you have finished ...* . **(1 KS 61c)**（参见第 2 册 61 课关键句型 c）

3 *They chipped through a wall. It was eighteen inches thick. They found a man. He had been trapped in the chimney.* (ll.17-18) Join these sentences together to make a single sentence. Compare your answer with the sentence in the passage. **(1 KS 49)**（参见第 2 册第 49 课关键句型）

4 *they found that a man had been trapped in the chimney*. (l.18) What is the plural of the following words: *chimney, valley, baby, day, hobby, army, money, victory, turkey* and *storey.* **(SD 18)**（参见第 18 课难点）

5 Give the correct form of the verbs in parentheses. Do not refer to the passage until you finish the exercise.
The sorry-looking, blackened figure that emerged, ________ (admit) at once that he ________ (try) to break into the shop during the night but ________ (get) stuck in the chimney. He ________ (be) there for nearly ten hours. Justice ________ (do) even before the man was handed over to the police. (ll.20-22) **(1 KS 38)**（参见第 2 册第 38 课关键句型）

Multiple choice questions 选择题

Choose the correct answers to the following questions.

Comprehension 理解

1 In what circumstances may justice take effect outside the courts of law?
(*a*) When a judge has proved neither eminent nor wise.
(*b*) When it has not been possible to prove a man's guilt beyond any doubt.
(*c*) When justice has been done without the interference of a human agent.
(*d*) When, for example, a man is caught and handed over to the police.

2 Why did the manager ring up the fire brigade?

(*a*) He thought that one of the chimneys was on fire.

(*b*) He expected them to be of most help in the circumstances.

(*c*) He had not realized there was a criminal on the premises.

(*d*) He thought whoever was stuck might be a member of the fire brigade.

3 The fire fighters ascertained which chimney the man was in by ________ .

(*a*) deciding which of the many cries came from the right chimney

(*b*) listening for the man's response to their taps on the walls

(*c*) chipping through a wall which was eighteen inches thick

(*d*) cutting a huge hole in the wall

Structure 结构

4 ________ wise or eminent, judges are human and can make mistakes. (ll.5-6)

(*a*) Whether (*b*) Either (*c*) How much (*d*) No matter how

5 In our use of a phrase like 'it serves him right' ________ , in part, admitting ... (ll.8-10)

(*a*) is (*b*) it is (*c*) we are (*d*) and in

6 The staff must have found it impossible ________ to say 'it serves him right'. (ll.11-12)

(*a*) they were not tempted (*b*) for them not to be tempted

(*c*) to be tempted (*d*) not to be tempted

7 ________ several times, she ran to tell the manager. (l.14)

(*a*) Repeating the cry (*b*) While the cry was repeated

(*c*) The cry being repeated (*d*) Having repeated the cry

8 – admitted that ________ to break into the shop during the night, he had got stuck in the chimney. (ll.20-21)

(*a*) although he had tried (*b*) while he has tried

(*c*) in trying (*d*) it was he who had tried

Vocabulary 词汇

9 She ________ the cry several times, so she ran ... (ll.14-15)

(*a*) heard (*b*) listened to (*c*) listened for (*d*) earmarked

10 They located the chimney ________ by tapping ... (ll.16-17)

(*a*) on the right (*b*) well (*c*) right away (*d*) correctly

11 The blackened figure that emerged was ________ sight. (l.20)

(*a*) an ugly (*b*) a sorry (*c*) an apologetic (*d*) a poor

12 The sorry-looking blackened figure that ________ , admitted at once ... (l.20)

(*a*) came to light (*b*) came up (*c*) went out (*d*) got out

LESSON

36 A chance in a million 百万分之一的机遇

Listen then answer the question below.

听录音，然后回答以下问题。

What was the chance in a million?

recently found a brother

We are less credulous than we used to be. In the nineteenth century, a novelist would bring his story to a conclusion by presenting his readers with a series of coincidences — most of them wildly improbable. Readers happily accepted the fact that an obscure maidservant was really the hero's mother. A long-lost brother, who was presumed dead, was really alive all the time and wickedly plotting to bring about the hero's downfall. And so on. Modern readers would find such naive solutions totally unacceptable. Yet, in real life, circumstances do sometimes conspire to bring about coincidences which anyone but a nineteenth century novelist would find incredible.

When I was a boy, my grandfather told me how a German taxi driver, Franz Bussman, found a brother who was thought to have been killed twenty years before. While on a walking tour with his wife, he stopped to talk to a workman. After they had gone on, Mrs. Bussman commented on the workman's close resemblance to her husband and even suggested that he might be his brother. Franz poured scorn on the idea, pointing out that his brother had been killed in action during the war. Though Mrs. Bussman was fully acquainted with this story, she thought that there was a chance in a million that she might be right. A few days later, she sent a boy to the workman to ask him if his name was Hans Bussman. Needless to say, the man's name was Hans Bussman and he really was Franz's long-lost brother. When the brothers were reunited, Hans explained how it was that he was still alive. After having been wounded towards the end of the war, he had been sent to hospital and was separated from his unit. The hospital had been bombed and Hans had made his way back into Western Germany on foot. Meanwhile, his unit was lost and all records of him had been destroyed. Hans returned to his family home, but the house had been bombed and no one in the neighbourhood knew what had become of the inhabitants. Assuming that his family had been killed during an air raid, Hans settled down in a village fifty miles away where he had remained ever since.

New words and expressions 生词和短语

credulous (l.1)	/ˈkredjʊləs/	*adj.*	轻信的
improbable (l.4)	/ɪmˈprɒbəbəl/	*adj.*	不大可能的
obscure (l.4)	/əbˈskjʊə/	*adj.*	不起眼的
maidservant (l.5)	/ˈmeɪdˌsɜːvənt/	*n.*	女仆，女佣
presume (l.6)	/prɪˈzjuːm/	*v.*	假定
wickedly (l.6)	/ˈwɪkɪdli/	*adv.*	心眼坏地，居心叵测地
plot (l.7)	/plɒt/	*v.*	密谋
downfall (l.7)	/ˈdaʊnfɔːl/	*n.*	倒台，垮台
naive (l.8)	/naɪˈiːv/	*adj.*	天真的
unacceptable (l.8)	/ˌʌnəkˈseptəbəl/	*adj.*	不能接受的
conspire (l.9)	/kənˈspaɪə/	*v.*	（事件）巧合促成
incredible (l.9)	/ɪnˈkredəbəl/	*adj.*	难以置信的
resemblance (l.13)	/rɪˈzembləns/	*n.*	相似
scorn (l.13)	/skɔːn/	*n.*	嘲弄，挖苦
acquaint (l.15)	/əˈkweɪnt/	*v.*	使了解
reunite (l.18)	/ˌriːjuːˈnaɪt/	*v.*	使团聚
assume (l.22)	/əˈsjuːm/	*v.*	假定，认为

Notes on the text 课文注释

1 bring ... to a conclusion, 作“使……结束”讲。

2 bring about, 造成，导致。

3 and so on, 等等，诸如此类。

4 do sometimes conspire 中，do 为助动词，对谓语动词起强调作用。

5 while on a walking tour ...,
while 后面省略了主谓结构 he was。在表示时间、地点、条件、让步等的状语从句中，从句的主语如与主句的主语相同，常省略从句的主语和谓语。

6 pour scorn on ..., 作“讥笑……”讲。

7 point out, 指出，提请注意。

8 be acquainted with, 已知道。

9 needless to say, 不用说，当然。

10 become of, 结果如何，发生了……情况。

参考译文

我们不再像以往那样轻易相信别人了。在 19 世纪，小说家常在小说结尾处给读者准备一系列巧合——大部分是牵强附会，极不可能的。当时的读者却愉快地接受这样一些事实：一个低贱的女佣实际上是主人公的母亲；主人公一位长期失散的兄弟，大家都以为死了，实际上一直活着，并且正在策划暗算主人公；如此等等。现代读者会觉得这种天真的结局完全无法接受。不过，在现实生活中，有时确实会出现一些巧合。这些巧合除了 19 世纪小说家外谁也不会相信。

当我是个孩子的时候，我祖父给我讲了一位德国出租汽车司机弗朗兹·巴斯曼如何找到了据说已在 20 年前死去的兄弟的事。一次，他与妻子徒步旅行。途中，他停下来与一个工人交谈，接着他们继续往前走去。巴斯曼夫人说那工人与她丈夫相貌很像，甚至猜测他可能就是她丈夫的兄弟。弗朗兹对此不屑一顾，指出他兄弟已经在战争中阵亡了。尽管巴斯曼夫人熟知这个情况，但她仍然认为自己的想法有百万分之一的可能性。几天后，她派了一个男孩去问那人是否叫汉斯·巴斯曼。不出巴斯曼夫人所料，那人的名字真是汉斯·巴斯曼，他确实是弗朗兹失散了多年的兄弟。兄弟俩团聚时，汉斯说明了他活下来的经过。战争即将结束时，他负伤被送进医院，并与部队失去联系。医院遭到轰炸，汉斯步行回到了西德。与此同时，他所在的部队被击溃，他的所有档案材料全部毁于战火。汉斯重返故里，但他的家已被炸毁，左邻右舍谁也不知原住户的下落。汉斯以为全家人都在空袭中遇难，于是便在距此 50 英里外的一座村子里定居下来。

Comprehension 理解

Give short answers to these questions in your own words as far as possible. Use one complete sentence for each answer.

1 How did many nineteenth century novels end?

2 Why was Mrs. Bussman struck by the workman's appearance?

3 How did Mrs. Bussman find out the identity of the workman?

Vocabulary 词汇

Explain the meanings of the following words and phrases as they are used in the passage: credulous (l.1); a conclusion (l.2); improbable (l.4); presumed (l.6); plotting (l.7); totally (l.8); bring about (l.9).

Summary writing 摘要写作

In not more than 80 words write an account of what happened to Hans Bussman from the time he was wounded to the time he was reunited with his brother. Use your own words as far as possible. Do not include anything that is not in the last paragraph.

Composition 作文

In not more than 250 words write an imaginary account of Franz Bussman's life story up to the time he was reunited with his brother. Use the ideas given below. Do not write more than four paragraphs.

Title: The past.

Introduction: Tried to get information about Hans — none available — gave up search.

Development: Found it hard to settle down — moved from place to place and from job to job — how he met Mrs. Bussman — marriage — settled down at last — became a cook — disliked the work — went into partnership with a friend — became a taxi driver — once visited home town — block of flats where his house used to be — no one remembered him.

Conclusion: Future plans now that Hans has been found.

Letter writing 书信写作

Write a letter of about 100 words in three paragraphs to your employer informing him that you will be absent from work for a few days because you are ill. Point out anything important that should be attended to in your absence and say when you hope to be back.

Key structures and Special difficulties 关键句型和难点

Exercises 练习

1 *We are less credulous than we used to be. In the nineteenth century, a novelist would bring his story ... .* (ll.1-2) Supply *used to* and *would* in the following:
When I was young I ________ have a lot more free time than I do now. I ________ live near my work and ... always get home early. Sometimes I ________ do a bit of gardening or go for a long walk. **(1 KS 55b)**（参见第 2 册第 55 课关键句型 b）

2 *Readers happily accepted the fact.* (l.4) Write two sentences illustrating the difference between *accept* and *agree*. **(1 SD 65b)**（参见第 2 册第 65 课难点 b）

3 *the hero's mother*. (l.5) Supply apostrophes in the following: *Georges umbrella; that womans handbag; Keats poetry; the childrens clothes; the soldiers uniforms; in six hours time; a hundred pounds worth.* **(1 SD 13)**（参见第 2 册第 13 课难点）

4 *After having been wounded ... .* (l.18) Write two sentences beginning with *After having been ... .* **(1 KS 69)**（参见第 2 册第 69 课关键句型）

Multiple choice questions 选择题

Choose the correct answers to the following questions.

Comprehension 理解

1 What would a modern reader find totally unacceptable in a novel today?
(*a*) Having for a hero a man once presumed dead.
(*b*) The happiness a hero might feel on being reunited with his mother.
(*c*) Any character being so wicked as to plot against the hero.
(*d*) Two brothers, each presuming the other long since dead, meeting again by chance.

2 When Mrs. Bussman suggested that the workman might be Franz's brother ________ .
(*a*) she was told for the first time that Hans had been killed
(*b*) Franz objected to the idea of being associated with a workman
(*c*) Franz was so sure his brother was dead he did not take her seriously
(*d*) they were both too shy to ask the workman if this was so themselves

3 What did Hans Bussman do immediately after the war was over?
(*a*) He went to hospital to have his wounds attended to.
(*b*) He deserted his unit and walked back to his home town.
(*c*) He inquired after his family's whereabouts but found no trace of them.
(*d*) He settled in a village near his home, hoping his family would find him.

Structure 结构

4 – his readers with a series of coincidences ________ wildly improbable. (ll.2-4)
(*a*) mostly being (*b*) most of which were
(*c*) most of them were (*d*) which would be most

5 A long-lost brother had not in fact died and ________ to bring about the hero's downfall. (ll.5-7)
(*a*) wickedly plotting (*b*) wickedly plotted
(*c*) been wickedly plotting (*d*) had been wickedly plotting

6 He stopped ________ . (ll.11-12)
(*a*) in order to talk to a workman (*b*) a workman for a talk
(*c*) talking to a workman (*d*) so that he talked to a workman

7 She sent a boy to ask the workman ________ . (l.16)
(*a*) what was he called (*b*) what he was called
(*c*) how he was called (*d*) if he was called

8 Meanwhile his unit was lost and ________ had been destroyed. (ll.20-21)
(*a*) each of his records (*b*) all records of him (*c*) all records of his (*d*) every record of his

Vocabulary 词汇

9 He found a brother who was thought to have been killed twenty years ________ . (ll.10-11)
(*a*) ago (*b*) back (*c*) before hand (*d*) previously

10 Mrs. Bussman told her husband that he and the workman ________ ... (ll.12-13)
(*a*) had a close look (*b*) had the same look
(*c*) looked very alike (*d*) looked the same way

11 – there was the ________ chance she might be right. (l.15)
(*a*) remotest (*b*) scarcest (*c*) greatest (*d*) lightest

12 – how it had ________ that he was still alive. (l.18)
(*a*) become (*b*) arrived (*c*) resulted (*d*) come about

LESSON

37 The Westhaven Express

开往威斯特海温的快车

Listen then answer the question below.

听录音，然后回答以下问题。

What was the mistake the author made?

an unshakable faith in timetables

We have learnt to expect that trains will be punctual. After years of conditioning, most of us have developed an unshakable faith in railway timetables. Ships may be delayed by storms; flights may be cancelled because of bad weather; but trains must be on time. Only an exceptionally heavy snowfall might temporarily dislocate railway services. It is all too easy to blame the railway authorities when something does go wrong. The truth is that when mistakes occur, they are more likely to be *ours* than *theirs*.

After consulting my railway timetable, I noted with satisfaction that there was an express train to Westhaven. It went direct from my local station and the journey lasted a mere hour and seventeen minutes. When I boarded the train, I could not help noticing that a great many local people got on as well. At the time, this did not strike me as odd. I reflected that there must be a great many people besides myself who wished to take advantage of this excellent service. Neither was I surprised when the train stopped at Widley, a tiny station a few miles along the line. Even a mighty express train can be held up by signals. But when the train dawdled at station after station, I began to wonder. It suddenly dawned on me that this express was not roaring down the line at ninety miles an hour, but barely chugging along at thirty. One hour and seventeen minutes passed and we had not even covered half the distance. I asked a passenger if this was the Westhaven Express, but he had not even heard of it. I determined to lodge a complaint as soon as we arrived. Two hours later, I was talking angrily to the station master at Westhaven. When he denied the train's existence, I borrowed his copy of the timetable. There was a note of triumph in my voice when I told him that it was there in black and white. Glancing at it briefly, he told me to look again. A tiny asterisk conducted me to a footnote at the bottom of the page. It said: 'This service has been suspended.'

New words and expressions 生词和短语

express (title)	/ɪk'spres/	*n.*	快车	dislocate (l.5)	/'dɪsləkeɪt/	*v.*	打乱（计划等）
		adj.	高速的	blame (l.6)	/bleɪm/	*v.*	责怪
punctual (l.1)	/'pʌŋktʃuəl/	*adj.*	准时的	consult (l.9)	/kən'sʌlt/	*v.*	请教，查阅
condition (l.2)	/kən'dɪʃən/	*v.*	使习惯于	direct (l.10)	/dɪ'rekt/	*adv.*	径直地
unshakable (l.2)	/ʌn'ʃeɪkəbəl/	*adj.*	不可动摇的	odd (l.12)	/ɒd/	*adj.*	奇怪的，异常的
faith (l.2)	/feɪθ/	*n.*	信任	reflect (l.12)	/rɪ'flekt/	*v.*	细想
cancel (l.4)	/'kænsəl/	*v.*	取消	advantage (l.13)	/əd'vɑːntɪdʒ/	*n.*	优势
exceptionally (l.5)	/ɪk'sepʃənəli/	*adv.*	极其，非常	mighty (l.14)	/'maɪti/	*adj.*	强大的，有力的

dawdle (l.15)	/ˈdɔːdl/	v.	慢吞吞地动或做
chug (l.16)	/tʃʌg/	v.	咔嚓咔嚓地响
lodge (l.18)	/lɒdʒ/	v.	提出
complaint (l.18)	/kəmˈpleɪnt/	n.	抱怨
triumph (l.20)	/ˈtraɪəmf/	n.	胜利
asterisk (l.21)	/ˈæstərɪsk/	n.	星号（*）
conduct (l.21)	/kənˈdʌkt/	v.	引向，引导

Notes on the text 课文注释

1 they are more likely to be *ours* than *theirs*, 这些错误往往是我们而不是铁路当局造成的。

they 指 mistakes；*ours, theirs* 此处用斜体字表示强调，应该重读。

2 I could not help noticing that ..., 我不禁注意到……，can't help doing 是"禁不住……"的意思。

3 strike me as odd, 使我感到奇怪。

4 take advantage of, 利用。

5 Neither was I surprised, 这是以 neither 开头的句子，要用倒装语序。

6 It suddenly dawned on me ..., 我突然明白了，……。

7 a note of triumph, 胜利者的调子。

8 in black and white, 白纸黑字。

参考译文

我们已经习惯于相信火车总是准点的。经过多年的适应，大多数人对火车时刻表产生了一种不可动摇的信念。轮船船期可能因风暴而推延，飞机航班可能因恶劣天气而取消，唯有火车必然是准点的。只有非同寻常的大雪才可能暂时打乱铁路运行。因此，一旦铁路上真出了问题，人们便不假思索地责备铁路当局。事实上，出错的很可能是我们自己，而不是铁路当局。

我查看了列车时刻表，满意地了解到有一趟去威斯特海温的快车。这是趟直达车，旅途总共才需 1 小时 17 分钟。上车后，我不禁注意到许多当地人也上了车。一开始，我并不感到奇怪，我想除我之外，想利用快车之便的也一定大有人在。火车开出几英里即在一个叫威德里的小站停了下来。对此，我也不觉得奇怪，因为即便是特别快车也可能被信号拦住。但是，当火车一站接着一站往前蠕动时，我便产生了怀疑。我突然感到这趟快车并没以时速 90 英里的速度呼啸前进，而是咔嚓咔嚓地向前爬行，时速仅 30 英里。1 小时 17 分过去了，走了还不到一半路程。我问一位乘客，这是不是开往威斯特海温的那趟快车，他说从未听说过有这么一趟快车。我决定一到目的地就给铁路部门提意见。两小时后，我气呼呼地同威斯特海温站站长说起此事。他说根本没有这趟车。于是我借了他本人的列车时刻表，我带着一种胜利者的口吻告诉他那趟车白纸黑字、明明白白印在时刻表上。他迅速地扫视了一眼，让我再看一遍。一个小小的星形符号把我的目光引到了那页底部的一个说明上。上面写着："此趟列车暂停运营。"

Comprehension 理解

Give short answers to these questions in your own words as far as possible. Use one complete sentence for each answer.

1 Why have we developed an unshakable faith in railway timetables?

2 How long was the journey from the writer's village to Westhaven supposed to take by express train?

3 How did the writer explain the fact that many local people boarded the train at the same time as he did?

Vocabulary 词汇

Explain the meanings of the following words and phrases as they are used in the passage: punctual (l.1); unshakable faith (l.2); delayed (l.3); cancelled (l.4); temporarily dislocate (l.5); consulting (l.9); a mere (l.10).

Summary writing 摘要写作

In not more than 80 words write an account of the writer's experiences from the moment he boarded the train. Use your own words as far as possible. Do not include anything that is not in the last paragraph.

Composition 作文

In not more than 250 words describe a journey by train. Though you wished to take a slow train, you accidentally got on a fast one. Expand the ideas given below into a plan and provide a suitable title. Your composition should not be more than four paragraphs.

Ideas: Got on train — expected it to stop — prepared to alight — it went straight on — very fast — you asked passengers — learnt it was an express — ticket collector came along — you explained situation — had to pay full fare — journey lasted two hours — arrived miles away from destination — no fast train back — had to board a slow one!

Letter writing 书信写作

A young couple you know have just had their first child: a baby girl. Write a letter of about 100 words in three paragraphs congratulating them. Inquire about the health of mother and child and say that you hope to be able to visit them soon.

Key structures and Special difficulties 关键句型和难点

Exercises 练习

1 *It is all too easy to blame the railway authorities.* (l.6) Note this pattern. Join the following sentences using the words in parentheses: **(1 SD 85)** (参见第 2 册第 85 课难点)

The wall is high. I cannot climb it. (too)

The wall is low. I can climb it. (enough)

2 *I could not help noticing.* (l.11) Complete the following sentences. **(1 KS 68)** (参见第 2 册第 68 课关键句型)

I can't stand ________ .

I don't mind ________ .

3 *Neither was I surprised* ... . (l.13) Write sentences beginning with the following words: *Never* ...; *Hardly* ...; *Little* ... . **(SD 5)** (参见第 5 课难点)

4 *seventeen minutes passed.* (ll.16-17) Write two sentences illustrating the difference between *passed* and *past*. **(1 SD 33a)** (参见第 2 册第 33 课难点 a)

5 *he denied the train's existence.* (l.19) Write two sentences illustrating the difference between *refuse* and *deny*. **(1 SD 29a)** (参见第 2 册第 29 课难点 a)

6 *I borrowed his copy of the timetable.* (ll.19-20) Write two sentences illustrating the difference between *borrow* and *lend*. **(1 SD 11b)** (参见第 2 册第 11 课难点 b)

Multiple choice questions 选择题

Choose the correct answers to the following questions.

Comprehension 理解

1 When the writer consulted his railway timetable ________ .

(*a*) he wanted to find out how long the express train to Westhaven took

(*b*) he wanted to know the quickest way of getting to Westhaven by rail

(*c*) he did not notice how many stations there were on the way to Westhaven

(*d*) he misread the information concerning the time the journey took

2 At what point did the writer realize that the train was not travelling at the speed of an express train?

(*a*) When the train had reached the station after Widley.

(*b*) When the train had been held up by signals.

(*c*) After the train had stopped at several small stations.

(*d*) After the train had covered a distance of thirty miles.

3 When the writer went to the station master, he complained about ________ .

(*a*) the train scheduled as an express train having in fact been a slow one

(*b*) the lack of colour in the timetable

(*c*) the lack of any express trains from his local station to Westhaven

(*d*) the fact that the Westhaven express had been suspended from service

Structure 结构

4 We have learnt to expect ________ punctual. (l.1)

(*a*) trains being (*b*) trains to be (*c*) of trains being (*d*) trains are going to be

5 ________ exceptionally heavily might railway services be temporarily dislocated. (ll.5-6)

(*a*) If only it snowed (*b*) Only in case it snows

(*c*) Only were it to snow (*d*) Only when snow

6 The express train went direct from my local station to Westhaven ________ a mere hour and seventeen minutes. (l.10)

(*a*) in (*b*) lasting (*c*) a journey which lasted (*d*) a journey of

7 One hour and seventeen minutes passed ________ still to cover half the distance. (ll.16-17)

(*a*) before we had (*b*) before having (*c*) when we had (*d*) and we had

8 When he denied the train's existence, I asked if I ________ borrow his copy. (ll.19-20)

(*a*) can (*b*) may (*c*) might (*d*) was able to

Vocabulary 词汇

9 Even a mighty express train can be ________ by signals. (l.14)

(*a*) halted (*b*) retarded (*c*) slowed up (*d*) delayed

10 I determined to lodge a complaint ________ on arrival. (l.18)

(*a*) firstly (*b*) punctually (*c*) straight (*d*) immediately

11 ________ , I told him that it was there in black and white. (ll.20-21)

(*a*) Noting my triumph (*b*) Sounding triumphant

(*c*) On a triumphant note (*d*) In my triumphant voice

12 Glancing at it briefly, he told me I should ________ . (l.21)

(*a*) take another look (*b*) review it (*c*) overlook it (*d*) have second sight

LESSON

38 The first calendar 最早的日历

Listen then answer the question below.

听录音，然后回答以下问题。

What is the importance of the dots, lines, and symbols engraved on stone, bones and ivory?

Future historians will be in a unique position

Future historians will be in a unique position when they come to record the history of our own times. They will hardly know which facts to select from the great mass of evidence that steadily accumulates. What is more, they will not have to rely solely on the written word. Films, videos, CDs and CD-ROMs are just some of the bewildering amount of information they will have. They will be able, as it were, to see and hear us in action. But the historian attempting to reconstruct the distant past is always faced with a difficult task. He has to deduce what he can from the few scanty clues available. Even seemingly insignificant remains can shed interesting light on the history of early man.

Up to now, historians have assumed that calendars came into being with the advent of agriculture, for then man was faced with a real need to understand something about the seasons. Recent scientific evidence seems to indicate that this assumption is incorrect.

Historians have long been puzzled by dots, lines and symbols which have been engraved on walls, bones, and the ivory tusks of mammoths. The nomads who made these markings lived by hunting and fishing during the last Ice Age which began about 35,000 B.C. and ended about 10,000 B.C. By correlating markings made in various parts of the world, historians have been able to read this difficult code. They have found that it is connected with the passage of days and the phases of the moon. It is, in fact, a primitive type of calendar. It has long been known that the hunting scenes depicted on walls were not simply a form of artistic expression. They had a definite meaning, for they were as near as early man could get to writing. It is possible that there is a definite relation between these paintings and the markings that sometimes accompany them. It seems that man was making a real effort to understand the seasons 20,000 years earlier than has been supposed.

New words and expressions 生词和短语

calendar (title)	/'kælɪndə/	*n.*	历法，日历
historian (l.1)	/hɪ'stɔːriən/	*n.*	历史学家
unique (l.1)	/juː'niːk/	*adj.*	无与伦比的
steadily (l.3)	/'stedɪli/	*adv.*	不断地
solely (l.4)	/'səʊl-li/	*adv.*	唯一地
video (l.5)	/'vɪdiəʊ/	*n.*	录像
CD-ROM (l.5)	/ˌsiː-diː-'rɒm/	*n.*	（只读）光盘驱动器
bewildering (l.6)	/bɪ'wɪldərɪŋ/	*adj.*	令人眼花缭乱的
deduce (l.8)	/dɪ'djuːs/	*v.*	推断，推理
scanty (l.8)	/'skænti/	*adj.*	不足的，贫乏的
clue (l.8)	/kluː/	*n.*	线索
insignificant (l.9)	/ˌɪnsɪg'nɪfɪkənt/	*adj.*	不重要的
shed (l.9)	/ʃed/	*v.*	使流出，泻
advent (l.10)	/'ædvent/	*n.*	出现，到来，来临

agriculture (l.10)	/ˈæɡrɪˌkʌltʃə/	*n.*	农业
assumption (l.12)	/əˈsʌmpʃən/	*n.*	假定，设想
dot (l.13)	/dɒt/	*n.*	小圆点
symbol (l.13)	/ˈsɪmbəl/	*n.*	符号
engrave (l.13)	/ɪnˈɡreɪv/	*v.*	雕刻
ivory (l.14)	/ˈaɪvəri/	*n.*	象牙制品
tusk (l.14)	/tʌsk/	*n.*	獠牙，长牙，象牙
mammoth (l.14)	/ˈmæməθ/	*n.*	（古）长毛象
nomad (l.14)	/ˈnəʊmæd/	*n.*	游牧民
correlate (l.15)	/ˈkɒrɪleɪt/	*v.*	使相互联系
phase (l.17)	/feɪz/	*n.*	月相，天相
primitive (l.17)	/ˈprɪmɪtɪv/	*adj.*	原始的
depict (l.18)	/dɪˈpɪkt/	*v.*	描画，描绘

Notes on the text 课文注释

1 what is more, 作“而且”、“再者”解，是插入语。

2 CD-ROM, 是 compact disc read-only memory 的缩写。

3 as it were, “可以说”，是插入语。

4 be faced with, 作“面临”、“面对”解。

5 shed light on ..., 使……清楚地显出来，揭示。

6 come into being, 产生，形成。

7 Ice Age, 冰川时期。

参考译文

未来的历史学家在写我们这一段历史的时候会别具一格。对于逐渐积累起来的庞大材料，他们几乎不知道选取哪些好，而且，也不必完全依赖文字材料。电影、录像、光盘和光盘驱动器只是能为他们提供令人眼花缭乱的大量信息的几种手段。他们能够身临其境般地观看我们做事，倾听我们讲话。但是，历史学家企图重现遥远的过去可是一项艰巨的任务，他们必须根据现有的不充分的线索进行推理。即使看起来微不足道的遗物，也可能揭示人类早期历史中的一些有趣的内容。

历史学家迄今认为日历是随农业的出现而产生的，因为当时人们面临着了解四季的实际需要。但近期科学研究发现，这种假设好像是不正确的。

长期以来，历史学家一直对雕刻在墙壁上、骨头上、古代长毛象的象牙上的点、线和形形色色的符号感到困惑不解。这些痕迹是游牧人留下的，他们生活在从公元前约 35,000 年到公元前 10,000 年的冰川期的末期，以狩猎、捕鱼为生。历史学家通过把世界各地留下的这种痕迹放在一起研究，终于弄懂了这种费解的代码。他们发现代码与昼夜更迭和月亮圆缺有关，事实上是一种最原始的日历。大家早就知道，画在墙上的狩猎图景并不是单纯的艺术表现形式，它们有着一定的含义，因为它们已接近古代人的文字形式。有时，这种图画与墙壁上的刻痕共存，它们之间可能有一定的联系。看来人类早就致力于探索四季变迁了，比人们想象的要早 20,000 年。

Comprehension 理解

Give short answers to these questions in your own words as far as possible. Use one complete sentence for each answer.

1 Why will future historians not have to rely entirely on the written word when they come to record the history of our own times?

2 Why do historians who write about the distant past have a difficult task?

3 When was it believed that calendars were first used?

Vocabulary 词汇

Explain the meanings of the following words and phrases as they are used in the passage: record (l.2); select (l.3); great mass of evidence (l.3); accumulates (l.4); solely (l.4); bewildering (l.6); insignificant (l.9).

Summary writing 摘要写作

In not more than 80 words describe what historians have learnt from the strange markings made by early man. Use your own words as far as possible. Do not include anything that is not in the last paragraph.

Composition 作文

In not more than 250 words describe some of the things future historians will be able to learn about us. Use the ideas given below. Do not write more than four paragraphs.

Title: Studying the past.

Introduction: The future historian's sources: films, video, CDs, CD-ROMs.

Development: Social and political history: how we dressed — what we ate — what houses we lived in — what our cities were like — the forms of entertainment we enjoyed — the news day by day — the way we fought our wars — great moments in history — leading figures of the time as well as ordinary people.

Conclusion: Study of history will provide interest and excitement — the past will be brought to life.

Letter writing 书信写作

For several years you have been writing to a penfriend whom you have never met in person. Write him a letter of about 100 words in three paragraphs telling him that you will be visiting his country soon and expressing pleasure that you will be able to meet each other for the first time.

Key structures and Special difficulties 关键句型和难点

Exercises 练习

1 Give the correct form of the verbs in parentheses. Do not refer to the passage until you finish the exercise.
Up to now, historians ________ (assume) that calendars ________ (come) into being with the advent of agriculture, for then man ________ (face) with a real need to understand something about the seasons. Recent scientific evidence ________ (seem) to indicate that this assumption ________ (be) incorrect. Historians ________ long ________ (puzzle) by dots, lines and symbols which ________ (engrave) on walls, bones, and the ivory tusks of mammoths. The nomads who ________ (make) these markings ________ (live) by hunting and fishing during the last Ice Age which ________ (begin) about 35,000 B.C. and ________ (end) about 10,000 B.C. (ll.10-15) **(Mainly 1 KS 29)**（主要参见第 2 册第 29 课关键句型）

2 *it is connected with*. (l.17) Put *with* or *for* after the following verbs: *agree, account, mistake, cope, correspond, apologize, blame, reason, satisfy(fied), quarrel, wait, search*. **(1 KS 46)**（参见第 2 册第 46 课关键句型）

3 *between these paintings and the markings*. (l.20) Write two sentences illustrating the difference between *between* and *among*. **(1 SD 76b)**（参见第 2 册第 76 课难点 b）

Multiple choice questions 选择题

Choose the correct answers to the following questions.

Comprehension 理解

1 In assuming that calendars came into being with the advent of agriculture, historians made the mistake of ________ .

(*a*) relying solely on the written word

(*b*) disregarding the markings that early man had been responsible for

(*c*) supposing that nomadic man had no reason to understand the seasons

(*d*) not connecting the passage of days with the phases of the moon

2 The scientific evidence that has recently come to light is that ________ .

(*a*) nomads engraved the bones and tusks of the animals they killed

(*b*) nomads lived by hunting and fishing

(*c*) nomads travelled widely in various parts of the world

(*d*) the markings made by various nomadic groups all have a definite pattern

3 The paintings which have been found on the walls of nomadic dwelling places ________ .

(*a*) have taught historians something about the nomadic way of life

(*b*) have no other content than their artistic merit

(*c*) are not thought to be connected with an ancient calendar system

(*d*) are invariably accompanied by odd dots, lines and symbols

Structure 结构

4 It ________ as if they could see and hear us in action. (ll.6-7)

(*a*) was (*b*) were (*c*) should be (*d*) will be

5 Even ________ seem insignificant remains can shed interesting ... (ll.8-9)

(*a*) they (*b*) which (*c*) what (*d*) those to

6 Historians are now able to read this difficult code ________ markings made in ... (ll.15-16)

(*a*) with correlating (*b*) having correlated (*c*) which correlates (*d*) for they correlate

7 ________ be a definite relation between these paintings and the ... (ll.19-21)

(*a*) It could (*b*) There can (*c*) There may (*d*) It might

Vocabulary 词汇

8 Historians have long tried to ________ dots, lines and ... (l.13)

(*a*) puzzle (*b*) puzzle out (*c*) riddle (*d*) detect

9 By correlating markings made in ________ parts of the world ... (ll.15-16)

(*a*) different (*b*) several (*c*) many (*d*) other

10 – historians have been able to read ________ . (l.16)

(*a*) these puzzling signs (*b*) this hard law

(*c*) these difficult signals (*d*) this uneasy letter

11 Until recently historians assumed that calendars ________ with the advent of agriculture. (l.10)

(*a*) came to existence (*b*) came to existing (*c*) came to exist (*d*) were existential

12 The people who lived by hunting and fishing during the last Ice Age ________ . (ll.14-15)

(*a*) wandered from place to place (*b*) lived in villages

(*c*) first learnt to write (*d*) learnt how to farm the land

LESSON

39 Nothing to worry about 不必担心

Listen then answer the question below.

听录音，然后回答以下问题。

What was the difference between Bruce's behaviour and that of other people?

Bruce was not in the least perturbed

The rough road across the plain soon became so bad that we tried to get Bruce to drive back to the village we had come from. Even though the road was littered with boulders and pitted with holes, Bruce was not in the least perturbed. Glancing at his map, he informed us that the next village was a mere twenty miles away. It was not that Bruce always underestimated difficulties. He simply had no sense of danger at all. No matter what the conditions were, he believed that a car should be driven as fast as it could possibly go.

As we bumped over the dusty track, we swerved to avoid large boulders. The wheels scooped up stones which hammered ominously under the car. We felt sure that sooner or later a stone would rip a hole in our petrol tank or damage the engine. Because of this, we kept looking back, wondering if we were leaving a trail of oil and petrol behind us.

What a relief it was when the boulders suddenly disappeared, giving way to a stretch of plain where the only obstacles were clumps of bushes. But there was worse to come. Just ahead of us there was a huge fissure. In response to renewed pleadings, Bruce stopped. Though we all got out to examine the fissure, he remained in the car. We informed him that the fissure extended for fifty yards and was two feet wide and four feet deep. Even this had no effect. Bruce went into a low gear and drove at a terrifying speed, keeping the front wheels astride the crack as he followed its zigzag course. Before we had time to worry about what might happen, we were back on the plain again. Bruce consulted the map once more and told us that the village was now only fifteen miles away. Our next obstacle was a shallow pool of water about half a mile across. Bruce charged at it, but in the middle, the car came to a grinding halt. A yellow light on the dashboard flashed angrily and Bruce cheerfully announced that there was no oil in the engine!

New words and expressions 生词和短语

rough (l.1)	/rʌf/	*adj.*	崎岖不平的	scoop (l.9)	/skuːp/	*v.*	挖出
boulder (l.3)	/ˈbəʊldə/	*n.*	大石块	hammer (l.10)	/ˈhæmə/	*v.*	（用锤）击打，锤打
pit (l.3)	/pɪt/	*v.*	使……变得坑坑洼洼	ominously (l.10)	/ˈɒmɪnəsli/	*adv.*	有预兆地，不祥地
				rip (l.10)	/rɪp/	*v.*	划破，撕，扯
perturbed (l.4)	/pəˈtɜːbd/	*adj.*	不安的	petrol (l.11)	/ˈpetrəl/	*n.*	汽油
underestimate (l.6)	/ˌʌndərˈestɪmeɪt/	*v.*	低估	stretch (l.13)	/stretʃ/	*n.*	一大片（平地或水）
swerve (l.9)	/swɜːv/	*v.*	急转向	obstacle (l.14)	/ˈɒbstəkəl/	*n.*	障碍

clump (l.14)	/klʌmp/	*n.*	丛，簇
fissure (l.14)	/ˈfɪʃə/	*n.*	（石、地的）深缝
renewed (l.15)	/rɪˈnjuːd/	*adj.*	重复的
pleading (l.15)	/ˈpliːdɪŋ/	*n.*	恳求
gear (l.17)	/ɡɪə/	*n.*	（汽车）排挡
astride (l.18)	/əˈstraɪd/	*prep.*	跨在……上
crack (l.18)	/kræk/	*n.*	缝隙
zigzag (l.18)	/ˈzɪɡzæɡ/	*n.*	"之"字形
shallow (l.20)	/ˈʃæləʊ/	*adj.*	浅的
grinding (l.21)	/ˈɡraɪndɪŋ/	*adj.*	（机器部件的摩擦声）持续而刺耳的
halt (l.21)	/hɔːlt/	*n.*	停
dashboard (l.21)	/ˈdæʃbɔːd/	*n.*	（汽车上的）仪表盘

Notes on the text 课文注释

1 get sb. to do sth., 说服某人做某事。

2 not in the least, 一点儿也不，完全不。

3 It was not that Bruce always underestimated difficulties. 这并不是说布鲁斯总是低估困难。

4 sooner or later, 作"迟早"、"总有一天"讲。

5 giving way to a stretch of plain, 出现了一片平原。

give way to ..., 此处作"为……所代替"解。

6 charge at, 冲向。

参考译文

穿越平原的道路高低不平，开车走了不远，路面愈加崎岖。我们想劝说布鲁斯把车开回到我们出发的那个村庄去。尽管路面布满石头，坑坑洼洼，但布鲁斯却一点儿不慌乱。他瞥了一眼地图，告诉我们前面再走不到 20 英里就有一个村庄。这并不是说布鲁斯总是低估困难，而是他压根儿没有一点儿危险感。他认为不管路面情况如何，车必须以最高速度前进。

我们在尘土飞扬的道路上颠簸，车子东拐西弯，以躲开那些大石块。车轮搅起的石块锤击车身，发出不祥的锤击声。我们相信迟早会飞起一个石块把油箱砸开一个窟窿，或者把发动机砸坏。因此，我们不时地掉过头，想知道车后是否留下了机油和汽油的痕迹。

突然大石块不见了，前面是一片平地，唯一的障碍是一簇簇灌木丛。这使我们长长地松了口气。但是更糟糕的事情在等着我们，离我们不远处，出现了一个大裂缝。我们再次央求布鲁斯小心，他这才把车停了下来。我们纷纷下车察看那个大裂缝，他却待在车上。我们告诉他那个大裂缝长 50 码，宽 2 英尺，深 4 英尺。这也没有对他产生任何影响。布鲁斯挂上慢挡，把两只前轮分别搁在裂缝的两边，顺着弯弯曲曲的裂缝，以发疯的速度向前开去。我们还未来得及担心后果，车已重新开上了平地。布鲁斯又看了一眼地图，告诉我们那座村庄离我们只有 15 英里了。下一个障碍是一片约半英里宽的浅水塘。布鲁斯向水塘冲去，但车开到水塘当中，嘎吱一声停住了。仪表盘上一盏黄灯闪着刺眼的光芒，布鲁斯兴致勃勃地宣布发动机里没油了！

Comprehension 理解

Give short answers to these questions in your own words as far as possible. Use one complete sentence for each answer.

1 Why did the passengers try to get Bruce to drive back to the village they had come from?

2 Why was Bruce not perturbed by the bad state of the road?

3 Why did the passengers keep looking back as Bruce swerved to avoid boulders?

Vocabulary 词汇

Explain the meanings of the following words and phrases as they are used in the passage: boulders (l.3); perturbed (l.4); underestimated (l.6); bumped (l.9); swerved (l.9); hammered (l.10); ominously (l.10).

Summary writing 摘要写作

In not more than 80 words describe what happened from the time when the car got past the boulders to the moment it stopped in the shallow pool. Use your own words as far as possible. Do not include anything that is not in the last paragraph.

Composition 作文

In not more than 250 words write a continuation to the passage. Expand the ideas given below into a plan and provide a suitable title. Your composition should be in four paragraphs.

Ideas: Got out — tried to push car — impossible — walked to next village — tried to get a taxi — no driver would take us over rough road — paid a large sum of money to rent a jeep — pulled car out of water — found engine badly damaged — Bruce undismayed.

Letter writing 书信写作

You are on holiday and are running out of money. Write an urgent letter to your father in about 100 words in three paragraphs, asking him to help you out of your difficulties.

Key structures and Special difficulties 关键句型和难点

Exercises 练习

1 *we tried to get Bruce to drive back to the village.* (ll.1-2) Write these sentences again using *got* in place of *made*. **(1 SD 66)**（参见第 2 册第 66 课难点）

I made him tell me the truth.

He made me translate the article into English.

2 *he believed that a car should be driven.* (l.7) Write two sentences beginning: *He suggested that ...; He insisted that ...* . **(1 KS 63)**（参见第 2 册第 63 课关键句型）

3 *wondering if we were leaving.* (l.11) Complete the following sentences. **(1 KS 63d)**（参见第 2 册第 63 课关键句型练习 d）

Can he wait a few minutes longer? I wonder if ________ .

When will he arrive? I wonder when ________ .

4 *What a relief it was ...* . (l.13) Write these sentences again beginning each one with *What*. **(1 SD 2)**（参见第 2 册第 2 课难点）

This is a wonderful garden!

It is a terrible day!

5 *we all got out.* (l.15) Write sentences using the following: *get on; get over;* and *get through*. **(1 SD 74a)**（参见第 2 册第 74 课难点 a）

6 *Bruce ... told us.* (l.19) Write two sentences illustrating the difference between *say* and *tell*. **(1 KS 15)**（参见第 2 册第 15 课关键句型）

Multiple choice questions 选择题

Choose the correct answers to the following questions.

Comprehension 理解

1 Why were the passengers so relieved when the boulders disappeared?
(*a*) Bruce could now drive even faster.
(*b*) They had covered the greater part of the distance to the village.
(*c*) It seemed less likely that they would meet with disaster.
(*d*) They had seen the huge fissure that lay ahead of them.

2 When they reached the fissure, Bruce stopped the car because ________ .
(*a*) the passengers had begged him to do so
(*b*) he wanted to know the exact dimensions of the fissure
(*c*) he thought it was safer to drive across it without the passengers
(*d*) he was not sure whether the car was wide enough to bridge it

3 Bruce's reaction to the final episode shows that ________ .
(*a*) he was not the sort of person to be perturbed by anything
(*b*) he was extremely brave in face of danger
(*c*) he had underestimated the depth of the pool
(*d*) when it came to crossing water, his driving was not good enough

Structure 结构

4 He believed ________ a car as fast as it could possibly go. (ll.7-8)
(*a*) driving in (*b*) he would drive (*c*) to drive (*d*) in driving

5 ________ when the boulders suddenly disappeared. (l.13)
(*a*) How relieved we felt (*b*) What a relief we were feeling
(*c*) So relieved we felt (*d*) How we felt relieved

6 Bruce ________ when the car came to a grinding halt. (l.21)
(*a*) had charged through it midway (*b*) charged through it to the middle
(*c*) charged midway through it (*d*) was in the middle of charging through it

7 Bruce cheerfully announced that the engine ________ out of oil. (l.22)
(*a*) ran (*b*) had run (*c*) was running (*d*) has run

Vocabulary 词汇

8 Glancing at his map, he informed us that the next village was ________ twenty miles away. (ll.4-5)
(*a*) simply (*b*) boringly (*c*) only (*d*) in significantly

9 – where nothing could ________ but clumps of trees. (ll.13-14)
(*a*) hinder our progress (*b*) spoil our course (*c*) hold up our train (*d*) harm our way

10 When we pleaded ________ , Bruce stopped. (l.15)
(*a*) afresh (*b*) aloud (*c*) repeatedly (*d*) forcibly

11 He said: 'It's fifteen miles ________ the village.' (ll.19-20)
(*a*) until (*b*) to (*c*) from (*d*) before

12 – obstacle was a shallow pool of water half a mile ________ . (ll.20-21)
(*a*) side by side (*b*) from top to bottom (*c*) from side to side (*d*) up and down

LESSON

40 Who's who 真假难辨

Listen then answer the question below.
听录音，然后回答以下问题。

How did the policeman discover that the whole thing was a joke?

The police attempted to seize the drill

It has never been explained why university students seem to enjoy practical jokes more than anyone else. Students specialize in a particular type of practical joke: the hoax. Inviting the fire brigade to put out a nonexistent fire is a crude form of deception which no self-respecting student would ever indulge in. Students often create amusing situations which are funny to everyone except the victims.

When a student recently saw two workmen using a pneumatic drill outside his university, he immediately telephoned the police and informed them that two students dressed up as workmen were tearing up the road with a pneumatic drill. As soon as he had hung up, he went over to the workmen and told them that if a policeman ordered them to go away, they were not to take him seriously. He added that a student had dressed up as a policeman and was playing all sorts of silly jokes on people. Both the police and the workmen were grateful to the student for this piece of advance information.

The student hid in an archway nearby where he could watch and hear everything that went on. Sure enough, a policeman arrived on the scene and politely asked the workmen to go away. When he received a very rude reply from one of the workmen, he threatened to remove them by force. The workmen told him to do as he pleased and the policeman telephoned for help. Shortly afterwards, four more policemen arrived and remonstrated with the workmen. As the men refused to stop working, the police attempted to seize the pneumatic drill. The workmen struggled fiercely and one of them lost his temper. He threatened to call the police. At this, the police pointed out ironically that this would hardly be necessary as the men were already under arrest. Pretending to speak seriously, one of the workmen asked if he might make a telephone call before being taken to the station. Permission was granted and a policeman accompanied him to a pay phone. Only when he saw that the man was actually telephoning the police did he realize that they had all been the victims of a hoax.

New words and expressions 生词和短语

hoax (l.3)	/həʊks/	n.	骗局，戏弄
deception (l.4)	/dɪˈsepʃən/	n.	欺骗，骗局
self-respecting (l.5)	/ˌself rɪˈspektɪŋ/	adj.	自重的
indulge (l.5)	/ɪnˈdʌldʒ/	v.	沉迷
pneumatic (l.7)	/njuːˈmætɪk/	adj.	气动的
drill (l.8)	/drɪl/	n.	钻
silly (l.11)	/ˈsɪli/	adj.	无意义的，无聊的
advance (l.12)	/ədˈvɑːns/	adj.	预先的，事先获得的
archway (l.13)	/ˈɑːtʃweɪ/	n.	拱形门廊
remonstrate (l.17)	/ˈremənstreɪt/	v.	规劝，告诫
ironically (l.19)	/aɪˈrɒnɪkli/	adv.	讽刺地
permission (l.21)	/pəˈmɪʃən/	n.	许可
grant (l.21)	/grɑːnt/	v.	同意，准予

Notes on the text 课文注释

1 It has never been explained why ..., 在这个句子中真正的主语是以 why 引导的主语从句。

2 specialize in, 专门从事。

3 inviting the fire brigade, 是动名词短语，此处作主语。put out 作“扑灭”、“熄灭”讲。

4 dress up as, 装扮成。

5 they were not to take him seriously, （他们）不要把他当回事。
take 此处作“对待”讲，多指对人、对事物的态度和反应。

6 grateful to the student for this piece of advance information, 对这个学生事先通报情况表示感谢。
be grateful to sb. for sth., 对某人因某事表示感谢。

7 as he pleased, 是方式状语从句，后面省略了 to do，可译作“随他的便”。

8 be under arrest, 被逮捕，拘禁。

9 Only when ... did he realize that ... . 在这句话中，only 加上状语从句放在句首，因此主句的主谓语要用倒装的句式。

参考译文

谁也弄不清为什么大学生好像比任何人都更喜欢恶作剧。大学生擅长一种特殊的恶作剧——戏弄人。请消防队来扑灭一场根本没有的大火是一种低级骗局，有自尊心的大学生决不会去做。大学生们常常做的是制造一种可笑的局面，使大家笑上一场，当然受害者是笑不出来的。

最近有个学生看见两个工人在大学校门外用风钻干活，马上打电话报告警察，说有两个学生装扮成工人，正在用风钻破坏路面。挂上电话后，他又马上来到工人那儿，告诉他们若有个警察来让他们走开，不要把他当回事；还对工人说，有个学生常装扮成警察无聊地同别人开玩笑。警察与工人都对那个学生事先通报情况表示感谢。

那学生躲在附近一拱形门廊里，在那儿可以看见、听到现场发生的一切。果然，警察来了，有礼貌地请工人离开此地；但其中一个工人粗鲁地回了几句。于是警察威胁要强行使他们离开。工人说，悉听尊便。警察去打电话叫人。一会儿工夫，又来了 4 个警察，规劝工人离开。由于工人拒绝停下手中的活，警察想夺风钻。两个工人奋力抗争，其中一个发了火，威胁说要去叫警察。警察听后讥讽地说，这大可不必，因为他俩已被逮捕了。其中一个工人装模作样地问道，在被带往警察局之前，是否可以打一个电话。警察同意了，陪他来到一个投币电话前。当他看到那个工人真的是给警察挂电话，才恍然大悟，原来他们都成了一场骗局的受害者。

Comprehension 理解

Give short answers to these questions in your own words as far as possible. Use one complete sentence for each answer.

1 What sort of practical joke do students specialize in?

2 What did the student tell the police?

3 What did the student tell the workmen?

Vocabulary 词汇

Explain the meanings of the following words and phrases as they are used in the passage: a particular type (ll.2-3); put out (l.4); deception (l.4); victims (l.6); hung up (l.9); silly (l.11); grateful (l.12).

Summary writing 摘要写作

In not more than 80 words describe what happened after the student hid in an archway. Use your own words as far as possible. Do not include anything that is not in the last paragraph.

Composition 作文

Imagine that the policeman who accompanied the workman to the pay phone did not realize that they had all been victims of a practical joke. In not more than 250 words describe what happened. Use the ideas given below. Do not write more than four paragraphs.

Title: Arrest the police!

Introduction: Policeman and worker returned — the other workman still quarrelling with police — resisting arrest.

Development: More police arrived — workmen told them that the first lot of policemen were students — the second lot of police threatened to arrest the first lot — asked for identity cards — the first lot said that the workmen were students — workers had to prove their identity.

Conclusion: Realized they were victims of a hoax.

Letter writing 书信写作

A friend has written to you offering you a place in his car on a long trip he intends to make, providing that you are willing to share expenses. In not more than 100 words write a letter accepting his offer. Do not write more than three paragraphs.

Key structures and Special difficulties 关键句型和难点

Exercises 练习

1 *to put out a nonexistent fire*. (l.4) Write sentences using the following: *put up, put someone up, put up with* and *put off*. **(1 SD 27)**（参见第 2 册第 27 课难点）

2 *funny to everyone except the victims*. (l.6) Write three sentences illustrating the use of the following: *except, except for* and *apart from*. **(1 SD 14b)**（参见第 2 册第 14 课难点 b）

3 *dressed up*. (l.11) Write two sentences illustrating the difference between *dress* and *dress up*. **(1 SD 65c)**（参见第 2 册第 65 课难点 c）

4 *he could watch*. (l.13) Write two sentences illustrating the difference between *watch* and *follow*. **(1 SD 36a)**（参见第 2 册第 36 课难点 a）

5 *one of them lost his temper*. (l.18) Write sentences using the following: *in a good temper, in a good mood, in a bad temper* and *in the mood*. **(1 SD 83)**（参见第 2 册第 83 课难点）

Multiple choice questions 选择题

Choose the correct answers to the following questions.

Comprehension 理解

1 A good hoax is a joke which depends on ________ .

(*a*) deceiving people into behaving in a way which amuses everyone but themselves

(*b*) doing something like calling the fire brigade to a nonexistent fire

(*c*) at least two parties being led to believe the other is fraudulent

(*d*) people disguising themselves to look like other people

2 When the policeman first arrived outside the university ________ .

(*a*) the student hid in an archway to see what happened next

(*b*) he told the workmen if they disobeyed him he would call four policemen

(*c*) the workmen refused to take his request that they should move seriously

(*d*) he was polite to the workmen as he had expected them to be students

3 When did it become clear to the police that the workmen were not students?

(*a*) When one of the workmen angrily said he was going to call the police.

(*b*) Not until one of the workmen asked if he could telephone the police.

(*c*) When the policeman saw whom the workman was ringing from the pay phone.

(*d*) Only after they had arrested the workmen and taken them to the station.

Structure 结构

4 – why students seem ________ practical jokes than anyone else. (ll.1-2)

(*a*) entertained by more (*b*) to have been entertained more by

(*c*) more to be entertained by (*d*) to be more entertained by

5 – and told them that ________ order them to go away they were not to take them seriously. (ll.10-11)

(*a*) should the police (*b*) the police might

(*c*) if the policeman did (*d*) was a policeman to

6 – were grateful to the student for ________ in advance. (l.12)

(*a*) they had been informed this (*b*) having informed them this

(*c*) being informed of this (*d*) informing them of this

7 The workmen told him to do ________ ... (ll.15-16)

(*a*) as it pleased him (*b*) how he pleased (*c*) as he pleased (*d*) that pleased him

8 Only then ________ that it had been a trick. (ll.22-23)

(*a*) he realized (*b*) he understood (*c*) did he realize (*d*) he did realize

Vocabulary 词汇

9 – a student had dressed up as a policeman and was amusing himself ________ . (ll.11-12)

(*a*) by joking with people (*b*) at other people's expense

(*c*) by making fun of people (*d*) to other people's surprise

10 When he received a very ________ from one of the workmen ... (ll.14-15)

(*a*) impolite retort (*b*) harsh response (*c*) rough report (*d*) sharp return

11 Four more policemen arrived to protest ________ the workmen's behaviour. (ll.16-17)

(*a*) with (*b*) for (*c*) to (*d*) against

12 The police attempted to ________ the pneumatic drill. (ll.17-18)

(*a*) get hold of (*b*) keep hold of (*c*) hold back (*d*) hold on to

Unit 3

Unit 3

INSTRUCTIONS TO THE STUDENT

No language exercises have been included in Unit 3. You should now be able to write continuous English prose entirely on your own.

How to work

Carry out the detailed instructions given in the Introduction to Unit 2 (p.101). They are very important. Here is a brief summary:

Comprehension

Write complete answers in your own words as far as possible.

Vocabulary

Explain each word or phrase as it is used in the passage.

Summary writing

Make out a list of Points, a Rough draft, and a Fair copy. Do not exceed the word limit. At the end of your Fair copy, write the number of words you have used.

Composition

Make out a full plan which contains an Introduction, a Development and a Conclusion. Write essays of about 300 words in three or four paragraphs.

Letter writing

Pay close attention to the Layout of each letter. Answer each question closely. Do not exceed the word limit.

Example

Work carefully through this past First Certificate paper. Note how the questions have been answered.

Read the following passage carefully and complete Comprehension, Vocabulary and Summary writing.

As I stepped out of the train I felt unusually solitary, since I was the only passenger to alight. I was accustomed to arriving in the summer, when holiday makers throng coastal resorts, and this was my first visit when the season was over. My destination was a little village eight miles distant by the road, but only four if you took the cliff path over the moor. This I always did, unless it was raining: and I left my luggage at the bus office beside the railway station, to be conveyed for me on the next bus, so that I could enjoy my walk unhampered by a suitcase.

It took me only a few minutes to come to the foot of the cliff path. Half way up I paused to enjoy the sight of the purple hills stretching away to my right and to my left the open sea. When I reached the top I had left all signs of habitation behind me. The moorland turf was springy under my feet, the air was like wine and I felt rejuvenated and intoxicated with it. Glancing seaward a minute or two later, I was surprised to notice that the sky was already aflame with the sunset. The air grew perceptibly cooler and I began to look forward to the delectable hot meal I should have when I reached the inn. It seemed to be getting dark amazingly quickly. I did not think that I had walked unduly slowly and I was at a loss to account for the exceptionally early end of daylight, until I recollected that on previous visits I had walked in high summer and now it was October and the nights were drawing in.

All at once it was night. The track was grassy and even in daylight showed up hardly at all against the moor, so it was difficult to keep on it now. If only I had been a smoker with matches always to hand, or if my torch had been in my pocket instead of in the suitcase, I could have walked with more assurance. As it was, I was terrified of hurtling over the edge of the cliff to the rocks below. When I did stray, however, it was towards the hills. I felt my feet squelching and sticking in something soggy. There was no bog to my knowledge near the track, so I must have wandered a long way off my course. I extricated myself with difficulty and very cautiously edged myself towards the sound of the sea. Then I bumped into a little clump of trees that suddenly loomed up in front of me. This was providential rest and shelter until the moon rose. I climbed up the nearest trunk and managed to find a tolerably comfortable fork in which to sit. The waiting seemed interminable and was relieved only by my attempts to identify the little stirrings and noises of animal life that I could hear. I grew colder and colder and managed to sleep only in uneasy, fitful starts, waking when my position got cramped. At last, when the moon came up, I discovered that I was not more than fifty yards from the track and I was soon on my way again.

Comprehension

Give short answers to each of the following questions in your own words as far as possible, using only material contained in the passage. Use *one* complete sentence for each answer.

1 How was the author's arrival at the station this time different from his arrival on other occasions?

2 Why did the author leave his luggage in the bus office?

3 Why was the author surprised at the darkness coming so soon?

Vocabulary

Choose five of the following words and phrases and give for each another word or phrase of similar meaning to that in which the word or phrase is used in the passage: coastal resorts (l.2); all signs of habitation (l.9); rejuvenated (l.10); glancing seaward (l.10); perceptibly (l.11); unduly (l.13); account for (l.13); recollected (l.14).

Summary writing

Give an account *in not more than 85 words* of the author's experiences on the moor after it had become completely dark. Use your own words as far as possible. Do not include anything that is not in the last paragraph.

Possible answers

Comprehension

1 The author's arrival at the station this time was different from his arrival on other occasions because this was the first time he had ever visited the coastal resort after the holiday season had passed.

2 The author left his luggage in the bus office so that he could enjoy his walk without having to carry anything.

3 The author was surprised at the darkness coming so soon because at first he failed to realize that the days were now shorter because summer had passed.

Vocabulary

coastal resorts: places near the seashore where people spend their holidays.
rejuvenated: young again.
perceptibly: noticeably.
unduly: excessively.
recollected: remembered.

Summary writing

Points (The author's experiences)

1 Difficult to keep on track.
2 Strayed — hills.
3 Feet stuck — something soggy.
4 Off course.
5 Extricated himself.
6 Went — sound of sea.
7 Bumped — clump of trees.
8 Climbed nearest trunk.
9 Sat in fork.
10 Waited — long time.
11 Felt cold.
12 Slept — fitful starts.
13 Moon rose — able to see track.
14 Continued on his way.

Rough draft (Joining the Points)

In the darkness, the author could not follow the track and wandered towards the hills. When he got stuck in soggy soil, he knew he had lost his way. After extricating himself, he walked towards the sound of the sea. It was then that he bumped into a clump of trees so he climbed up the nearest trunk and sat in a branch. He waited there for a long time, and even though he felt very cold, he slept for short intervals. When the moon rose, he was able to see the track a short way off and he continued on his way. (103 words)

Fair copy (Corrected draft)

Unable to follow the track in the darkness, the author wandered off his course towards the hills where he got stuck in a bog. After extricating himself, he walked towards the sea. When he bumped into a clump of trees, he climbed up the nearest trunk, sat on a branch and waited there for a long time. Though he felt cold, he managed to get a little sleep. Later, when the moon rose, he saw the track and continued on his way.

(82 words)

Key structures and Special difficulties

In this exercise you will be asked to rewrite a sentence taken from the passage without changing its meaning. This exercise tests your ability to use your English to express yourself in a restricted way.

Multiple choice questions

You will again find comprehension questions in which you are asked to choose the correct answer from a number of suggested answers. This exercise tests your ability to understand the meaning of the passage you have read and also to recognize grammatical and lexical errors in English.

LESSON

41 Illusions of pastoral peace

宁静田园生活的遐想

Listen then answer the question below.

听录音，然后回答以下问题。

What particular anxiety spoils the country dweller's visit to the theatre?

the gentle pace of living

The quiet life of the country has never appealed to me. City born and city bred, I have always regarded the country as something you look at through a train window, or something you occasionally visit during the weekend. Most of my friends live in the city, yet they always go into raptures at the mere mention of the country. Though they extol the virtues of the peaceful life, only one of them has ever gone to live in the country and he was back in town within six months. Even he still lives under the illusion that country life is somehow superior to town life. He is forever talking about the friendly people, the clean atmosphere, the closeness to nature and the gentle pace of living. Nothing can be compared, he maintains, with the first cockcrow, the twittering of birds at dawn, the sight of the rising sun glinting on the trees and pastures. This idyllic pastoral scene is only part of the picture. My friend fails to mention the long and friendless winter evenings in front of the TV — virtually the only form of entertainment. He says nothing about the poor selection of goods in the shops, or about those unfortunate people who have to travel from the country to the city every day to get to work. Why people are prepared to tolerate a four-hour journey each day for the dubious privilege of living in the country is beyond me. They could be saved so much misery and expense if they chose to live in the city where they rightly belong.

If you can do without the few pastoral pleasures of the country, you will find the city can provide you with the best that life can offer. You never have to travel miles to see your friends. They invariably live nearby and are always available for an informal chat or an evening's entertainment. Some of my acquaintances in the country come up to town once or twice a year to visit the theatre as a special treat. For them this is a major operation which involves considerable planning. As the play draws to its close, they wonder whether they will ever catch that last train home. The city dweller never experiences anxieties of this sort. The latest exhibitions, films, or plays are only a short bus ride away. Shopping, too, is always a pleasure. There is so much variety that you never have to make do with second best. Country people run wild when they go shopping in the city and stagger home loaded with as many of the exotic items as they can carry. Nor is the city without its moments of beauty. There is something comforting about the warm glow shed by advertisements on cold wet winter nights. Few things could be more impressive than the peace that descends on deserted city streets at weekends when the thousands that travel to work every day are tucked away in their homes in the country. It has always been a mystery to me why city dwellers, who appreciate all these things, obstinately pretend that they would prefer to live in the country.

New words and expressions 生词和短语

illusion (title)	/ɪ'luːʒən/	n.	幻想，错觉
pastoral (title)	/'pɑːstərəl/	adj.	田园的
breed (l.2)	/briːd/ (bred /bred/, bred)	v.	培育
rapture (l.5)	/'ræptʃə/	n.	欣喜
extol (l.6)	/ɪk'stəʊl/	v.	赞美，颂扬
superior (l.8)	/suː'pɪəriə/	adj.	优越的
cockcrow (l.10)	/'kɒk-krəʊ/	n.	鸡叫
twitter (l.10)	/'twɪtə/	v.	（鸟）吱吱叫，喊喊喳喳叫
glint (l.10)	/glɪnt/	v.	闪烁
pasture (l.11)	/'pɑːstʃə/	n.	牧场
idyllic (l.11)	/ɪ'dɪlɪk/	adj.	田园诗的
virtually (l.12)	/'vɜːtʃuəli/	adv.	几乎，差不多
dubious (l.15)	/'djuːbiəs/	adj.	可疑的，怀疑的
privilege (l.15)	/'prɪvɪlɪdʒ/	n.	特权
misery (l.15)	/'mɪzəri/	n.	苦难
acquaintance (l.20)	/ə'kweɪntəns/	n.	熟人
treat (l.20)	/triːt/	n.	难得的乐事，享受
dweller (l.22)	/'dwelə/	n.	居住者
stagger (l.25)	/'stægə/	v.	摇晃，蹒跚
exotic (l.25)	/ɪg'zɒtɪk/	adj.	异乎寻常的；外来的
glow (l.26)	/gləʊ/	n.	白炽光
descend (l.28)	/dɪ'send/	v.	下落；降临
tuck (l.28)	/tʌk/	v.	缩进；隐藏
obstinately (l.30)	/'ɒbstɪnɪtli/	adv.	固执地，顽固地

Notes on the text 课文注释

1 city born and city bred, 城里生，城里长。

这是由“名词 + 过去分词”构成的合成形容词，此处作原因状语。

2 go into raptures, 变得欣喜若狂起来。

at the mere mention of, 一提到。

3 be under an illusion, 作“有……的错觉”讲，原文中 that 引导的是同位语从句。

4 beyond me, 我所无法理解的。

5 do without ..., 没有……也行。

6 draw to a close, 结束，告终。

7 you never have to make do with second best, 你从来不必用二等品来凑合。

make do with ..., 凑合着用……。

参考译文

宁静的乡村生活从来没有吸引过我。我生在城市，长在城市，总认为乡村是透过火车车窗看到的那个样子，或偶尔周末去游玩一下的景象。我的许多朋友都住在城市，但他们只要一提起乡村，马上就会变得欣喜若狂。尽管他们都交口称赞宁静的乡村生活的种种优点，但其中只有一人真去农村住过，而且不足 6 个月就回来了。即使他也仍存有幻觉，好像乡村生活就是比城市生活优越。他滔滔不绝地大谈友好的农民、洁净的空气、贴近大自然的环境和悠闲的生活节奏。他坚持认为，凌晨雄鸡第一声啼叫，黎明时分小鸟吱喳欢叫，冉冉升起的朝阳染红树木、牧场，此番美景无与伦比。但这种田园诗般的乡村风光仅仅是一个侧面。我的朋友没有提到在电视机前度过的漫长寂寞的冬夜——电视是唯一的娱乐形式。他也不说商店货物品种单调，以及那些每天不得不从乡下赶到城里工作的不幸的人们。人们为什么情愿每天在路上奔波 4 个小时去换取值得怀疑的乡间的优点，我是无法理解的。要是他们愿意住在本来属于他们的城市，则可以让他们省去诸多不便与节约大量开支。

如果你愿舍弃乡下生活那一点点乐趣的话，那么你会发现城市可以为你提供生活中最美好的东西。你去看朋友根本不用跋涉好几英里，因为他们都住在附近，你随时可以同他们聊天或在晚上一起娱乐。我在乡村有一些熟人，他们每年进城来看一回或几回戏，并把此看作一种特殊的享受。看戏在他们是件大事，需要精心计划。当戏快演完时，他们又为是否能赶上末班火车回家而犯愁。这种焦虑，城里人是从未体验过的。坐公共汽车几站路，就可看到最新的展览、电影、戏剧。买东西也是一种乐趣。物品品种繁多，从来不必用二等品来凑合。乡里人进城采购欣喜若狂，每次回家时都买足了外来商品，直到拿不动方才罢休，连走路都摇摇晃晃的。城市也并非没有良辰美景。寒冷潮湿的冬夜里，广告灯箱发出的暖光，会给人某种安慰。周末，当成千上万进城上班的人回到了他们的乡间寓所之后，空旷的街市笼罩着一种宁静的气氛，没有什么能比此时的宁静更令人难忘了。城里人对这一切心里很明白，却偏要执拗地装出他们喜欢住在乡村的样子，这对我来说一直是个谜。

Comprehension 理解

Give short answers to these questions in your own words as far as possible. Use one complete sentence for each answer.

1 How long did one of the author's city friends live in the country?

2 Why does the author find fault with his friend's description of the country?

3 Why does the author consider people who have to travel from the country to the city every day unfortunate?

Vocabulary 词汇

Explain the meanings of the following words and phrases as they are used in the passage: extol the virtues (l.6); illusion (l.7); superior to (l.8); maintains (l.9); glinting (l.10); tolerate (l.14); beyond me (l.15).

Summary writing 摘要写作

In not more than 80 words give an account of the advantages which the author attributes to living in the city. Use your own words as far as possible. Do not include anything that is not in the last paragraph.

Composition 作文

Write a composition in about 300 words on one of the following:

a Write an answer to the above passage pointing out the advantages of living in the country and the disadvantages of living in the city.

b Which part of your country would you prefer to live in and why?

Letter writing 书信写作

A friend of yours who lives in the country intends to come to town for a few days and has written to you asking if you could put him up. Write him a letter of about 100 words offering him the use of your guestroom.

Key structures and Special difficulties 关键句型和难点

Rewrite the following sentence without changing the meaning. Then refer to ll.14-15.

I can't understand why people are prepared to tolerate a four-hour journey each day for the dubious privilege of living in the country.

Why people ...

Multiple choice questions 选择题

Choose the correct answers to the following questions.

Comprehension 理解

1 What is the main difference between the writer and most of his friends?

(*a*) They often visit the country but he has only spent one weekend there.

(*b*) Unlike them, being brought up in the city, he can appreciate its worth.

(*c*) In contrast to them, he finds city people friendlier than country people.

(*d*) He thinks them hypocritical to maintain a preference for country life.

2 What advantage has the city dweller over the country dweller in terms of entertainment?

(*a*) He can entertain his country friends more often than they can him.

(*b*) His choice of entertainment is wide and within easy reach of him.

(*c*) As he travels by bus and not by train, he can see the latest plays.

(*d*) He does not need a major operation when planning a visit to the theatre.

3 When he speaks of the beauty to be found in the city, the writer ________ .

(*a*) alludes to the comparative cheerlessness of winter nights in the country

(*b*) means that if more people settled in the city they would find peace

(*c*) advertises the fact that the city is a warmer place than the country

(*d*) implies that the country is less peaceful than the city at weekends

Structure 结构

4 I ________ and bred in the city and have always regarded ... (ll.1-2)

(*a*) being born (*b*) had been born (*c*) was born (*d*) am born

5 He ________ talking about the friendly people ... (ll.8-9)

(*a*) never tires of (*b*) is never tiring of (*c*) is never tired (*d*) is never tiring when

6 The latest exhibitions, films or plays are only ________ . (l.23)

(*a*) by bus a short distance away (*b*) a short distance by bus away

(*c*) a short distance away by bus (*d*) the distance of a short bus away

7 – and stagger home loaded with ________ exotic items as they can carry. (ll.25-26)

(*a*) as many of the (*b*) as many (*c*) so many (*d*) the most

8 I have always been mystified ________ city dwellers, who ... (ll.29-30)

(*a*) why (*b*) by the fact that (*c*) for what (*d*) with

Vocabulary 词汇

9 ________ the only form of entertainment (l.12)

(*a*) pretty well (*b*) altogether (*c*) certainly (*d*) in particular

10 If you can ________ without the few pastoral pleasures of the country ... (l.17)

(*a*) make (*b*) manage (*c*) succeed (*d*) pass

11 As the play ________ ... (ll.21-22)

(*a*) reaches its climax (*b*) nears its end (*c*) ends its run (*d*) draws the curtain

12 Few things can have such an ________ as the peace ... (ll.27-28)

(*a*) impact (*b*) imposition (*c*) imprint (*d*) impression

LESSON 42

Modern cavemen 现代洞穴人

Listen then answer the question below.

听录音，然后回答以下问题。

With what does the writer compare the Gouffre Berger?

... can only be dimly understood

Cave exploration, or pot-holing, as it has come to be known, is a relatively new sport. Perhaps it is the desire for solitude or the chance of making an unexpected discovery that lures people down to the depths of the earth. It is impossible to give a satisfactory explanation for a pot-holer's motives. For him, caves have the same peculiar fascination which high mountains have for the climber. They arouse instincts which can only be dimly understood.

Exploring really deep caves is not a task for the Sunday afternoon rambler. Such undertakings require the precise planning and foresight of military operations. It can take as long as eight days to rig up rope ladders and to establish supply bases before a descent can be made into a very deep cave. Precautions of this sort are necessary, for it is impossible to foretell the exact nature of the difficulties which will confront the pot-holer. The deepest known cave in the world is the Gouffre Berger near Grenoble. It extends to a depth of 3,723 feet. This immense chasm has been formed by an underground stream which has tunnelled a course through a flaw in the rocks. The entrance to the cave is on a plateau in the Dauphiné Alps. As it is only six feet across, it is barely noticeable. The cave might never have been discovered had not the entrance been spotted by the distinguished French pot-holer, Berger. Since its discovery, it has become a sort of pot-holers' Everest. Though a number of descents have been made, much of it still remains to be explored.

A team of pot-holers recently went down the Gouffre Berger. After entering the narrow gap on the plateau, they climbed down the steep sides of the cave until they came to a narrow corridor. They had to edge their way along this, sometimes wading across shallow streams, or swimming across deep pools. Suddenly they came to a waterfall which dropped into an underground lake at the bottom of the cave. They plunged into the lake, and after loading their gear on an inflatable rubber dinghy, let the current carry them to the other side. To protect themselves from the icy water, they had to wear special rubber suits. At the far end of the lake, they came to huge piles of rubble which had been washed up by the water. In this part of the cave, they could hear an insistent booming sound which they found was caused by a small waterspout shooting down into a pool from the roof of the cave. Squeezing through a cleft in the rocks, the pot-holers arrived at an enormous cavern, the size of a huge concert hall. After switching on powerful arc lights, they saw great stalagmites — some of them over forty feet high — rising up like tree-trunks to meet the stalactites suspended from the roof. Round about, piles of limestone glistened in all the colours of the rainbow. In the eerie silence of the cavern, the only sound that could be heard was made by water which dripped continuously from the high dome above them.

New words and expressions 生词和短语

caveman (title)	/ˈkeɪvmæn/	*n.*	（远古）洞穴人
pot-holing (l.1)	/ˈpɒt-ˌhəʊlɪŋ/	*n.*	洞穴探险，洞穴探险运动
solitude (l.2)	/ˈsɒlɪtjuːd/	*n.*	孤独，寂寞
lure (l.3)	/lʊə/	*v.*	引诱，诱惑
pot-holer (l.5)	/ˈpɒt-ˌhəʊlə/	*n.*	洞穴探险者
rambler (l.8)	/ˈræmblə/	*n.*	漫步者，散步者
undertaking (l.8)	/ˌʌndəˈteɪkɪŋ/	*n.*	任务，工作
foresight (l.9)	/ˈfɔːsaɪt/	*n.*	预见；深谋远虑
foretell (l.11)	/fɔːˈtel/ (foretold /fɔːˈtəʊld/, foretold)	*v.*	预言
Grenoble (l.12)	/grɪˈnəʊbl/	*n.*	格勒诺布尔
chasm (l.13)	/ˈkæzəm/	*n.*	断层，裂口，陷坑
flaw (l.14)	/flɔː/	*n.*	小裂缝
distinguished (l.16)	/dɪˈstɪŋgwɪʃt/	*adj.*	杰出的，著名的
Everest (l.17)	/ˈevərɪst/	*n.*	珠穆朗玛峰（即 Qomolangma）
wade (l.20)	/weɪd/	*v.*	涉水，蹚水
waterfall (l.21)	/ˈwɔːtəfɔːl/	*n.*	瀑布
gear (l.22)	/gɪə/	*n.*	一套用具
inflatable (l.22)	/ɪnˈfleɪtəbəl/	*adj.*	可充气的
rubble (l.24)	/ˈrʌbəl/	*n.*	碎石，瓦砾
insistent (l.25)	/ɪnˈsɪstənt/	*adj.*	连续的，不断的
boom (l.25)	/buːm/	*v.*	轰响
waterspout (l.25)	/ˈwɔːtəspaʊt/	*n.*	强大的水柱
cleft (l.26)	/kleft/	*n.*	裂隙，开口
cavern (l.27)	/ˈkævən/	*n.*	大洞穴
stalagmite (l.28)	/ˈstæləgmaɪt/	*n.*	石笋
stalactite (l.28)	/ˈstæləktaɪt/	*n.*	钟乳石
limestone (l.29)	/ˈlaɪmstəʊn/	*n.*	石灰石
glisten (l.29)	/ˈglɪsən/	*v.*	闪烁
eerie (l.29)	/ˈɪəri/	*adj.*	引起恐惧的，可怕的
dome (l.31)	/dəʊm/	*n.*	穹窿，圆顶

Notes on the text 课文注释

1 as it has come to be known, 正如已逐渐为人所了解的那样，此处作插入语。

2 it is the desire ... or the chance ... that ...

这是强调句式，被强调的部分是句子的主语 the desire ... or the chance ...

3 rig up, 装配，搭起。

4 Grenoble, 格勒诺布尔，是法国东南部伊泽尔河上的一座大城镇，尤以它的大学而著称。

5 The cave might never have been discovered had not the entrance been spotted by ..., 如果不是……偶然发现这个洞口的话，这个洞也许永远不会为人所知。这是表示与过去事实不相符的虚拟语气结构，句中的非真实条件句 had not the entrance been spotted by ... 由于省略了 if，因此要用倒装句式。

6 edge one's way, 此处作"侧身徐徐向前移动"讲。

7 which they found was caused ... of the cave.

which was caused ... of the cave 是定语从句，修饰 sound; they found 此处作插入语。shooting down ... of the cave 是现在分词短语作定语，修饰 waterspout。

参考译文

洞穴勘探——或洞穴探险——是一项比较新的体育活动，已逐渐被人们了解。寻求独居独处的愿望或寻求意外发现机会的欲望吸引着人们来到地下深处。要想对洞穴探险者的动机作出满意的解释是不可能的。对洞穴探险者来说，洞穴有一种特殊的魅力，就像高山对于登山者有特殊的魅力一样。为什么洞穴能引发人的那种探险本能，人们对此只能有一种模模糊糊的认识。

探测非常深的洞穴不是那些在星期日下午漫步的人所能胜任的。这种活动需要有军事行动般的周密部署和预见能力。有时需要花费整整 8 天时间来搭起绳梯，建立供应基地，然后才能下到一个很深的洞穴里。作出这样的准备是必要的，因为无法预见到洞穴探险者究竟会遇到什么性质的困难。世界上最深的洞穴是格勒诺布尔附近的高弗·伯杰洞，深达 3,723 英尺。这个深邃的洞穴是由一条地下暗泉冲刷岩石中的缝隙并使之慢慢变大而形成的。此洞的洞口在丹芬阿尔卑斯山的高原上，仅 6 英尺宽，很难被人发现。若不是法国著名洞穴探险家伯杰由于偶然的机会发现了这个洞口的话，这个洞也许永远不会为人所知。自从被发现以后，这个洞成了洞穴探险者的珠穆朗玛峰，人们多次进入洞内探险，但至今尚有不少东西有待勘探。

最近，一个洞穴探险队下到了高弗·伯杰洞里。他们从高原上的窄缝进去，顺着笔直陡峭的洞壁往下爬，来到了一条狭窄的走廊上。他们不得不侧着身子往前走，有时蹚过浅溪，有时蹚过深潭。突然，他们来到一道瀑布前，那瀑布奔泻而下，注入洞底一处地下湖里。他们跳入湖中，把各种器具装上一只充气橡皮艇，听任水流将他们带往对岸。湖水冰冷刺骨，他们必须穿上一种特制的橡皮服以保护自己。在湖的尽头，他们见到一大堆一大堆由湖水冲刷上岸的碎石。在这儿，他们可以听见一种连续不断的轰鸣声。后来他们发现这是由山洞顶部的一个小孔里喷出的水柱跌落到水潭中时发出的声音。洞穴探险者从岩石缝里挤身过去，来到一个巨大的洞里，其大小相当于一个音乐厅。他们打开强力弧光灯，看见一株株巨大的石笋，有的高达 40 英尺，像树干似地向上长着，与洞顶悬挂下来的钟乳石相接。周围是一堆堆石灰石，像彩虹一样闪闪发光。洞里有一种可怕的寂静，唯一可以听见的声响是高高的圆顶上不间断地滴水的滴答声。

Comprehension 理解

Give short answers to these questions in your own words as far as possible. Use one complete sentence for each answer.

1 Why does the exploration of a deep cave require careful planning?

2 How has the Gouffre Berger been formed?

3 Why might the entrance to the Gouffre Berger never have been discovered?

Vocabulary 词汇

Explain the meanings of the following words and phrases as they are used in the passage: relatively (l.2); desire for solitude (l.2); lures (l.3); arouse (l.6); precise (l.9); confront (l.11); is barely noticeable (l.15).

Summary writing 摘要写作

Give an account *in not more than 80 words* of the pot-holers' experiences after they entered the Gouffre Berger. Use your own words as far as possible. Do not include anything that is not in the last paragraph.

Composition 作文

Write a composition in about 300 words on one of the following:

a Describe a man's efforts to escape from a cave by the seashore in order to avoid the incoming tide.

b The most popular sport in your country.

Letter writing 书信写作

You had a party at your home recently but unintentionally neglected to invite a close friend of yours. Write him a letter of about 100 words apologizing for this and explaining how the mistake came about.

Key structures and Special difficulties 关键句型和难点

Rewrite the following sentence without changing the meaning. Then refer to ll.25-26.

The insistent booming sound they could hear was found to be caused by a small waterspout shooting down into a pool from the roof of the cave.

They could hear ... which they ...

Multiple choice questions 选择题

Choose the correct answers to the following questions.

Comprehension 理解

1 In undertaking the descent of a really deep cave, a pot-holer ________ .

(*a*) must be motivated by the desire to make an unexpected discovery

(*b*) is prepared to spend a whole weekend away from his home

(*c*) needs military co-operation in making preparations for the descent

(*d*) may have to spend as much as a week planning his descent

2 The cave discovered by the French pot-holer, Berger ________ .

(*a*) represents the ultimate challenge to any pot-holer who is truly dedicated

(*b*) was recently explored for the first time since its discovery

(*c*) has to be approached by following a stream which leads underground

(*d*) consists of a large cavern, the size of a huge concert hall

3 On reaching the enormous cavern, the pot-holers ________ .

(*a*) had to squeeze into a cleft in the rocks at the side

(*b*) lit it up by using the arc lights they had carried down with them

(*c*) saw a rainbow shedding its light on the limestone around them

(*d*) could still hear the waterspout falling into the pool behind them

Structure 结构

4 – or the chance that they ________ an unexpected discovery that ... (ll.2-3)

(*a*) would make (*b*) can make (*c*) may make (*d*) might have made

5 It can take as long as eight days getting rope ladders rigged up and ________ before ... (ll.9-10)

(*a*) to establish bases supplied (*b*) supplying bases established

(*c*) establishing supply bases (*d*) bases established and supplied

6 After ________ the narrow gap, they climbed down the steep sides of the cave. (ll.18-19)

(*a*) they were entering (*b*) entering (*c*) entered (*d*) they will enter

7 – let ________ the current to the other side. (ll.22-23)

(*a*) them be carried with (*b*) their being carried by

(*c*) themselves carry (*d*) themselves be carried by

8 No other sound could be heard ________ made by water ... (ll.30-31)

(*a*) except it was (*b*) than that (*c*) that was (*d*) but this was

Vocabulary 词汇

9 It can take ________ eight days to rig up ... (l.9)

(*a*) around (*b*) more than (*c*) up to (*d*) at least

10 – has tunnelled a course through a ________ in the rocks. (ll.13-14)

(*a*) fault (*b*) gap (*c*) cleft (*d*) fissure

11 They had to ________ along this ... (ll.19-20)

(*a*) sidle nervously (*b*) file sideways (*c*) walk sharply (*d*) move cautiously

12 To protect themselves from the ________ water, they wore special rubber suits. (l.23)

(*a*) frozen (*b*) freezing (*c*) chilly (*d*) iced

LESSON 43

Fully insured 全保险

Listen then answer the question below.

听录音，然后回答以下问题。

Who owned the pie dish and why?

it was an unusual pie dish

Insurance companies are normally willing to insure anything. Insuring public or private property is a standard practice in most countries in the world. If, however, you were holding an open air garden party or a fete it would be equally possible to insure yourself in the event of bad weather. Needless to say, the bigger the risk an insurance company takes, the higher the premium you will have to pay. It is not uncommon to hear that a shipping company has made a claim for the cost of salvaging a sunken ship. But the claim made by a local authority to recover the cost of salvaging a sunken pie dish must surely be unique.

Admittedly it was an unusual pie dish, for it was eighteen feet long and six feet wide. It had been purchased by a local authority so that an enormous pie could be baked for an annual fair. The pie committee decided that the best way to transport the dish would be by canal, so they insured it for the trip. Shortly after it was launched, the pie committee went to a local inn to celebrate. At the same time, a number of teenagers climbed on to the dish and held a little party of their own. Dancing proved to be more than the dish could bear, for during the party it capsized and sank in seven feet of water.

The pie committee telephoned a local garage owner who arrived in a recovery truck to salvage the pie dish. Shivering in their wet clothes, the teenagers looked on while three men dived repeatedly into the water to locate the dish. They had little difficulty in finding it, but hauling it out of the water proved to be a serious problem. The sides of the dish were so smooth that it was almost impossible to attach hawsers and chains to the rim without damaging it. Eventually chains were fixed to one end of the dish and a powerful winch was put into operation. The dish rose to the surface and was gently drawn towards the canal bank. For one agonizing moment, the dish was perched precariously on the bank of the canal, but it suddenly overbalanced and slid back into the water. The men were now obliged to try once more. This time they fixed heavy metal clamps to both sides of the dish so that they could fasten the chains. The dish now had to be lifted vertically because one edge was resting against the side of the canal. The winch was again put into operation and one of the men started up the truck. Several minutes later, the dish was successfully hauled above the surface of the water. Water streamed in torrents over its sides with such force that it set up a huge wave in the canal. There was a danger that the wave would rebound off the other side of the bank and send the dish plunging into the water again. By working at tremendous speed, the men managed to get the dish on to dry land before the wave returned.

New words and expressions 生词和短语

insure (title)	/ɪnˈʃʊə/	v.	投保
fete (l.4)	/feɪt/	n.	游园会
premium (l.6)	/ˈpriːmiəm/	n.	保险费
recover (l.8)	/rɪˈkʌvə/	v.	使……得到补偿，弥补
admittedly (l.10)	/ədˈmɪtɪdli/	adv.	公认地
purchase (l.10)	/ˈpɜːtʃɪs/	v.	买
annual (l.11)	/ˈænjuəl/	adj.	一年一度的
teenager (l.13)	/ˈtiːneɪdʒə/	n.	（13至19岁的）青少年
capsize (l.15)	/kæpˈsaɪz/	v.	（船）翻
shiver (l.17)	/ˈʃɪvə/	v.	打颤，发抖
dive (l.17)	/daɪv/	v.	（头向下）跳水
haul (l.18)	/hɔːl/	v.	拖，拉
hawser (l.19)	/ˈhɔːzə/	n.	粗缆绳
rim (l.20)	/rɪm/	n.	（圆形物品的）外沿，边
winch (l.20)	/wɪntʃ/	n.	绞车
agonizing (l.22)	/ˈægənaɪzɪŋ/	adj.	精神紧张的，提心吊胆的
perch (l.22)	/pɜːtʃ/	v.	处于（高处）
precariously (l.22)	/prɪˈkeəriəsli/	adv.	危险地，不稳固地
overbalance (l.22)	/ˌəʊvəˈbæləns/	v.	失去平衡
clamp (l.24)	/klæmp/	n.	夹钳，夹板
vertically (l.24)	/ˈvɜːtɪkəli/	adv.	垂直地
torrent (l.27)	/ˈtɒrənt/	n.	激流，洪流
rebound (l.28)	/rɪˈbaʊnd/	v.	弹回

Notes on the text 课文注释

1 in the event of, 作“倘若”、“万一”、“如果发生”讲。

2 the bigger the risk an insurance company takes, the higher the premium you will have to pay. 保险公司承担的风险越大，你付的保险费就越高。这里又是一个“the + 形容词比较级，the + 形容词比较级”的例子，汉语可译成“越……越……”。

3 make a claim for ..., 作“要求得到……”讲。

4 put into operation, 使……运转。

5 for one agonizing moment, 在令人忐忑不安的瞬间。

6 set up, 激起。

参考译文

保险公司一般说来愿意承保一切东西。承办公共财产或私人财产保险是世界上大部分国家的正常业务。如果你要举办一次露天游园会或盛宴，为避免碰上不好的天气而遭受损失也同样可以投保。不用说，保险公司承担的风险越大，你付的保险费也就越高。航运公司为打捞沉船而提出索赔，这是常有的事，但某地当局为打捞一只焙制馅饼的盘子提出索赔，倒是件新鲜事儿。

这个馅饼盘子确实少见，有18英尺长，6英尺宽。某地方当局买下它用来焙制一个巨大的馅饼为一年一度的交易会助兴。馅饼委员会确定运输这只盘子的最佳方案是通过运河水运。于是，他们对这只盘子的运输安全投了保。盘子下水后不久，馅饼委员会成员们来到当地一家小酒店庆贺。就在这个时候，许多十几岁的孩子爬上盘子举行他们自己的集会。他们跳起了舞，但盘子难以承受。在舞会进行过程中，盘子倾覆，沉入了7英尺深的水中。

馅饼委员会给当地汽车修理厂的老板打电话，他闻讯后开着一辆急修车前来打捞盘子。那些孩子们穿着湿衣服浑身哆嗦，看着3个工人轮番潜入水中以确定盘子的位置。他们没费多大事儿就找到了盘子，可是要把盘子捞出却是一个很大的难题。盘子四边十分光滑，要在盘边拴上绳索或链条而同时又不损坏它是很难办到的。不过，他们终于将链条固定在盘子的一端，一台大功率的绞车开动起来。盘子慢慢浮出水面，被轻轻地拽向运河岸边。在令人忐忑不安的瞬间，盘子晃晃悠悠地上了岸，但它突然失去了平衡，又跌回水中。工人们只得再来一次。这次，他们用沉重的金属夹子把盘子夹住，以便往盘子上安装铁链。这次，盘子必须垂直吊出水面，因为盘子的一边紧靠着运河河岸。绞盘机再次启动，一位工人发动了急修车的引擎。几分钟后，盘子被成功地拽出了水面。波浪从盘子两侧急涌而出，在运河里掀起一股大浪。但是当波浪从河对岸折回来时，就有再次把盘子冲进水里的危险。工人们动作迅速，终于赶在那股大浪返回之前把盘子拽到了岸上。

Comprehension 理解

Give short answers to these questions in your own words as far as possible. Use one complete sentence for each answer.

1 How is a policy holder affected when an insurance company takes a big risk?

2 Why had the local authorities bought such a big pie dish?

3 Why did the pie dish capsize?

Vocabulary 词汇

Explain the meanings of the following words and phrases as they are used in the passage: a standard practice (l.2); in the event of (l.5); premium (l.6); salvaging (l.9); annual (l.11); launched (l.13); capsized (l.15).

Summary writing 摘要写作

Describe *in not more than 80 words* how the pie dish was recovered after it had been located in the water. Use your own words as far as possible. Do not include anything that is not in the last paragraph.

Composition 作文

Write a composition in about 300 words on one of the following:

a Write an imaginary account of how the pie dish capsized during the party held by the teenagers.

b Describe a day spent by the river or by the sea.

Letter writing 书信写作

You have just heard that a friend of yours was recently involved in a car accident but was not hurt. Write a letter of about 100 words telling him how you came to hear of the accident and expressing the hope that he has recovered from his unpleasant experience.

Key structures and Special difficulties 关键句型和难点

Rewrite the following sentence without changing the meaning. Then refer to ll.23-24.

This time heavy metal clamps were fixed to both sides of the dish so that the chains could be fastened.

This time they ...

Multiple choice questions 选择题

Choose the correct answers to the following questions.

Comprehension 理解

1 In the case of the pie dish, the insurance company concerned ________ .

(*a*) demanded a high premium in view of the unusual size of the dish

(*b*) was asked to pay the costs of the salvaging operation

(*c*) agreed to pay the cost of transporting the dish by canal

(*d*) arranged for the dish to be recovered from the canal

2 When the pie dish had capsized, the men who came to recover it ________ .
(*a*) had some difficulty finding it as they had been drinking locally
(*b*) had little difficulty finding it as it had not sunk to the bottom
(*c*) found it difficult to devise a way of getting it out of the water
(*d*) damaged the dish when they attached hawsers and chains to the rim

3 The huge wave in the canal was caused by ________ .
(*a*) the sinking of the pie dish
(*b*) the dish sliding back into the water
(*c*) the great quantity of water which poured off the dish when they were getting it out
(*d*) the party of teenagers

4 Eventually the dish was successfully recovered by ________ .
(*a*) resting one of its edges on the bank and attaching chains to the other
(*b*) securing the winch chains with metal clamps and lifting it vertically
(*c*) one of the men getting on to the truck so as to pull at the chains
(*d*) some men who hauled it to the surface of the water at tremendous speed

Structure 结构

5 The bigger the risk an insurance company takes, ________ to pay as a premium. (ll.5-7)
(*a*) the higher you will have (*b*) the more you will have
(*c*) more you will have (*d*) you will have higher

6 It is not uncommon to hear ________ a claim for ... (ll.7-8)
(*a*) of a shipping company making (*b*) a shipping company to have made
(*c*) the shipping company which has made (*d*) a shipping company making

7 The sides of the dish were so smooth that attaching hawsers and chains to the rim ________ almost certain to damage it. (ll.19-20)
(*a*) had (*b*) were (*c*) it was (*d*) was

8 There was a danger that when the wave ________ off the other side, it would send the dish plunging into the water again. (ll.28-29)
(*a*) was rebounding (*b*) has rebounded (*c*) rebounded (*d*) would rebound

Vocabulary 词汇

9 Three men dived ________ into the water. (ll.17-18)
(*a*) now and again (*b*) one after another (*c*) time and again (*d*) many a time

10 A powerful winch was ________ . (ll.20-21)
(*a*) got going (*b*) made to work (*c*) taken to task (*d*) given a function

11 For one ________ moment, the dish ... (ll.21-23)
(*a*) dangerous (*b*) frightening (*c*) exciting (*d*) painful

12 This time they put metal clamps ________ both sides of the dish. (ll.23-24)
(*a*) over (*b*) on to (*c*) astride (*d*) upon

LESSON

44 Speed and comfort 又快捷又舒适

... meet interesting people

Listen then answer the question below.

听录音，然后回答以下问题。

Which type of transport does the writer prefer, do you think?

People travelling long distances frequently have to decide whether they would prefer to go by land, sea, or air. Hardly anyone can positively enjoy sitting in a train for more than a few hours. Train compartments soon get cramped and stuffy. It is almost impossible to take your mind off the journey. Reading is only a partial solution, for the monotonous rhythm of the wheels clicking on the rails soon lulls you to sleep. During the day, sleep comes in snatches. At night, when you really wish to go to sleep, you rarely manage to do so. If you are lucky enough to get a sleeper, you spend half the night staring at the small blue light in the ceiling, or fumbling to find your ticket for inspection. Inevitably you arrive at your destination almost exhausted. Long car journeys are even less pleasant, for it is quite impossible even to read. On motorways you can, at least, travel fairly safely at high speeds, but more often than not, the greater part of the journey is spent on roads with few service stations and too much traffic. By comparison, ferry trips or cruises offer a great variety of civilized comforts. You can stretch your legs on the spacious decks, play games, meet interesting people and enjoy good food — always assuming, of course, that the sea is calm. If it is not, and you are likely to get seasick, no form of transport could be worse. Even if you travel in ideal weather, sea journeys take a long time. Relatively few people are prepared to sacrifice holiday time for the pleasure of travelling by sea.

Aeroplanes have the reputation of being dangerous and even hardened travellers are intimidated by them. They also have the disadvantage of being an expensive form of transport. But nothing can match them for speed and comfort. Travelling at a height of 30,000 feet, far above the clouds, and at over 500 miles an hour is an exhilarating experience. You do not have to devise ways of taking your mind off the journey, for an aeroplane gets you to your destination rapidly. For a few hours, you settle back in a deep armchair to enjoy the flight. The real escapist can watch a film and sip champagne on some services. But even when such refinements are not available, there is plenty to keep you occupied. An aeroplane offers you an unusual and breathtaking view of the world. You soar effortlessly over high mountains and deep valleys. You really see the shape of the land. If the landscape is hidden from view, you can enjoy the extraordinary sight of unbroken cloud plains that stretch out for miles before you, while the sun shines brilliantly in a clear sky. The journey is so smooth that there is nothing to prevent you from reading or sleeping. However you decide to spend your time, one thing is certain: you will arrive at your destination fresh and uncrumpled. You will not have to spend the next few days recovering from a long and arduous journey.

New words and expressions 生词和短语

positively	(l.3)	/ˈpɒzɪtɪvli/	*adv.*	绝对地，完全地
compartment	(l.4)	/kəmˈpɑːtmənt/	*n.*	列车客车厢内的分隔间（或单间）
cramped	(l.4)	/kræmpt/	*adj.*	窄小的
stuffy	(l.4)	/ˈstʌfi/	*adj.*	憋气的，闷气的
monotonous	(l.6)	/məˈnɒtənəs/	*adj.*	枯燥的，乏味的，单调的
rhythm	(l.6)	/ˈrɪðəm/	*n.*	有节奏的运动
click	(l.6)	/klɪk/	*v.*	发出咔嗒声
lull	(l.7)	/lʌl/	*v.*	催人欲睡
snatch	(l.7)	/snætʃ/	*n.*	短时，片段
sleeper	(l.8)	/ˈsliːpə/	*n.*	卧铺
fumble	(l.9)	/ˈfʌmbəl/	*v.*	乱摸，摸索
inspection	(l.9)	/ɪnˈspekʃən/	*n.*	检查
inevitably	(l.9)	/ɪˈnevətəbli/	*adv.*	必然地，不可避免地
destination	(l.9)	/ˌdestɪˈneɪʃən/	*n.*	目的地
exhausted	(l.10)	/ɪɡˈzɔːstɪd/	*adj.*	精疲力尽的
motorway	(l.11)	/ˈməʊtəweɪ/	*n.*	高速公路
ferry	(l.12)	/ˈferi/	*n.*	渡船
cruise	(l.13)	/kruːz/	*n.*	巡游船
civilized	(l.13)	/ˈsɪvəl-aɪzd/	*adj.*	文明的
spacious	(l.13)	/ˈspeɪʃəs/	*adj.*	宽敞的
seasick	(l.15)	/ˈsiːˌsɪk/	*adj.*	晕船的
intimidate	(l.18)	/ɪnˈtɪmɪdeɪt/	*v.*	恐吓，恫吓
disadvantage	(l.19)	/ˌdɪsədˈvɑːntɪdʒ/	*n.*	短处，缺点
exhilarating	(l.21)	/ɪɡˈzɪləreɪtɪŋ/	*adj.*	使人高兴的，令人兴奋的
escapist	(l.23)	/ɪˈskeɪpɪst/	*n.*	逍遥者
sip	(l.23)	/sɪp/	*v.*	呷，啜
champagne	(l.23)	/ʃæmˈpeɪn/	*n.*	香槟酒
refinement	(l.24)	/rɪˈfaɪnmənt/	*n.*	精心的安排
breathtaking	(l.25)	/ˈbreθˌteɪkɪŋ/	*adj.*	激动人心的；不寻常的
soar	(l.25)	/sɔː/	*v.*	高飞，翱翔
effortlessly	(l.25)	/ˈefətləsli/	*adv.*	不费力地
landscape	(l.26)	/ˈlændskeɪp/	*n.*	景色
fresh	(l.29)	/freʃ/	*adj.*	精神饱满的
uncrumpled	(l.29)	/ʌnˈkrʌmpld/	*adj.*	没有垮下来的

Notes on the text 课文注释

1 take your mind off the journey, 摆脱旅途的困扰。take one's mind off sth. 是"把某人的注意力从某事上移开"的意思。

2 in snatches, 断断续续地。

3 more often than not, 经常。

4 But nothing can match them for speed and comfort.
但就速度和舒适而论，什么也不能和飞机相比。介词 for 此处作"就……而论"讲。

5 keep you occupied, 使你有事可做。

参考译文

出远门的人常常需要决定是走旱路、水路，还是坐飞机。很少有人能够真正喜欢坐几个小时以上的火车。车厢很快就变得拥挤、闷热，想摆脱开旅途的困扰是很难的。看书只能解决部分问题。车轮与铁轨间单调的咔嗒声很快就会送你进入梦乡。白天是忽睡忽醒，到了夜晚，你真想睡了，却很难入睡。即使你走运弄到一个卧铺，夜间有一半时间你会盯着车顶那盏小蓝灯而睡不着觉；要不然就为查票摸索你的车票。一旦抵达目的地，你总是疲惫不堪。乘汽车作长途旅行则更加不舒服，因为连看书都几乎不可能。在高速公路上还好，你至少能以相当快的速度安全地向前行进。但旅行的大部分时间都花在普通道路上，而且只有很少的服务设施，交通也很拥挤。相比之下，坐船旅行或环游可以得到文明世界的各种享受。你可以在宽敞的甲板上伸展四肢，做游戏，还能见到各种有趣的人，能享用各种美味佳肴——当然，这一切只有在大海风平浪静的情况下才有可能。如果大海肆虐起来，你就可能晕船，那种难受劲儿是任何一种别的旅行方式都不会有的。即便风平浪静，坐船旅行也要占用很长时间。没有多少人会为了享受坐船旅行的乐趣而牺牲假期的时间。

飞机以危险而著称，连老资格的旅行者也怕飞机。飞机的另一个缺点是昂贵。但就速度与舒适而言，飞机是无与伦比的。腾云驾雾，在 30,000 英尺高空以 500 英里的时速旅行，这种经历令人心旷神怡。你不必想办法去摆脱旅途的困扰，因为飞机会迅速地把你送到目的地。几小时之内，你躺在扶手椅上，享受着旅途的欢乐。真正会享受的人还可以在某些航班上看一场电影和喝香槟。即使没有这些消遣条件，也总是有事可做。飞机上，你可以观察世界上非同寻常的奇妙的美景。你毫不费劲地飞越高山幽谷，你确能饱览大地的风貌。如果这种景色被遮住了，你便可以观赏一下展现在你面前的、一望数英里的、连绵不断的云海，同时阳光灿烂，天空清澈明朗。旅途平稳，丝毫不妨碍你阅读或睡眠。不管你打算如何消磨时间，有件事是可以肯定的，即当你抵达目的地时，你感到精神焕发，毫无倦意，用不着因为漫长旅途的辛苦而花几天时间休息来恢复精神。

Comprehension 理解

Give short answers to these questions in your own words as far as possible. Use one complete sentence for each answer.

1 Why is it difficult to read on a train?

2 What makes long car journeys unpleasant?

3 What are the two disadvantages of travelling by sea?

Vocabulary 词汇

Explain the meanings of the following words and phrases as they are used in the passage: cramped and stuffy (l.4); monotonous (l.6); lulls (l.7); in snatches (l.7); destination (l.9); stretch your legs (l.13); sacrifice (l.16).

Summary writing 摘要写作

In not more than 80 words give an account of the advantages of travelling by air. Use your own words as far as possible. Do not include anything that is not in the last paragraph.

Composition 作文

Write a composition in about 300 words on one of the following:

a Which form of transport do you prefer for long distance journeys: train, car, or ship?

b The disadvantages of travelling by air.

Letter writing 书信写作

You had bought a ticket to the theatre but now find that you will be unable to go. Write a letter of about 100 words to a friend enclosing the ticket and explaining why you are sending it to him.

Key structures and Special difficulties 关键句型和难点

Rewrite the following sentence without changing the meaning. Then refer to l.28.

You travel so smoothly that there is nothing to prevent you from reading or sleeping.

The journey ...

Multiple choice questions 选择题

Choose the correct answers to the following questions.

Comprehension 理解

1 The great disadvantage shared by train and car travel alike is ________ .
(*a*) the fact that one cannot get to sleep on either form of transport
(*b*) the fact that one cannot concentrate on what one is reading
(*c*) the monotony of travelling at fast speeds along railway lines or roads
(*d*) the tedium and discomfort of the journey

2 An aeroplane journey invariably provides such distractions as ________ .
(*a*) the thought that one has not long to wait before arriving
(*b*) the exhilarating quality of the air one breathes at 30,000 feet
(*c*) being able to watch a film or drink champagne
(*d*) the marvellous views of land or clouds you can see from the plane

3 Having arrived at your destination by air, you will ________ .
(*a*) not feel exhausted as you will have had plenty of sleep
(*b*) feel the expense was worth the comfort and speed of the 500-mile flight
(*c*) have the satisfaction of knowing you could not have got there any faster
(*d*) at least feel fresh though your clothes might be a mess

Structure 结构

4 People travelling long distances frequently have to decide ________ they would prefer to go by land, sea or air. (ll.1-2)
(*a*) which (*b*) how (*c*) what (*d*) if

5 If you are ________ a sleeper ... (ll.8-9)
(*a*) luckily getting (*b*) lucky and get (*c*) to get luckily (*d*) so lucky to get

6 – and enjoy good food ________ , of course, that the sea is calm. (ll.13-14)
(*a*) provided (*b*) in the event (*c*) in case (*d*) if only

7 In addition, it ________ their being the most expensive form of transport. (l.19)
(*a*) has been a grave disadvantage (*b*) is the great disadvantage that
(*c*) is a great disadvantage (*d*) has been the great disadvantage of

Vocabulary 词汇

8 If it is not, and you are ________ , no form of transport could be worse. (ll.14-15)
(*a*) probably seasick (*b*) bad at sailing (*c*) sick of the sea (*d*) prone to seasickness

9 Nothing can ________ aeroplanes for speed and comfort. (ll.19-20)
(*a*) match with (*b*) equal (*c*) equal with (*d*) equal to

10 For a few hours, you ________ a deep armchair to enjoy the flight. (ll.22-23)
(*a*) relax in (*b*) sit up in (*c*) sit on (*d*) install

11 You can enjoy the extraordinary ________ of unbroken cloud plains ... (ll.26-27)
(*a*) scene (*b*) vision (*c*) spectacle (*d*) scenery

12 You won't spend the next few days getting ________ a long and arduous journey. (ll.29-30)
(*a*) above (*b*) over (*c*) up from (*d*) away from

LESSON

45 The power of the press

新闻报道的威力

Listen then answer the question below.

听录音，然后回答以下问题。

Does the writer think the parents were lucky or unlucky to gain prosperity in this way? Why?

The rise to fame was swift

In democratic countries any efforts to restrict the freedom of the press are rightly condemned. However, this freedom can easily be abused. Stories about people often attract far more public attention than political events. Though we may enjoy reading about the lives of others, it is extremely doubtful whether we would equally enjoy reading about ourselves. Acting on the contention that facts are sacred, reporters can cause untold suffering to individuals by publishing details about their private lives. Newspapers exert such tremendous influence that they can not only bring about major changes to the lives of ordinary people but can even overthrow a government.

The story of a poor family that acquired fame and fortune overnight, dramatically illustrates the power of the press. The family lived in Aberdeen, a small town of 23,000 inhabitants in South Dakota. As the parents had five children, life was a perpetual struggle against poverty. They were expecting their sixth child and were faced with even more pressing economic problems. If they had only had one more child, the fact would have passed unnoticed. They would have continued to struggle against economic odds and would have lived in obscurity. But they suddenly became the parents of quintuplets, four girls and a boy, an event which radically changed their lives. The day after the birth of the five children, an aeroplane arrived in Aberdeen bringing sixty reporters and photographers.

The rise to fame was swift. Television cameras and newspapers carried the news to everyone in the country. Newspapers and magazines offered the family huge sums for the exclusive rights to publish stories and photographs. Gifts poured in not only from unknown people, but from baby food and soap manufacturers who wished to advertise their products. The old farmhouse the family lived in was to be replaced by a new $500,000 home. Reporters kept pressing for interviews so lawyers had to be employed to act as spokesmen for the family at press conferences. While the five babies were still quietly sleeping in oxygen tents in a hospital nursery, their parents were paying the price for fame. It would never again be possible for them to lead normal lives. They had become the victims of commercialization, for their names had acquired a market value. Instead of being five new family members, these children had immediately become a commodity.

New words and expressions 生词和短语

democratic	(l.1)	/ˌdeməˈkrætɪk/	*adj.*	民主的
restrict	(l.1)	/rɪˈstrɪkt/	*v.*	限制
abuse	(l.3)	/əˈbjuːz/	*v.*	滥用
contention	(l.6)	/kənˈtenʃən/	*n.*	论点
untold	(l.7)	/ˌʌnˈtəʊld/	*adj.*	数不尽的，无限的
South Dakota	(l.11)	/ˌsaʊθ-dəˈkəʊtə/		南达科他州（美国）

perpetual (l.12)	/pəˈpetʃuəl/	*adj.*	永久的	nursery (l.24)	/ˈnɜːsəri/	*n.*	育婴室，保育室
obscurity (l.15)	/əbˈskjʊərɪti/	*n.*	默默无闻	commercialization (l.25)	/kəˌmɜːʃəlaɪˈzeɪʃən/	*n.*	商品化
quintuplet (l.15)	/ˈkwɪntjʊplɪt/	*n.*	五胞胎之一	commodity (l.26)	/kəˈmɒdɪti/	*n.*	商品
radically (l.16)	/ˈrædɪkli/	*adv.*	彻底地，完全地				
exclusive (l.19)	/ɪkˈskluːsɪv/	*adj.*	独占的，独家的				

Notes on the text 课文注释

1 read about (= of) ..., 作“读到……”讲。

2 it is extremely doubtful whether ... ourselves.

it 是先行主语，替代以 whether 引导的主语从句。

3 act on ..., 根据……行动。

4 bring about, 带来。

5 South Dakota, 南达科他，美国中北部的一个州。面积 77,047 平方英里（约 200,000 平方公里）。这个州以粮食生产和矿产著称。

6 struggle against ... odds, 与厄运搏斗。

7 If they had only had one more child, the fact would have passed unnoticed. 如果他们只是添了 1 个孩子，这件事就不会引起任何人的注意。这是虚拟语气，用来表示与过去的事实相反的假设。unnoticed 是过去分词作方式状语，修饰 passed。

8 The rise to fame was swift. 出名太快了。

to fame 作 rise 的定语。

9 the exclusive rights to publish, 独家报道（出版）权。

10 pour in, 作“大量流入”、“源源而来”解。

11 press for ..., 作“迫切要求……”讲。

参考译文

在民主国家里，任何限制新闻自由的企图都理所当然地受到谴责。然而，这种自由很容易被滥用。常人轶事往往比政治事件更能引起公众注意。我们都喜欢看关于别人生活的报道，但是否同样喜欢看关于自己生活的报道，就很难说了。记者按事实至上的论点行事，发表有关别人私生活的细节，有时会给当事人造成极大的痛苦。新闻具有巨大的威力。它们不仅可以给寻常人家的生活带来重大的变化，甚至还能推翻一个政府。

下面这户穷人一夜之间出名发财的故事戏剧性地说明了新闻报道的威力。这户人家住在南达科他州一个人口为 23,000 的小镇上，镇名为阿伯丁。家里已有 5 个孩子，全家人常年在贫困中挣扎。第 6 个孩子即将问世，他们面临着更为严峻的经济问题。如果他们只是添了 1 个孩子，这件事就不会引起任何人的注意。这家人会继续为克服经济上的拮据而奋斗，并默默无闻地活下去。但是他们出人意料地生了个五胞胎，4 女 1 男。这事使他们的生活发生了根本的变化。五胞胎降生第二天，一架飞机飞抵阿伯丁，随机带来 60 名记者与摄影师。

这一家迅速出了名。电视摄像机和报纸把消息传送到全国。报纸、杂志出高价向他们购买文字、图片的独家报道权。不但素昧平生的人寄来了大量的礼物，而且婴儿食品、婴儿肥皂制造厂商为了替自己产品做广告也寄来了大量的礼物。这家人住的旧农舍将由一座价值 50 万美元的新住宅所取代。由于记者们纷纷要求会见，他们不得不请了律师充当他们家的发言人举行记者招待会。眼下，五胞胎还静静地躺在医院婴儿室的氧气帐里，他们的父母却为这名声付出了代价，他们再也无法过正常的生活。他们成了商业化的受害者，因为他们的名字具有了市场价值。这些孩子立即成了商品，而不是 5 个新的家庭成员。

Comprehension 理解

Give short answers to these questions in your own words as far as possible. Use one complete sentence for each answer.

1 How can newspapermen cause untold suffering to ordinary people?

2 What event made the poor family in South Dakota famous?

3 What happened the day after the birth of the children?

Vocabulary 词汇

Explain the meanings of the following words and phrases as they are used in the passage: restrict (l.1); equally (l.5); contention (l.6); untold (l.7); acquired (l.10); perpetual struggle (l.12); in obscurity (l.15).

Summary writing 摘要写作

Describe *in not more than 80 words* how the birth of the five children affected the family and the town. Use your own words as far as possible. Do not include anything that is not in the last paragraph.

Composition 作文

Write a composition in about 300 words on one of the following:

a Write a 'human interest' story about a person who suddenly acquired fame because he won a lot of money from football pools.

b Describe the newspaper you most enjoy reading.

Letter writing 书信写作

Write a letter of about 100 words to the Editor of a newspaper complaining about an article that was published recently. Begin 'Dear Sir' and end 'Yours faithfully'.

Key structures and Special difficulties 关键句型和难点

Rewrite the following sentence without changing the meaning. Then refer to ll.19-20.

The family were offered huge sums by newspapers and magazines.

Newspapers and magazines ...

Multiple choice questions 选择题

Choose the correct answers to the following questions.

Comprehension 理解

1 The Press will argue that they have the right to publish a story, although it may seriously affect the individual concerned, because ________ .

(*a*) in a democracy, the individual deserves more attention than politics

(*b*) facts in themselves, however unpleasant they may be, must be respected

(*c*) people not only enjoy reading about others but about themselves as well

(*d*) they only use their power to influence events of national importance

2 News editors and reporters wanted to publish the story because ________ .
(*a*) they always defend the freedom of the Press
(*b*) they know that stories about people sell a lot of newspapers
(*c*) they wanted to change the lives of these poor people
(*d*) they believed it was the right thing to do

3 The interest that was taken in the family was ________ .
(*a*) of national importance because of the rise in the birth rate
(*b*) charitable, for people of all kinds were concerned about their poverty
(*c*) so overwhelming that even lawyers attended their press conferences
(*d*) mainly from commercial organizations who wanted to promote their sales

Structure 结构

4 The public are often far more interested ________ political events. (ll.3-4)
(*a*) in people's stories than
(*b*) in stories about people than in
(*c*) with stories about people than
(*d*) by people's stories than by

5 The influence of newspapers is ________ bring about major changes in the lives of ordinary people but they can even overthrow a government. (ll.8-9)
(*a*) such that not only can they
(*b*) so that not only they can
(*c*) such that they cannot only
(*d*) so that not only can they

6 A sixth child ________ expected so they were faced ... (ll.12-13)
(*a*) was (*b*) being (*c*) having (*d*) had been

7 While the five babies ________ in oxygen tents ... (ll.23-24)
(*a*) were remaining quietly sleeping
(*b*) remained quietly sleeping
(*c*) remained to sleep quietly
(*d*) remaining were quietly sleeping

Vocabulary 词汇

8 Stories about people are often ________ . (l.3)
(*a*) of great interest to everyone
(*b*) in the public interest
(*c*) a matter of publicity
(*d*) publicly attended

9 Newspapers ________ tremendous influence over the lives of ordinary people. (ll.8-9)
(*a*) press (*b*) invoke (*c*) impose (*d*) wield

10 Reporters ________ interviews ... (l.22)
(*a*) went on strike for
(*b*) went on printing
(*c*) made repeated requests for
(*d*) were continually hurrying to

11 Lawyers were employed to act as spokesmen ________ the family. (ll.22-23)
(*a*) on account of (*b*) instead of (*c*) on behalf of (*d*) for the sake of

12 Instead of being five new family members, these children had become ________ . (l.26)
(*a*) victims of commercialization
(*b*) something to be bought and sold
(*c*) a public convenience
(*d*) a product of the market

LESSON

46 Do it yourself 自己动手

Listen then answer the question below.

听录音，然后回答以下问题。

Did the writer repair his lawn mower in the end? Why/Why not?

wives assume their husbands will put things right

So great is our passion for doing things for ourselves, that we are becoming increasingly less dependent on specialized labour. No one can plead ignorance of a subject any longer, for there are countless do-it-yourself publications. Armed with the right tools and materials, newlyweds gaily embark on the task of decorating their own homes. Men, particularly, spend hours of their leisure time installing their own fireplaces, laying out their own gardens; building garages and making furniture. Some really keen enthusiasts go so far as to build their own computers. Shops cater for the do-it-yourself craze not only by running special advisory services for novices, but by offering consumers bits and pieces which they can assemble at home. Such things provide an excellent outlet for pent up creative energy, but unfortunately not all of us are born handymen.

Some wives tend to believe that their husbands are infinitely resourceful and can fix anything. Even men who can hardly drive a nail in straight are supposed to be born electricians, carpenters, plumbers and mechanics. When lights fuse, furniture gets rickety, pipes get clogged, or vacuum cleaners fail to operate, some women assume that their husbands will somehow put things right. The worst thing about the do-it-yourself game is that sometimes even men live under the delusion that they can do anything, even when they have repeatedly been proved wrong. It is a question of pride as much as anything else.

Last spring my wife suggested that I call in a man to look at our lawn mower. It had broken down the previous summer, and though I promised to repair it, I had never got round to it. I would not hear of the suggestion and said that I would fix it myself. One Saturday afternoon, I hauled the machine into the garden and had a close look at it. As far as I could see, it needed only a minor adjustment: a turn of a screw here, a little tightening up there, a drop of oil and it would be as good as new. Inevitably the repair job was not quite so simple. The mower firmly refused to mow, so I decided to dismantle it. The garden was soon littered with chunks of metal which had once made up a lawn mower. But I was extremely pleased with myself. I had traced the cause of the trouble. One of the links in the chain that drives the wheels had snapped. After buying a new chain I was faced with the insurmountable task of putting the confusing jigsaw puzzle together again. I was not surprised to find that the machine still refused to work after I had reassembled it, for the simple reason that I was left with several curiously shaped bits of metal which did not seem to fit anywhere. I gave up in despair. The weeks passed and the grass grew. When my wife nagged me to do something about it, I told her that either I would have to buy a new mower or let the grass grow. Needless to say our house is now surrounded by a jungle. Buried somewhere in deep grass there is a rusting lawn mower which I have promised to repair one day.

New words and expressions 生词和短语

plead (l.3)	/pliːd/	*v.*	找（借口），辩解
ignorance (l.3)	/ˈɪɡnərəns/	*n.*	无知，不懂
publication (l.4)	/ˌpʌblɪˈkeɪʃən/	*n.*	出版物
newlyweds (l.5)	/ˈnjuːliwedz/	*n.*	（复数）新婚夫妇
gaily (l.5)	/ˈɡeɪli/	*adv.*	愉快地，高兴地
leisure (l.6)	/ˈleʒə/	*n.*	空闲
keen (l.8)	/kiːn/	*adj.*	热心的，渴望的
advisory (l.9)	/ədˈvaɪzəri/	*adj.*	咨询的
novice (l.9)	/ˈnɒvɪs/	*n.*	新手
consumer (l.9)	/kənˈsjuːmə/	*n.*	消费者，顾客
assemble (l.10)	/əˈsembəl/	*v.*	装配，组装
outlet (l.10)	/ˈaʊtlet/	*n.*	出路
creative (l.10)	/kriˈeɪtɪv/	*adj.*	创造性的
handyman (l.11)	/ˈhændimæn/	*n.*	手巧的人，能工巧匠
resourceful (l.12)	/rɪˈzɔːsfəl/	*adj.*	足智多谋的
fuse (l.14)	/fjuːz/	*v.*	由于烧断保险丝而短路
rickety (l.14)	/ˈrɪkɪti/	*adj.*	要散架的，晃动的
clog (l.14)	/klɒɡ/	*v.*	堵塞
delusion (l.16)	/dɪˈluːʒən/	*n.*	错觉
lawn mower (l.18)	/ˈlɔːn-ˌməʊə/		割草机
adjustment (l.21)	/əˈdʒʌstmənt/	*n.*	调整
screw (l.21)	/skruː/	*n.*	螺丝钉
dismantle (l.23)	/dɪsˈmæntl/	*v.*	拆卸
chunk (l.24)	/tʃʌŋk/	*n.*	（厚）块
snap (l.25)	/snæp/	*v.*	绷断
insurmountable (l.26)	/ˌɪnsəˈmaʊntəbəl/	*adj.*	不能克服的，难以对付的
jigsaw (l.26)	/ˈdʒɪɡsɔː/	*n.*	拼板玩具
nag (l.29)	/næɡ/	*v.*	唠叨不休
rust (l.31)	/rʌst/	*v.*	生锈

Notes on the text 课文注释

1 So great is our passion for doing ..., 这句话的基本句型是 so ... that ... 引导的结果状语从句，为了强调 great 这个词，把 so great 提到句首，因此主谓语要倒装。
2 embark on, 开始干。
3 lay out, 布置。
4 go so far as to (do), 竟到了……的程度。
5 cater for, 迎合。
6 get round to, 抽出时间，腾空。
7 I would not hear, 我不愿意听。
8 jigsaw puzzle, 拼板玩具。

参考译文

现在我们自己动手做事的热情很高，结果对于专业工人的依赖越来越少了。由于出版了不计其数的教人自己动手做事的书报杂志，没有人再能说对某事一无所知。新婚夫妇找来合适的工具和材料，喜气洋洋地开始布置新房。特别是男人，常利用空闲时间安装壁炉，布置花园，建造车库，制作家具。有些热衷于自己动手的人甚至自己组装电脑。为了满足自己动手热的需要，商店不仅为初学者提供专门的咨询服务，而且为顾客准备了各种零件，供他们买回家去安装。这些东西为人们潜在的创造力提供了一个绝妙的用武之地。但遗憾的是，我们并非人人都是天生的能工巧匠。

妻子常常认为她们的丈夫无比聪明能干。甚至那些连一枚钉子都钉不直的男人都被认为是天生的电工、木匠、水管工和机械师。每当电灯保险丝烧断、家具榫头松动、管道堵塞、吸尘器出故障时，有些妻子认为丈夫总有办法。自己动手的例子中最糟糕的是，有时甚至是男人尽管接连失败却还误以为自己什么都行，原因就是要面子。

去年春天，妻子让我请人检查一下我家的割草机。那台割草机去年夏天就坏了，尽管我答应修，但一直没抽出时间。我不愿听妻子的建议，说我自己会修。一个星期六的下午，我把割草机拉到了花园里，仔细检查了一番。在我看来，只需稍加调整即可。这儿紧紧螺丝，那儿固定一下，再加几滴油，它就会像新的一样了。事实上，修理工作远不是那么简单。修完后割草机还是纹丝不动。于是，我决定把它拆开。一会儿工夫，割草机便被拆成一个个金属零件，乱七八糟地堆在花园里。但我却非常高兴，因为我找到了毛病所在。驱动轮子的链条断了一节。我买来一根新链条后，面临的就是如何把这些令人眼花缭乱的拼板重新组装起来。等我装完后，那台割草机仍然一动不动，对此我倒并不感到吃惊。原因很简单，因为还剩下几个形状奇特的零件似乎哪里也装不上去。我无可奈何，只好罢休。几个星期过去了，草长了起来。妻子喋喋不休地让我想点办法。我告诉她，要么买一台新割草机，要么让草长下去。不用说，我家现在已被丛林包围。深草丛中的某个地方有一台正在生锈的割草机，那就是我曾答应某日要修理的割草机。

Comprehension 理解

Give short answers to these questions in your own words as far as possible. Use one complete sentence for each answer.

1 Why do we not rely on specialized labour so much nowadays?

2 How do shops encourage people to do things for themselves?

3 What do some women tend to believe about their husbands?

Vocabulary 词汇

Explain the meanings of the following words and phrases as they are used in the passage: increasingly (l.2); plead ignorance (l.3); gaily embark on the task (l.5); installing (l.7); novices (l.9); repeatedly (l.17).

Summary writing 摘要写作

Describe *in not more than 80 words* the author's efforts to repair his lawn mower. Use your own words as far as possible. Do not include anything that is not in the last paragraph.

Composition 作文

Write a composition in about 300 words on one of the following:

a Describe a similar 'do-it-yourself' experience of your own.

b Your favourite hobby.

Letter writing 书信写作

Write a letter of about 100 words to an uncle who gave you some good advice two years ago which you acted on. This enabled you to do very well in your work. Thank him and give news of yourself.

Key structures and Special difficulties 关键句型和难点

Rewrite the following sentence without changing the meaning. Then refer to l.20.

'I shall fix it myself,' I said.

I said that ...

Multiple choice questions 选择题

Choose the correct answers to the following questions.

Comprehension 理解

1 Why did the writer's wife suggest calling in a man to look at the mower?
(*a*) To get her husband to mend it, believing him to be a born carpenter.
(*b*) She had forgotten that her husband had promised to mend it.
(*c*) She suspected it would otherwise remain unrepaired and the grass uncut.
(*d*) Her husband had repeatedly tried mending it already without success.

2 The writer decided to dismantle the mower because ________ .
(*a*) it was a Saturday and he had the time to spare
(*b*) he had discovered the cause of the trouble
(*c*) he thought it was a sure way of proving it would not work
(*d*) what repairs he had already carried out had not proved adequate

3 The writer's house is now surrounded by a jungle because ________ .
(*a*) he lost several pieces of the mower in the process of dismantling it
(*b*) by now the lawn mower is too rusty to cut the grass with
(*c*) besides not having cut the grass, he has failed to cut down the trees
(*d*) his wife was not prepared to let him buy a new lawn mower

Structure 结构

4 – that we are ________ dependent on specialized labour as we used to be. (ll.1-2)
(*a*) increasingly less (*b*) becoming not so (*c*) not nearly as (*d*) becoming less

5 Whatever it is, a fused light, ________ furniture, a clogged pipe, a broken-down vacuum cleaner, wives automatically assume ... (ll.14-15)
(*a*) shaked (*b*) a shaken (*c*) a shaky (*d*) shaky

6 – my wife said to me: 'Darling, ________ call someone in to look at the lawn mower?' (l.18)
(*a*) why don't you (*b*) why you don't (*c*) would you be kind to (*d*) do you kindly

7 – which I have promised to get round ________ one day. (l.19)
(*a*) to repair it (*b*) to repairing (*c*) repairing (*d*) to repairing it

Vocabulary 词汇

8 To plead ignorance of a subject is no longer a ________ , for there are ... (ll.2-4)
(*a*) wise precaution (*b*) literary discussion (*c*) legitimate excuse (*d*) reasonable allowance

9 Men, ________ spend hours of their leisure time on do-it-yourself. (ll.6-7)
(*a*) mostly (*b*) especially (*c*) rather (*d*) specially

10 Some women assume that their husbands will somehow put things ________ . (ll.14-15)
(*a*) in order (*b*) well (*c*) in straight (*d*) correctly

11 I was left with bits of metal which did not seem to ________ anywhere. (l.28)
(*a*) fasten (*b*) suit (*c*) go (*d*) fix

12 ________ , our house is now surrounded by a jungle. (ll.30-31)
(*a*) As a matter of fact (*b*) As you can imagine
(*c*) As a result (*d*) As a last resort

LESSON

47 Too high a price? 代价太高？

Listen then answer the question below.

听录音，然后回答以下问题。

What does the writer describe as an 'amusing old-fashioned source of noise'?

an insidious kind of pollution

Pollution is the price we pay for an overpopulated, over-industrialized planet. When you come to think about it, there are only four ways you can deal with rubbish: dump it, burn it, turn it into something you can use again, attempt to produce less of it. We keep trying all four methods, but the sheer volume of rubbish we produce worldwide threatens to overwhelm us.

Rubbish, however, is only part of the problem of polluting our planet. The need to produce ever-increasing quantities of cheap food leads to a different kind of pollution. Industrialized farming methods produce cheap meat products: beef, pork and chicken. The use of pesticides and fertilizers produces cheap grain and vegetables. The price we pay for cheap food may be already too high: Mad Cow Disease (BSE) in cattle, salmonella in chicken and eggs, and listeria in dairy products. And if you think you'll abandon meat and become a vegetarian, you have the choice of very expensive organically-grown vegetables or a steady diet of pesticides every time you think you're eating fresh salads and vegetables, or just having an innocent glass of water!

However, there is an even more insidious kind of pollution that particularly affects urban areas and invades our daily lives, and that is noise. Burglar alarms going off at any time of the day or night serve only to annoy passers-by and actually assist burglars to burgle. Car alarms constantly scream at us in the street and are a source of profound irritation. A recent survey of the effects of noise revealed (surprisingly?) that dogs barking incessantly in the night rated the highest form of noise pollution on a scale ranging from 1 to 7. The survey revealed a large number of sources of noise that we really dislike. Lawn mowers whining on a summer's day, late-night parties in apartment blocks, noisy neighbours, vehicles of all kinds, especially large container trucks thundering through quiet villages, planes and helicopters flying overhead, large radios carried round in public places and played at maximum volume. New technology has also made its own contribution to noise. A lot of people object to mobile phones, especially when they are used in public places like restaurants or on public transport. Loud conversations on mobile phones invade our thoughts or interrupt the pleasure of meeting friends for a quiet chat. The noise pollution survey revealed a rather surprising and possibly amusing old-fashioned source of noise. It turned out to be snoring! Men were found to be the worst offenders. It was revealed that 20% of men in their mid-thirties snore. This figure rises to a staggering 60% of men in their sixties. Against these figures, it was found that only 5% of women snore regularly, while the rest are constantly woken or kept awake by their trumpeting partners. Whatever the source of noise, one thing is certain: silence, it seems, has become a golden memory.

New words and expressions 生词和短语

pollution (l.1)	/pəˈluːʃən/	n.	污染
overpopulated (l.1)	/ˌəuvəˈpɒpjuleɪtɪd/	adj.	人口过多的
over-industrialized (l.2)	/ˌəuvəɪnˈdʌstriəlaɪzd/	adj.	过度工业化的
sheer (l.5)	/ʃɪə/	adj.	纯粹的，不掺杂的
worldwide (l.6)	/ˌwɜːldˈwaɪd/	adv.	在全世界
overwhelm (l.6)	/ˌəuvəˈwelm/	v.	制服；使不知所措
pollute (l.7)	/pəˈluːt/	v.	污染
pesticide (l.9)	/ˈpestɪsaɪd/	n.	杀虫剂
fertilizer (l.9)	/ˈfɜːtɪlaɪzə/	n.	肥料
salmonella (l.11)	/ˌsælməˈnelə/	n.	沙门氏菌
listeria (l.11)	/lɪˈstɪəriə/	n.	利斯特杆菌
vegetarian (l.12)	/ˌvedʒɪˈteəriən/	n.	吃素的人
organically-grown (l.12)	/ɔːˈgænɪkli-grəun/	adj.	有机培植的（不施化肥和其他化学药品培植）
insidious (l.15)	/ɪnˈsɪdiəs/	adj.	暗中为害的
urban (l.15)	/ˈɜːbən/	adj.	城市的
burglar (l.16)	/ˈbɜːglə/	n.	窃贼
burgle (l.17)	/ˈbɜːgəl/	v.	入室偷窃
scream (l.17)	/skriːm/	v.	尖叫
profound (l.18)	/prəˈfaund/	adj.	极度的
irritation (l.18)	/ˌɪrɪˈteɪʃən/	n.	烦躁
incessantly (l.19)	/ɪnˈsesəntli/	adv.	连续不断地
whine (l.20)	/waɪn/	v.	发呜呜声
helicopter (l.22)	/ˈhelɪkɒptə/	n.	直升机
maximum (l.23)	/ˈmæksɪməm/	adj.	最大的
technology (l.23)	/tekˈnɒlədʒi/	n.	技术
contribution (l.23)	/ˌkɒntrɪˈbjuːʃən/	n.	贡献
mobile (l.24)	/ˈməubaɪl/	adj.	可移动的
snore (l.27)	/snɔː/	v.	打鼾
offender (l.27)	/əˈfendə/	n.	冒犯者
staggering (l.28)	/ˈstægərɪŋ/	adj.	令人惊愕的
trumpet (l.30)	/ˈtrʌmpɪt/	v.	吹号
partner (l.30)	/ˈpɑːtnə/	n.	伙伴

Notes on the text 课文注释

1 pay for, 付出代价，得到报应。

2 Mad Cow Disease (BSE), 疯牛病。

这是牛得的一种病的医学名称的缩写，全称为牛海绵状组织病。这种病的首例在 20 世纪 80 年代末发生在英国，很难彻底治愈。此病俗称“疯牛病”，因为患病的动物无法控制自身的行为。

3 you have the choice of very expensive organically-grown vegetables or a steady diet of pesticides every time you think you're eating fresh salads and vegetables, 你可以两者择一：或是选用价格昂贵、有机培植的蔬菜，或是当你认为在享用新鲜色拉和新鲜蔬菜的时候，实际上每次都不断地吃进杀虫剂。

the choice of ... or ..., 在……和……之间选择。

4 burglar alarm, 防盗警报器；go off, 响起。

5 car alarm, 汽车防盗警报器。

6 large container truck, 运输大型集装箱的卡车。

7 mobile phone, 移动式电话，手机。

8 against these figures, 与这些数字相比。

参考译文

污染就是我们为这个人口过密、过度工业化的星球所付出的代价。当我们开始考虑垃圾问题时，我们只有 4 种对付垃圾的方法：倾倒、焚烧、把垃圾变成再生材料或试图少产生一些垃圾。我们一直在试这 4 种方式，但是，我们在世界范围内仅产生的垃圾的量就有把我们覆盖的危险。

然而，垃圾只是我们这个星球的污染问题的一个方面。日益增长的对廉价食物的需求导致了另一种形式的污染。工业化的农作方式生产出了廉价的肉类制品——牛肉、猪肉和鸡肉。使用杀虫剂和化肥生产出了廉价的谷物和蔬菜。为了廉价食物我们付出的代价已经太高了：牛肉中的疯牛病，鸡肉和鸡蛋中的沙门氏菌，奶制品中的利斯特杆菌。如果你想放弃肉类而变成一位素食者，那么你可以两者择一：或是选用价格昂贵、有机培植的蔬菜，或是当你认为在享用新鲜色拉和新鲜蔬菜或饮用一杯无害的水的时候，实际上每次都在吃进杀虫剂。

但是，还有一种更加隐蔽有害的污染，它专门影响城镇地区，侵袭我们的日常生活，那就是噪音。防盗警报器在白天和黑夜的任何时候都会响起来，它的作用只是骚扰过路行人，而实际上却帮助窃贼入室行窃。在街上，汽车的防盗警报不断对我们吼叫，这是人们极度烦躁的一个原因。最近一个有关噪音的作用的调查（令人吃惊地）指出，夜间连续不断的狗叫声，在一个从1级至7级的刻度表上应列为最严重的噪音污染。这个调查揭示了我们所不喜欢的大量的噪音的来源：夏天呜呜作响的割草机，公寓楼里深夜聚会的喧哗声，大声吵闹的邻居，各式各样的车辆，特别是穿越寂静的村庄的集装箱卡车，从头顶飞过的飞机和直升机，被带到公共场所、音量开到最大的大功率收音机。新技术也为噪音作出了它的贡献。许多人都反对移动式电话，特别是在如饭店、公共交通车等公共场所使用移动电话。用移动电话大声交谈干扰我们的思路，破坏我们和朋友在一起轻声聊天所得到的乐趣。这个有关噪声污染的调查还揭示了一种出人意外而同时可能会引人发笑的老式噪声源。它竟然是鼾声。男人是这方面的罪魁祸首。调查指出，20%的35岁左右的男人打鼾；而到60岁这个年龄段，这个数字上升到令人惊愕的60%。与这些数字相比，只有5%的女性经常打鼾，而其余的则经常被与她们同睡、像吹号似地打着呼噜的男人吵醒或弄得睡不着。不管噪声来自何方，有一点是肯定的：看来寂静已变成一种珍贵的回忆。

Comprehension 理解

Give short answers to these questions in your own words as far as possible. Use one complete sentence for each answer.

1 What is meant by the clause 'the sheer volume of rubbish we produce worldwide threatens to overwhelm us'?

2 What do farmers do to produce meat products cheaply?

3 Why wouldn't you necessarily avoid pollution if you became a vegetarian?

Vocabulary 词汇

Explain the meanings of the following words and phrases as they are used in the passage: dump (1.3); sheer volume (1.5); rubbish (1.5); leads to (1.8); dairy (1.11); abandon (1.11); organically-grown (1.12).

Summary writing 摘要写作

In not more than 80 words give an account of noise pollution. Do not include anything that is not in the last paragraph.

Composition 作文

Write a composition in about 300 words on one of the following:

a 'You are what you eat.' What do you think this means and how does it apply to you or the people you know?

b Write about any serious pollution problems in this country.

Letter writing 书信写作

In not more than 100 words write a letter which you would very much like to receive.

Key structures and Special difficulties 关键句型和难点

Rewrite the following sentence without changing the meaning. Then refer to ll.15-16.

Noise is an even more insidious kind of pollution which affects urban areas and invades our daily lives.

There is ...

Multiple choice questions 选择题

Choose the correct answers to the following questions.

Comprehension 理解

1 – the sheer volume of rubbish we produce worldwide ________ .

(*a*) is heaped up like a great mountain (*b*) is spread over the world like a blanket

(*c*) is already beyond our control (*d*) is like a tide that will rise and drown us

2 The root cause of pollution in agriculture is ________ .

(*a*) the intensive use of pesticides and fertilizers

(*b*) the twin pressures to produce more food and at lower cost

(*c*) the conflict between good hygiene and cheap meat production

(*d*) the unrealistic price of organically-grown vegetables

3 For most people, the most distressing form of noise pollution is ________ .

(*a*) dogs barking all night (*b*) people using mobile phones

(*c*) heavy trucks in quiet villages (*d*) noisy neighbours having parties

4 Snoring causes a severe noise problem for ________ .

(*a*) young males in particular (*b*) a majority of middle-aged men

(*c*) women of all ages (*d*) young women especially

Structure 结构

5 – there are only four ways ________ rubbish. (ll.2-3)

(*a*) of dealing with (*b*) which to deal with (*c*) can be dealt with (*d*) to be dealing with

6 We keep trying ________ methods. (ll.4-5)

(*a*) these all four (*b*) of these all four (*c*) all of these four (*d*) all these of four

7 Burglar alarms ________ at any time of the day or night serve only to annoy ... (ll.16-17)

(*a*) that go off (*b*) that are going off (*c*) go off (*d*) which going off

8 A recent survey revealed that ________ dogs barking incessantly in the night that we dislike most. (ll.18-19)

(*a*) it is (*b*) is (*c*) there be (*d*) there are

Vocabulary 词汇

9 New technology has also ________ in noise pollution. (l.23)

(*a*) done its bit (*b*) done a share (*c*) played a role (*d*) given its all

10 A lot of people ________ to mobile phones, especially in public places. (l.24)

(*a*) except (*b*) offend (*c*) take exception (*d*) take offence

11 The noise pollution survey ________ a rather surprising source of noise. (ll.26-27)

(*a*) brought to light (*b*) gave birth to (*c*) came to be (*d*) took the lid off

12 ________ these figures, it was found that only 5% of women snore. (l.29)

(*a*) Comparing with (*b*) By comparison with (*c*) In comparing (*d*) In comparing with

LESSON 48

The silent village 沉默的村庄

Listen then answer the question below.
听录音，然后回答以下问题。

Why was the village silent?

hostile to travellers

In this much-travelled world, there are still thousands of places which are inaccessible to tourists. We always assume that villagers in remote places are friendly and hospitable. But people who are cut off not only from foreign tourists, but even from their own countrymen can be hostile to travellers. Visits to really remote villages are seldom enjoyable — as my wife and I discovered during a tour through the Balkans.

We had spent several days in a small town and visited a number of old churches in the vicinity. These attracted many visitors, for they were not only of great architectural interest, but contained a large number of beautifully preserved frescoes as well. On the day before our departure, several bus loads of tourists descended on the town. This was more than we could bear, so we decided to spend our last day exploring the countryside. Taking a path which led out of the town, we crossed a few fields until we came to a dense wood. We expected the path to end abruptly, but we found that it traced its way through the trees. We tramped through the wood for over two hours until we arrived at a deep stream. We could see that the path continued on the other side, but we had no idea how we could get across the stream. Suddenly my wife spotted a boat moored to the bank. In it there was a boatman fast asleep. We gently woke him up and asked him to ferry us to the other side. Though he was reluctant to do so at first, we eventually persuaded him to take us.

The path led to a tiny village perched on the steep sides of a mountain. The place consisted of a straggling unmade road which was lined on either side by small houses. Even under a clear blue sky, the village looked forbidding, as all the houses were built of grey mud bricks. The village seemed deserted, the only sign of life being an ugly-looking black goat on a short length of rope tied to a tree in a field nearby. Sitting down on a dilapidated wooden fence near the field, we opened a couple of tins of sardines and had a picnic lunch. All at once, I noticed that my wife seemed to be filled with alarm. Looking up I saw that we were surrounded by children in rags who were looking at us silently as we ate. We offered them food and spoke to them kindly, but they remained motionless. I concluded that they were simply shy of strangers. When we later walked down the main street of the village, we were followed by a silent procession of children. The village which had seemed deserted, immediately came to life. Faces appeared at windows. Men in shirt sleeves stood outside their houses and glared at us. Old women in black shawls peered at us from doorways. The most frightening thing of all was that not a sound could be heard. There was no doubt that we were unwelcome visitors. We needed no further warning. Turning back down the main street, we quickened our pace and made our way rapidly towards the stream where we hoped the boatman was waiting.

New words and expressions 生词和短语

inaccessible	(l.2)	/ˌɪnək'sesəbəl/	*adj.*	难接近的，达不到的
hospitable	(l.3)	/'hɒspɪtəbəl/	*adj.*	好客的
hostile	(l.5)	/'hɒstaɪl/	*adj.*	不友好的，有敌意的
vicinity	(l.8)	/vɪ'sɪnɪti/	*n.*	周围，近邻
architectural	(l.9)	/ˌɑːkɪ'tektʃərəl/	*adj.*	建筑的
fresco	(l.10)	/'freskəʊ/	*n.*	壁画
abruptly	(l.13)	/ə'brʌptli/	*adv.*	突然地，意外地
tramp	(l.13)	/træmp/	*v.*	徒步行进
moor	(l.16)	/mʊə/	*v.*	（用绳、链、锚）系（船）
ferry	(l.16)	/'feri/	*v.*	（用渡船）运
straggle	(l.18)	/'strægəl/	*v.*	蔓延，散乱分布
dilapidated	(l.22)	/dɪ'læpɪdeɪtɪd/	*adj.*	陈旧破烂的，倒塌的
sardine	(l.22)	/ˌsɑː'diːn/	*n.*	沙丁鱼，沙丁鱼罐头
rag	(l.24)	/ræg/	*n.*	破烂衣服
motionless	(l.25)	/'məʊʃənləs/	*adj.*	不动的
procession	(l.26)	/prə'seʃən/	*n.*	行列，成队的人群
shawl	(l.28)	/ʃɔːl/	*n.*	披巾，围巾
peer	(l.28)	/pɪə/	*v.*	凝视，盯着
quicken	(l.30)	/'kwɪkən/	*v.*	加快

Notes on the text 课文注释

1 much-travelled world, 经常有游客往来的世界。

2 be inaccessible to ..., 是……难以到达的。

3 be cut off from ..., 与……隔绝。

4 Balkans, 巴尔干半岛，它位于欧洲东南部，包括阿尔巴尼亚、保加利亚、希腊、罗马尼亚东南部分、土耳其欧洲部分和前南斯拉夫各州。

5 descend on, 突然到来。

6 taking a path which led out of the town 是现在分词短语作时间状语，which 引导定语从句修饰 path。意即“走上了一条出镇的小路”。

7 (be) fast asleep, 熟睡，此处作定语，修饰 boatman。

8 the only sign of life being an ugly-looking black goat, 这是一个由名词和分词组成的独立主格结构，作状语，说明 seemed deserted。

9 be shy of ..., 作“对……畏缩”、“害怕……”解。

10 come to life, 苏醒过来，活跃起来。

参考译文

在这个旅游频繁的世界上，仍有成千上万个游人足迹未至的地方。人们总是以为偏僻地方的村民们热情好客。但是，那些不但与外国旅游者隔绝，而且与本国同胞隔绝的人们有可能对游客抱有敌意。到真正偏僻的村庄去旅游并不是一件愉快的事情，我与妻子在一次周游巴尔干半岛时对此深有体会。

我们在一座小镇上逗留了几天，参观了附近的许多古老的教堂。这些教堂吸引了大量游客，不仅是因为建筑风格奇特，而且还存有大量保存完好的壁画。我们离开小镇的前一天，镇上来了几辆满载游客的公共汽车。人多得使我们难以忍受，于是我们决定利用最后一天去乡间一游。我们走上了一条出镇的小路，穿过几块农田，来到一片茂密的树林。我们原以为小路会到此突然终止，没想到它在树林中继续向前延伸。我们在树林中跋涉了两个多小时，到了一条深溪边。我们可以看到小路在深溪对岸继续向前伸展，但却不知如何越过这道深溪。突然，妻子发现岸边泊着一条小船，船上有一船夫在呼呼大睡。我们轻轻地把他唤醒，请他把我们摆渡过溪。一开始，他很不愿意，但经劝说，终于同意了。

顺着小路，我们来到一个坐落在陡峭山坡上的小村庄。这儿有一条未经修筑的弯弯曲曲的道路，路两边排列着一些矮小的农舍。农舍全用灰色的土坯建成，因此，即使在晴朗的蓝天底下，村庄看上去也会令人感到难以亲近。村里似乎无人居住，唯一的生命迹象是附近田里一只面目可憎的黑山羊，用一截短绳拴在一棵树上。我们在田边一堵东倒西歪的篱笆墙上坐了下来，打开几听沙丁鱼罐头，吃了一顿野外午餐。

突然，我注意到妻子十分惊恐。我抬头一看，发现我们被一群衣衫褴褛的小孩团团围住了，他们在默不作声地看着我们吃饭。我们给他们东西吃，客客气气地同他们交谈，但他们却一动也不动。我认为这不过是他们在陌生人面前表现出的害羞。后来，我们在村里的主要街道上行走的时候，一队默不作声的孩子跟在我们后头。刚才还似乎空荡荡的村庄一下子活跃了起来，窗口露出了一张张面孔，只穿着衬衣的男人们站在屋子外面凶狠地盯着我们，披黑纱巾的老妇人站在门口偷偷地瞅着我们。最令人害怕的是到处没有一点声音。毫无疑问，我们的来访是不受欢迎的。我们不需要进一步的警告了，便掉转身子，沿着那条大道加快步伐，快速地朝深溪边走去，希望船夫还在那儿等着我们。

Comprehension 理解

Give short answers to these questions in your own words as far as possible. Use one complete sentence for each answer.

1 Why are visits to really remote villages seldom enjoyable?
2 Why did the author and his wife decide to spend their last day exploring the countryside?
3 How did the author and his wife get across the stream?

Vocabulary 词汇

Explain the meanings of the following words and phrases as they are used in the passage: inaccessible (l.2); hospitable (l.3); hostile (l.5); vicinity (l.8); end abruptly (l.13); traced (l.13); eventually (l.17).

Summary writing 摘要写作

Describe *in not more than 80 words* the experiences of the author and his wife when they visited a remote village in the Balkans. Use your own words as far as possible. Do not include anything that is not in the last paragraph.

Composition 作文

Write a composition in about 300 words on one of the following:

a Describe any village you know well.
b Continue the above passage. Imagine the boatman was not waiting for the author and his wife. Describe what happened.

Letter writing 书信写作

Write a letter in not more than 100 words to a very old man congratulating him on the occasion of his eighty-fifth birthday.

Key structures and Special difficulties 关键句型和难点

Rewrite the following sentence without changing the meaning. Then refer to ll.26-27.

Though the village had seemed deserted, it immediately came to life.

The village ...

Multiple choice questions 选择题

Choose the correct answers to the following questions.

Comprehension 理解

1 On the last day of their visit to a Balkan town, the writer and his wife ________ .

(*a*) followed a path which they found to their surprise led them into a wood

(*b*) went exploring for churches further afield, having seen those nearby

(*c*) decided to visit a small village some distance away from the town

(*d*) discovered their own countrymen to be hostile when they are cut off

2 The village looked forbidding in that ________ .

(*a*) the road leading up to it was so steep and rough

(*b*) it had a deserted and gloomy appearance

(*c*) the mountain threw its shadow over the small brick houses

(*d*) there was nobody in the village

3 What made the writer and his wife feel they were unwelcome visitors?

(*a*) Apart from the children, no one had come out to greet them.

(*b*) When they had first gone through the village, the people had hidden.

(*c*) Nobody said a single word as they watched them walk down the street.

(*d*) The men were too shy to speak to them and the women too shy to come out.

Structure 结构

4 ________ that the path continued on the other side, we wondered how we could get across the stream. (ll.14-15)

(*a*) Being able to see (*b*) It could be seen (*c*) At the sight of (*d*) Seeing

5 Though he was reluctant to ________ at first, we ... (l.17)

(*a*) ferry us across (*b*) ferry (*c*) take to the other side (*d*) do that

6 – unmade road ________ small houses lining it on either side. (ll.18-19)

(*a*) with (*b*) which (*c*) by (*d*) and

7 ________ of all was that not a sound could be heard. (l.29)

(*a*) It frightened us most (*b*) The thing that most frightened us

(*c*) What frightened us most (*d*) We were most frightened by

8 – where we hoped the boatman was waiting and ________ us back. (ll.30-31)

(*a*) was ferrying (*b*) ferrying (*c*) ferried (*d*) would ferry

Vocabulary 词汇

9 In it there was a boatman ________ asleep. (l.16)

(*a*) dead (*b*) sound (*c*) quickly (*d*) hard

10 The fence the writer and his wife sat down on was ________ ... (l.22)

(*a*) no longer in use (*b*) sheltered by trees

(*c*) in a state of disrepair (*d*) made of very hard timber

11 All at once, I noticed that my wife ________ to be filled with alarm. (l.23)

(*a*) came (*b*) appeared (*c*) turned (*d*) looked

12 Men stood outside their houses and ________ angrily at us. (ll.27-28)

(*a*) stared (*b*) frowned (*c*) grimaced (*d*) winked

LESSON

49 The ideal servant 理想的仆人

Listen then answer the question below.

听录音，然后回答以下问题。

What was Bessie's 'little weakness'?

this occasioned great mirth among the guests

It is a good thing my aunt Harriet died years ago. If she were alive today she would not be able to air her views on her favourite topic of conversation: domestic servants. Aunt Harriet lived in that leisurely age when servants were employed to do housework. She had a huge, rambling country house called 'The Gables'. She was sentimentally attached to this house, for even though it was far too big for her needs, she persisted in living there long after her husband's death. Before she grew old, Aunt Harriet used to entertain lavishly. I often visited The Gables when I was a boy. No matter how many guests were present, the great house was always immaculate. The parquet floors shone like mirrors; highly polished silver was displayed in gleaming glass cabinets; even my uncle's huge collection of books was kept miraculously free from dust. Aunt Harriet presided over an invisible army of servants that continuously scrubbed, cleaned, and polished. She always referred to them as 'the shifting population', for they came and went with such frequency that I never even got a chance to learn their names. Though my aunt pursued what was, in those days, an enlightened policy, in that she never allowed her domestic staff to work more than eight hours a day, she was extremely difficult to please. While she always criticized the fickleness of human nature, she carried on an unrelenting search for the ideal servant to the end of her days, even after she had been sadly disillusioned by Bessie.

Bessie worked for Aunt Harriet for three years. During that time she so gained my aunt's confidence, that she was put in charge of the domestic staff. Aunt Harriet could not find words to praise Bessie's industriousness and efficiency. In addition to all her other qualifications, Bessie was an expert cook. She acted the role of the perfect servant for three years before Aunt Harriet discovered her 'little weakness'. After being absent from The Gables for a week, my aunt unexpectedly returned one afternoon with a party of guests and instructed Bessie to prepare dinner. Not only was the meal well below the usual standard, but Bessie seemed unable to walk steadily. She bumped into the furniture and kept mumbling about the guests. When she came in with the last course — a huge pudding — she tripped on the carpet and the pudding went flying through the air, narrowly missed my aunt, and crashed on the dining table with considerable force. Though this caused great mirth among the guests, Aunt Harriet was horrified. She reluctantly came to the conclusion that Bessie was drunk. The guests had, of course, realized this from the moment Bessie opened the door for them and, long before the final catastrophe, had had a difficult time trying to conceal their amusement. The poor girl was dismissed instantly. After her departure, Aunt Harriet discovered that there were piles of empty wine bottles of all shapes and sizes neatly stacked in what had once been Bessie's wardrobe. They had mysteriously found their way there from the wine cellar!

New words and expressions 生词和短语

rambling (l.5)	/'ræmblɪŋ/	adj.	杂乱无章的
sentimentally (l.6)	/ˌsentɪ'mentli/	adv.	感情上；多情地
lavishly (l.8)	/'lævɪʃli/	adv.	慷慨地，大方地
immaculate (l.9)	/ɪ'mækjʊlɪt/	adj.	清洁的，无污点的
parquet (l.10)	/'pɑːkeɪ/	n.	镶木地板
gleaming (l.10)	/gliːmɪŋ/	adj.	发亮的，闪光的
preside (l.11)	/prɪ'zaɪd/	v.	指挥
invisible (l.11)	/ɪn'vɪzɪbəl/	adj.	看不见的，无形的
scrub (l.12)	/skrʌb/	v.	擦拭，刷洗
enlightened (l.14)	/ɪn'laɪtənd/	adj.	开明的
fickleness (l.16)	/'fɪkəlnɪs/	n.	变化无常
unrelenting (l.16)	/ˌʌnrɪ'lentɪŋ/	adj.	不屈不挠的，不松懈的
disillusion (l.17)	/ˌdɪsɪ'luːʒən/	v.	使幻想破灭
industriousness (l.20)	/ɪn'dʌstriəsnɪs/	n.	勤奋
qualification (l.20)	/ˌkwɒlɪfɪ'keɪʃən/	n.	资格，能力
mirth (l.27)	/mɜːθ/	n.	欢笑，高兴
stack (l.31)	/stæk/	v.	整齐地堆放
cellar (l.32)	/'selə/	n.	地窖

Notes on the text 课文注释

1 air one's views on ..., 作“对……发表意见”讲。

2 be attached to, 喜爱，喜欢。

3 persist in doing sth., 坚持做某事。

4 free from dust, 一尘不染。

5 Aunt Harriet presided over an invisible army of servants ... 句中的 preside over 是“统辖”、“指挥”的意思。由于她雇用过许多仆人，人数之多已可称作一支队伍（army）；而由于她不断解雇又不断雇用，因此这支队伍在一定程度上也就变得无形了。

6 refer to them as, 把他们称作……。

7 what was, ..., an enlightened policy, 算得上是一项开明政策。in that 是书面用语，作“因为”、“既然”讲。

8 While she always criticized ...,
while 作“虽然”讲，引导让步状语从句；to the end of her days, 直到她去世前。

参考译文

我的姑妈哈丽特好多年前就去世了，这倒是件好事。如果她活到今天，她将不能就她热衷的话题“佣人”发表意见了。哈丽特生活在一个悠闲的年代，家务事都由雇来的佣人代劳。她在乡下有一幢巨大杂乱的房子，叫作“山墙庄园”。她对这幢房子在感情上难舍难分。房子实在太大了，但在丈夫去世多年后，她仍然执意长年住在那儿。哈丽特姑妈年轻时，喜欢大摆宴席，招待宾客。我小时候常去“山墙庄园”作客。不管去多少宾客，大房子里总是收拾得干干净净。镶木地板洁如明镜，擦得发亮的银器陈列在明亮的玻璃柜里，连姑夫的大量藏书也保存得很好，奇迹般地一尘不染。哈丽特姑妈统率着一支看不见的佣人大军，他们不停地擦拭、清扫、刷洗。她称这些佣人叫“流动人口”，因为他们来去匆匆，所以我甚至都没有机会知道他们的姓名。姑妈待佣人在当时算是开明的，从来不让佣人每天工作超过 8 小时，但他们很难使她称心如意。她一方面总批评人的本性朝三暮四，另一方面她又持之以恒地寻找一个理想的佣人。即使在贝西大大地伤了她的心之后，她还在找，一直到她死去。

贝西在哈丽特家干了 3 年。在此期间，她赢得了姑妈的赏识，甚至当上了大管家。哈丽特不知该用什么言辞来赞扬贝西的勤奋与高效。贝西除了有各种本领以外，还是一个烹饪大师。她担任“理想仆人”角色 3 年之后，哈丽特终于发现了她有“小小的弱点”。一次，姑妈有一个星期没在“山墙庄园”住。一天下午，她出其不意地回来了，带来一大批客人，吩咐贝西准备晚饭。结果，不仅饭菜远不如平时做得好，而且贝西走起路来似乎东倒西歪。她撞到了家具上，嘴里还不断咕咕哝哝议论客人。当她端着最后一道菜——一大盘布丁——走进屋来时，在地毯上绊了一跤。布丁飞到半空，从姑妈身边擦过，然后狠狠地砸在餐桌上。

这件事引起了客人们的欢笑，但哈丽特却着实吓了一跳。她不得不认定贝西是喝醉了。客人们自然从贝西为他们开门那一刻起就看出来了，在好长一段时间里，即最后这个乱子发生前，他们努力克制才没笑出声来。贝西当即被解雇了。贝西走后，哈丽特姑妈发现在贝西以前用过的衣柜里整整齐齐地放着一堆堆形状各异、大小不一的酒瓶子。这些酒瓶神不知鬼不觉地从酒窖来到了这里。

Comprehension 理解

Give short answers to these questions in your own words as far as possible. Use one complete sentence for each answer.

1 What did Aunt Harriet most like to talk about?

2 Why did Aunt Harriet continue to live in The Gables after her husband's death?

3 Why did Aunt Harriet always refer to her servants as 'the shifting population'?

Vocabulary 词汇

Explain the meanings of the following words and phrases as they are used in the passage: air her views (l.2); favourite (l.2); persisted in (l.7); immaculate (l.9); invisible (l.11); enlightened (l.14); domestic staff (l.15).

Summary writing 摘要写作

In not more than 80 words describe what happened after Aunt Harriet unexpectedly returned to The Gables with a party of guests. Use your own words as far as possible. Do not include anything that is not in the last paragraph.

Composition 作文

Write a composition in about 300 words on one of the following:

a Write an imaginary account of how Bessie's 'little weakness' went undetected for three years.

b 'It is a good thing that domestic servants have become a great rarity.' What is your opinion?

Letter writing 书信写作

Write a letter of thanks to an aunt who has sent you a generous amount of money for your twenty-first birthday. Say what you intend to do with the money. Do not write more than 100 words.

Key structures and Special difficulties 关键句型和难点

Rewrite the following sentence without changing the meaning. Then refer to ll.21-23.

My aunt had been absent from The Gables for a week when she unexpectedly returned one afternoon with a party of guests.

After ... my aunt ...

Multiple choice questions 选择题

Choose the correct answers to the following questions.

Comprehension 理解

1 In the days when the writer used to visit 'The Gables' ________ .

(*a*) his aunt would employ a great many servants whenever she invited guests

(*b*) he always found the house spotlessly clean

(*c*) he never stayed long enough to learn the names of the servants

(*d*) his aunt was hard to please if her staff only worked an eight-hour day

2 Bessie was made responsible for the domestic staff ________ .

(*a*) as a result of her hard work

(*b*) because she was loyal to my aunt

(*c*) because she had such good qualifications

(*d*) because my aunt trusted her

3 When the pudding crashed on the table, Aunt Harriet was horrified ________ .

(*a*) to see how weak Bessie had become during her absence

(*b*) because the guests all found the incident very amusing

(*c*) because the pudding was not up to Bessie's usual standard of cooking

(*d*) because it was only then that she realized how drunk Bessie was

4 After Bessie's dismissal, Aunt Harriet ________ .

(*a*) still hoped to find a servant who would please her in every respect

(*b*) was so disillusioned by Bessie that she gave up entertaining lavishly

(*c*) found a great many bottles of wine in Bessie's wardrobe

(*d*) could not understand how so many bottles had disappeared from her cellar

Structure 结构

5 ________ guests were present, the great house ... (l.9)

(*a*) No matter the number of (*b*) Whatever many

(*c*) Whoever the many (*d*) However many

6 Though my aunt pursued a policy, ________ , in those days, enlightened, in that she never allowed her domestic staff ... (ll.14-15)

(*a*) that it was (*b*) what was (*c*) which was (*d*) being

7 Bessie seemed ________ steadily. (ll.23-24)

(*a*) impossible to walk (*b*) incapable to walk

(*c*) incapable of walking (*d*) not possible for walking

8 – came to the conclusion that Bessie had ________ . (ll.27-28)

(*a*) been drinking (*b*) drunk (*c*) drank (*d*) some drinks

Vocabulary 词汇

9 ________ Aunt Harriet in her praise of Bessie's industriousness ... (ll.19-20)

(*a*) Not a word was said by (*b*) Words were lost on

(*c*) Words failed (*d*) Word did not come to

10 – could not find words to praise Bessie's ________ and efficiency. (ll.19-20)

(*a*) factory (*b*) hard work (*c*) dusting (*d*) business

11 She ________ the carpet and the pudding went ... (l.25)

(*a*) fell over (*b*) slipped on (*c*) trespassed (*d*) stumbled on

12 – and, ________ the final catastrophe, the guests had had a difficult time ... (ll.28-29)

(*a*) far in front of (*b*) much behind (*c*) well before (*d*) long ahead of

LESSON 50 New Year resolutions 新年的决心

Listen then answer the question below.

听录音，然后回答以下问题。

What marked the end of the writer's New Year resolutions?

my enthusiasm waned

The New Year is a time for resolutions. Mentally, at least, most of us could compile formidable lists of 'dos' and 'don'ts'. The same old favourites recur year in year out with monotonous regularity. We resolve to get up earlier each morning, eat less, find more time to play with the children, do a thousand and one jobs about the house, be nice to people we don't like, drive carefully, and take the dog for a walk every day. Past experience has taught us that certain accomplishments are beyond attainment. If we remain inveterate smokers, it is only because we have so often experienced the frustration that results from failure. Most of us fail in our efforts at self-improvement because our schemes are too ambitious and we never have time to carry them out. We also make the fundamental error of announcing our resolutions to everybody so that we look even more foolish when we slip back into our bad old ways. Aware of these pitfalls, this year I attempted to keep my resolutions to myself. I limited myself to two modest ambitions: to do physical exercises every morning and to read more of an evening. An all-night party on New Year's Eve provided me with a good excuse for not carrying out either of these new resolutions on the first day of the year, but on the second, I applied myself assiduously to the task.

The daily exercises lasted only eleven minutes and I proposed to do them early in the morning before anyone had got up. The self-discipline required to drag myself out of bed eleven minutes earlier than usual was considerable. Nevertheless, I managed to creep down into the living room for two days before anyone found me out. After jumping about on the carpet and twisting the human frame into uncomfortable positions, I sat down at the breakfast table in an exhausted condition. It was this that betrayed me. The next morning the whole family trooped in to watch the performance. That was really unsettling, but I fended off the taunts and jibes of the family good-humouredly and soon everybody got used to the idea. However, my enthusiasm waned. The time I spent at exercises gradually diminished. Little by little the eleven minutes fell to zero. By January 10th, I was back to where I had started from. I argued that if I spent less time exhausting myself at exercises in the morning, I would keep my mind fresh for reading when I got home from work. Resisting the hypnotizing effect of television, I sat in my room for a few evenings with my eyes glued to a book. One night, however, feeling cold and lonely, I went downstairs and sat in front of the television pretending to read. That proved to be my undoing, for I soon got back to my old bad habit of dozing off in front of the screen. I still haven't given up my resolution to do more reading. In fact, I have just bought a book entitled *How to Read a Thousand Words a Minute*. Perhaps it will solve my problem, but I just haven't had time to read it!

New words and expressions 生词和短语

resolution (title)	/ˌrezəˈluːʃən/	*n.*	决心
mentally (l.1)	/ˈmentli/	*adv.*	内心里
compile (l.2)	/kəmˈpaɪl/	*v.*	编辑，编制
formidable (l.2)	/ˈfɔːmɪdəbəl/	*adj.*	令人畏惧的
recur (l.3)	/rɪˈkɜː/	*v.*	再发生，又出现
regularity (l.3)	/ˌregjʊˈlærɪti/	*n.*	规律性
accomplishment (l.8)	/əˈkʌmplɪʃmənt/	*n.*	成就
attainment (l.8)	/əˈteɪnmənt/	*n.*	达到
inveterate (l.8)	/ɪnˈvetərɪt/	*adj.*	根深蒂固的
self-improvement (l.9)	/ˌself-ɪmˈpruːvmənt/	*n.*	自我完善
scheme (l.10)	/skiːm/	*n.*	简单的计划，方案
ambitious (l.10)	/æmˈbɪʃəs/	*adj.*	雄心勃勃的
pitfall (l.12)	/ˈpɪtfɔːl/	*n.*	意外的困难，易犯的错误
modest (l.13)	/ˈmɒdɪst/	*adj.*	要求不过分的
assiduously (l.15)	/əˈsɪdjuəsli/	*adv.*	刻苦地
self-discipline (l.18)	/ˌself-ˈdɪsɪplɪn/	*n.*	自我约束
frame (l.20)	/freɪm/	*n.*	躯体
betray (l.21)	/bɪˈtreɪ/	*v.*	暴露，显露
troop (l.22)	/truːp/	*v.*	成群结队地走动
unsettling (l.22)	/ʌnˈsetlɪŋ/	*adj.*	令人不安的
taunt (l.23)	/tɔːnt/	*n.*	嘲笑，奚落人的话
jibe (l.23)	/dʒaɪb/	*n.*	嘲弄，挖苦
good-humouredly (l.23)	/ˌgʊdˈhjuːmədli/	*adv.*	和气地，心情好地
wane (l.24)	/weɪn/	*v.*	逐渐变小，变弱
diminish (l.24)	/dɪˈmɪnɪʃ/	*v.*	减少，缩小
hypnotize (l.27)	/ˈhɪpnətaɪz/	*v.*	使欲睡，使蒙眬
undoing (l.29)	/ʌnˈduːɪŋ/	*n.*	祸根，毁灭的原因
screen (l.30)	/skriːn/	*n.*	电视机屏幕

Notes on the text 课文注释

1 dos and don'ts, 要做的事和不要做的事。

2 year in year out, 年复一年。

3 a thousand and one, 许许多多。

4 beyond attainment, 做不到的，达不到的。

5 carry out, 实行，照办，执行。

6 slip back into our bad old ways, 滑回到那些坏的老习惯上去。

7 keep ... to oneself, 作“将……秘而不宣”、“保密”讲。

8 of an evening = in the evenings。

9 apply oneself to, 全力以赴地干。

10 It was this that betrayed me.

这是强调句型，被强调的部分 this 指 sat down ... in an exhausted condition。

11 fend off, 挡回，避开。

12 doze off, 打瞌睡。

参考译文

新年是下决心的时候，至少在大多数人的心里会编排出一份“应做什么”和“不应做什么”的令人生畏的单子。相同的决心以单调的规律年复一年地出现。我们决心每天早晨起得早些；吃得少些；多花点时间与孩子们一起做游戏；做大量的家务；对不喜欢的人友善一些；小心驾车；每天都要带着狗散步等等。以往的经验告诉我们有些事是办不到的。如果我们烟瘾大，戒不掉，那是因为屡戒屡败，失去了信心。我们大多数人想自我完善却遭到失败，这是因为我们的规划过于宏大，而又根本没有时间去实施。我们还犯有一个根本性的错误，即把我们的决心向大家宣布。这样一旦滑回到那些坏的老习惯上去，我们在别人眼里会显得更加难堪。我深知这些问题，于是，今年我对自己的计划要严加保密，只给自己定下两项适中的任务：每天早上锻炼身体，每天晚上多看点书。新年除夕举办的一次通宵晚会，使我理直气壮地在新年头一天免去了这两项任务。不过，新年第二天，我全力以赴地照着去做了。

早锻炼一共只有 11 分钟，我打算在别人起床之前进行。这就要求我比平日早 11 分钟把自己从床上拽起来，这种自我约束是很艰苦的。不过开头两天我还是成功地蹑手蹑脚地来到楼下起居室，没被人发现。我在地毯上跳过来蹦过去，扭曲身子，摆出各种姿势，弄得浑身不舒服，然后坐到桌边吃早饭，一副筋疲力尽的样子。正是这副模样泄露了我的秘密。第二天早晨全家人结队来到起居室看我表演。这真叫人不好意思，但我心平气和地顶住了全家人的嘲笑和奚落。不久，大家对我习以为常了，而这时我的热情却减退了。我花在锻炼上的时间逐渐减少，慢慢地从 11 分钟减到了零。到了 1 月 10 日，我恢复了原来的作息时间。我辩解说，早晨少耗费精力锻炼，晚上下班回家看书时头脑更清醒些。有几天晚上，我极力摆脱了电视的诱惑，坐在自己房间里，两眼盯在书上。可是，有一天夜里，我感到又冷又孤单，便来到楼下坐在电视机前假装看书。这下我可完了，因为不一会儿，我就恢复了以前的坏习惯，在屏幕前打起瞌睡来。但我还没有放弃多看些书的决心。事实上，我刚买来一本叫《一分钟读一千字的诀窍》的书。也许这本书能解决我的问题，但我一直还没时间去看这本书！

Comprehension 理解

Give short answers to these questions in your own words as far as possible. Use one complete sentence for each answer.

1 What has past experience of New Year resolutions taught us?

2 Why is it a basic mistake to announce our resolutions to everybody?

3 Why did the writer not carry out his resolutions on New Year's Day?

Vocabulary 词汇

Explain the meanings of the following words and phrases as they are used in the passage: mentally (l.1); formidable (l.2); recur year in year out (l.3); beyond attainment (l.8); inveterate (l.8); frustration (l.9); carrying out (l.14).

Summary writing 摘要写作

In not more than 80 words describe the efforts the writer made to carry out his resolutions after New Year's Day. Use your own words as far as possible. Do not include anything that is not in the last paragraph.

Composition 作文

Write a composition in about 300 words on one of the following:

a Write an account of resolutions you have made in the past and failed to keep.

b Describe New Year celebrations in your country.

Letter writing 书信写作

Before you went abroad, you promised your parents that you would write once a week. Since then, you have failed to keep your promise. Write a letter to them explaining why it has been impossible for you to write more often. Do not write more than 100 words.

Key structures and Special difficulties 关键句型和难点

Rewrite the following sentence without changing the meaning. Then refer to ll.31-32.

It may solve my problem, but I just haven't had time to read it!

Perhaps ...

Multiple choice questions 选择题

Choose the correct answers to the following questions.

Comprehension 理解

1 In making his New Year resolutions, the writer ________ .

(*a*) decided against choosing any of his old favourites

(*b*) did not tell his family of them in case they announced them in public

(*c*) was careful to choose two which he thought were within his scope

(*d*) underestimated the time it would take him to get up in the mornings

2 The family realized what one of his resolutions was when they ________ .

(*a*) noticed how tired he looked when he came to breakfast

(*b*) heard him jumping about on the carpet in the living room

(*c*) came down earlier than usual and saw him doing his exercises

(*d*) saw him reading instead of looking at television

3 The writer's efforts to read more have so far failed because ________ .

(*a*) he is not able to read quickly enough in the time he has available

(*b*) he enjoys watching television more than he does reading

(*c*) his room is too cold for comfort and he misses his family

(*d*) he has not been able to resist the hypnotic effects of television

Structure 结构

4 Past experience has taught us that we ________ certain accomplishments. (ll.7-8)

(*a*) never attain (*b*) would never attain (*c*) are never attaining (*d*) will never attain

5 – we look even more foolish than we ________ when we slip back into our old ways. (ll.11-12)

(*a*) would (*b*) should (*c*) need (*d*) ought

6 I jumped about on the carpet and ________ uncomfortable positions that I sat down exhausted. (ll.20-21)

(*a*) so twisted me into (*b*) so twisted myself into

(*c*) twisted myself into such (*d*) twisted me into such

7 I argued that ________ less time exhausting myself, I would ... (ll.25-26)

(*a*) to spend (*b*) by spending (*c*) my spending (*d*) to have spent

Vocabulary 词汇

8 This year I attempted to keep my resolutions ________ . (ll.12-13)

(*a*) private (*b*) personal (*c*) intimate (*d*) solitary

9 ________ , I managed to creep down into the living room ... (l.19)

(*a*) Meanwhile (*b*) Little by little (*c*) Just the same (*d*) By all means

10 The whole family ________ to watch the performance. (ll.21-22)

(*a*) gathered round (*b*) marched by (*c*) flocked in (*d*) joined in

11 My enthusiasm for my new resolutions soon ________ . (ll.23-24)

(*a*) faded (*b*) evaporated (*c*) ran out (*d*) fell out

12 I soon ________ into my old habit of dozing off ... (ll.29-30)

(*a*) returned (*b*) slipped back (*c*) went back (*d*) took again

LESSON

51 Predicting the future 预测未来

providing information about traffic jam

Listen then answer the question below.

听录音，然后回答以下问题。

What was the 'future' electronic development that Leon Bagrit wasn't able to foresee?

Predicting the future is notoriously difficult. Who could have imagined, in the mid 1970s, for example, that by the end of the 20th century, computers would be as common in people's homes as TV sets? In the 1970s, computers were common enough, but only in big business, government departments, and large organizations. These were the so-called mainframe machines. Mainframe computers were very large indeed, often occupying whole air-conditioned rooms, employing full-time technicians and run on specially-written software. Though these large machines still exist, many of their functions have been taken over by small powerful personal computers, commonly known as PCs.

In 1975, a primitive machine called the Altair, was launched in the USA. It can properly be described as the first 'home computer' and it pointed the way to the future. This was followed, at the end of the 1970s, by a machine called an Apple. In the early 1980s, the computer giant, IBM produced the world's first Personal Computer. This ran on an 'operating system' called DOS, produced by a then small company named Microsoft. The IBM Personal Computer was widely copied. From those humble beginnings, we have seen the development of the user-friendly home computers and multimedia machines which are in common use today.

Considering how recent these developments are, it is even more remarkable that as long ago as the 1960s, an Englishman, Leon Bagrit, was able to predict some of the uses of computers which we know today. Bagrit dismissed the idea that computers would learn to 'think' for themselves and would 'rule the world', which people liked to believe in those days. Bagrit foresaw a time when computers would be small enough to hold in the hand, when they would be capable of providing information about traffic jams and suggesting alternative routes, when they would be used in hospitals to help doctors to diagnose illnesses, when they would relieve office workers and accountants of dull, repetitive clerical work. All these computer uses have become commonplace. Of course, Leon Bagrit could not possibly have foreseen the development of the Internet, the worldwide system that enables us to communicate instantly with anyone in any part of the world by using computers linked to telephone networks. Nor could he have foreseen how we could use the Internet to obtain information on every known subject, so we can read it on a screen in our homes and even print it as well if we want to. Computers have become smaller and smaller, more and more powerful and cheaper and cheaper. This is what makes Leon Bagrit's predictions particularly remarkable. If he, or someone like him, were alive today, he might be able to tell us what to expect in the next fifty years.

New words and expressions 生词和短语

notoriously (l.1)	/nəʊˈtɔːriəsli/	*adv.*	（尤指因坏事）众所周知地
mainframe (l.6)	/ˈmeɪnfreɪm/	*n.*	主机，中央处理机
full-time (l.8)	/ˌfʊlˈtaɪm/	*adj.*	专职的
technician (l.8)	/tekˈnɪʃən/	*n.*	技师
software (l.8)	/ˈsɒftweə/	*n.*	软件
IBM (l.12)	/ˈaɪ biː em/		（美国）国际商用机器公司（International Business Machines）
DOS (l.13)	/dɒs/	*n.*	磁盘操作系统（Disk Operating System）
Microsoft (l.13)	/ˈmaɪkrəʊsɒft/		（美国）微软公司
user-friendly (l.15)	/ˌjuːzə-ˈfrendli/	*adj.*	容易操作的，好用的
multimedia (l.15)	/ˌmʌltiˈmiːdiə/	*adj.*	多媒体的
alternative (l.21)	/ɔːlˈtɜːnətɪv/	*adj.*	选择的
diagnose (l.21)	/ˈdaɪəgnəʊz/	*v.*	诊断
relieve (l.22)	/rɪˈliːv/	*v.*	减轻
accountant (l.22)	/əˈkaʊntənt/	*n.*	会计
repetitive (l.22)	/rɪˈpetɪtɪv/	*adj.*	重复的
clerical (l.22)	/ˈklerɪkəl/	*adj.*	办公室工作的
Internet (l.24)	/ˈɪntənet/	*n.*	因特网
network (l.25)	/ˈnetwɜːk/	*n.*	网络

Notes on the text 课文注释

1 in the mid 1970s, 在 20 世纪 70 年代中叶。

2 so-called, 号称，所谓的。

3 Mainframe computers were very large indeed ... software. 在这句话中，现在分词短语 occupying ... 和 employing ... 以及过去分词短语 run ... 均作主语 mainframe computers 的修饰成分。

4 take over, 接收，接管。

5 home computer, 家庭电脑。

6 a then small company, 那时候规模尚小的一个公司。

7 dismiss the idea that ..., 不考虑……这个想法。

8 the Internet, the worldwide system that ..., 后面的这个短语用来进一步说明名词 the Internet，是它的同位语，这种用法在科技类的文章中很常见。

参考译文

众所周知，预测未来是非常困难的。举个例子吧，在 20 世纪 70 年代中叶又有谁能想象得到在 20 世纪末的时候，家庭用的计算机会像电视机一样普遍？在 70 年代，计算机已经相当普及了，但只用在大的公司、政府部门和大的组织之中，它们被称为主机。计算机主机确实很大，常常占据了装有空调的多间房间，雇用专职的技师，而且得用专门编写的软件才能运行。虽然这种大计算机仍然存在，但是它们的许多功能已被体积小但功能齐全的个人电脑——即我们常说的 PC 机——所代替了。

1975 年，美国推出了一台被称为“牛郎星”的原始机型。严格地说起来，它可以被称为第一台“家用电脑”，而且它也指出了今后的发展方向。70 年代末，在牛郎星之后又出现了一种被称为“苹果”的机型。80 年代初，计算机行业的王牌公司美国国际商用机器公司（IBM）生产出了世界上第一台个人电脑。这种电脑采用了一种被称为磁盘操作系统（DOS）的工作程序，而这种程序是由当时规模不大的微软公司生产的。IBM 的个人电脑被大规模地仿制。从那些简陋的初级阶段，我们看到了现在都已普及的、使用简便的家用电脑和多媒体的微机的发展。

想一想这些发展的时间多么短，就更觉得英国人莱昂·巴格瑞特有着非凡的能力。他在 60 年代就能预言我们今天知道的计算机的一些用途。巴格瑞特根本不接受计算机可以学会自己去“思考”和计算机可以“统治世界”这种想法，而这种想法是当时的人们都愿意相信的。巴格瑞特预见有一天计算机可以小到拿在手上，计算机可以提供有关交通阻塞的信息，并建议可供选择的其他路线，计算机在医院里可以帮助医生诊断病情，计算机可以使办公室人员和会计免除那些枯燥、重复的劳动。计算机的所有这些功能现在都变得很平常。当然了，莱昂·巴格瑞特根本没有可能预测到因特网——就是把计算机连接到电话线路上，以便和世界上任何一个地方的人立即进行联系的一个世界范围的通讯系统——的发展。他也无法预测到我们可以利用因特网获取有关任何已知专题的信息，以便在家里的屏幕上阅读，如果愿意的话甚至可以将其打印出来。计算机已经变得体积越来越小，功能越来越多，价格越来越低，这就是莱昂·巴格瑞特的预测非凡的地方。如果他或是像他一样的什么人今天还活着的话，他大概可以告诉我们下一个 50 年后会发生什么事情。

Comprehension 理解

Give short answers to these questions in your own words as far as possible. Use one complete sentence for each answer.

1 How have PCs affected the use of mainframe computers?

2 What was the first home computer called and when was it produced?

3 What did the first Personal Computer need to make it run?

Vocabulary 词汇

Explain the meanings of the following words and phrases as they are used in the passage: predicting (1.1); imagined (1.2); whole (1.7); functions (1.9); primitive (1.10); humble (1.14); in common use (1.15).

Summary writing 摘要写作

In not more than 80 words describe what computer developments Leon Bagrit was able to predict and what he failed to predict. Do not include anything that is not in the last paragraph.

Composition 作文

Write a composition in about 300 words on one of the following:

a Predict the next 20 years in computer development.

b Describe your attitude to computers and give reasons for it.

Letter writing 书信写作

You have arranged to place your house at the disposal of a friend of yours while you are away on holiday. You are now about to leave. Write him or her a letter in about 100 words telling him or her what final arrangements you have made.

Key structures and Special difficulties 关键句型和难点

Rewrite the following sentence without changing the meaning. Then refer to ll.7-8.

Indeed, very large were those mainframe computers which often occupied whole air-conditioned rooms, were required to employ full-time technicians and ran on specially-written software.

Mainframe computers ...

Multiple choice questions 选择题

Choose the correct answers to the following questions.

Comprehension 理解

1 In the mid 1970s, computers were ________ .

(*a*) notoriously unreliable (*b*) rather rare

(*c*) in widespread use (*d*) not at all common

2 The importance of the Altair was that it ________ .

(*a*) did not need specially-written software to run it

(*b*) put computing power within the reach of ordinary people

(*c*) helped to establish Microsoft DOS as the standard system

(*d*) was widely copied by IBM and other big manufacturers

3 Leon Bagrit foresaw that before long, ________ .

(*a*) we would be able to teach computers to think like human beings

(*b*) computers would bring about the development of the Internet

(*c*) computers in hospitals would diagnose illnesses and prescribe treatments

(*d*) computers in commerce would take over many repetitive tasks

4 Leon Bagrit's most important insight into the future development of computers was in terms of their ________ .

(*a*) ability to relieve people of boring tasks (*b*) size, power and cost

(*c*) use in traffic management (*d*) commonplace use in offices and hospitals

Structure 结构

5 It is notoriously difficult ________ the future. (l.1)

(*a*) when predicting (*b*) the prediction of (*c*) to predict (*d*) that we predict

6 Who could have imagined that ________ as many computers as TV sets? (ll.1-4)

(*a*) there would be (*b*) there to be (*c*) their being (*d*) there were

7 People in those days liked to believe in computers ________ the world. (ll.18-19)

(*a*) taking over and ruling (*b*) that took over and ruled

(*c*) take over and rule (*d*) to take over and rule

8 ________ Bagrit's predictions so remarkable is their accuracy. (l.28)

(*a*) What makes (*b*) Why are (*c*) How many are (*d*) They make

Vocabulary 词汇

9 Bagrit ________ the idea that computers would rule the world. (ll.18-19)

(*a*) refuted (*b*) refused (*c*) rejected (*d*) discharged

10 Bagrit foresaw that computers would become ________ small to hold in the hand. (ll.19-20)

(*a*) adequately (*b*) sufficiently (*c*) capably (*d*) possibly

11 All these computer uses have become ________ . (ll.22-23)

(*a*) relatively normal (*b*) more or less frequent

(*c*) taken for granted (*d*) unexceptionable

12 The Internet enables us to ________ instantly with anyone in any part of the world. (ll.24-25)

(*a*) get in touch (*b*) contact (*c*) send a message (*d*) convey an idea

LESSON

52 Mud is mud 实事求是

all sorts of weird concoctions

Listen then answer the question below.

听录音，然后回答以下问题。

Why did Harry decide to give up his little game?

My cousin, Harry, keeps a large curiously-shaped bottle on permanent display in his study. Despite the fact that the bottle is tinted a delicate shade of green, an observant visitor would soon notice that it is filled with what looks like a thick, greyish substance. If you were to ask Harry what was in the bottle, he would tell you that it contained perfumed mud. If you expressed doubt or surprise, he would immediately invite you to smell it and then to rub some into your skin. This brief experiment would dispel any further doubts you might have. The bottle really does contain perfumed mud. How Harry came into possession of this outlandish stuff makes an interesting story which he is fond of relating. Furthermore, the acquisition of this bottle cured him of a bad habit he had been developing for years.

Harry used to consider it a great joke to go into expensive cosmetic shops and make outrageous requests for goods that do not exist. He would invent fanciful names on the spot. On entering a shop, he would ask for a new perfume called 'Scented Shadow' or for 'insoluble bath cubes'. If a shop assistant told him she had not heard of it, he would pretend to be considerably put out. He loved to be told that one of his imaginary products was temporarily out of stock and he would faithfully promise to call again at some future date, but of course he never did. How Harry managed to keep a straight face during these performances is quite beyond me.

Harry does not need to be prompted to explain how he bought his precious bottle of mud. One day, he went to an exclusive shop in London and asked for 'Myrolite'. The shop assistant looked puzzled and Harry repeated the word, slowly stressing each syllable. When the woman shook her head in bewilderment, Harry went on to explain that 'myrolite' was a hard, amber-like substance which could be used to remove freckles. This explanation evidently conveyed something to the woman who searched shelf after shelf. She produced all sorts of weird concoctions, but none of them met with Harry's requirements. When Harry put on his act of being mildly annoyed, the assistant promised to order some for him. Intoxicated by his success, Harry then asked for perfumed mud. He expected the assistant to look at him in blank astonishment. However, it was his turn to be surprised, for the woman's eyes immediately lit up and she fetched several bottles which she placed on the counter for Harry to inspect. For once, Harry had to admit defeat. He picked up what seemed to be the smallest bottle and discreetly asked the price. He was glad to get away with a mere twenty pounds and he beat a hasty retreat, clutching the precious bottle under his arm. From then on, Harry decided that this little game he had invented might prove to be expensive. The curious bottle, which now adorns the bookcase in his study, was his first and last purchase of rare cosmetics.

New words and expressions 生词和短语

permanent (l.2)	/ˈpɜːmənənt/	*adj.*	永久的
tint (l.3)	/tɪnt/	*v.*	给……染色
delicate (l.3)	/ˈdelɪkət/	*adj.*	淡色的
shade (l.3)	/ʃeɪd/	*n.*	色度
observant (l.3)	/əbˈzɜːvənt/	*adj.*	观察力敏锐的
greyish (l.4)	/ˈgreɪ-ɪʃ/	*adj.*	浅灰色的
dispel (l.8)	/dɪˈspel/	*v.*	驱散，消除
outlandish (l.9)	/aʊtˈlændɪʃ/	*adj.*	稀奇古怪的
acquisition (l.10)	/ˌækwɪˈzɪʃən/	*n.*	获得
cosmetic (l.12)	/kɒzˈmetɪk/	*n.*	化妆品
outrageous (l.12)	/aʊtˈreɪdʒəs/	*adj.*	无理的，令人不能容忍的
fanciful (l.13)	/ˈfænsɪfəl/	*adj.*	想象出来的
insoluble (l.14)	/ɪnˈsɒljʊbəl/	*adj.*	不可溶解的
prompt (l.19)	/prɒmpt/	*v.*	敦促，激励
exclusive (l.20)	/ɪkˈskluːsɪv/	*adj.*	专售高档商品的
syllable (l.21)	/ˈsɪləbəl/	*n.*	音节
bewilderment (l.21)	/bɪˈwɪldəmənt/	*n.*	迷惑，糊涂
freckle (l.22)	/ˈfrekəl/	*n.*	雀斑
evidently (l.23)	/ˈevɪdəntli/	*adv.*	显然地，明显地
weird (l.24)	/wɪəd/	*adj.*	奇异的，古怪的
concoction (l.24)	/kənˈkɒkʃən/	*n.*	调制品
intoxicate (l.25)	/ɪnˈtɒksɪkeɪt/	*v.*	（使）陶醉，（使）得意忘形
blank (l.26)	/blæŋk/	*adj.*	无表情的，茫然的
discreetly (l.29)	/dɪˈskriːtli/	*adv.*	谨慎地
clutch (l.30)	/klʌtʃ/	*v.*	抓住
adorn (l.31)	/əˈdɔːn/	*v.*	装饰，打扮

Notes on the text 课文注释

1 a delicate shade of green, 淡绿色。

2 If you were to ask, 这里用 was/were 加动词不定式来表示过去预计发生并且发生了的事情。

3 come into possession of, 占有，得到。

4 cure someone of ..., 治好某人的……。

5 on the spot, 当场。

6 put out, 烦恼，不安，不高兴。

7 out of stock, 脱销。

8 keep a straight face, 板着面孔，一本正经。

参考译文

我的堂兄哈里在他的书房里一直摆着一只形状古怪的大瓶子。尽管那只瓶子呈淡绿色，但细心的客人很快就会发现瓶里装的是一种看上去黏稠、颜色发灰的东西。要是你问哈里瓶里装着什么，他会告诉你是香水泥。如果你表示怀疑或惊奇，他会立即请你闻一闻，然后取出一些抹在你的皮肤上。这一简单的试验会消除你可能存有的一切疑虑。瓶里装的的确是香水泥。哈里是如何得到这种稀奇古怪的东西的，这里有个有趣的故事，而且他挺爱把它讲给别人听。此外，得到这瓶香水泥还治好了他多年的一个坏习惯。

哈里曾认为走进一家名贵化妆品商店，荒唐地提出要买一种根本不存在的商品是件很开心的事儿。他会当场编造出一些稀奇古怪的货名。他走进商店后，会提出要一种名叫“香影”的新型香水或者什么“不溶浴皂”。要是女售货员告诉他从未听说过这些东西，他会装出十分遗憾和不安的样子。他爱听售货员说他想象出来的那种东西暂时脱销，于是他就煞有介事地许诺改天再来光顾。当然，他再也不会来了。我实在想象不出哈里在这些表演中是怎样装出一本正经的样子的。

无需暗示，哈里就会向你讲起他买下那瓶珍贵香水泥的经过。一天，他去伦敦一家高级商店要买一种叫“密诺莱特”的东西，店员露出诧异的神色。哈里又慢慢地、一字一顿地说了一遍这个词，那个女售货员还是迷惑不解地摇了摇头。哈里便进一步解释“密诺莱特”是一种质地坚硬、状似琥珀的东西，可以用来除去雀斑。他的解释显然对女售货员有些启示。她一个货架接着一个货架地寻找，拿出各种各样稀奇古怪的化妆品，但没有一样能够符合哈里的要求。哈里装出不高兴的样子时，女售货员答应为他订货。哈里为他的恶作剧成功而感到洋洋得意，又提出要买香水泥。他原想女售货员会惊奇地望着他，不知所措，没料到这回该轮到他自己吃惊了。因为那女售货员听完哈里的话后，马上眼睛一亮，拿出几瓶东西放在柜台上让哈里挑选。哈里只好认输。他挑出一个看上去最小的瓶子，谨慎地问了价。他庆幸自己只破费了 20 英镑便得以脱身。他把那只宝贵的瓶子放在腋下夹着，赶紧溜之大吉。从那以后，他认识到自己发明的小小恶作剧是要付出很大代价的。在他书房的书柜里摆着的那瓶形状古怪的香水泥就是他第一次也是最后一次购买的稀有化妆品。

Comprehension 理解

Give short answers to these questions in your own words as far as possible. Use one complete sentence for each answer.

1 What does the curiously-shaped bottle which Harry keeps in his study contain?

2 Why did Harry often visit cosmetic shops?

3 What would he do when he was told that one of his imaginary products was temporarily out of stock?

Vocabulary 词汇

Explain the meanings of the following words and phrases as they are used in the passage: delicate (l.3); observant (l.3); came into possession (l.9); stuff (l.9); insoluble (l.14); to keep a straight face (l.17); is quite beyond me (ll.17-18).

Summary writing 摘要写作

In not more than 80 words describe Harry's experiences on the day he bought a bottle of perfumed mud. Use your own words as far as possible. Do not include anything that is not in the last paragraph.

Composition 作文

Write a composition in about 300 words on one of the following:

a A day's shopping.

b The strangest person I have ever met.

Letter writing 书信写作

Your house was damaged during a recent thunderstorm. Write a letter of about 100 words to a friend telling him what happened.

Key structures and Special difficulties 关键句型和难点

Rewrite the following sentence without changing the meaning. Then refer to ll.21-22.

'"Myrolite" is a hard, amber-like substance and you can use it to remove freckles,' Harry went on to explain.

Harry went on to explain that 'myrolite' ... which ...

Multiple choice questions 选择题

Choose the correct answers to the following questions.

Comprehension 理解

1 The essence of the joke, from Harry's point of view, was that ________ .

(*a*) he would take up the shop assistants' time without having to buy anything

(*b*) he enjoyed inventing fanciful names for outlandish products

(*c*) the shop assistants usually tried very hard not to disappoint him

(*d*) he was amused at the idea that he knew something the shop assistants didn't

2 On Harry's visits to expensive cosmetics shops, he ________ .

(*a*) always thought up a name for some nonexistent item before going into the shop

(*b*) would walk out angrily if the assistant did not entertain his request

(*c*) was delighted if the shop assistant believed the product actually existed

(*d*) seldom bought the products he asked for as they were out of stock

3 When Harry was presented with several bottles of perfumed mud, he ________ .

(*a*) was surprised, as he had only expected one such bottle to be produced

(*b*) told the shop assistant he was defeated

(*c*) felt obliged to offer twenty pounds for the smallest bottle

(*d*) picked up the smallest bottle, hoping it wouldn't be too expensive

Structure 结构

4 The bottle is filled with what ________ a thick, greyish substance. (l.4)

(*a*) must be (*b*) seems to be (*c*) would be (*d*) would appear

5 He thought ________ funny to ask for goods that do not exist. (ll.12-13)

(*a*) that was (*b*) it being (*c*) it (*d*) they were

6 He requested goods that do not exist, ________ he would invent names on the spot. (ll.12-13)

(*a*) when (*b*) to which (*c*) for what (*d*) for which

7 He loved ________ that the product was out of stock. (ll.15-16)

(*a*) when he was told (*b*) it when he was told (*c*) it to be told (*d*) that he was told

8 It was then that Harry decided the game he had invented might prove expensive and ________ since. (ll.30-31)

(*a*) he has not played it (*b*) had not played it (*c*) he does not play it (*d*) did not play it

Vocabulary 词汇

9 He likes to relate how he came into possession of this ________ stuff. (ll.9-10)

(*a*) foreign (*b*) rural (*c*) weird (*d*) unlikely

10 This explanation evidently ________ something to the woman ... (l.23)

(*a*) sensed (*b*) reminded (*c*) informed (*d*) meant

11 Harry put on his act of being ________ annoyed ... (ll.24-25)

(*a*) slightly (*b*) little (*c*) barely (*d*) grossly

12 He felt that for a mere twenty pounds, he had ________ . (ll.29-30)

(*a*) got a real bargain (*b*) made a fortunate choice

(*c*) little to lose (*d*) had a lucky escape

LESSON

53 In the public interest 为了公众的利益

Listen then answer the question below.

听录音，然后回答以下问题。

What could not be reported in the official files?

refer to him as the 'J.O.'

The Scandinavian countries are much admired all over the world for their enlightened social policies. Sweden has evolved an excellent system for protecting the individual citizen from high-handed or incompetent public officers. The system has worked so well that it has been adopted in other countries too.

The Swedes were the first to recognize that public officials like civil servants, police officers, health inspectors or tax-collectors can make mistakes or act over-zealously in the belief that they are serving the public. As long ago as 1809, the Swedish Parliament introduced a scheme to safeguard the interest of the individual. A parliamentary committee representing all political parties appoints a person who is suitably qualified to investigate private grievances against the State. The official title of the person is 'Justiteombudsman', but the Swedes commonly refer to him as the 'J.O.' or 'Ombudsman'. The Ombudsman is not subject to political pressure. He investigates complaints large and small that come to him from all levels of society. As complaints must be made in writing, the Ombudsman receives an average of 1,200 letters a year. He has eight lawyer assistants to help him and he examines every single letter in detail. There is nothing secretive about the Ombudsman's work, for his correspondence is open to public inspection. If a citizen's complaint is justified, the Ombudsman will act on his behalf. The action he takes varies according to the nature of the complaint. He may gently reprimand an official or even suggest to parliament that a law be altered. The following case is a typical example of the Ombudsman's work.

A foreigner living in a Swedish village wrote to the Ombudsman complaining that he had been ill-treated by the police, simply because he was a foreigner. The Ombudsman immediately wrote to the Chief of Police in the district asking him to send a record of the case. There was nothing in the record to show that the foreigner's complaint was justified and the Chief of Police strongly denied the accusation. It was impossible for the Ombudsman to take action, but when he received a similar complaint from another foreigner in the same village, he immediately sent one of his lawyers to investigate the matter. The lawyer ascertained that a policeman had indeed dealt roughly with foreigners on several occasions. The fact that the policeman was prejudiced against foreigners could not be recorded in the official files. It was only possible for the Ombudsman to find this out by sending one of his representatives to check the facts. The policeman in question was severely reprimanded and was informed that if any further complaints were lodged against him, he would be prosecuted. The Ombudsman's prompt action at once put an end to an unpleasant practice which might have gone unnoticed.

New words and expressions 生词和短语

evolve (l.2)	/ɪˈvɒlv/	v.	逐渐形成
high-handed (l.4)	/ˌharˈhændɪd/	adj.	高压的，专横的
incompetent (l.4)	/ɪnˈkɒmpɪtənt/	adj.	不够格的，不称职的
over-zealously (l.8)	/ˌəuvəˈzeləsli/	adv.	过分热情地
safeguard (l.9)	/ˈseɪfgɑːd/	v.	保护
parliamentary (l.9)	/ˌpɑːləˈmentəri/	adj.	国会的
qualified (l.10)	/ˈkwɒlɪfaɪd/	adj.	合格的
grievance (l.11)	/ˈgriːvəns/	n.	不平，冤屈
Justiteombudsman (l.11)	/ˈdʒʌstaɪtˌɒmbʊdzmən/	n.	（瑞典的）司法特派员
ombudsman (l.12)	/ˈɒmbʊdzmən/	n.	（瑞典和英国的）司法特派员
secretive (l.15)	/ˈsiːkrɪtɪv/	adj.	保密的
correspondence (l.16)	/ˌkɒrɪˈspɒndəns/	n.	来往信件
alter (l.18)	/ˈɔːltə/	v.	改变
accusation (l.23)	/ˌækjʊˈzeɪʃən/	n.	谴责，指控
ascertain (l.25)	/ˌæsəˈteɪn/	v.	查出，查明
prejudiced (l.27)	/ˈpredʒʊdɪst/	adj.	有偏见的，不公平的
prompt (l.30)	/prɒmpt/	adj.	及时的

Notes on the text 课文注释

1 in the interest of, 符合……的利益。
2 in the belief that ..., 自以为……。
3 be qualified to do sth., 胜任做某事。
4 be subject to ..., 受……的控制，应服从……。
5 complaints large and small, 程度不同的怨言，large and small 作名词 complaints 的定语。这样两个意义相反的形容词并用时要置于被修饰的词之后。
6 in writing, 以书面形式。
7 in detail, 详细地。
8 on one's behalf, 代表某人。
9 in question, 当事的，所涉及的。
10 put an end to, 制止，结束。

参考译文

斯堪的纳维亚半岛各国实行的开明的社会政策，受到全世界的推崇。在瑞典，已逐渐形成了一种完善的制度以保护每个公民不受专横的和不称职的政府官员的欺压。这种制度由于行之有效，已被其他国家采纳。

是瑞典人首先认识到政府工作人员如文职人员、警官、卫生稽查员、税务人员等等也会犯错误或者自以为在为公众服务而把事情做过了头。早在 1809 年，瑞典议会就建立了一个保护公民利益的制度。议会内有一个代表各政党利益的委员会，由它委派一位称职的人选专门调查个人对国家的意见。此人官衔为“司法特派员”，但瑞典人一般都管他叫“J.O.”或“特派员”。司法特派员不受任何政治压力的制约。他听取社会各阶层的各种大小意见，并进行调查。由于意见均需用书面形式提出，司法特派员每年平均收到 1,200 封信。他有 8 位律师做他的助手协助工作，每封信都详细批阅。司法特派员的工作没有什么秘密可言，他的信件是公开的，供公众监督。如果公民的意见正确，司法特派员便为他伸张正义。司法特派员采取的行动因意见的性质不同而有所不同。他可以善意地批评某位官员，甚至可以向议会提议修改某项法律。下述事件是司法特派员工作的一个典型例子。

一个住在瑞典乡村的外国人写信给司法特派员，抱怨说他受到警察虐待，就是因为他是个外国人。司法特派员立即写信给当地的警察局长，请他寄送与此事有关的材料。材料中没有任何文字记载证明外国人所说的情况符合事实，因此警察局长矢口否认这一指控。这使得司法特派员很难采取行动。但是，当他又收到住在同一村庄的另一个外国人写的一封内容类似的投诉信时，他立即派出一位律师前去调查。律师证实有个警察确实多次粗鲁地对待外国人。警察歧视外国人的事在官方档案中不可能加以记载，司法特派员只有派他的代表去核对事实才能了解真相。当事的警察受到严厉斥责，并被告知，如果再有人投诉他，他将受到起诉。司法特派员及时采取的行动，迅速制止了这一起不愉快的事件，不然这件事可能因未得到人们注意而不了了之。

Comprehension 理解

Give short answers to these questions in your own words as far as possible. Use one complete sentence for each answer.

1 Why did Sweden introduce the institution of Ombudsman?

2 How is an Ombudsman chosen in Sweden?

3 How can the public find out about the Ombudsman's work?

Vocabulary 词汇

Explain the meanings of the following words and phrases as they are used in the passage: evolved an excellent system (ll.2-3); safeguard (l.9); grievances (l.11); investigates (l.12); correspondence (l.16); altered (l.18).

Summary writing 摘要写作

In not more than 80 words write an account of the action the Ombudsman took when he received a complaint from a foreigner in a Swedish village. Use your own words as far as possible. Do not include anything that is not in the last paragraph.

Composition 作文

Write a composition in about 300 words on one of the following:

a Explain whether the Ombudsman institution is or would be useful in your country.

b Describe the work of any one of the following: a policeman, a civil servant, a health officer, a social worker.

Letter writing 书信写作

Write an imaginary letter of about 100 words to an Ombudsman complaining about postal services in your district. Begin 'Dear Sir' and end 'Yours faithfully'.

Key structures and Special difficulties 关键句型和难点

Rewrite the following sentence without changing the meaning. Then refer to ll.26-27.

The policeman's prejudice against foreigners could not be recorded in the official files.

The fact that ...

Multiple choice questions 选择题

Choose the correct answers to the following questions.

Comprehension 理解

1 In what respect does the institution of Ombudsman reflect enlightened social policy?

(*a*) Other countries have followed the Swedish example.

(*b*) Each party appoints its own Ombudsman to ensure equal representation.

(*c*) It admits the possibility of official oppression and guards against it.

(*d*) It aims to eliminate prejudice against foreigners living in Sweden.

2 The authority exercised by the Ombudsman is impartial in that ________ .

(*a*) the complaints he deals with come from all levels of society

(*b*) he will only take action if written evidence justifies a complaint

(*c*) every letter of complaint receives legal attention

(*d*) his decisions are not influenced by any one political party

3 What happened to the policeman in the case?

(*a*) He was sent to prison.

(*b*) He was prosecuted.

(*c*) He was officially rebuked.

(*d*) He was dismissed from the police force.

4 The case taken as an example of the Ombudsman's work shows that ________ .

(*a*) an official may not be prosecuted until a law is altered by parliament

(*b*) the Ombudsman cannot take action if he lacks supporting evidence

(*c*) it needs two similar complaints before the Ombudsman can take action

(*d*) the Swedish police are corrupt and prejudiced against foreigners

Structure 结构

5 ________ recognized that public officials like civil servants can make mistakes. (ll.6-8)

(*a*) It was the Swedes who first (*b*) They were Swedes who had first

(*c*) The Swedes were the first who have (*d*) First it was the Swedes that

6 If a citizen has ________ , the Ombudsman will act on his behalf. (ll.16-17)

(*a*) the complaint justifiably (*b*) the justified complaint

(*c*) a justified complaint (*d*) justified his complaint

7 The policeman was informed that ________ complaints were lodged against him, he ... (ll.28-30)

(*a*) the next time any (*b*) after any further (*c*) unless no further (*d*) furthermore

8 If the Ombudsman hadn't acted promptly, this unpleasant practice ________ . (ll.30-31)

(*a*) might have continued (*b*) might continue

(*c*) will continue (*d*) would continue

Vocabulary 词汇

9 – protecting the individual citizen from ________ and incompetent ... (ll.3-4)

(*a*) efficient (*b*) quick-tempered (*c*) officious (*d*) handy

10 The action he takes ________ the nature of the complaint. (l.17)

(*a*) depends on (*b*) alternates with (*c*) differs from (*d*) agrees with

11 The Chief of Police in the district ________ denied the accusation. (l.23)

(*a*) bitterly (*b*) firmly (*c*) mildly (*d*) roughly

12 The policeman ________ was severely reprimanded ... (ll.28-29)

(*a*) questioned (*b*) concerned (*c*) described (*d*) interrogated

LESSON

54 Instinct or cleverness?

是本能还是机智？

Listen then answer the question below.

听录音，然后回答以下问题。

Was the writer successful in protecting his peach tree? Why not?

We enjoy staring at them

We have been brought up to fear insects. We regard them as unnecessary creatures that do more harm than good. We continually wage war on them, for they contaminate our food, carry diseases, or devour our crops. They sting or bite without provocation; they fly uninvited into our rooms on summer nights, or beat against our lighted windows. We live in dread not only of unpleasant insects like spiders or wasps, but of quite harmless ones like moths. Reading about them increases our understanding without dispelling our fears. Knowing that the industrious ant lives in a highly organized society does nothing to prevent us from being filled with revulsion when we find hordes of them crawling over a carefully prepared picnic lunch. No matter how much we like honey, or how much we have read about the uncanny sense of direction which bees possess, we have a horror of being stung. Most of our fears are unreasonable, but they are impossible to erase. At the same time, however, insects are strangely fascinating. We enjoy reading about them, especially when we find that, like the praying mantis, they lead perfectly horrible lives. We enjoy staring at them, entranced as they go about their business, unaware (we hope) of our presence. Who has not stood in awe at the sight of a spider pouncing on a fly, or a column of ants triumphantly bearing home an enormous dead beetle?

Last summer I spent days in the garden watching thousands of ants crawling up the trunk of my prize peach tree. The tree has grown against a warm wall on a sheltered side of the house. I am especially proud of it, not only because it has survived several severe winters, but because it occasionally produces luscious peaches. During the summer, I noticed that the leaves of the tree were beginning to wither. Clusters of tiny insects called aphids were to be found on the underside of the leaves. They were visited by a large colony of ants which obtained a sort of honey from them. I immediately embarked on an experiment which, even though it failed to get rid of the ants, kept me fascinated for twenty-four hours. I bound the base of the tree with sticky tape, making it impossible for the ants to reach the aphids. The tape was so sticky that they did not dare to cross it. For a long time, I watched them scurrying around the base of the tree in bewilderment. I even went out at midnight with a torch and noted with satisfaction (and surprise) that the ants were still swarming around the sticky tape without being able to do anything about it. I got up early next morning hoping to find that the ants had given up in despair. Instead, I saw that they had discovered a new route. They were climbing up the wall of the house and then on to the leaves of the tree. I realized sadly that I had been completely defeated by their ingenuity. The ants had been quick to find an answer to my thoroughly unscientific methods!

New words and expressions 生词和短语

insect (l.1)	/ˈɪnsekt/	*n.*	昆虫；虫子
wage (l.3)	/weɪdʒ/	*v.*	进行（斗争）
contaminate (l.3)	/kənˈtæmɪneɪt/	*v.*	弄脏
provocation (l.4)	/ˌprɒvəˈkeɪʃən/	*n.*	惹怒
spider (l.7)	/ˈspaɪdə/	*n.*	蜘蛛
wasp (l.7)	/wɒsp/	*n.*	黄蜂
moth (l.7)	/mɒθ/	*n.*	飞蛾
ant (l.8)	/ænt/	*n.*	蚂蚁
revulsion (l.9)	/rɪˈvʌlʃən/	*n.*	厌恶
horde (l.10)	/hɔːd/	*n.*	群
uncanny (l.11)	/ʌnˈkæni/	*adj.*	神秘的，不可思议的
erase (l.12)	/ɪˈreɪz/	*v.*	擦，抹去
praying mantis (ll.13-14)	/ˌpreɪɪŋ ˈmæntɪs/		螳螂
entranced (l.14)	/ɪnˈtrɑːnst/	*adj.*	出神的
beetle (l.16)	/ˈbiːtl/	*n.*	甲虫
sheltered (l.18)	/ˈʃeltəd/	*adj.*	伤不着的，无危险的
luscious (l.19)	/ˈlʌʃəs/	*adj.*	甘美的
cluster (l.20)	/ˈklʌstə/	*n.*	一簇
aphid (l.21)	/ˈeɪfɪd/	*n.*	蚜虫
underside (l.21)	/ˈʌndəsaɪd/	*n.*	底面，下侧
colony (l.21)	/ˈkɒləni/	*n.*	一群
sticky (l.24)	/ˈstɪki/	*adj.*	黏的
scurry (l.25)	/ˈskʌri/	*v.*	小步跑
swarm (l.27)	/swɔːm/	*v.*	聚集
ingenuity (l.30)	/ˌɪndʒəˈnjuːɪti/	*n.*	机灵

Notes on the text 课文注释

1 do more harm than good, 害多益少。

2 wage war on, 对……开战。

3 does nothing to prevent, 不能阻止……。

4 go about ..., 做……。

5 stand in awe, 肃然起敬。

参考译文

我们自幼就在对昆虫的惧怕中长大。我们把昆虫当作害多益少的无用东西。人类不断地同昆虫斗争，因为昆虫弄脏我们的食物，传播疾病，吞噬庄稼。它们无缘无故地又叮又咬；夏天的晚上，它们未经邀请便飞到我们房间里，或者对着露出亮光的窗户乱扑乱撞。在日常生活中，我们不但憎恶如蜘蛛、黄蜂之类令人讨厌的虫子，而且憎恶并无大害的飞蛾等。阅读有关昆虫的书能增加我们对它们的了解，却不能消除我们的恐惧心理。即使知道勤奋的蚂蚁生活在具有高度组织性的社会里，当看到大群蚂蚁在我们精心准备的午间野餐上爬行时，我们也无法抑制对它们的反感。不管我们多么爱吃蜂蜜，或读过多少关于蜜蜂具有神秘的识别方向的灵感的书，我们仍然十分害怕被蜂蜇。我们的恐惧大部分是没有道理的，但却无法消除。同时，不知为什么昆虫又是迷人的。我们喜欢看有关昆虫的书，尤其是当我们了解到螳螂等过着一种令人生畏的生活时，就更加爱读有关昆虫的书了。我们喜欢入迷地看它们做事，它们不知道（但愿如此）我们就在它们身边。当看到蜘蛛扑向一只苍蝇时，一队蚂蚁抬着一只巨大的死甲虫凯旋时，谁能不感到敬畏呢？

去年夏天，我花了好几天时间站在花园里观察成千只蚂蚁爬上我那棵心爱的桃树的树干。那棵树是靠着房子有遮挡的一面暖墙生长的。我为这棵树感到特别自豪，不仅因为它度过了几个寒冬终于活了下来，而且还因为它有时结出些甘甜的桃子来。到了夏天，我发现树叶开始枯萎，结果在树叶背面找到成串的叫作蚜虫的小虫子。蚜虫遭到了一窝蚂蚁的攻击，蚂蚁从它们身上可以获得一种蜜。我当即动手做了一项试验，这项试验尽管没有使我摆脱这些蚂蚁，却使我着迷了 24 小时。我用一条胶带把桃树底部包上，不让蚂蚁接近蚜虫。胶带极黏，蚂蚁不敢从上面爬过。在很长一段时间里，我看见蚂蚁围着大树底部来回转悠，不知所措。半夜，我还拿着电筒来到花园里，满意地（同时惊奇地）发现那些蚂蚁还在围着胶带团团转，无能为力。第二天早上，我起床后希望看到蚂蚁已因无望而放弃了尝试，结果却发现它们又找到一条新的路径。

它们正在顺着房子的外墙往上爬，然后爬上树叶。我懊丧地感到败在了足智多谋的蚂蚁手下。蚂蚁已很快找到了相应的对策，来对付我那套完全不科学的办法！

Comprehension 理解

Give short answers to these questions in your own words as far as possible. Use one complete sentence for each answer.

1 What is our attitude to insects?

2 Why does man try to exterminate insects?

3 What do we enjoy most when reading about insects?

Vocabulary 词汇

Explain the meanings of the following words as they are used in the passage: contaminate (l.3); devour (l.4); provocation (l.4); dispelling (l.8); industrious (l.8); revulsion (l.9); pouncing (l.15).

Summary writing 摘要写作

Describe *in not more than 80 words* what the writer saw and did when he tried to prevent the ants from climbing up his peach tree. Use your own words as far as possible. Do not include anything that is not in the last paragraph.

Composition 作文

Write a composition in about 300 words on one of the following:

a Write an account of any insect you have read about or observed.

b Describe man's efforts to control pests.

Letter writing 书信写作

A friend took some amusing photographs of you when you were on holiday together some time ago. Write him a letter of about 100 words asking him what he has been doing since then and requesting that he send you copies of the photographs he took.

Key structures and Special difficulties 关键句型和难点

Rewrite the following sentence without changing the meaning. Then refer to ll.24-25.

The tape was sticky and they did not dare to cross it.

The tape was so ...

Multiple choice questions 选择题

Choose the correct answers to the following questions.

Comprehension 理解

1 We may learn more about the behaviour of insects ________ .

(*a*) and become so fascinated by them that we are no longer moved by them

(*b*) but we are no less likely to lose our irrational fear of them

(*c*) provided they remain unaware of our presence while we observe them

(*d*) as long as they only harm each other and not us

2 The ant is an insect which ________ .

(*a*) will eat its way through anything from picnic lunches to aphids

(*b*) lives in a highly organized society which we find disgusting

(*c*) once it has killed its prey, will bear it home in a triumphal column

(*d*) shows great ingenuity at finding its way round any obstacle in its path

3 Had the peach tree been planted on the opposite side of the house ________ .

(*a*) it might not have survived the severe winters

(*b*) the writer would not have spent days looking at it

(*c*) the ants would have had further to go before reaching it

(*d*) the ants would not have found another route of access to the leaves

4 The reason for the ants' swarming up and down the tree was that ________ .

(*a*) they collected a kind of honey from the leaves

(*b*) they fed on a kind of honey contained in the sap of the tree

(*c*) they were milking a kind of honey from the aphids on the leaves

(*d*) they needed to go back to their nest in the branches of the tree

Structure 结构

5 By reading about them, we may increase our understanding but ________ dispel our fears. (ll.7-8)

(*a*) we will not (*b*) it does not (*c*) this will not (*d*) not

6 Most of our fears are unreasonable, but we find ________ . (l.12)

(*a*) it impossible to erase them (*b*) that they cannot erase

(*c*) them to erase impossible (*d*) erasing them impossible

7 – an experiment which, ________ failure to get rid of the ants, kept me fascinated. (ll.22-23)

(*a*) even though it was (*b*) in spite of the (*c*) despite its (*d*) was a

8 ________ long to find an answer to ... (ll.30-31)

(*a*) The ants have not been (*b*) The ants had not been

(*c*) The ants had not spent (*d*) It had not taken the ants

Vocabulary 词汇

9 Even when we know that the ant is an industrious creature which leads a highly organized life, we cannot ________ being filled with ... (ll.8-10)

(*a*) refuse (*b*) help (*c*) prevent (*d*) lose

10 – we have read about the ________ sense of direction which bees possess ... (l.11)

(*a*) unknown (*b*) mysterious (*c*) infinite (*d*) disabled

11 The tree occasionally produces ________ fruit. (ll.19-20)

(*a*) deliciously fresh (*b*) sweet and juicy (*c*) tender (*d*) exotic

12 I had been completely defeated by the ________ . (ll.29-30)

(*a*) speedy swarms (*b*) hungry hordes (*c*) inventive creatures (*d*) ingenuous insects

LESSON

55 From the earth: Greetings

来自地球的问候

Listen then answer the question below.
听录音，然后回答以下问题。
Which life forms are most likely to develop on a distant planet?

'little green men'

Recent developments in astronomy have made it possible to detect planets in our own Milky Way and in other galaxies. This is a major achievement because, in relative terms, planets are very small and do not emit light. Finding planets is proving hard enough, but finding life on them will prove infinitely more difficult. The first question to answer is whether a planet can actually support life. In our own solar system, for example, Venus is far too hot and Mars is far too cold to support life. Only the Earth provides ideal conditions, and even here it has taken more than four billion years for plant and animal life to evolve.

Whether a planet can support life depends on the size and brightness of its star, that is its 'sun'. Imagine a star up to twenty times larger, brighter and hotter than our own sun. A planet would have to be a very long way from it to be capable of supporting life. Alternatively, if the star were small, the life-supporting planet would have to have a close orbit round it and also provide the perfect conditions for life forms to develop. But how would we find such a planet? At present, there is no telescope in existence that is capable of detecting the presence of life. The development of such a telescope will be one of the great astronomical projects of the twenty-first century.

It is impossible to look for life on another planet using earth-based telescopes. Our own warm atmosphere and the heat generated by the telescope would make it impossible to detect objects as small as planets. Even a telescope in orbit round the earth, like the very successful Hubble telescope, would not be suitable because of the dust particles in our solar system. A telescope would have to be as far away as the planet Jupiter to look for life in outer space, because the dust becomes thinner the further we travel towards the outer edges of our own solar system. Once we detected a planet, we would have to find a way of blotting out the light from its star, so that we would be able to 'see' the planet properly and analyse its atmosphere. In the first instance, we would be looking for plant life, rather than 'little green men'. The life forms most likely to develop on a planet would be bacteria. It is bacteria that have generated the oxygen we breathe on earth. For most of the earth's history they have been the only form of life on our planet. As Earth-dwellers, we always cherish the hope that we will be visited by little green men and that we will be able to communicate with them. But this hope is always in the realms of science fiction. If we were able to discover lowly forms of life like bacteria on another planet, it would completely change our view of ourselves. As Daniel Goldin of NASA observed, 'Finding life elsewhere would change everything. No human endeavour or thought would be unchanged by it.'

New words and expressions 生词和短语

astronomy (l.1)	/əˈstrɒnəmi/	n.	天文学
relative (l.3)	/ˈrelətɪv/	adj.	相对的
infinitely (l.5)	/ˈɪnfɪnɪtli/	adv.	无限地，无穷地
solar (l.7)	/ˈsəʊlə/	adj.	太阳系的
Venus (l.7)	/ˈviːnəs/	n.	金星
Mars (l.7)	/mɑːz/	n.	火星
orbit (l.13)	/ˈɔːbɪt/	n.	运行轨道
astronomical (l.15)	/ˌæstrəˈnɒmɪkəl/	adj.	天文学的
generate (l.18)	/ˈdʒenəreɪt/	v.	产生
particle (l.20)	/ˈpɑːtɪkəl/	n.	微粒，粒子
Jupiter (l.20)	/ˈdʒuːpɪtə/	n.	木星
blot (l.22)	/blɒt/	v.	遮暗
analyse (l.23)	/ˈænəlaɪz/	v.	分析
bacteria (l.25)	/bækˈtɪəriə/	n.	细菌
oxygen (l.25)	/ˈɒksɪdʒən/	n.	氧气
realm (l.28)	/relm/	n.	领域
endeavour (l.30)	/ɪnˈdevə/	n.	努力

Notes on the text 课文注释

1 Milky Way, 银河。

2 Whether a planet can support life depends on ..., 一颗行星是否能支持生命取决于……。在这句话中，以 whether 引导的名词性从句作句子的主语。

3 up to, 直到。

4 earth-based telescopes, 放置在地球上的望远镜。

5 in the realms of science fiction, 在科幻小说中存在。

6 NASA, 这是美国国家航空航天局的首字母缩写（也可作 N.A.S.A. 或 Nasa）。这个机构成立于 1958 年，负责组织美国的航空宇航研究。它的巨大成功之一便是 1969 年 7 月 21 日把人类送上了月球。

参考译文

天文学方面的最新发展使得我们能够在银河系和其他星系发现行星。这是一个重要的成就，因为相对来说，行星很小，而且也不发光。寻找行星已证明相当困难，但是要在行星上发现生命则是难上加难。第一个需要解答的问题是一颗行星是否有能够维持生命的条件。举例来说，在我们的太阳系里，对于生命来说，金星的温度太高，而火星的温度则太低。只有地球提供了理想的条件，而即使在这里，植物和动物的进化也用了 40 多亿年的时间。

一颗行星是否能够维持生命取决于它的恒星——即它的“太阳”——的大小和亮度。设想一下，有这么一颗恒星，它的大小、亮度和热度都是太阳的 20 倍，那么一颗行星为了维持生命就要离它的恒星非常远。反之，如果恒星很小，维持生命的行星就要在离恒星很近的轨道上运行，而且要有极好的条件才能使生命得以发展。但是，我们如何才能找到这样一颗行星呢？现在，没有一台现存的望远镜可以发现生命的存在。而开发这样一台望远镜将会是 21 世纪天文学的一个重要的研究课题。

使用放置在地球上的望远镜是无法观察到其他行星上的生命的。地球周围温暖的大气层和望远镜散出的热量使得我们根本不可能找到比行星更小的物体。即使是一台放置在围绕地球的轨道上的望远镜——如非常成功的哈勃望远镜——也因为太阳系中的尘埃微粒而无法胜任。望远镜要放置在木星那样遥远的行星上才有可能在外层空间搜寻生命，因为我们越是接近太阳系的边缘，尘埃就越稀薄。一旦我们找到这样一颗行星，我们就要想办法将它的恒星射过来的光线遮暗，这样我们就能彻底“看见”这颗行星，并分析它的大气层。首先我们要寻找植物，而不是“小绿人”。在行星上最容易生存下来的是细菌。正是细菌生产出我们在地球上呼吸的氧气。在地球发展的大部分进程中，细菌是地球上唯一的生命形式。作为地球上的居民，我们总存有这样的希望：小绿人来拜访我们，而我们可以和他们交流。但是，这种希望总是只在科幻小说中存在。如果我们能够在另一颗行星上找到诸如细菌那种低等生命，那么这个发现将彻底改变我们对我们自己的看法。正如美国国家航空航天局的丹尼尔·戈尔丁指出的：“在其他地方发现生命会改变一切。任何人类的努力和想法都会发生变化。”

Comprehension 理解

Give short answers to these questions in your own words as far as possible. Use one complete sentence for each answer.

1 Why is it a major achievement to be able to find new planets in space?

2 Why can't all planets support life?

3 What will be one of the great astronomical projects of the twenty-first century?

Vocabulary 词汇

Explain the meanings of the following words and phrases as they are used in the passage: detect (l.1); in relative terms (l.3); emit (l.4); ideal conditions (l.8); capable of (l.12); alternatively (l.12); presence (l.15).

Summary writing 摘要写作

In not more than 80 words describe what would have to be done to find life on a distant planet and what kind of life this might be. Do not include anything that is not in the last paragraph.

Composition 作文

Write a composition in about 300 words on one of the following:

a Extra terrestrials.

b Suppose the time came when we could send pictures of life on earth to intelligent creatures on other planets, what sorts of pictures do you think would be most interesting to them?

Letter writing 书信写作

You borrow from a friend a travel guide which you are now returning. Write him or her a letter of about 100 words thanking him or her for having lent it to you and saying how useful you found it.

Key structures and Special difficulties 关键句型和难点

Rewrite the following sentence without changing the meaning. Then refer to ll.20-21.

A telescope would have to be far away — for instance round the planet Jupiter — to look for life in outer space.

A telescope would ... as the planet Jupiter ...

Multiple choice questions 选择题

Choose the correct answers to the following questions.

Comprehension 理解

1 Why are planets in other solar systems so much more difficult to detect than stars?

(*a*) Because of the dust particles in our own solar system.

(*b*) Because of the limitations of earth-based telescopes.

(*c*) Because even the Hubble is not powerful enough to see beyond the Milky Way.

(*d*) Because planets are small and dark, and stars are large and radiant.

2 What do we know about the kind of planet, other than our own, that might be able to support life?

(*a*) It will orbit closely round its star.

(*b*) It will be at least four billion years old.

(*c*) Its distance from its star will be such that it has a moderate temperature.

(*d*) It will have an atmosphere capable of supporting bacteria.

3 A telescope capable of finding life on other planets would have to be ________ .

(*a*) far enough from the centre of our solar system not to be affected by dust

(*b*) infinitely more powerful than even the very successful Hubble

(*c*) orbiting in a different solar system a long way away from our own

(*d*) on the planet Jupiter, on the edge of our solar system

Structure 结构

4 It has become possible ________ recent developments in astronomy to ... (l.1)

(*a*) caused by (*b*) through (*c*) as regards (*d*) for

5 Venus is far too hot and Mars is too cold ________ there to be any life. (ll.7-8)

(*a*) than (*b*) whether (*c*) for (*d*) nor

6 A planet would have to be a very long way from ________ . (ll.11-12)

(*a*) so big a star (*b*) such big star (*c*) a like star (*d*) a star as this

7 At present, the telescope ________ that is capable of detecting life. (ll.14-15)

(*a*) does not exist (*b*) no exist (*c*) cannot exist (*d*) won't exist

8 ________ in human endeavour or thought would be unchanged. (ll.30-31)

(*a*) All things (*b*) Everything (*c*) Nothing (*d*) None

Vocabulary 词汇

9 Imagine a star ________ twenty times larger than our own sun. (ll.10-11)

(*a*) as much as (*b*) as well as (*c*) such as (*d*) as if

10 The oxygen we breathe on earth has been ________ by bacteria. (l.25)

(*a*) manufactured (*b*) fabricated (*c*) produced (*d*) given being

11 As Earth-dwellers, we ________ that we will be visited by little green men. (ll.26-27)

(*a*) like to know (*b*) fondly dream (*c*) love to expect (*d*) profoundly believe

12 No human endeavour or thought would be ________ by it. (ll.30-31)

(*a*) unaltered (*b*) ineffective (*c*) unchallenged (*d*) unchecked

LESSON

56 Our neighbour, the river

河流，我们的邻居

Listen then answer the question below.

听录音，然后回答以下问题。

Why had the neighbours left their farm?

just as beekeepers with their bees

The river which forms the eastern boundary of our farm has always played an important part in our lives. Without it we could not make a living. There is only enough spring water to supply the needs of the house, so we have to pump from the river for farm use. We tell the river all our secrets. We know instinctively, just as beekeepers with their bees, that misfortune might overtake us if the important events of our lives were not related to it.

We have special river birthday parties in the summer. Sometimes we go upstream to a favourite backwater, sometimes we have our party at the boathouse, which a predecessor of ours at the farm built in the meadow hard by the deepest pool for swimming and diving. In a heat wave we choose a midnight birthday party and that is the most exciting of all. We welcome the seasons by the riverside, crowning the youngest girl with flowers in the spring, holding a summer festival on Midsummer Eve, giving thanks for the harvest in the autumn, and throwing a holly wreath into the current in the winter.

After a long period of rain the river may overflow its banks. This is a rare occurrence as our climate seldom goes to extremes. We are lucky in that only the lower fields, which make up a very small proportion of our farm, are affected by flooding, but other farms are less favourably sited, and flooding can sometimes spell disaster for their owners.

One bad winter we watched the river creep up the lower meadows. All the cattle had been moved into stalls and we stood to lose little. We were, however, worried about our nearest neighbours, whose farm was low lying and who were newcomers to the district. As the floods had put the telephone out of order, we could not find out how they were managing. From an attic window we could get a sweeping view of the river where their land joined ours, and at the most critical juncture we took turns in watching that point. The first sign of disaster was a dead sheep floating down. Next came a horse, swimming bravely, but we were afraid that the strength of the current would prevent its landing anywhere before it became exhausted. Suddenly a raft appeared, looking rather like Noah's ark, carrying the whole family, a few hens, the dogs, a cat, and a bird in a cage. We realized that they must have become unduly frightened by the rising flood, for their house, which had sound foundations, would have stood stoutly even if it had been almost submerged. The men of our family waded down through our flooded meadows with boathooks, in the hope of being able to grapple a corner of the raft and pull it out of the current towards our bank. We still think it a miracle that they were able to do so.

New words and expressions 生词和短语

boundary (l.1)	/ˈbaʊndəri/	*n.*	界线；边界	spell (l.17)	/spel/	*v.*	招致，带来
pump (l.4)	/pʌmp/	*v.*	用泵抽	stall (l.19)	/stɔːl/	*n.*	牲口棚
overtake (l.6)	/ˌəʊvəˈteɪk/	*v.*	突然降临	attic (l.21)	/ˈætɪk/	*n.*	顶楼
backwater (l.8)	/ˈbækwɔːtə/	*n.*	回水河汊	sweeping (l.21)	/ˈswiːpɪŋ/	*adj.*	范围广大的
predecessor (l.9)	/ˈpriːdɪsesə/	*n.*	前任，前辈	critical (l.22)	/ˈkrɪtɪkəl/	*adj.*	危急的
meadow (l.9)	/ˈmedəʊ/	*n.*	草地，草场	juncture (l.22)	/ˈdʒʌŋktʃə/	*n.*	时刻，关头
crown (l.11)	/kraʊn/	*v.*	给……戴花环	raft (l.25)	/rɑːft/	*n.*	木筏
holly (l.13)	/ˈhɒli/	*n.*	一种冬青植物	unduly (l.26)	/ʌnˈdjuːli/	*adv.*	过度地
wreath (l.13)	/riːθ/	*n.*	花环	foundations (l.27)	/faʊnˈdeɪʃənz/	*n.*	（复数）地基
occurrence (l.14)	/əˈkʌrəns/	*n.*	偶发事件	stoutly (l.27)	/ˈstaʊtli/	*adv.*	牢固地
proportion (l.15)	/prəˈpɔːʃən/	*n.*	部分	submerge (l.27)	/səbˈmɜːdʒ/	*v.*	浸没
site (l.16)	/saɪt/	*v.*	使位于	grapple (l.28)	/ˈgræpəl/	*v.*	抓住

Notes on the text 课文注释

1 Without it we could not make a living. 没有它我们就无法生存下去。without it 起非真实条件句的作用。make a living, 谋生。

2 hard by ..., 在……近旁。

3 in a heat wave, 在大热天。

4 stand to lose, 处于损失的境况之中。

5 put ... out of order, 使……出故障。

6 Noah's ark, 诺亚方舟。这是摘自《圣经·旧约》《创世记》中的典故。诺亚是故事中上帝用洪水消灭人类后的新始祖；诺亚借助一方形大船，与他家属及每种动物雌雄各一逃脱了洪水之灾。

参考译文

形成我们农场东部边界的一条河流一直在我们生活中发挥着重要作用。要是没有这条河，我们就无法生存下去。泉水只能满足家庭生活用水，因此我们必须从河里抽水以用于农业生产。我们向那条河倾诉我们的秘密。我们本能地懂得，就像养蜂人和他们的蜜蜂那样，要是我们不把生活中的重大事件告诉那条河，就可能大祸临头。

夏天，我们为这条河举办特殊的生日宴会。有时，我们溯流而上来到我们喜爱的回水河汊举办；有时在船坞举办。那船坞是农场的一位前辈在一块草地上盖的，草地紧挨一个专供游泳、跳水的深水池。天气炎热时，我们便选择在半夜举办生日聚会，这种聚会是最令人激动的。我们在河边迎接一年四季。春天在河边为最年轻的姑娘戴上花冠，夏天在河边欢庆“仲夏前夜”，秋天在河边为丰收而感恩，冬天往河中抛撒一个冬青花环。

久雨之后，河水会泛滥成灾，但是在我们这里，气候很少发生异常，河水极少泛滥。值得庆幸的是，只有低洼地受到洪水影响，而低洼地在我们农场比例很小。其他农场地势欠佳，洪水有时会给农场主带来灾难。

有一年冬天，天气不好，我们眼看着河水浸没了地势较低的草场。所有的牲口已提前转移到畜圈里，没有造成什么损失。不过，我们很为我们的近邻担心。他们的农场地势低洼，而且他们又是新来乍到。由于洪水造成了电话中断，我们无法了解他们的情况。从顶楼窗口看去，我们农场与他们农场接壤处的那段河流一览无余。在最紧急的时刻，我们轮流监视那段河流的险情。灾难的第一个迹象是一只死羊顺流而下，接着是一匹活马勇敢地与水搏击。但我们担心，洪水的力量将使它在上岸之前就筋疲力尽了。突然，出现了一只筏子，看起来很像诺亚方舟，上面载着他们全家老小，还有几只母鸡、几只狗、一只猫与一只鸟笼，笼里有一只小鸟。我们意识到他们一定是被不断上涨的洪水吓坏了。因为他们的房子地基牢固，即使洪水几乎灭顶也不会倒塌。我家的男人们手拿船篙蹚过被水淹没的草场，希望能够钩住筏子一角，将它拽出激流，拖回岸边。他们终于成功了。至今我们仍认为这是个奇迹。

Comprehension 理解

Give short answers to each of the following questions in your own words as far as possible, using only material contained in the passage. Use one complete sentence for each answer.

1 Why were the family so dependent on the river for their livelihood?

2 For what occasions did they hold festivities by the river?

3 In what was the position of their farm fortunate?

Vocabulary 词汇

Choose five of the following words or phrases and give for each another word or phrase of similar meaning to that in which the word or phrase is used in the passage: instinctively (l.5); overtake (l.6); predecessor (l.9); hard by (l.10); in a heat wave (l.10); a rare occurrence (l.14); goes to extremes (l.15); favourably (l.16).

Summary writing 摘要写作

Give an account *in not more than 80 words* of the author's description of events during the bad flood, as narrated in the last paragraph. Use your own words as far as possible. Do not include anything that is not in the last paragraph.

Composition 作文

Write a composition on one of the following subjects; the length should be between 250 and 350 words.

a What the world would be like without newspapers, radio, films and television.

b 'It was a dark and gloomy street.' Continue the story of an adventure you had in this street.

Letter writing 书信写作

Write a letter of between 80 and 100 words in length on one of the following subjects. You should make the beginning and ending like those of an ordinary letter, but the address is not to be counted in the total number of words.

a You have accidentally broken a window of the house (or flat) next door. As your neighbour is not in when you call, write a letter of apology, offering to make good the damage.

b Write a letter inviting a friend to go with you to a theatre, opera or ballet performance.

Key structures and Special difficulties 关键句型和难点

Rewrite the following sentence without changing the meaning. Then refer to ll.20-21.

There was no way of finding out how they were managing, for the floods had put the telephone out of order.

As the floods ... we could ...

Multiple choice questions 选择题

Choose the correct answers to the following questions.

Comprehension 理解

1 People whose property was less favourably situated than the writer's ________ .
(*a*) had no means of pumping water away from the river
(*b*) farmed land which for the most part lay on a level with the river banks
(*c*) lived where the climate was more variable and the rainfall heavier
(*d*) had land which lay upstream where the river current was stronger

2 The writer's family suspected that their nearest neighbours might have trouble managing ________ .
(*a*) as their farm was liable to flooding and they had not lived there long
(*b*) because the floods had put the telephone out of order
(*c*) when they saw the river sweep over the boundary between the two farms
(*d*) as soon as they saw a dead sheep floating down the river

3 When the writer's family saw a raft appear along the river, they ________ .
(*a*) thought their neighbour's house must have been submerged
(*b*) rowed their boats down to the bank and pulled the raft in with the oars
(*c*) managed to get down to the river in time to save their neighbours
(*d*) were surprised that their neighbours had been able to save themselves

Structure 结构

4 ________ is only enough to supply the needs of the house. (ll.3-4)
(*a*) Water of the spring (*b*) The water in spring
(*c*) The water from the spring (*d*) Spring water

5 We have parties at the boathouse, built in the meadow ________ . (ll.9-10)
(*a*) at the farm by a predecessor of ours (*b*) for us at the farm by a predecessor
(*c*) by our predecessor at the farm (*d*) by one of our predecessors at the farm

6 After it ________ for a long time, the river may overflow its banks. (l.14)
(*a*) is raining (*b*) rained (*c*) has rained (*d*) had rained

7 The strength of the current would prevent ________ anywhere before it ... (l.24)
(*a*) that it landed (*b*) it from landing (*c*) it to land (*d*) the landing of it

Vocabulary 词汇

8 We ________ the seasons by the riverside ... (l.11)
(*a*) greet (*b*) go out to greet
(*c*) celebrate the arrival of (*d*) invoke the start of

9 We were, however, ________ our nearest neighbours ... (l.19)
(*a*) concerned for (*b*) occupied with (*c*) agitated by (*d*) distressed about

10 – and ________ we took turns in watching that point. (l.22)
(*a*) in the peak of condition (*b*) in place of the most severe critic
(*c*) at the most dangerous boundary (*d*) when the flood was at its height

11 – and pull it towards our bank before the current carried it ________ ... (ll.28-29)
(*a*) out (*b*) in (*c*) off (*d*) under

12 ________ we think it a miracle that they were able to do so. (ll.29-30)
(*a*) To this day (*b*) Up till now (*c*) As yet (*d*) Even so

LESSON

57 Back in the old country 重返故里

Listen then answer the question below.

听录音，然后回答以下问题。

Did the narrator find his mother's grave?

everything seemed alien

I stopped to let the car cool off and to study the map. I had expected to be near my objective by now, but everything still seemed alien to me. I was only five when my father had taken me abroad, and that was eighteen years ago. When my mother had died after a tragic accident, he did not quickly recover from the shock and loneliness. Everything around him was full of her presence, continually reopening the wound. So he decided to emigrate. In the new country he became absorbed in making a new life for the two of us, so that he gradually ceased to grieve. He did not marry again and I was brought up without a woman's care; but I lacked for nothing, for he was both father and mother to me. He always meant to go back one day, but not to stay. His roots and mine had become too firmly embedded in the new land. But he wanted to see the old folk again and to visit my mother's grave. He became mortally ill a few months before we had planned to go and, when he knew that he was dying, he made me promise to go on my own.

I hired a car the day after landing and bought a comprehensive book of maps, which I found most helpful on the cross-country journey, but which I did not think I should need on the last stage. It was not that I actually remembered anything at all. But my father had described over and over again what we should see at every milestone, after leaving the nearest town, so that I was positive I should recognize it as familiar territory. Well, I had been wrong, for I was now lost.

I looked at the map and then at the milometer. I had come ten miles since leaving the town, and at this point, according to my father, I should be looking at farms and cottages in a valley, with the spire of the church of our village showing in the far distance. I could see no valley, no farms, no cottages and no church spire — only a lake. I decided that I must have taken a wrong turning somewhere. So I drove back to the town and began to retrace the route, taking frequent glances at the map. I landed up at the same corner. The curious thing was that the lake was not marked on the map. I felt as if I had stumbled into a nightmare country, as you sometimes do in dreams. And, as in a nightmare, there was nobody in sight to help me. Fortunately for me, as I was wondering what to do next, there appeared on the horizon a man on horseback, riding in my direction. I waited till he came near, then I asked him the way to our old village. He said that there was now no village. I thought he must have misunderstood me, so I repeated its name. This time he pointed to the lake. The village no longer existed because it had been submerged, and all the valley too. The lake was not a natural one, but a man-made reservoir.

New words and expressions 生词和短语

alien (l.2)	/ˈeɪliən/	*adj.*	异国的，外国的
emigrate (l.7)	/ˈemɪgreɪt/	*v.*	移居（国外）
absorb (l.8)	/əbˈsɔːb/	*v.*	全神贯注于
embedded (l.11)	/ɪmˈbedɪd/	*adj.*	扎牢的
mortally (l.12)	/ˈmɔːtəl-i/	*adv.*	致命地
comprehensive (l.14)	/ˌkɒmprɪˈhensɪv/	*adj.*	广泛的；丰富的
milestone (l.17)	/ˈmaɪlstəʊn/	*n.*	里程碑
territory (l.18)	/ˈterɪtəri/	*n.*	领地；地区
milometer (l.19)	/maɪˈlɒmɪtə/	*n.*	计程表
spire (l.20)	/spaɪə/	*n.*	（教堂的）塔尖
retrace (l.23)	/rɪˈtreɪs/	*v.*	返回，重走
stumble (l.24)	/ˈstʌmbəl/	*v.*	趔趄地走
horizon (l.26)	/həˈraɪzən/	*n.*	地平线
reservoir (l.30)	/ˈrezəvwɑː/	*n.*	水库

Notes on the text 课文注释

1 I had expected to be near my objective by now, 我本以为这时已经接近目的地了。
"expect 的过去完成时 + 不定式的一般式"，表示过去想做而未做的事。

2 become（be）absorbed in ..., 作"专心致志于……"、"全神贯注于……"讲。

3 lack for nothing, 什么也不缺。

4 he made me promise to go on my own, 他要我答应一定单独回故乡一趟。
promise 是不带 to 的动词不定式，作宾语补足语；on one's own 作"单独"、"靠自己的力量"解。

5 It was not that ... at all. 和下文的 But ... territory. 这两个句子实际用的是一个完整的句型：not that ... but that（不是因为……而是因为……）。

参考译文

我停下车，让汽车发动机冷却一下，同时查看一下地图。我原以为离目的地已经不远，但周围一切对我仍很陌生。我 5 岁那年，父亲就带我出了国，那是 18 年前的事了。当时我母亲在一次事故中惨死，父亲未能很快从悲痛与孤独中恢复过来。他身边的一切都有母亲的影子，不断地勾起他的伤感。于是他决定移居他国。在这个新的国家里，父亲专心致志地为我们俩开创一种新的生活，慢慢地不伤心了。父亲没有再娶，因此，我在没有母亲的环境里长大成人。但我却什么都不缺，因为他既当父亲又当母亲。他总想将来回国看看，但却不愿长期住下去，因为他与我一样已经把根深深地扎在了异国的土地上。但是，他想看一看家乡的父老乡亲，为我的母亲扫墓。就在他计划回国的前几个月，他突然身患绝症。他知道自己已奄奄一息，于是要我答应一定单独回故乡一趟。

我下飞机后租了一辆车，并买了一本详尽的地图册。在乡间行车途中，我觉得它非常有用，但快到家了，我倒觉得它没什么用了。这倒并非是我背熟了地图，而是父亲曾反复向我描述，在过了离故乡最近的那个小镇后，在每一个路标处可见到些什么。因此，我相信这段路对我来说会是很熟悉的。唉，实际我错了，我现在迷路了。

我看了看地图，又查了一下里程表。从小镇出来，我走了 10 英里。照父亲的说法，我面前应是一个山谷，有农场与村舍，还可远远望见老家村子里的教堂的尖顶。可现在我却看不到山谷，看不见农舍，也看不见教堂尖顶，看见的只是一片湖水。我想一定是在什么地方拐错了弯儿。于是我驾车返回小镇，重新按路线行驶，还不停地查看地图。结果又来到刚才那个拐弯处。奇怪的是那个湖没有在地图上标出。我感到自己就像平时做梦那样迷迷糊糊地闯进了噩梦境地。就像在噩梦里一样，见不到一个人可以帮助我。不过，我是幸运的，正当我走投无路之时，从天边出现一个骑马的人向我骑来。等他走近了，我问他去老家的路。他说那村子已经没有了。我想他一定误解了我的意思，于是又说了一遍村庄的名字。这次他用手指了一下那个湖。村庄已不复存在，因为已经为水所淹，山谷也被水淹没了。这不是一个天然湖，而是一座人工修建的水库。

Comprehension 理解

Give short answers to each of the following questions in your own words as far as possible, using only material contained in the passage. Use one complete sentence for each answer.

1 Why did the author's father emigrate?

2 Why had the author come back to the land of his birth?

3 What made the author think that he would not need a map for the last part of his journey?

Vocabulary 词汇

Choose five of the following words and phrases and give for each another word or phrase of similar meaning to that in which the word or phrase is used in the passage: objective (l.2); seemed alien (l.2); lacked for nothing (l.9); embedded (l.11); mortally (l.12); comprehensive (l.14); positive (l.17); familiar territory (ll.17-18).

Summary writing 摘要写作

Give an account *in not more than 80 words* of the author's search for the village, as narrated in the last paragraph. Use your own words as far as possible. Do not include anything that is not in the last paragraph.

Composition 作文

Write a composition on one of the following subjects; the length should be between 250 and 350 words.

a The house you wish to own.

b A day spent by the sea or by a lake or river.

Letter writing 书信写作

Write a letter of between 80 and 100 words in length on one of the following subjects. You should make the beginning and ending like those of an ordinary letter. Write the postal address in full at the head of your letter, but do not count this address in the total number of words.

a You are ill and cannot go to work for a few days. Write explaining your absence and making arrangements for your work while you are absent.

b You have received a gift from an old friend abroad. Write a letter of thanks, say how you will make use of the gift and briefly give news of yourself.

Key structures and Special difficulties 关键句型和难点

Rewrite the following sentence without changing the meaning. Then refer to ll.21-22.

It wasn't possible for me to see any valley, any farms, any cottages and any church spire — only a lake.

I could see ...

Multiple choice questions 选择题

Choose the correct answers to the following questions.

Comprehension 理解

1 When the author thought he was near his objective, he stopped because ________ .

(*a*) it was too hot for him to concentrate on where he was going

(*b*) he wanted to find his way back to the nearest town

(*c*) he realized that he must have taken a wrong turning

(*d*) he did not recognize any familiar landmarks

2 Why did the author's father want his son to go back on his own?

(*a*) He feared that his wound would reopen if he were to return himself.

(*b*) He wanted to hear what had happened to his village before dying.

(*c*) He was too ill to accompany his son on the cross-country journey.

(*d*) He had always intended that his son should see the land of their birth.

3 What made the author feel he had stumbled into a nightmare country?

(*a*) According to his father, he should already have reached the village.

(*b*) Nothing he saw corresponded to what he had expected to see.

(*c*) He did not know how he could get to the other side of the lake.

(*d*) He was curious to know more about the lake but there was no one to ask.

Structure 结构

4 I was only five when I ________ , and that was eighteen years ago. (ll.3-4)

(*a*) had been taken abroad by my father (*b*) took abroad with my father

(*c*) had taken with my father abroad (*d*) was taken by my father abroad

5 – and I was brought up ________ . (l.9)

(*a*) without a care of women (*b*) without care by a woman

(*c*) without a woman to care for me (*d*) careless of a woman

6 – leaving the town. It was here that my father had told me I ________ farms and cottages ... (ll.19-20)

(*a*) could see (*b*) would see (*c*) would be seeing (*d*) should have seen

7 I waited for his approach ________ I asked him ... (l.27)

(*a*) until (*b*) when (*c*) before (*d*) so that

8 I asked him ________ to our old village. (l.27)

(*a*) what way it was (*b*) if he knows the way (*c*) which way to go (*d*) how to get

Vocabulary 词汇

9 Everything around him ________ , continually reopening ... (ll.6-7)

(*a*) reminded him of her (*b*) presented her to him

(*c*) recalled him to her (*d*) remembered her for him

10 But my father had described ________ what we should see ... (ll.16-18)

(*a*) incessantly (*b*) overmuch (*c*) repeatedly (*d*) extensively

11 – the lake was not ________ on the map. (l.24)

(*a*) signed (*b*) written (*c*) shown (*d*) spotted

12 The lake was not a natural one. It was ________ one. (ll.29-30)

(*a*) an unnatural (*b*) a man-made (*c*) an unreal (*d*) a manufactured

LESSON 58

A spot of bother 一点儿小麻烦

Listen then answer the question below.

听录音，然后回答以下问题。

What did the old lady find when she got home?

what she described as a little spot of bother

The old lady was glad to be back at the block of flats where she lived. Her shopping had tired her and her basket had grown heavier with every step of the way home. In the lift her thoughts were on lunch and a good rest; but when she got out at her own floor, both were forgotten in her sudden discovery that her front door was open. She was thinking that she must reprimand her home help the next morning for such a monstrous piece of negligence, when she remembered that she had gone shopping after the home help had left and she knew that she had turned both keys in their locks. She walked slowly into the hall and at once noticed that all the room doors were open, yet following her regular practice she had shut them before going out. Looking into the drawing room, she saw a scene of confusion over by her writing desk. It was as clear as daylight then that burglars had forced an entry during her absence. Her first impulse was to go round all the rooms looking for the thieves, but then she decided that at her age it might be more prudent to have someone with her, so she went to fetch the porter from his basement. By this time her legs were beginning to tremble, so she sat down and accepted a cup of very strong tea, while he telephoned the police. Then, her composure regained, she was ready to set off with the porter's assistance to search for any intruders who might still be lurking in her flat.

They went through the rooms, being careful to touch nothing, as they did not want to hinder the police in their search for fingerprints. The chaos was inconceivable. She had lived in the flat for thirty years and was a veritable magpie at hoarding; and it seemed as though everything she possessed had been tossed out and turned over and over. At least sorting out the things she should have discarded years ago was now being made easier for her. Then a police inspector arrived with a constable and she told them of her discovery of the ransacked flat. The inspector began to look for fingerprints, while the constable checked that the front door locks had not been forced, thereby proving that the burglars had either used skeleton keys or entered over the balcony. There was no trace of fingerprints, but the inspector found a dirty red bundle that contained jewellery which the old lady said was not hers. So their entry into this flat was apparently not the burglars' first job that day and they must have been disturbed. The inspector then asked the old lady to try to check what was missing by the next day and advised her not to stay alone in the flat for a few nights. The old lady thought he was a fussy creature, but since the porter agreed with him, she rang up her daughter and asked for her help in what she described as a little spot of bother.

New words and expressions 生词和短语

lift (l.3)	/lɪft/	*n.*	电梯
monstrous (l.7)	/ˈmɒnstrəs/	*adj.*	极大的，可怕的
negligence (l.7)	/ˈneglɪdʒəns/	*n.*	粗心大意
prudent (l.13)	/ˈpruːdənt/	*adj.*	谨慎的
composure (l.15)	/kəmˈpəʊʒə/	*n.*	镇静，沉着
intruder (l.16)	/ɪnˈtruːdə/	*n.*	入侵者（尤指欲行窃者）
lurk (l.16)	/lɜːk/	*v.*	潜藏
hinder (l.17)	/ˈhɪndə/	*v.*	妨碍
fingerprint (l.18)	/ˈfɪŋgəˌprɪnt/	*n.*	指纹
chaos (l.18)	/ˈkeɪ-ɒs/	*n.*	混乱，无秩序
inconceivable (l.18)	/ˌɪnkənˈsiːvəbəl/	*adj.*	不可思议的
veritable (l.19)	/ˈverɪtəbəl/	*adj.*	真正的，地地道道的
magpie (l.19)	/ˈmægpaɪ/	*n.*	喜欢收藏物品的人
toss (l.19)	/tɒs/	*v.*	扔
discard (l.20)	/dɪsˈkɑːd/	*v.*	丢弃
constable (l.21)	/ˈkʌnstəbəl/	*n.*	警察
ransack (l.22)	/ˈrænsæk/	*v.*	洗劫
balcony (l.24)	/ˈbælkəni/	*n.*	阳台
fussy (l.28)	/ˈfʌsi/	*adj.*	大惊小怪的，小题大做的

Notes on the text 课文注释

1 with every step of the way home, 这里介词 with 引导的短语作状语，表示“随……（情况发生某种变化）”。

2 her thoughts were on lunch and a good rest, 她只想着午餐和好好休息。

3 reprimand sb. for ..., 因为……而训斥某人。

4 yet following her regular practice, 然而按照她的惯例。
这是现在分词短语作方式状语，修饰 had shut。

5 as clear as daylight, 十分清楚。

6 it might be more prudent to have someone with her, 有人陪伴她可能更谨慎一些。
it 是形式主语，不定式短语 to have someone with her 是真正的主语。

7 being careful to touch nothing 是现在分词短语作方式状语，修饰 went through。

8 skeleton key, 万能钥匙。

参考译文

老妇人回到了她居住的公寓楼，心里很高兴。去商店买东西把她搞得筋疲力尽；在回家的路上，她每走一步，就感到手里的篮子又重了一点。她乘上电梯后，只想着午餐和好好休息一下。但她到了自己的楼层走出电梯后，就把这两件事忘了个干净，因为她突然发现她家的大门开着。她心想明天上午一定要好好训斥那个干家务的帮手，她竟如此疏忽大意。但突然她记起来了，帮手是在她出去买东西之前走的，她还记得曾用了两把钥匙把大门锁上了。她慢慢地走进前厅，立即发现所有的房门都敞开着，而她记得在出门买东西前，她按老规矩是把房门一一锁上的。她往起居室里看去，写字台边一片狼藉。事情很清楚，在她外出时，窃贼曾闯进家门。她第一个念头是到各个房间里搜寻一下窃贼，但转念一想，像她这个年纪，最好是找个人一起去。于是她到地下室去找看门的人。这时，她两腿累得开始发抖，于是坐了下来，喝了一杯浓茶。与此同时，看门的人给警察挂了电话。此刻老妇人也镇定了下来，准备在看门人的协助下搜寻可能仍躲藏在她房里的窃贼。

他俩搜遍了每一个房间，小心翼翼地不接触任何东西，因为他们怕妨碍警察寻找指纹。房间里的紊乱状况是无法想象的。老妇人在这套公寓里住了 30 年，她又是个名副其实的收藏家。看来她的每一件东西都被翻了出来，并且被里里外外看了个遍。这样一来，她倒是容易将那些几年前就该扔掉的东西找出来了。过了一会儿，一位巡官带着一名警察来了。她向他们讲述了发现公寓遭劫的经过。巡官开始搜寻指纹，警察经检查发现大门锁头并无撬过的迹象。由此可以证明，窃贼或者是用了万能钥匙，或者是翻越阳台进来的。巡官没有发现指纹，却发现了一个装有珠宝的、肮脏的红包袱。老妇人说那不是她的。很明显，闯进这套公寓的窃贼那天并不是首次作案，而且他们一定是受了惊吓。巡官请老妇人在次日之前设法查清丢了些什么，并劝她几夜之内不要独自一人在公寓过夜。老妇人觉得巡官大惊小怪，但既然看门人也同意他的意见，她只得打电话向女儿求援，说她碰到了一点儿小麻烦。

Comprehension 理解

Give short answers to each of the following questions in your own words as far as possible, using only material contained in the passage. Use one complete sentence for each answer.

1 Why was the old lady surprised to find her front door open?

2 What made her realize that burglars had entered the flat?

3 Why did she go down to the basement?

Vocabulary 词汇

Choose five of the following words and phrases and give for each another word or phrase of similar meaning to that in which the word or phrase is used in the passage: reprimand (l.6); piece of negligence (l.7); regular practice (l.10); as clear as daylight (l.11); prudent (l.13); her composure regained (l.15); intruders (l.16); lurking (l.16).

Summary writing 摘要写作

Give an account *in not more than 80 words* of what took place in the flat after the old lady had returned to it with the porter. Use your own words as far as possible. Do not include anything that is not in the last paragraph.

Composition 作文

Write a composition on one of the following subjects; the length should be between 250 and 350 words.

a Public festivals in your own country.

b Your adventures when you first visited a foreign country.

Letter writing 书信写作

Write a letter of between 80 and 100 words in length on one of the following subjects. You should make the beginning and ending like those of an ordinary letter, but the address is not to be counted in the total number of words.

a You are ill and cannot meet a friend (who has no telephone) as arranged. Write explaining why you cannot meet, and invite him or her to visit you.

b An English friend has written asking you to help in finding, for a seventeen-year-old English student, a school or place for training or study in your country. Answer the letter giving any helpful information.

Key structures and Special difficulties 关键句型和难点

Rewrite the following sentence without changing the meaning. Then refer to ll.26-27.

'Try to check what's missing by tomorrow and don't stay alone in the flat for a few nights,' the inspector said.

The inspector asked the old lady ... and advised her ...

Multiple choice questions 选择题

Choose the correct answers to the following questions.

Comprehension 理解

1 The old lady's thoughts were on lunch and a good rest ________ .

(*a*) because she had done so much shopping on her way home

(*b*) as she climbed the steps to the floor her flat was on

(*c*) but the sight of the open front door put them both out of her mind

(*d*) until she remembered she had gone shopping after the home help had left

2 When the old lady and the porter got back to the scene of the crime ________ .

(*a*) he made her a cup of strong tea and then telephoned the police

(*b*) they searched the rooms for any burglars who might not have escaped

(*c*) they took care not to touch anything the burglars had touched

(*d*) they waited for the police before going into every room in the flat

3 What made the police think the burglars had been disturbed?

(*a*) They had been forced to leave the front door open.

(*b*) There was no trace of their fingerprints.

(*c*) They had made no attempt to disguise the fact they had been there.

(*d*) They had left behind some jewellery which did not belong to the lady.

Structure 结构

4 She was thinking that she ________ reprimand her home help ... (l.6)

(*a*) would have to (*b*) had to (*c*) was having to (*d*) has to

5 – the room doors were open, yet she never went out ________ ... (ll.9-10)

(*a*) without shutting them (*b*) before she shut them

(*c*) except to have shut them (*d*) in case they were not shut

6 – so she went ________ to fetch the porter. (ll.13-14)

(*a*) down to the basement (*b*) below to his basement

(*c*) from his basement (*d*) along to the basement

7 At least it was now being made easier ________ out the things she should have discarded years ago. (ll.20-21)

(*a*) than she sorted (*b*) that she sorted (*c*) for her to sort (*d*) sorting

8 – locks had not been forced, ________ that the burglars ... (ll.23-24)

(*a*) which proved (*b*) by this proving (*c*) so that he proved (*d*) in that it proved

Vocabulary 词汇

9 – for thirty years and had hoarded ________ ... (ll.18-19)

(*a*) anything of value (*b*) every conceivable article

(*c*) quite a few items of interest (*d*) odd bits and pieces

10 – and advised her not to stay ________ in the flat ... (ll.26-27)

(*a*) single (*b*) on her own (*c*) lonely (*d*) selfish

11 The old lady thought he was ________ concerned. (ll.27-28)

(*a*) rather (*b*) quite (*c*) hardly (*d*) unduly

12 In describing the burglary as 'a little spot of bother', the old lady was ________ . (l.29)

(*a*) underestimating her losses (*b*) undercharging the burglars

(*c*) underlining the evidence (*d*) understating the case

LESSON

59 Collecting 收藏

Listen then answer the question below.

听录音，然后回答以下问题。

What in particular does a person gain when he or she becomes a serious collector?

associations with the past

People tend to amass possessions, sometimes without being aware of doing so. Indeed they can have a delightful surprise when they find something useful which they did not know they owned. Those who never have to move house become indiscriminate collectors of what can only be described as clutter. They leave unwanted objects in drawers, cupboards and attics for years, in the belief that they may one day need just those very things. As they grow old, people also accumulate belongings for two other reasons, lack of physical and mental energy, both of which are essential in turning out and throwing away, and sentiment. Things owned for a long time are full of associations with the past, perhaps with relatives who are dead, and so they gradually acquire a value beyond their true worth.

Some things are collected deliberately in the home in an attempt to avoid waste. Among these I would list string and brown paper, kept by thrifty people when a parcel has been opened, to save buying these two requisites. Collecting small items can easily become a mania. I know someone who always cuts sketches out from newspapers of model clothes that she would like to buy if she had the money. As she is not rich, the chances that she will ever be able to afford such purchases are remote; but she is never sufficiently strong-minded to be able to stop the practice. It is a harmless habit, but it litters up her desk to such an extent that every time she opens it, loose bits of paper fall out in every direction.

Collecting as a serious hobby is quite different and has many advantages. It provides relaxation for leisure hours, as just looking at one's treasures is always a joy. One does not have to go outside for amusement, since the collection is housed at home. Whatever it consists of, stamps, records, first editions of books, china, glass, antique furniture, pictures, model cars, stuffed birds, toy animals, there is always something to do in connection with it, from finding the right place for the latest addition, to verifying facts in reference books. This hobby educates one not only in the chosen subject, but also in general matters which have some bearing on it. There are also other benefits. One wants to meet like-minded collectors, to get advice, to compare notes, to exchange articles, to show off the latest find. So one's circle of friends grows. Soon the hobby leads to travel, perhaps to a meeting in another town, possibly a trip abroad in search of a rare specimen, for collectors are not confined to any one country. Over the years, one may well become an authority on one's hobby and will very probably be asked to give informal talks to little gatherings and then, if successful, to larger audiences. In this way self-confidence grows, first from mastering a subject, then from being able to talk about it. Collecting, by occupying spare time so constructively, makes a person contented, with no time for boredom.

New words and expressions 生词和短语

amass (l.1)	/əˈmæs/	*v.*	积聚
indiscriminate (l.4)	/ˌɪndɪˈskrɪmɪnɪt/	*adj.*	不加选择的
clutter (l.5)	/ˈklʌtə/	*n.*	一堆杂物
string (l.12)	/strɪŋ/	*n.*	细线
requisite (l.13)	/ˈrekwɪzɪt/	*n.*	必需品
mania (l.13)	/ˈmeɪniə/	*n.*	癖好
sketch (l.13)	/sketʃ/	*n.*	草图，图样
remote (l.15)	/rɪˈməʊt/	*adj.*	（机会、可能性）少的，小的
strong-minded (ll.15-16)	/ˌstrɒŋ ˈmaɪndɪd/	*adj.*	意志坚强的
relaxation (l.18)	/ˌriːlækˈseɪʃən/	*n.*	休息，娱乐
verify (l.22)	/ˈverɪfaɪ/	*v.*	查证，核实
bearing (l.24)	/ˈbeərɪŋ/	*n.*	关系，联系
like-minded (l.24)	/ˌlaɪkˈmaɪndɪd/	*adj.*	志趣相投的
specimen (l.27)	/ˈspesɪmɪn/	*n.*	标本
constructively (l.30)	/kənˈstrʌktɪvli/	*adv.*	有益地，积极地
contented (l.31)	/kənˈtentɪd/	*adj.*	心满意足的
boredom (l.31)	/ˈbɔːdəm/	*n.*	烦恼，无聊

Notes on the text 课文注释

1 in the belief that, 这个介词短语在句子中作谓语动词 leave 的状语。

2 those very things, 就是那些东西，very 在这里起强调作用，可译作“正是那个（些）”，“正是所要的”。

3 for two other reasons, lack of physical and mental energy, ... and sentiment, 在这个句子中，lack of ... 和 sentiment 是两个并列的成分，作 reasons 的同位语，而 both of which ... 是 physical and mental energy 的非限定性定语从句。

4 beyond their true worth, 超过它们的实际价值。

5 to such an extent that, 达到了这样的程度，that 后面的从句作 extent 的同位语。

6 as just looking at one’s treasures is always a joy, 因为欣赏自己收藏的珍品总会充满了乐趣。as 是连词，引导原因状语从句。

7 have some bearing on it, 与它有关。

参考译文

人们喜欢收藏东西，有时并没有意识到自己在这样做。确实，一旦无意之中从自己的收藏品中找到某件有用的东西时，可以给人一种惊喜的感觉。那些从来不必搬家的人们成了一种无所不收的收藏家。他们专门收藏那些只能被称作杂货的东西。他们在抽屉里、碗柜中、阁楼上堆放着一些不用的东西，一放就是好几年，相信总有一天需要的正好是那些东西。人们年老之后也喜欢收藏东西，不过是出于两个不同的原因：一是体力、精力均告不佳，这二者是清除无用的东西必不可少的因素；另一个原因是感情因素。东西搁得时间久了，便会充满着与过去岁月的联系，比方说与死去的亲戚有关。因此这些东西慢慢获得了一种超出它本身的价值。

居家度日，有目的地收藏某些东西是为了防止浪费。这些东西中我想以细绳和包装纸为例。节俭的人们打开包裹后便把这两样必备的东西收藏起来，省得日后去买。收集小玩意儿很容易着迷。我认识一个人，她总喜欢从报纸上剪下流行服装的图样，等以后有钱时去买这些服装。由于她并不富裕，她买得起这些服装的可能性十分渺茫。但她又缺乏足够坚强的意志把这一收集活动停下来。这种习惯无害，只是把写字台里堆得满满当当，以致每次打开抽屉总能带出许多纸片四处飞扬。

作为一种严肃的业余爱好的收藏活动完全是另外一回事，它具有许多益处。它可以使人在闲暇中得到休息，因为欣赏自己收藏的珍品总会充满了乐趣。人们不必走到户外去寻求娱乐，因为收藏品都是存放在家中。不管收藏品是什么，邮票、唱片、头版书籍、瓷器、玻璃杯、老式家具、绘画、模型汽车、鸟类标本，还是玩具动物，从为新增添的收藏品寻找摆放位置到核对参考书中的事实，总归有事可做。这种爱好不仅能使人从选择的专题中受到教育，而且也能从与之有关的一般事物中获得长进。除此之外，还有其他的益处。收藏者要会见情趣相投的收藏者，以获取教益，交流经验，交换收藏品，炫耀自己的最新收藏。朋友的圈子就这样不断扩大。用不了多久，有这种爱好的人便开始旅行，也许是去另一个城市参加会议，也可能是出国寻找一件珍品，因为收藏活动是没有国界的。一个人积累了多年经验会成为自己这种爱好的权威，很可能应邀在小型集会上作非正式的讲话。如果讲得好，便可能向更多的人发表演说。这样，你的自信心不断增强，先是因为掌握了一门学问，接下来是因为能够就此发表见解。收藏活动通过富有建设性地利用业余时间使人感到心满意足，不再有无聊之日。

Comprehension 理解

Give short answers to each of the following questions in your own words as far as possible, using only material contained in the passage. Use one complete sentence for each answer.

1 Why do some people tend to hoard things which they never use?

2 What special reasons cause old people to keep possessions which they no longer need?

3 Why was it not very sensible of the author's friend to collect sketches of model clothes?

Vocabulary 词汇

Choose five of the following words and phrases and give for each another word or phrase of similar meaning to that in which the word or phrase is used in the passage: amass (l.1); being aware (l.1); move house (l.4); attics (l.6); gradually acquire (l.10); thrifty (l.12); in every direction (l.17).

Summary writing 摘要写作

Give an account *in not more than 80 words* of the advantages which the author attributes to having collecting as a hobby. Use your own words as far as possible. Do not include anything that is not in the last paragraph.

Composition 作文

Write a composition on one of the following subjects; the length should be between 250 and 350 words.

a If you could choose, in which country would you like to live and why?

b Write a short story beginning 'There was a knock on the window ...'

Letter writing 书信写作

Write a letter of between 80 and 100 words in length on one of the following subjects. You should make the beginning and ending like those of an ordinary letter, but the address is not to be counted in the total number of words.

a A friend is coming to visit you. Write a short letter giving him (or her) directions for finding your house.

b Write a letter to a friend explaining that, through illness, you will be unable to go to stay with him (or her) as previously arranged. Say how you are progressing and suggest alternative arrangements.

Key structures and Special difficulties 关键句型和难点

Rewrite the following sentence without changing the meaning. Then refer to ll.27-28.

Over the years, it is quite likely that one will become an authority on one's hobby.

Over the years one ...

Multiple choice questions 选择题

Choose the correct answers to the following questions.

Comprehension 理解

1 What differentiates the indiscriminate collector from the serious one?

(*a*) What he collects is only of personal rather than communal interest.

(*b*) He lacks the physical and mental energy to go out and about.

(*c*) His possessions are varied but over the years they gain in value.

(*d*) He confines his collection to the home and therefore does not travel.

2 The author's friend is typical of the indiscriminate collector in that ________ .

(*a*) she keeps newspapers in the hope that one day they may come in useful

(*b*) she collects sketches of clothes to save herself the cost of buying them

(*c*) she is too narrow-minded to be able to stop a sentimental practice

(*d*) she never gets round to sorting out the clutter she has accumulated

3 The serious collector can spend his leisure time ________ .

(*a*) at home, as his collection is sufficient entertainment in itself

(*b*) at the same time as looking joyfully at his treasures

(*c*) educating himself and others by verifying facts in reference books

(*d*) occupying himself by constructing a house for his collection

Structure 结构

4 ________ belongings people accumulate. There are two reasons for this ... (ll.7-9)

(*a*) As they get older more (*b*) In getting older there are more

(*c*) Only when they get older, do more (*d*) The older they get the more

5 ________ in the home in an attempt to avoid waste. (l.11)

(*a*) People deliberately collect (*b*) People deliberately collect some things

(*c*) People collect deliberately (*d*) People collect deliberately some things

6 – but it litters up her desk ________ that every time she opens it ... (ll.16-17)

(*a*) so far (*b*) as long as (*c*) in as much (*d*) so much

7 – something to do, from finding the right place ________ the latest addition to ... (ll.21-22)

(*a*) where he puts (*b*) in order to put (*c*) for to put (*d*) to put

8 – and then, if ________ successful, to larger audiences. (ll.28-29)

(*a*) they will be (*b*) one is (*c*) it has been (*d*) they were

Vocabulary 词汇

9 Some things are collected ________ in the home so as to avoid waste. (l.11)

(*a*) systematically (*b*) intentionally (*c*) purposefully (*d*) organizationally

10 Collecting as a serious hobby is ________ and has many advantages. (l.18)

(*a*) altogether separate (*b*) rather unlike (*c*) fairly diverse (*d*) very distinguished

11 – the right place for the latest addition to ________ facts in reference books. (ll.22-23)

(*a*) insuring (*b*) certifying (*c*) identifying (*d*) checking

12 – but also in general matters which ________ . (ll.23-24)

(*a*) stand up to it (*b*) relate to it (*c*) bear it out (*d*) carry it off

LESSON 60 Too early and too late 太早和太晚

Listen then answer the question below.

听录音，然后回答以下问题。

Why did the young girl miss the train?

half an hour too soon

Punctuality is a necessary habit in all public affairs in civilized society. Without it, nothing could ever be brought to a conclusion; everything would be in a state of chaos. Only in a sparsely-populated rural community is it possible to disregard it. In ordinary living, there can be some tolerance of unpunctuality. The intellectual, who is working on some abstruse problem, has everything coordinated and organized for the matter in hand. He is therefore forgiven if late for a dinner party. But people are often reproached for unpunctuality when their only fault is cutting things fine. It is hard for energetic, quick-minded people to waste time, so they are often tempted to finish a job before setting out to keep an appointment. If no accidents occur on the way, like punctured tyres, diversions of traffic, sudden descent of fog, they will be on time. They are often more industrious, useful citizens than those who are never late. The over-punctual can be as much a trial to others as the unpunctual. The guest who arrives half an hour too soon is the greatest nuisance. Some friends of my family had this irritating habit. The only thing to do was ask them to come half an hour later than the other guests. Then they arrived just when we wanted them.

If you are catching a train, it is always better to be comfortably early than even a fraction of a minute too late. Although being early may mean wasting a little time, this will be less than if you miss the train and have to wait an hour or more for the next one; and you avoid the frustration of arriving at the very moment when the train is drawing out of the station and being unable to get on it. An even harder situation is to be on the platform in good time for a train and still to see it go off without you. Such an experience befell a certain young girl the first time she was travelling alone.

She entered the station twenty minutes before the train was due, since her parents had impressed upon her that it would be unforgivable to miss it and cause the friends with whom she was going to stay to make two journeys to meet her. She gave her luggage to a porter and showed him her ticket. To her horror he said that she was two hours too soon. She felt in her handbag for the piece of paper on which her father had written down all the details of the journey and gave it to the porter. He agreed that a train did come into the station at the time on the paper and that it did stop, but only to take on mail, not passengers. The girl asked to see a timetable, feeling sure that her father could not have made such a mistake. The porter went to fetch one and arrived back with the station master, who produced it with a flourish and pointed out a microscopic 'o' beside the time of the arrival of the train at his station; this little 'o' indicated that the train only stopped for mail. Just at that moment the train came into the station. The girl, tears streaming down her face, begged to be allowed to slip into the guard's van. But the station master was adamant: rules could not be broken. And she had to watch that train disappear towards her destination while she was left behind.

New words and expressions 生词和短语

punctuality (l.1)	/ˌpʌŋktʃuˈælɪti/	n.	准时
rural (l.4)	/ˈrʊərəl/	adj.	农村的
disregard (l.4)	/ˌdɪsrɪˈɡɑːd/	v.	不顾，无视
intellectual (l.5)	/ˌɪntɪˈlektʃuəl/	n.	知识分子
abstruse (l.6)	/əbˈstruːs/	adj.	深奥的
coordinate (l.6)	/kəʊˈɔːdɪneɪt/	v.	协调
reproach (l.8)	/rɪˈprəʊtʃ/	v.	责备
puncture (l.10)	/ˈpʌŋktʃə/	v.	刺破（轮胎）
diversion (l.10)	/daɪˈvɜːʃən/	n.	改道，绕道
trial (l.12)	/ˈtraɪəl/	n.	讨厌的事或人
fraction (l.16)	/ˈfrækʃən/	n.	很小一点儿
flourish (l.29)	/ˈflʌrɪʃ/	n.	挥舞（打手势）
microscopic (l.29)	/ˌmaɪkrəˈskɒpɪk/	adj.	微小的
adamant (l.32)	/ˈædəmənt/	adj.	坚定的，不动摇的

Notes on the text 课文注释

1 Only in a sparsely-populated ... is it possible ..., 这是一个倒装句，因为 only 放在句首。

2 for the matter in hand, 为手中的事。

3 if late for a dinner party,

在以 if, when, though 等连词引导的从句中，当其谓语为 be 时，而主语又与主句的主语相同，从句中往往可以将主语和谓语省去。上句 if 后就省略了 he is。

4 cut things fine, 把时间安排得不留余地。

5 The over-punctual can be as much a trial to others as the unpunctual.

到得过早的人和迟到的人同样使人无法忍受。as much as, 和……一样。

6 half an hour too soon（= half an hour earlier）, 早到半个小时。

7 in good time, 作“适当地”、“及时地”讲。

参考译文

准时是文明社会中进行一切社交活动时必须养成的习惯。不准时将一事无成，事事都会陷入混乱不堪的境地。只有在人口稀少的农村，才可以忽视准时的习惯。在日常生活中，人们可以容忍一定程度的不准时。一个专心钻研某个复杂问题的知识分子，为了搞好手头的研究，要把一切都协调一致、组织周密。因此，他要是赴宴迟到了会得到谅解。但有些人不准时常常是因为掐钟点所致，他们常常会受到责备。精力充沛、头脑敏捷的人极不愿意浪费时间，因此他们常想做完一件事后再去赴约。要是路上没有发生如爆胎、改道、突然起雾等意外事故，他们是决不会迟到的。他们与那些从不迟到的人相比，常常是更勤奋有用的公民。早到的人同迟到的人一样令人讨厌。客人提前半小时到达是最令人讨厌的。我家有几个朋友就有这种令人恼火的习惯。唯一的办法就是请他们比别的客人晚来半小时。这样，他们可以恰好在我们要求的时间到达。

如果赶火车，早到总比晚到好，哪怕早到一会儿也好。虽然早到可能意味着浪费一点时间，但这比误了火车、等上一个多小时坐下一班车浪费的时间要少，而且可以避免那种正好在火车驶出站时赶到车站，因上不去车而感到的沮丧。更难堪的情况是虽然及时赶到站台上，却眼睁睁地看着那趟火车启动，把你抛下。一个小姑娘第一次单独出门就碰到了这种情况。

在火车进站 20 分钟前她就进了车站。因为她的父母再三跟她说，如果误了这趟车，她的东道主朋友们就得接她两趟，这是不应该的。她把行李交给搬运工并给他看了车票。搬运工说她早到了两个小时，她听后大吃一惊。她从钱包里摸出一张纸条，那上面有她父亲对这次旅行的详细说明，她把这张纸条交给了搬运工。搬运工说，正如纸条上所说，确有一趟火车在那个时刻到站，但它只停站装邮件，不载旅客。姑娘要求看一下时刻表，因为她相信父亲不会把这么大的事给弄错。搬运工跑回去取时刻表，同时请来了站长。站长拿着时刻表一挥手，指着那趟列车到站时刻旁边的一个很小的圆圈标记。这个标记表示列车是为装邮件而停车。正在这时，火车进站了。女孩泪流满面，央求让她悄悄地到押车员车厢里去算了。但站长态度坚决，规章制度不能破坏，姑娘只得眼看着那趟火车撇下她消逝在她要去的方向。

Comprehension 理解

Give short answers to each of the following questions in your own words as far as possible, using only material contained in the passage. Use one complete sentence for each answer.

1 What are the dangers of leaving the bare minimum of time for appointments?

2 Why did the author's family ask some guests to come half an hour later than others invited for the same day?

3 Why, according to the author, is it better to choose to wait on the platform before the train arrives than to be forced to wait after it has gone?

Vocabulary 词汇

Choose five of the following words and phrases and give for each another word or phrase of similar meaning to that in which the word or phrase is used in the passage: a state of chaos (l.3); sparsely-populated (l.3); disregard (l.4); reproached (l.8); setting out (l.10); diversions (l.10); industrious (l.11); destination (l.33).

Summary writing 摘要写作

Give an account *in not more than 80 words* of the girl's experience on the railway station, when she was not allowed to get on the train. Use your own words as far as possible. Do not include anything that is not in the last paragraph.

Composition 作文

Write a composition on one of the following subjects; the length should be between 250 and 350 words.

a Write a short story beginning 'A piece of paper was blowing in the wind ...'

b What science has done to make our lives easier and more comfortable.

Letter writing 书信写作

Write a letter of between 80 and 100 words in length on one of the following subjects. You should make the beginning and ending like those of an ordinary letter, but the address is not to be counted in the total number of words.

a Write a letter informing your employer (or the Principal of your school) that you have to be absent for a few days and explaining why this is necessary.

b A friend with several young children has fallen ill. Write offering help or suggesting a way in which help can be obtained.

Key structures and Special difficulties 关键句型和难点

Rewrite the following sentence without changing the meaning. Then refer to ll.27-28.

'May I see the timetable, please?' the girl asked.

The girl asked ...

Multiple choice questions 选择题

Choose the correct answers to the following questions.

comprehension 理解

1 The only people who can afford to neglect the exercise of punctuality are ________ .

(*a*) ordinary citizens who have nothing to do with publicity

(*b*) people who live in remote places where there are few people

(*c*) intellectuals who have to deal with unexpected problems

(*d*) people who are forced to work overtime in order to finish a job

2 People who cut things fine are usually ________ .

(*a*) delayed by accidents on the roads

(*b*) energetic, quick-minded people

(*c*) no more irritating than the over-punctual

(*d*) reproached for being late for appointments

3 The girl was very upset when the train came into the station because ________ .

(*a*) her parents would not forgive her for missing it

(*b*) she had two hours to wait before the next train arrived

(*c*) she was going to have to make a second journey to reach her destination

(*d*) the station master insisted that passengers were not allowed on to it

Structure 结构

4 Without it, it would be impossible ________ to a conclusion. (l.2)

(*a*) to have ever brought anything (*b*) ever to bring anything

(*c*) to bring nothing ever (*d*) nothing to be brought ever

5 The time you ________ waste through being early will be less than ... (l.17)

(*a*) must (*b*) might (*c*) should (*d*) can

6 If you are catching a train, you ________ comfortably early than ... (ll.16-17)

(*a*) are better being (*b*) would be better (*c*) had better be (*d*) will be better to be

7 – the frustration of arriving ________ the train is drawing out ... (ll.18-19)

(*a*) just as (*b*) immediately that (*c*) in a while (*d*) as soon as

8 And she had to watch that train disappear towards her destination ________ . (l.33)

(*a*) and left her behind (*b*) and leave behind her

(*c*) leaving her behind (*d*) while it left behind her

Vocabulary 词汇

9 In ordinary living, unpunctuality can be tolerated ________ . (ll.4-5)

(*a*) out of kindness (*b*) on occasion (*c*) to a certain extent (*d*) in varying degrees

10 The over-punctual can be just as ________ to others as the unpunctual. (l.12)

(*a*) detestable (*b*) trying (*c*) provident (*d*) inconsiderate

11 – since her parents had ________ that it would be unforgivable ... (ll.22-23)

(*a*) stressed the point (*b*) given the impression (*c*) marked it down (*d*) given notice

12 ________ the train came into the station. (l.31)

(*a*) Only then (*b*) Instantly (*c*) At that very moment (*d*) Precisely

Appendix 1: Personal names
附录 1：人名中英文对照表

英文（课）	译文	英文（课）	译文
Alan Fielding (32)	艾伦·菲尔丁	Hans Bussman (36)	汉斯·巴斯曼
Aleko (16)	阿列科	Harriet (49)	哈丽特
Alf (4)	艾尔弗	Harry (52)	哈里
Alfred Bloggs (4)	艾尔弗雷德·布洛格斯	Hubert Latham (20)	休伯特·莱瑟姆
Bessie (49)	贝西	Jackson (21)	杰克逊
Bill Wilkins (2)	比尔·威尔金斯	Jane Butlin (7)	简·巴特林
Bob (30)	鲍勃	Joe (30)	乔
Bruce (39)	布鲁斯	John (7)	约翰
Byron (21)	拜伦（姓）	John Hawkwood (14)	约翰·霍克伍德
Charlie Chaplin (29)	查理·卓别林	Leon Bagrit (51)	莱昂·巴格瑞特
Correggio (34)	柯勒乔（姓）	Louis Bleriot (20)	路易斯·布莱里奥
Daniel Goldin (55)	丹尼尔·戈尔丁	Mary (16)	玛丽
Daniel Mendoza (21)	丹尼尔·门多萨	Noah (56)	诺亚
Dickie (31)	迪基	Northcliffe (20)	诺斯克利夫（姓）
Dimitri (16)	迪米特里	Othman Ammann (17)	奥斯马·阿曼
Eleanor Ramsay (19)	埃莉诺·拉姆齐	Richard Colson (31)	理查德·科尔森
Eric Cox (30)	埃里克·考科斯	Richard Humphries (21)	理查德·汉弗莱斯
Frank Halliday (34)	弗兰克·哈利戴	Richards (13)	理查兹（姓）
Franz Bussman (36)	弗朗兹·巴斯曼	Robert (23)	罗伯特
George (15)	乔治	Robinson Crusoe (12)	鲁滨逊·克鲁索
George Carlton (24)	乔治·卡尔顿	Sabrina (9)	萨伯瑞娜
Giovanni Acuto (14)	乔凡尼·阿库托	Sebastian (24)	塞巴斯蒂安
Giovanni Haukodue (14)	乔凡尼·阿库托	Taylor (6)	泰勒（姓）
Gouffre Berger (42)	高弗·伯杰	Verrazano (17)	维拉萨诺（姓）

Appendix 2: Geographical names
附录 2：地名中英文对照表

英文（课）	译文	英文（课）	译文
Aberdeen (45)	阿伯丁	Italy (8)	意大利
America (1)	美洲	Java (25)	爪哇
Angoulême (17)	安古拉姆（纽约的旧称）	Kea (3)	基亚岛
Asia (8)	亚洲	London (1)	伦敦
Australia (25)	澳大利亚	Mediterranean, the (23)	地中海
Ayia Irini (3)	阿伊亚·依里尼	Miami (12)	迈阿密
Balkans, the (48)	巴尔干半岛	New York (city) (9)	纽约（市）
Barents Sea, the (32)	巴伦支海	Newcastle (7)	纽卡斯尔
Bastille, the (22)	巴士底狱	North Atlantic, the (10)	北大西洋
Britain (7)	英国	Parramatta (33)	帕拉马塔
Brooklyn (17)	布鲁克林	Perachora (16)	波拉考拉
Calais (20)	加来	Persia (28)	波斯
Caribbean, the (12)	加勒比海	Piccadilly (6)	皮卡迪利
Chicago (14)	芝加哥	Russia (32)	俄国
China (25)	中国	Shanghai (25)	上海
Dauphiné Alps, the (42)	丹芬阿尔卑斯山	Southampton (10)	南安普敦
Dover (20)	多佛尔	South Dakota (45)	南达科他州
Endley Farm (30)	恩得利农场	St. Bernard Monastery, the (8)	圣伯纳德修道院
England (7)	英国（泛指）	St. Bernard Pass (8)	圣伯纳德山口
English Channel, the (20)	英吉利海峡	Staten Island (17)	斯塔顿岛
Europe (8)	欧洲	Stilton (21)	斯蒂尔顿
Everest, Mount (42)	珠穆朗玛峰（即 Qomolangma, Mount）	Sweden (53)	瑞典
		Switzerland (8)	瑞士
Florence (14)	佛罗伦萨	Sydney (33)	悉尼
Gouffre Berger, the (42)	高弗·伯杰洞	U.S., the (29)	美国
Greece (16)	希腊	Virgin Islands (12)	维尔京群岛
Greenwich (25)	格林尼治	Western Germany (36)	西德
Grenoble (42)	格勒诺布尔	Westhaven (37)	威斯特海温
India (28)	印度	Widley (37)	威德里
Indian Ocean, the (25)	印度洋		

Appendix 3: Measures and weights
附录 3：英制和公制计量单位对照表

长度单位	重量单位
1 inch (英寸) = 2.54 cm (厘米)	1 pound (磅) = 0.4536 kg (千克)
1 foot (英尺) = 0.3048 m (米)	1 ton (英吨) = 1.016 tonnes (吨)
1 yard (码) = 0.9144 m (米)	
1 mile (英里) = 1.609 km (千米)	

新概念英语系列产品目录

书名	书号
新概念英语智慧版 1	978-7-5213-3670-2
新概念英语智慧版 2	978-7-5213-3671-9
新概念英语智慧版 3	978-7-5213-3672-6
新概念英语智慧版 4	978-7-5213-3673-3
新概念英语练习册 1	978-7-5600-1840-9
新概念英语练习册 2	978-7-5600-1723-5
新概念英语练习册 3	978-7-5600-2482-0
新概念英语练习册 4	978-7-5600-2775-3
新概念英语教师用书 1	978-7-5600-1350-3
新概念英语教师用书 2	978-7-5600-1351-0
新概念英语教师用书 3	978-7-5600-1771-6
新概念英语教师用书 4	978-7-5600-1841-6
新概念英语自学导读 1	978-7-5600-1799-0
新概念英语自学导读 2	978-7-5600-1733-4
新概念英语自学导读 3	978-7-5600-1940-6
新概念英语自学导读 4	978-7-5600-2512-4
新概念英语练习详解 1	978-7-5600-2225-3
新概念英语练习详解 2	978-7-5600-1812-6
新概念英语练习详解 3	978-7-5600-1873-7
新概念英语练习详解 4	978-7-5600-2329-8
新概念英语词汇练习 1	978-7-5600-4208-4
新概念英语词汇练习 2	978-7-5600-5632-6
新概念英语词汇练习 3	978-7-5600-4390-6
新概念英语口语练习 1	978-7-5600-4391-3
新概念英语口语练习 2	978-7-5600-4573-3
新概念英语语法练习 1	978-7-5600-3304-4
新概念英语语法练习 2	978-7-5600-4591-7
新概念英语语法手册	978-7-5600-4230-5
新概念英语词汇随身听速记手册 1	978-7-5600-3063-0
新概念英语词汇随身听速记手册 2	978-7-5600-3150-7
新概念英语词汇随身听速记手册 3	978-7-5600-3151-4
新概念英语词汇大全	978-7-5600-1727-3
新概念英语青少版	
新概念英语青少版学生用书 入门级 A	978-7-5600-9855-5
新概念英语青少版学生用书 入门级 B	978-7-5135-0287-0
新概念英语青少版学生用书 1A	978-7-5600-7354-5

书名	书号
新概念英语青少版学生用书 1B	978-7-5600-7356-9
新概念英语青少版学生用书 2A	978-7-5600-7371-2
新概念英语青少版学生用书 2B	978-7-5600-7372-9
新概念英语青少版学生用书 3A	978-7-5600-7373-6
新概念英语青少版学生用书 3B	978-7-5600-7374-3
新概念英语青少版学生用书 4A	978-7-5600-9567-7
新概念英语青少版学生用书 4B	978-7-5600-9711-4
新概念英语青少版学生用书 5A	978-7-5600-9746-6
新概念英语青少版学生用书 5B	978-7-5135-8435-7
新概念英语青少版练习册入门级 A	978-7-5600-9956-9
新概念英语青少版练习册入门级 B	978-7-5135-0419-5
新概念英语青少版练习册 1A	978-7-5600-7355-2
新概念英语青少版练习册 1B	978-7-5600-7357-6
新概念英语青少版练习册 2A	978-7-5600-7375-0
新概念英语青少版练习册 2B	978-7-5600-7376-7
新概念英语青少版练习册 3A	978-7-5600-7377-4
新概念英语青少版练习册 3B	978-7-5600-7378-1
新概念英语青少版练习册 4A	978-7-5600-9648-3
新概念英语青少版练习册 4B	978-7-5600-9647-6
新概念英语青少版练习册 5A	978-7-5600-9681-0
新概念英语青少版练习册 5B	978-7-5600-9680-3
新概念英语青少版教师用书 入门级	978-7-5135-1390-6
新概念英语青少版教师用书 1	978-7-5600-7368-2
新概念英语青少版教师用书 2	978-7-5600-7369-9
新概念英语青少版教师用书 3	978-7-5600-7370-5
新概念英语青少版教师用书 4	978-7-5135-0771-4
新概念英语青少版教师用书 5	978-7-5135-1386-9
新概念英语青少版同步测试 入门级 A	978-7-5135-7572-0
新概念英语青少版同步测试 入门级 B	978-7-5135-6954-5
新概念英语青少版同步测试 1A	978-7-5135-5982-9
新概念英语青少版同步测试 1B	978-7-5135-6451-9
新概念英语青少版同步测试 2A	978-7-5135-6438-0
新概念英语青少版同步测试 2B	978-7-5135-6010-8
新概念英语青少版同步测试 3A	978-7-5135-6845-6
新概念英语青少版同步测试 3B	978-7-5135-7055-8